A Special Issue of
The European Journal of Cognitive Psychology

Ageing and Executive Control

Edited by

Ulrich Mayr
University of Oregon, Eugene, USA

Daniel H. Spieler
Stanford University, CA, USA

and

Reinhold Kliegl
University of Potsdam, Germany

Routledge
Taylor & Francis Group

LONDON AND NEW YORK

First published 2001 by Psychology Press Ltd,

Published 2018 by Routledge
2 Park Square, Milton Park, Abingdon, Oxon, OX14 4RN
52 Vanderbilt Avenue, New York, NY 10017

First issued in paperback 2018

Routledge is an imprint of the Taylor & Francis Group, an informa business

Typeset by Acorn Bookwork, Salisbury, Wiltshire

A catalogue record for this book is available from the British Library

ISBN 13: 978-1-138-88324-6 (pbk)
ISBN 13: 978-1-84169-908-0 (hbk)
ISSN 0954-1446

Contents*

Introduction
Ulrich Mayr, Daniel H. Spieler, and Reinhold Kliegl   1

Frontal tests and models for cognitive ageing
Patrick Rabbitt, Christine Lowe, and Val Shilling   5

A research strategy for investigating group differences in a cognitive
    construct: Application to ageing and executive processes
Timothy A. Salthouse   29

Is there an age deficit in the selection of mental sets?
Ulrich Mayr and Thomas Liebscher   47

Adult age differences in goal activation and goal maintenance
Ritske De Jong   71

The transient nature of executive control processes in younger and older
    adults
Robert West   91

Inhibitory control over the present and the past
Cindy Lustig, Lynn Hasher, and Simon T. Tonev   107

Executive-process interactive control: A unified computational theory for
    answering 20 questions (and more) about cognitive ageing
*David E. Meyer, Jennifer M. Glass, Shane T. Mueller, Travis L.
Seymour, and David E. Kieras*   123

Modelling cognitive control in task switching and ageing
Nachshon Meiran and Alex Gotler   165

* This book is also a special issue of the *European Journal of Cognitive
Psychology* which forms Issues 1 and 2 of Volume 13 (2001).

Beyond resources: Formal models of complexity effects and age
  differences in working memory
Klaus Oberauer and Reinhold Kliegl   187

Modelling age-related changes in information processing
Daniel H. Spieler   217

Age-related changes in brain–behaviour relationships: Evidence
  from event-related functional MRI studies
Bart Rypma and Mark D'Esposito   235

Neurocognitive ageing and storage of executive processes
Patricia A. Reuter-Lorenz, Christy Marshuetz, John Jonides,
Edward E. Smith, Alan Hartley, and Robert Koeppe   257

The impact of aerobic activity on cognitive function in older adults:
  A new synthesis based on the concept of executive control
Courtney D. Hall, Alan L. Smith, and Steven W. Keele   279

Subject index   301

EUROPEAN JOURNAL OF COGNITIVE PSYCHOLOGY, 2001, *13* (1/2), 1–4

Introduction

Ulrich Mayr
University of Oregon, Eugene, USA

Daniel H. Spieler
Stanford University, USA

Reinhold Kliegl
University of Potsdam, Germany

The papers assembled in this special issue were authored by a group of researchers representing a diverse set of theoretical perspectives and empirical emphases. Each one of them has been critically involved in research on cognitive ageing, executive control, and/or the integration of these two areas. Initially most of the authors were brought together by a conference on the same topic held in Potsdam, Germany, in October 1999 (funded by the Deutsche Forschungsgemeinschaft). The goal was to foster discussion on the empirical status and the theoretical perspectives on one particular hypothesis, namely that decrements in executive control may play a particularly critical part in cognitive development across the adult life span. To this end, we made a deliberate effort to include both researchers who promote some version of the ageing-and-executive-control hypothesis and researchers with a more sceptical stance. Also, we did not want to simply provide a collection of empirical papers as one would find in the relevant specialised journals. Rather, our goal was to bring the ideas driving the empirical work to the foreground. Therefore, we had asked authors to emphasise theoretical integration over the presentation of new data.

Requests for reprints should be addressed to Dr. Ulrich Mayr, University of Oregon, Dept of Psychology, College of Arts & Sciences, 1227 University of Oregon, Eugene OR 97403-1227, USA.

http://www.tandf.co.uk/journals/pp/09541446.html   DOI:10.1080/09541440042000188

Why "ageing and executive control"? This is an exciting time for cognitive ageing research but also a time where theoretical tensions are becoming increasingly apparent. Much of this tension arises from a potential mismatch between the traditional assumptions underlying the standard cognitive research and the subject matter of this research. On the one hand there is the standard cognitive(-neuroscience) paradigm with its focus on functionally dissociable processing components. On the other hand, there is the "messy" nature of ageing phenomenon, which often do not seem to fall neatly into the functional categories assumed by general cognitive research. Instead, ageing may affect more general parameters that cut across at least some of these categories as reflected in conceptualisations of general slowing or neural noise. For several reasons, the "ageing-and-executive-control" hypothesis may represent a productive middle-ground between these two view points.

First, there is sufficient anatomical evidence regarding specific age effects in the frontal lobes (e.g., Raz, 2000) as well as behavioural evidence indicating particularly large age differences in executively demanding tasks (e.g., Mayr & Kliegl, 1993) to warrant serious consideration of this hypothesis, even from contenders of a "general-parameter" explanation of age-related deficits (Salthouse, this issue).

Second, given the general, modulatory role of executive control in almost all cognitive processing (Shallice & Burgess, 1998), an executive-control deficit could be responsible for the type of seemingly undifferentiated age effects that "general-parameter accounts" of cognitive ageing try to explain.

Third, frontal-executive and working-memory processes have been a prominent topic of recent neuro-imaging work, both generally (e.g., Smith & Jonides, 1999) and with respect to ageing (Reuter-Lorenz et al., this issue; Rypma & D'Esposito, this issue). Therefore, the executive-control theme seems particularly suited for fostering cross-fertilisation between cognitive-behavioural and brain-imaging work.

Finally, what may seem like a weakness of the executive-control construct, namely its resistance to clear operational definitions (e.g., Monsell, 1996) also offers great potential for future interesting developments. The current vagueness of the construct, despite its undeniable importance, provides a strong motivation for theoretical developments targeted at more precise models (e.g., Meyer & Kieras, 1997). Evidence from work on the ageing-and-executive-control hypothesis will be an important force for stimulating such developments.

The papers in the special issue can be loosely grouped into the following five categories: First, general issues of how to go about testing the executive-control hypothesis are addressed in the papers by Rabbitt, Lowe, and Shilling, and Salthouse. Whereas Rabbitt et al. deal mainly with the unique methodological problems that may arise from use of "frontal/executive" tasks, Salthouse is most concerned with an efficient research strategy to address problems of inferring construct-specific age-related deficits in the face of a rather unspecific pattern of decline.

Second, different approaches to the experimental analysis of executive-control processes are presented in the papers by Mayr and Liebscher, De Jong, and West. Two common themes seem to be emerging here. On the one hand, it is certainly not executive control in general that is affected by ageing. On the other hand, there may be a characteristic pattern of decline when high-level prescriptions of actions (intentions, goals, or task sets) need to be maintained across time and when competing or more salient prescriptions are present. The paper by Lustig, Hasher, and Tonev discusses evidence in favour of one candidate mechanism behind such an age-related problem, namely a general inhibitory deficit.

Third, formal models of age-related processes are still an exception in cognitive-ageing research. A unique feature of the current special issue is that we were able to assemble four papers by (i) Meiran and Gotler, (ii) Meyer, Glass, Mueller, Seymour, and Kieras, (iii) Oberauer and Kliegl, and (iv) Spieler which all use formal models as a tool for identifying sources of age-related cognitive decline. The experimental paradigms modelled and the type of models used differ widely across papers. But in each case, new and in part surprising insights are revealed (which in some instances also convey a cautionary note regarding the executive-control hypothesis).

Fourth, there is no question that cognitive ageing is to a large degree a biologically driven process. Therefore, important insights are to be expected from the application of brain imaging methods to cognitive ageing phenomena. Progress in this area, and also the complex relationship between brain-activation and performance, is documented in the papers by Rypma and D'Esposito and Reuter-Lorenz et al. Noteworthy in both papers is the way in which novel, theoretically stimulating accounts are inspired through the consideration of neuroimaging evidence.

Finally, we end with an optimistic note regarding the practical benefits that may arise from the pursuit of the executive-control hypothesis of age-related decline. In the paper by Hall, Smith, and Keele evidence is reviewed suggesting that executive deficits may be particularly sensitive to positive effects of physical fitness.

It is too early to tell whether or not the ageing and executive-control hypothesis will hold up in the end. However, we believe this special issue demonstrates that much interesting work has been stimulated in this context and that a better understanding of cognitive ageing and a better understanding of executive control may develop in synchrony.

Manuscript received September 2000

REFERENCES

Mayr, U., & Kliegl, R. (1993). Sequential and coordinative complexity: Age-based processing limitations in figural transformations. *Journal of Experimental Psychology: Learning, Memory, and Cognition, 19,* 1297–1320.

Meyer, D.E., & Kieras, D.E. (1997). A computational theory of executive cognitive processes and multiple-task performance: I. Basic mechanisms. *Psychological Review, 104,* 3–65.

Monsell, S. (1996). Control of mental processes. In V. Bruce (Ed.), *Unsolved mysteries of the mind* (pp. 93–148). Hove, UK: Lawrence Erlbaum Associates Ltd.

Raz, N. (2000). Aging of the brain and its impact on cognitive performance: An integration of structural and functional findings. In F.I.M. Craik & T.A. Salthouse (Eds.), *The handbook of aging and cognition* (2nd ed.). Mahwah, NJ: Lawrence Erlbaum Associates Inc.

Shallice, T., & Burgess, P. (1998). The domain of supervisory processes and the temporal organization of behavior. In A.C. Roberts, T.W. Robbins, & L. Weiskrantz (Eds.), *The prefrontal cortex* (pp. 22–35). Oxford, UK: Oxford University Press.

Smith, E.E., & Jonides, J. (1999). Storage and executive processes in the frontal lobes. *Science, 283,* 1657–1661.

EUROPEAN JOURNAL OF COGNITIVE PSYCHOLOGY, 2001, *13* (1/2), 5–28

Frontal tests and models for cognitive ageing

Patrick Rabbitt, Christine Lowe, and Val Shilling

Age and Cognitive Performance Research Centre, University of Manchester, UK

Results of investigations of how specific behavioural changes in old age may be related to local changes in the brain have been discrepant because of neglect of methodological issues. Among these are neglect of the reliability and validity of frontal and executive tests; the operational definition and construct validity of hypothetical functional processes such as "inhibition"; the nature and origins of mutual relationships between tests; the relationships of test performance to higher order constructs of general mental ability such as "gf" and, most importantly, problems of cohort selection arising from imprecise definitions of the models of the ageing process. These problems are illustrated by a discussion of the results of several experiments in which younger and older groups of people are compared on frontal and executive tests.

A main goal of cognitive gerontology has been to use behavioural tests to identify cognitive changes that occur in old age and to relate these to concurrent changes in the brain. Models for these relationships have become polarised. "Single factor global models" (SFGMs), encouraged perhaps by illusions of parsimony of description, suggest that all cognitive changes occur at similar rates because they are consequences of global decline in a single, fundamental, functional performance characteristic of the entire brain. "Modular multifactor models" (MMMs), encouraged by anatomical and physiological evidence that particular parts of the brain may "age" faster than others, predict patterned rather than uniform decline such that mental abilities supported by age-vulnerable areas will decline faster than those supported by age-robust areas. Perhaps the clearest evidence for this relates to changes in the frontal cortex. Two decades of post-mortem and brain-imaging studies suggest that age-

Requests for reprints should be addressed to P.M.A. Rabbitt, Age and Cognitive Performance Research Centre, University of Manchester, Oxford Road, Manchester M13 9PL, UK. Email: rabbitt@psy.man.ac.uk

http://www.tandf.co.uk/journals/pp/09541446.html   DOI:10.1080/09541440042000197

related loss of cortical volume is greater in the frontal lobes than for other brain areas (Haug & Eggers, 1991; Mittenberg, Seidenberg, O'Leary, & DiGuilio, 1989; Whelihan & Lesher, 1985), and that older adults show greater cell loss in the prefrontal than in other cortical regions (Scheibel & Scheibel, 1975). More pronounced decreases in cerebral blood flow have been reported in prefrontal versus posterior regions after the age of about 60 (Shaw et al., 1984) and age-related region-specific declines in the concentration, synthesis, and number of receptor sites for some neurotransmitters have also been reported (Goldman-Rakic & Brown, 1981). There is also evidence for frontal cellular loss (Scheibel & Scheibel, 1975), reduced cerebral blood flow to the anterior cortex (Gur, Gur, Orbist, Skolnick, & Reivick, 1987), a decline in levels of neurotransmitters such as dopamine (Arnsten, Cai, Murphy, & Goldman-Rakic, 1994) and loss of myelin (Albert, 1993). Consequently, searches for behavioural and cognitive sequelae of local brain changes have largely focused on comparisons between healthy elderly and young adults on neuropsychological tests of frontal deficits.

Prominent among functions supposed to be supported by prefrontal cortex is the ability to inhibit processing of perceptual and production of responses that are irrelevant to a current goal. Hasher and her associates have argued that many cognitive changes in old age may be explained in terms of declining efficiency of inhibition (Connelly, Hasher, & Zacks, 1991; Hasher, Quig, & May, 1997; Hasher & Zacks, 1988). This idea is consistent with suggestions that older people are more distractible and disinhibited in verbal fluency tasks (Birren, 1959), produce more intrusions from external items in free recall (Cohen, 1988), have greater difficulty suppressing previously generated, but no longer relevant, inferences in text recall (Hamm & Hasher, 1992), show a heightened rate of false recognition to semantic associates of actually presented words (Rankin & Kausler, 1979), may have inconveniently heightened memory for irrelevant information (Hartman & Hasher, 1991), are less able deliberately to forget items on demand (Zacks, Radvansky, & Hasher, 1996), find it more difficult to inhibit both well-practised and newly learned response patterns in order to acquire new ones (Kausler & Hakami, 1982), and are more distracted by irrelevant items adjacent to targets in visual displays (Shaw, 1991).

This evidence that older people may have difficulties in selecting appropriate and suppressing inappropriate percepts, memories, and responses contrasts with poor definition of what the construct of inhibition may be, in functional and operational terms. As Goel and Grafman (1995) have pointed out, the construct has been over-extended to cover an implausibly wide range of functions from very simple and automatic responses such as saccade suppression (Walker, Husain, Hodgson, Harrison, & Kennard,

1998) to complicated behaviours such as the ability to suppress unacceptable or unwise social responses. Rabbitt (1997) suggested that the imprecision of the common-language usage of the word "inhibition" has encouraged misleading analogies between quite disparate functional processes. For example, Kimberg and Farah (1993) have formally shown that human performance on four quite distinct tasks that have been widely regarded as measures of frontal function, including "inhibition" in the Stroop (1935) paradigm, can be successfully simulated by identical production-system models without incorporation of any process that resembles "inhibition" as understood in the neuropsychological literature.

The Stroop Test (Stroop, 1935) has been so often used to study "inhibition" that it has become an ostensive behavioural definition of the construct. It requires participants to respond to less salient, and to suppress responses to more salient, aspects of complex displays, as when naming the colours in which the names of other, different, colours are printed (Stroop, 1935). Many investigators report that older adults are disproportionately slow to resolve such response conflicts (e.g., Cohn, Dustman, & Bradford, 1984; Houx, Jolles, & Vreeling, 1993; Panek, Rush, & Slade, 1984). "Negative priming" is a logically related effect seen in tasks where successive complex displays immediately follow each other and where, it is found, decisions are slower when an item that has to be ignored on one trial recurs as a target item on the next. Many studies have found that older people experience less interference ("negative priming") from previously ignored items and this has been explained by the hypothesis that they inhibited these items less efficiently when they first occurred (Hasher, Stoltzfus, Zacks, & Rypma, 1991; Kane, Hasher, Stoltzfus, Zacks, & Connelly, 1994; McDowd & Oseas-Kreger, 1991).

In spite of such evidence, direct failures of replication, and inconsistencies in age effects on logically similar paradigms render the issue unclear. For example, some investigators have found age deficits in verbal fluency (e.g., Pendleton, Heaton, Lehman, & Hulihan, 1982; Whelihan & Lesher, 1985), but others have not (e.g., Axelrod & Henry, 1992; Daigneault, Braun, & Whitaker, 1992). Age-related increases in perseverative errors on the Wisconsin Card Sorting Test have been found by some (Daigneault et al., 1992; Heaton, 1981; Loranger & Misiak, 1960) but not by others (Boone, Miler, Lesser, Hill, & D'Elia, 1990; Nelson, 1976). In particular, empirical studies suggest that age-related differences in performance on the Stroop largely reflect changes in some single, fundamental, performance characteristic of the central nervous system, notably slowing of information processing rate (Salthouse, 1998; Salthouse, Fristoe, & Rhee, 1996; Salthouse & Meinz, 1995).

Consideration of some logical and methodological difficulties in investigations of relationships between brain ageing and cognitive performance may help to account for these discrepancies and suggest ways to re-appraise models for relationship of the incidence, and the correlated time courses of age-related changes in brain and cognitive performance. These difficulties can be categorised as problems of indices of measurement, problems of task familiarity, problems of task specificity and construct validity, and, finally, much-neglected problems of cohort selection, which stem from the particular model for the nature and time course of cognitive ageing that we choose to adopt.

PROBLEMS OF MEASUREMENT

The Age × Task complexity interaction first brought to attention by Birren (1956, 1959) is now one of the most thoroughly replicated in cognitive psychology, but Cerella's (1985) influential meta-analysis, suggesting that it may best be described as a linear scaling effect, is questionable (Perfect, 1994; Rabbitt, 1996b; Verhaegen & DeMeersman, 1998). However this interaction has important methodological conse-quences for interpretation of comparisons between young and older people on most of the tasks on which models of "frontal ageing" have been based. For example in the Stroop test (Stroop, 1935) the relative efficiency with which participants can inhibit irrelevant signals and responses is assessed by comparing the difference between their mean choice reaction times (CRTs) for easier and faster "baseline" conditions from their mean CRTs for more difficult and slower "interference" condi-tions. Unfortunately the ubiquity of Age × Task complexity effects ensures that age will always increase CRTs for harder and slower interfer-ence conditions more than for easier and faster baseline conditions. Age deficits in inhibition cannot be claimed unless CRTs for interference conditions are proportionately, as well as absolutely, greater for older than for younger adults. Some, but by no means most, investigators have taken this point. It has been less well recognised that even findings that simple percentage differences between baseline and interference conditions are evidence for an inhibitory deficit only if we assume that the Age × Task difficulty interaction is best described by a linear scaling function as Cerella (1985) first suggested. For example, if global functional changes bring about even a very modestly exponential increase in CRT with task difficulty, percentage increases for the slower mean CRTs for difficult interference conditions will be greater than for the faster mean CRTs for easy baseline conditions. There is still no agreement about the precise nature of the function that best describes the Age × Task difficulty inter-action. Thus we can test hypotheses only for local rather than for global changes by comparing the same groups of younger and older people both on tasks that involve inhibition and on other tasks that are more difficult, and so have slower CRTs, but do not involve inhibition. We can claim that age has a local and specific effect on inhibitory tasks only if the older groups show proportionately greater slowing of mean CRTs on faster tasks involving inhibition than on slower tasks that do not involve inhibition. Neglect of this point brings into question all studies that have argued for age-related loss of inhibitory inefficiency from evidence that, in proportional terms, age-related slowing is greater only in tasks that require inhibition of signals, and responses.

Rabbitt (1996a) tested 117 people aged from 75 to 85 years (M = 79.3, SD = 4.5) and 124 aged from 64 to 74 years (M = 67.3, SD = 5.1) on 15 different tasks. Age groups were matched on Mill Hill Vocabulary test scores (M = 29.2, SD = 11.1 and M = 26.1, SD = 10.2, respectively) but the younger group had significantly higher scores on the Cattell and Cattell (1960) intelligence test (young M = 36.8, SD = 9.1; old M = 27.6, SD = 14.3). A "Brinley plot" (Brinley, 1965) of mean CRTs for the older group over mean CRTs for the younger group was excellently fitted (R = .97) by a simple linear function with slope 1.34. This common pattern of results at first sight seems to confirm Cerella's (1985) conclusion that age linearly scales CRTs on all tasks by the same simple multiplicative constant. Note, however, that each of the data points to which the linear function was fitted represents a ratio of a mean CRT for the older group over a mean CRT for the younger group. These "Brinley ratios" for individual tasks varied over the wide range 1.1 to 1.6. The largest ratios were not for the most difficult tasks with the slowest mean CRTs but for the interference condition of the Stroop colour word test and for the switching condition of a version of the Trails test. Both these tasks are widely used as clinical markers of prefrontal cortical damage. This single comparison might be dismissed as an example of the large random error that is invariably found in psychological experiments. However, the rank order of Brinley ratios across tasks and, in particular, the finding of exceptionally large Brinley ratios for the Stroop and Trails tests remained stable when the experiment was repeated on different samples of older and younger and of more and less able individuals (for an example, see Rabbitt 1996a). This consistency across different comparisons between groups of younger and older adults confirmed that age does not scale all Brinley ratios for all tasks only in respect of the average duration of the decision times that they require but also in terms of the qualitative demands that they make. In particular, the critical conditions of two tasks that are known to be sensitive to prefrontal cortical damage seem to be especially sensitive to age differences.

PROBLEMS OF TASK FAMILIARITY

Burgess (1997) illuminatingly draws attention to two kinds of difficulties with neuropsychological tests designed to detect deficits in "frontal" systems. One is that, in clinical practice, frontal tasks can generally only be used once with any particular patient because their sensitivity depends on their novelty. The other is that a patient who fails on one frontal test may nevertheless succeed on "any number" of others. Thus we must conclude that either tests, or patients, or both, are inconsistent with respect to each other (pp. 81–116). Let us consider these problems in turn.

Lowe and Rabbitt (1997) tested the same groups of older and younger individuals twice on the same series of 15 different tests described by Rabbitt (1996a). As in the experiments described earlier, on first testing "Brinley ratios" for the Stroop and Trails tests were larger than for any of the other tasks. However, on second testing "Brinley ratios" for the Stroop and Trails tests declined more than for any others and no differences in ratios between tests were now significant. This is not just another illustration that the "Stroop effect" is abolished by practice. For both older and younger groups mean CRTs for the interference condition of the Stroop test and for the switching condition of the Trails test remained significantly greater than for the corresponding baseline conditions. The point is that the disproportionate age-related increase in CRTs for the critical conditions of these tests disappears before the main effects of interference are lost. This loss of specific test sensitivity to age effects is consistent with Burgess's observation that frontal tests can identify patients with well-defined frontal lesions only while they are novel. It also raises problems of theoretical interpretation because it suggests that, as practice continues, localised or "modular" age differences disappear and data are increasingly well explained by proportional slowing of all categories of decisions, so fitting a "global slowing" model. Inconsistencies in the literature between findings of age-related changes on the Stroop and on other neuropsychological tests may, at least partly, be explained by differences in the amounts of practice that different investigators have given their participants.

These findings also raise another methodological problem: Frontal tasks are likely to rank order groups of individuals in different ways on successive administrations and so, in psychometric terms, they are likely to have low test/re-test reliability. Lowe and Rabbitt (1998) analysed data from two batteries of neuropsychological and other tests, the excellent CANTAB (Sahakian & Owen, 1992) and the "ISPOCD" battery used in a large study of cognitive impairment following surgery and anaesthesia (Moller et al., 1998). Both batteries included examples of "frontal" or "executive" and of other tasks. Test/re-test correlations for the frontal and executive tests in these batteries were markedly lower than for other, equally difficult, "non-frontal" tasks, and were generally below levels considered acceptable in psychometric practice. It must be stressed that this does not mean that these batteries, or any of the particular tests that they include, are either poorly designed or ill-chosen. On the contrary it confirms Burgess's (1997) clinical observation that excellent frontal tests may depend for their sensitivity on their novelty. Obviously this has inconvenient practical implications for the design of studies of cognitive ageing. In particular, it perhaps means that the more efficiently a test detects front deficits the less useful it is for longitudinal studies of cognitive change.

PROBLEMS OF TASK VALIDITY

A basic criterion for acceptability of psychometric tests as measures of a hypothetical functional construct, such as intelligence, is that they must be shown to be "valid" in at least four senses: (1) Scores on tests of a particular functional construct must correlate with performance in everyday situations that provide ostensive definitions of that construct. (2) Individuals' scores on parallel versions of the same test must correlate robustly. (3) Scores on different tests that are supposed to assess the same functional construct must also correlate robustly. (4) Correlations between scores on different versions of the same test, or on different tests, should not be explainable in terms of individual differences in any functional property other than the one that they are supposed to measure.

Frontal tests are generally assumed to be valid in the first of these senses because they have been derived from clinical practice as reliable diagnostic markers of particular kinds of brain injury and not others. They may also be said to be valid in the third sense, in so far as some of them often successfully diagnose a "frontal syndrome" that includes behavioural deficits for which they do not directly test. Nevertheless this issue is not clear-cut. For the most part, the functional properties of frontal tests have been inferred either from studies of patients who have sustained focal frontal damage or from studies of controlled lesions in primates. Costa (1988, p. 4) points out that limitations to these studies may contribute to lack of clarity in the patterns of findings of links between performance on "frontal" measures and focal lesions. Linking loss of a particular function to a particular locus of damage in the brain loses sight of the effects of loss of the normal connections between that region and other brain areas. Removal or injury of particular parts of the cortex may cause secondary changes in regions that send projections to or receive from the damaged area. As a result, as Costa (1988) comments, "it is easy to find tests that are sensitive to frontal-lobe dysfunction and very difficult to find tests that are specific for it!"

Neuropsychological tests of frontal function generally do not meet the remaining two criteria of validity. Part of the problem stems from vagueness of conceptual boundaries. As Goldman-Rakic (1993) has remarked "such a bewildering array of behavioural deficits have been attributed to frontal lobe injury that a common functional denominator would appear elusive." (p. 13). Further, we still do not have empirical evidence that parallel, or slightly different versions of the same test, or different tests that are held to assess integrity of the same functional system, are mutually valid in the sense that they rank order individuals in the same way. As we shall see later, some investigations of mutual consistency have not been encouraging. Finally, as Duncan (1995) and Duncan, Burgess, and Emslie (1995) have pointed out, correlations between scores on some frontal tests may be entirely explained in terms of their mutual correlations with an extraneous functional construct that they are not designed to measure: general intellectual ability, as indexed by Spearman's (1927) statistical construct "gf". Similar claims have, of course, been made for another putative index of "global efficiency", "speed of processing". Neumann and DeSchepper (1992) found that the faster members of a group of participants showed higher levels of negative priming (indicating greater inhibitory efficiency) than did the slower members. Salthouse and Meinz (1995) found that almost all of the age differences found in three measures of Stroop interference were related to individual differences in processing speed rather than to individual differences in calendar age. As Salthouse et al. (1996) and Phillips (1998) remark, many previous studies have failed to take into account the point that age-related changes on frontal measures may be explained by global slowing.

EXPLORING CONSTRUCT VALIDITY

Apart from the specificity of tasks as measures of particular cognitive functions there is the issue of the validity of the "functional construct", that is, of the putative cognitive process or function, that they are supposed to test. To test the construct validity of the Stroop paradigm as a measure of inhibition, Shilling, Chetwynd, and Rabbitt (2000) gave four different versions of the Stroop test to the same groups of young–old and old–old normal elderly adults. The first was "Colour Word" test used by Stroop (1935). The second was a digit-counting task in which participants had to respond to the number, rather than to the values, of strings of digits. For example they responded "two" to the display "33" or "four" to the display "2222". The third version, used by Navon (1977), required participants to respond to the value of a large outline digit while suppressing their involuntary responses to the value of the smaller individual digits of which it was composed. The fourth, used by Shor (1970, 1971) required participants to respond, with the appropriate key press, to the direction of single outline arrows that pointed "up", "down", "left", or "right" while ignoring the discrepant words "up", "down", "left", or "right" printed within each arrow. Note that Shilling et al.'s (2000) experiment design did, in effect, account for the effects of age-related slowing of information-processing speed because it compared ratios of interference condition CRTs over baseline condition CRTs rather than absolute differences between conditions.

Shilling et al. (2000) found no evidence that the relative sizes of the proportional "Stroop" effects (i.e., ratios of CRTs to interference over CRTs to baseline conditions) that individuals showed on any of these tasks predicted the sizes of the effects that they showed on any of the others. That is to say, at the level of individual participants, there was no evidence for construct validity of inhibition, as defined by the Stroop paradigm. However, a random effect analysis testing for construct validity at the group level also compared outcomes when individuals were partitioned in terms of their ages and in terms of their unadjusted scores on the Cattell and Cattell (1960) "Culture Fair" intelligence test (CCF scores). There was evidence for consistency of group effects across tasks in terms of differences in CCF scores, but not for consistency of group effects in terms of differences in age. Thus there is some evidence for validity of the construct of inhibition as indexed by the Stroop paradigm, at the group level, but when individuals are selected in terms of individual differences in general intellectual ability rather than in terms of their ages.

It should be stressed that this finding does not simply replicate the many demonstrations that individuals' unadjusted intelligence test scores inversely predict their decision times on many different tasks (Jensen, 1982; Rabbitt, 1996b; Rabbitt & Goward, 1994; Vernon, 1985). Rabbitt (1996b) found that mean CRTs across a wide range of tasks vary inversely with CCF scores, but that this relationship was stronger for CRTs for the interference condition of the Stroop test and for the switching condition of the Trails test than for other, non-frontal, tasks. Shilling et al.'s data once again show that CCF scores consistently predict the proportional sizes of inhibitory effects across four different versions of the Stroop test.

The logic of this way of testing for "construct validity" depends on the assumption that the relative strengths of correlations between scores on different tasks directly reflect the extent to which they make demands on the same underlying functional process. This can be misleading because tasks may make demands on a common functional performance characteristic of the CNS such as "inhibition", "gf", or "information processing speed". For example, tasks that apparently make common demands on inhibitory processes may correlate entirely, or partly, because they also share other kinds of more general processing demands. Shilling et al. made a second experiment comparing two versions of the Stroop test that were almost identical in their peripheral demands: a version of the Shor (1970, 1971) test in which the arrows pointed either up or down and a version in which they pointed either left or right. Unsurprisingly, CRTs on these closely similar tasks correlated more strongly with each other than they did with CRTs for other versions of the Stroop paradigm. Further, in this case, there was evidence for construct validity at the level of individual participants: that is, particular individuals who showed large proportional "Stroop effects" on one of these conditions also did so on the other. There was again clear evidence for "construct validity" at the group level, as defined by Cattell Culture Fair scores but not as defined by age. It follows that successes and failures of inter-correlations between frontal tasks may reflect concordances and disparities between what investigators have regarded as the superficial, rather than the critical and "frontal" demands of the tasks that they have compared.

Several previous studies have found that, even when their slower information-processing speed has been taken into account, older people find it difficult to inhibit irrelevant and intrusive stimuli (e.g., Connelly & Hasher, 1993; Hasher & Zacks, 1988; Kramer, Humphrey, Larish, Logan, & Strayer, 1994, etc.). Shilling et al.'s (2000) experiments do not directly replicate these findings since they showed effects when individuals were grouped in terms of their unadjusted intelligence test scores, but not when they were grouped in terms of their ages. It is important to note that since people's unadjusted intelligence test scores markedly decline as they age this cannot be interpreted as a finding that "there are no age effects on the Stroop task". This finding means only that if individuals of different ages are matched in terms of intelligence test scores they will not differ in terms of their ability to cope with the "Stroop effect". In other words, individual differences in intelligence test scores pick up all of the age-related variance in sensitivity to tasks requiring inhibition. In this respect these results are reminiscent of Duncan's (1995), and Duncan et al.'s (1995) findings that, even within groups of patients with well-mapped frontal lesions, individual differences in performance on frontal tests can be largely, or entirely, accounted for by individual differences in CCF scores. Duncan (1995) also reported that differences in performance between frontal patients on his "goal neglect" test of executive function were also entirely accounted for by differences in CCF scores. When taken together these results suggest that CCF scores may be particularly sensitive measures of individual differences in the ability to cope with interference, whether these are due to brain changes associated with old age or with focal frontal damage. This makes it useful to consider (1) the extent to which age effects on other neuropsychological tests can also be explained in terms of measures of gf, and (2) how far correlations between neuropsychological tests can be explained by their mutual associations with gf.

Lowe (1998) gave the Spatial Working Memory task (SWM), the Tower of London (TOL), the Inter and Extra Dimension Shift task (ID/ ED), the Shape Recognition and Position Recognition Memory tasks, the Spatial Memory Span task, the Delayed Matching to Sample task (DMST), and the Paired Associates task (PA), all from the CANTAB neuropsychological test battery (Sahakian & Owen, 1992), to 162 individuals aged from 60 to 80 years ($M = 70$, SD $= 4.7$ years). She also gave four other sets of neuropsychological tests to groups of individuals aged from 60 to 85 years and in all cases she compared predictions of participants' scores on tests from their ages alone, from their scores on the Cattell Culture Fair (CCF) intelligence test alone, and from their ages after CCF scores had been included in the model. In the second experiment 90 people aged from 60 to 85 years ($M = 71$, SD $= 5.5$ years) were given a Dual Dimension Visual Search task (DDVS) in which they responded contingently to either one or two of the dimensions of visual stimuli (shape or number) on a printed sheet. In a third experiment 57 people aged from 60 to 80 years were given the same DDVS task, the Stroop Colour/Word test, a negative priming task and a Context Memory task. In a fourth experiment the same individuals were given an attention-switching task modeled on that used by Rogers and Monsell (1995), the DDVS task, a verbal fluency task, and a random generation task. Table 1 compares the outcomes of regressions in which the effects of age and CCT scorers were tested independently and the effects of age were tested when CCF scores had also been included in the regression equation.

In sum, across all experiments, age effects are found only in 7 out of 23 tasks and in only 1 of these cases do these effects survive after CCF scores are included. Thus these comparisons find little evidence for consistency between different neuropsychological tests which have been considered to be equally sensitive measures of age-related cognitive changes. It also seems that, in the majority of cases examined, age-related variance in performance on neuropsychological tests, including frontal tests, is entirely accounted for by variance in gf scores.

TABLE 1
Patterns of prediction for neuropsychological test batteries

Measure	Predictor Variables		
	Age	Age(after Fluid IQ added)	Fluid IQ
Exp. 1. (N = 162)			Yes
SWM	No		Yes
TOL	No		
ID/ED	No		
Shape recognition	Yes	No	
Position recognition	Yes	No	
Spatial span	Yes	No	
DMST	Yes	No	Yes
Paired association	Yes	Yes	
Exp. 2 (N = 90)			
DDVS (dual dimension visual search)	Yes	No	No
Exp. 3. (N = 57)			
DDVS	No	No	No
Stroop	No	No	No
Negative priming	No	No	No
Context memory	No	No	No
Exp. 4. (N = 50)			
Numerical "switch"	No	Yes	Yes
Verbal fluency	No	No	No
Alternating fluency	No	Yes	Yes
Exp. 5. (N = 50)			
Attention switch	No	No	No
DDVS	Yes	No	No
Verbal fluency	No	Yes	Yes
Random generation	No	No	No

ARE NEUROPSYCHOLOGICAL TESTS VALID IN THE SENSE THAT THEY SHOW ROBUST MUTUAL CORRELATIONS?

Burgess (1997) points out that in clinical practice individuals who perform poorly on one frontal test do not necessarily also perform poorly on others. He illustrates this with data collected by Wilson, Alderman, Burgess, Emslie, and Evans (1996) from between 74 and 216 normal adult controls on four different neuropsychological tests (as part of a much wider study); WCST, verbal fluency, cognitive estimates, and the Trails task, and on the NART test, which is also a rough measure of general intellectual ability. Within this group Wilson et al. found that all correlations between test scores were modest and few were statistically significant. Moreover, most of the significant associations between test scores disappeared when variance associated with individual differences in NART scores was partialled out. Although the NART is intended as a test of vocabulary, NART scores provide a useful, coarse, estimate of individual differences in general mental ability. Thus, comparisons within this group of normal adults provides little evidence for the mutual construct validity of these particular "frontal" tests. Those associations between tests that do occur seem to be strongly mediated by individual differences in general intellectual ability. Like the comparisons made by Lowe described previously, Burgess's (1997) data are consistent with Duncan's (1995) and Duncan et al.'s (1995) suggestions that CCF scores, or even coarse measures of intelligence, such as the NART, may predict frontal and executive function as well as do clinical tests which are used as specific diagnostic indices for this purpose.

However, as Reitan and Wolfson (1994) warn, it is unsafe to draw, from studies of "normal" participants of any age, conclusions about the extent to which mutual associations between different frontal tests reflect a common dependence on the same functional processes. They point out that many experimental studies have concluded that there are differences in frontal efficiency between younger and older children (e.g., Dempster, 1992; Harnishfeger & Bjorklund, 1993) or between young and elderly adults without any independent neurological evidence that the particular groups compared actually differed in frontal lobe integrity. The conclusions of such studies rest entirely on the assumption that because the tasks used had previously been validated as identifying patients with frontal brain lesions, individuals who performed more poorly on them were, necessarily, also frontally impaired.

This raises the possibility that the performance on frontal tasks of participants who do not suffer from focal deficits or damage will, as on most other tasks, be well-predicted by global task performance indices such as unadjusted intelligence test scores or measures of information processing speed. Note that scores on tests of gf are also good predictors of individual differences in information processing speed, even on tasks that are not thought to involve "frontal" or "executive" processes, such as simple CRT tasks. Within groups of individuals who do not have brain damage, correlations between scores on both frontal and non-frontal tasks may be equally determined by individual differences in levels of gf. In this case their common dependence on gf may mean that scores on frontal tasks correlate with scores on non-frontal tasks as often and as strongly as they do with scores on other frontal tasks. In contrast, within groups of people who suffer from similar frontal lesions, to the extent that frontal tests are successful at identifying these lesions, individuals who perform poorly on one frontal task will also perform poorly on others. We may argue that, in this case, performance on frontal tasks will be determined more strongly by extent and site of brain damage rather than on gf (and on the other functional characteristics that gf entails, such as information-processing speed). In contrast performance on other, better maintained, non-frontal tasks will still be well-predicted by gf. Consequently, the higher the incidence of local brain damage the stronger will be associations between scores on tests that are specifically sensitive to this damage, and the more weakly will the strength of these associations be determined by scores on tests of gf.

Note that these suggestions differ from speculations by Duncan (1995) and Duncan et al. (1995) because they imply that tests of gf are not, primarily, exceptionally sensitive tests of executive processes and so of prefrontal damage. Tests of gf have, rather, evolved to successfully pick up individual differences in performance across a wide variety of situations because they pick up a wide variety of different functional system performance characteristics including information-processing speed (Eysenck, 1986; Jensen, 1982; Vernon, 1985) and working memory efficiency. Among these performance characteristics they also pick up individual differences in goal neglect (Duncan, 1995) and, it seems, also in efficiency of inhibition of intrusive stimuli (Rabbitt, 1996b; Shilling et al., 2000).

This way of looking at things is consistent with later results reported in Burgess (1997). When Wilson et al. (1996) gave the same test battery to between 43 and 92 patients with mixed aetiology, they found that correlations between test scores were markedly higher than for normal controls and remained significant even after variance associated with individual differences in NART scores had been partialled out. This raised the possibility that if the proportion of individuals who experience marked frontal decrements increases with population age, the older the group we test the more likely we are to find the relationships that Wilson et al. discovered in their patient sample.

Lowe, Rabbitt, and Shilling (2000) tested this possibility by analysing data from the cognitive estimates, verbal fluency, Hayling sentence completion, category cue memory test, and the Baddeley "Doors" test of non-verbal recognition and Names recognition test. These had been given to two groups of individuals aged from 61 to 86 years, in Manchester (N = 93) and 63 to 87 years (N = 99) in Newcastle-upon-Tyne, in 1994 and again in 1999 (age range given is at second time of testing). Both samples were divided into old–old and young–old groups, with the cut-off point of 70 years of age. Tables 2a and 2b show matrices of correlations between 1994 test scores at first testing for the Manchester cohort, before

TABLE 2a
Correlations between measures at T1 for both age groups

	Category cue	Doors	Names	Cognitive estimates	Hayling
Doors	**.404***				
	.185				
Names	**.376***	**.434***			
	.147	.182			
Cognitive estimates	**−.219**	**−.163**	**−.321***		
	−.199	.132	−.162		
Hayling	**−.292**	**−.380***	**−.006**	**.209**	
	−.028	−.455*	−.014	.158	
Fluency	**.164**	**.299***	**.333***	**−.144**	**−.176**
	.165	.229	.277	.194	−.270

Young–old group, N = 45, mean age = 64 (3.5), correlations printed in bold typeface; old–old group, N = 48, mean age = 74 (3.2), correlations printed in regular typeface.
*Correlations significant at .05.

(Table 2a) and after (Table 2b) variance associated with Culture Fair intelligence test scores had been taken into consideration. Tables 3a and 3b show equivalent data for the same cohort tested 5 years later. From Table 2 we see that T1, when the old–old group was aged between 70 and 81 years, correlations between test scores were modest, and disap-

TABLE 2b
Partial correlations between measures at T1 for both age groups controlling for Culture Fair test scores

	Category cue	Doors	Names	Cognitive estimates	Hayling
Doors	**.202**				
	.109				
Names	**.301***	**.344***			
	.129	.096			
Cognitive estimates	**−.145**	**−.046**	**−.285**		
	−.150	−.060	−.176		
Hayling	**−.196**	**−.188**	**.112**	**.168**	
	.083	−.388*	.027	.106	
Fluency	**.044**	**.018**	**.244**	**−.106**	**−.003**
	.120	.219	.332*	−.095	−.232

Young–old group, correlations printed in bold typeface; old–old group, correlations printed in regular typeface.
*Correlations significant at .05.

TABLE 3a
Correlations between measures at T2 for both age groups

	Category cue	Doors	Names	Cognitive estimates	Hayling
Doors	**.414***				
	.455*				
Names	**.362***	**.195**			
	.388*	.511*			
Cognitive estimates	**−.154**	**−.247**	**−.029**		
	−.172	−.475*	−.155		
Hayling	**−.248**	**−.453***	**−.018**	**.359***	
	.397*	−.344*	−.395*	.243	
Fluency	**.210**	**.421***	**−.276**	**−.142**	**−.425***
	.388*	.309*	.452*	−.281	−.397*

Young–old group, N = 45, mean age = 69 (3.5), correlations printed in bold typeface; old–old group, N = 48, mean age = 79 (3.2), correlations printed in regular typeface.
*Correlations significant at .05.

peared when CCF scores were taken into consideration. Correlations in the young–old group were greater in number and magnitude than in the old–old group and, as expected, were largely non-significant after variance associated with CCF scores had been partialled out. Table 3 shows that 54 years later, when the old–old group were aged between 75

TABLE 3b
Partial correlations between measures at T2 for both age groups controlling for Culture Fair scores

	Category cue	Doors	Names	Cognitive estimates	Hayling
Doors	**.314***				
	.496*				
Names	**.292**	**−.015**			
	.535*	.429*			
Cognitive estimates	**−.066**	**−.070**	**.094**		
	−.163	−.393*	−.067		
Hayling	**−.141**	**−.265**	**.159**	**.254**	
	−.393*	−.311*	−.368*	.209	
Fluency	**.086**	**.196**	**.135**	**.015**	**−.274**
	.386*	.312*	.451*	−.271	−.389*

Young–old group, correlations printed in bold typeface; old–old group, correlations printed in regular typeface.
*Correlations significant at .05.

and 86 years, correlations between scores on different frontal tests had become stronger and were now independent of CCF scores. The pattern of correlations in the young–old group remained unchanged. This contrast resembles that between Wilson et al.'s control and patient groups and encourages the hypothesis that as this population aged it began to include increasing numbers of individuals whose performance resembled that of their patient group.

This result seems to neatly extend Wilson et al.'s findings with patients and to give a new slant to the progress of age-related cognitive changes. As people age they become increasingly likely to suffer from focal, frontal brain changes. However until these changes occur their levels of performance on nearly all tasks, including tests of frontal function, are largely determined by their levels of general intellectual ability as indexed by their scores on tests of gf. As a population ages those individuals who begin to suffer frontal deficits will tend to perform relatively poorly on frontal tasks. Individuals who perform poorly on one frontal test will also tend to perform poorly on others so that correlations between scores on different frontal tests will become more robust. Because, in elderly groups, exceptionally poor performance on frontal tests is increasingly likely to be due to damage to specific frontal systems rather than to global changes, correlations between test scores may be reduced, but will not vanish, when intelligence test scores are taken into consideration.

Unfortunately for this neat parallel with Wilson et al.'s (1996) findings, these results completely failed to replicate within the Newcastle sample. This failure of a longitudinal trend in relationships between test scores in one large sample to replicate in another, closely similar large sample means that we must turn to consider possible effects of absence of control of cohort selection which are related to poor specification of a model for the nature, and time course, of cognitive ageing in population samples.

MODELS FOR COGNITIVE AGEING AND THEIR CONSEQUENCES FOR COHORT SELECTION

An important issue that has not been acknowledged in discussions of "frontal ageing" is precisely how observations of CNS changes should be interpreted at the population level rather than at the individual level. We argue that it is essential to make a distinction between four different hypotheses about the ways in which brain changes occur in an ageing population. These represent the four alternatives resulting from combinations of two binary assumptions. First, whether we assume that patterns of brain changes invariably follow the same pattern in all individuals or that they may follow different patterns in different individuals. Second, whether we assume that local brain changes proceed continuously in all individuals as they age, or that as individuals grow old they may show some, general, intellectual decline but also become increasingly more likely to suffer abrupt focal decrements.

The first of these scenarios may be further expanded. One possibility is that the same, characteristic, patterns of brain changes invariably occur in all members of an ageing population, but that the rates at which these changes proceed, and so the balance and extent of their combined effects at any age differ between individuals. This may, albeit clumsily, be termed "universal, progressive, single pattern brain ageing". A second possibility is that patterns of local brain changes occur, and gradually progress, in all individuals, but that not only the rates, but also the particular patterns of change across brain sites may differ across individuals. This may be termed "universal, progressive multiple pattern brain ageing". Either of these scenarios may be modified by an additional assumption that apart from local changes that may occur continuously or suddenly, and which may be detected by changing patterns of performance across specific neuropsychological tests, there are also continuous global changes that affect performance on all tests of any kind.

The permutations of possible outcomes from these various scenarios are dauntingly complex, but it has been costly to ignore them for so long. In particular, they bring into question the conveniently simplistic assumption that there are two, separate, factors that are responsible for cognitive changes in ageing populations: the increasing, and accelerating accumulation throughout a lifetime's pathologies and "biological life events" (see Houx et al., 1993) and another process, which has been deemed to be aetiologically distinct, although it remains completely undefined both in terms of its biological causes and effects on the CNS: "normal" or "usual" ageing. Because processes of "usual" ageing have lacked any specific biological attribution it has been possible for them to be taken, without evidence, to be both continuous in their progress and global in their effects. The relatively abrupt effects of pathologies that become increasingly common in old age have, again without explicit acknowledgement or evidence, been regarded as necessarily being superimposed on these continuous and global changes.

This is an unsatisfactory state of affairs because it vitiates attempts to predicate, as so many investigators have done, models for age-related cognitive change on behavioural evidence alone. Even if we accept the simplistic distinction between the (undefined) continuous effects on the brain of "normal" ageing and the superimposed, relatively rapid effects of pathologies, a problem remains. Perhaps the most common cause of changes in the Central Nervous System in old age are cerebrovascular accidents or insufficiencies of cerebrovascular circulation. As Shaw et al.

(1984) have pointed out, these changes become more common as age increases and occur more frequently in the frontal lobes than in other areas of the brain. Some cerebrovascular problems will have relatively continuous and gradual effects, others will produce abrupt changes but the impacts of these conditions will, in general, occur over relatively short time spans compared to changes that have been attributed to the progress of "normal" ageing. On these grounds it is likely that the effect of focal brain changes, particularly in the frontal lobes, is best considered as a problem of increasing incidence of cases of particular kinds of local deficits rather than as a problem of continuous, and progressive unfolding of particular patterns of deficit in all, or most members of a population. The older the population we sample, the more individuals within it are likely to show focal "pathological" deficits in addition to global "normal" changes. It seems likely from the evidence cited above that these "pathological" deficits will, perhaps even most commonly, include frontal deficits.

Problems of self-selection bias and of drop-out are well recognised in large longitudinal studies. Comparisons of models for the aetiology of brain changes force us to recognise that they are equally pervasive and influential in small cross-sectional behavioural studies of modular changes in cognitive function in old age. In this respect it is comical that, without exception, authors of all small cross-sectional studies insistently make the point that the elderly groups that they tested were "healthy" or "well". As evidence that such individuals become increasingly rare as populations age we may consider that, in the United Kingdom, some 60% of males over the age of 70 are hospitalised, bed-ridden, or in sheltered accommodation and so are unavailable for laboratory testing. Evidence for the pervasiveness and diversity of brain pathology in so-called "normal, healthy community-resident samples" of older people is currently accumulating. For example a longitudinal study of 2616 individuals aged 75 and over found not only a sharp increasing incidence of brain lesions, but also an increasing heterogeneity of lesion sites with increasing age. This was coupled with increasing incidence of ischaemia, neuritic plaques, neurofibrillary tangles, and Lewy bodies that are characteristic of dementia, even in normal, self-maintaining community residents (Xureb et al., 2000).

Thus it seems certain that the older samples who have been assessed in all behavioural studies of cognitive changes in old age have been "elite" and atypical members of their age groups and that frailness and incapacity have filtered out precisely those individuals who might most clearly show "focal" or "modular" changes in cognition. It also seems likely that even among these rare elite survivors there is a very high incidence of "silent", undiagnosed focal lesions and of undiagnosed cerebrovascular disease and neuropathology which becomes greater the older the group that we sample.

An admission that modular brain ageing may be better described as a matter of increasing incidence of particular kinds of changes associated with various forms of pathology rather than continuous progression of "natural" and uniform patterns of change challenges vested interests in behavioural cognitive gerontology. More importantly it makes the design of further studies inconveniently complicated. We need to study much larger, and clinically better investigated samples. Indeed, it now begins to seem doubtful whether it is worthwhile to pursue research in this area without data from both structural and functional brain imaging. In recompense for these discomforts this recognition of diversity offers the advantage that it explains inconsistencies and conflicts in a very untidy literature. It entails acceptance of contrasts in the literature, similar to those discussed earlier, between the appearance in one sample of increasing coherency between frontal tests, and of their increasing independence of unadjusted intelligence test scores and the absence of similar changes in another. Like many other contrasting results, these seem to be down to the luck of the draw from populations that are differently weighted by initial self-selection and by selective drop-out over time. The effects of selection bias and of selective attrition have been often and very eloquently pointed out (e.g., Cooney, Schaie, & Willis, 1988; Siegler & Botwinick, 1979), perhaps it is time that we finally paid attention!

Manuscript received September 2000

REFERENCES

Albert, M. (1993). Neuropsychological and neurophysiological changes in healthy adult humans across the age range. *Neurobiology of Aging, 14,* 623.

Arnsten, A.F.T., Cai, J.X., Murphy, B.L., & Goldman-Rakic, P.S. (1994). Dopamine D1 receptor mechanisms in the cognitive functioning of young adults and aged monkeys. *Psychopharmacology, 116,* 143–151.

Axelrod, B.N., & Henry, R.R. (1992). Age-related performance on the Wisconsin card sorting, similarities and controlled oral word association tests. *The Clinical Neuropsychologist, 6,* 16–26.

Birren, J.E. (1956). The significance of age changes in speed of perception and psychomotor skills. In J.E. Anderson (Ed.), *Psychological aspects of aging.* Washington, DC: American Psychological Association.

Birren, J.E. (1959). Sensation, perception and modification of behavior in relation to the process of aging. In J.E. Birren, H.A. Imus, & W.F. Windle (Eds.), *The process of aging in the nervous system* (pp. 143–165). Springfield, IL: Charles C. Thomas.

Boone, K.B., Miler, B.L., Lesser, I.M., Hill, E., & D'Elia, L. (1990). Performance on frontal lobe tests in healthy older individuals. *Developmental Neuropsychology, 6,* 215–223.

Brinley, J.F. (1965). Cognitive sets, speed and accuracy of performance in the elderly. In

A.T. Welford & J.E. Birren (Eds.), *Behavior, aging and the nervous system* (pp. 114–149). Springfield, IL: Charles C. Thomas.

Burgess, P.W. (1997). Theory and methodology in executive function research. In P.M.A. Rabbitt (Ed.), *Methodology of frontal and executive function*. Hove, UK: Psychology Press.

Cattell, R.B., & Cattell, A.K.S. (1960). *The individual or group culture fair intelligence test*. Champaign, IL: IPAT.

Cerella, J. (1985). Information processing rates in the elderly. *Psychological Bulletin, 98*, 67–83.

Cohen, G. (1988). Age differences in memory for test: Production deficiency or processing limitations? In L. Light & D. Burke (Eds.), *Language, memory and aging* (pp. 171–190). Cambridge, UK: Cambridge University Press.

Cohn, N.B., Dustman, R.E., & Bradford, D.C. (1984). Age-related decrements in Stroop colour test performance. *Journal of Clinical Psychology, 40*, 1244–1250.

Connelly, S.L., & Hasher, L. (1993). Aging and the inhibition of spatial location. *Journal of Experimental Psychology: Human Perception and Performance, 19*, 1238–1250.

Connelly, S.L., Hasher, L., & Zacks, R.T. (1991). Age and reading: The impact of distraction. *Psychology and Aging, 6*, 533–541.

Cooney, T.M., Schaie, K.W., & Willis, S.L. (1988). The relationship between prior functioning on cognitive and personality dimensions and subject attrition in longitudinal research. *Journal of Gerontology, Psychological Sciences, 43*, P12–P17.

Costa, L. (1988). Clinical neuropsychology: Prospects and problems. *The Clinical Neuropsychologist, 2*, 3–11.

Daigneault, S., Braun, C.M.J., & Whitaker, H.A. (1992). Early effects of normal aging in perseverative and non-perseverative prefrontal measures. *Developmental Neuropsychology, 8*, 99–114.

Dempster, F.N. (1992). The rise and fall of the inhibitory mechanism: Towards a unified theory of cognitive development and ageing. *Developmental Review, 12*, 45–75.

Duncan, J. (1995). Attention, intelligence and the frontal lobes. In M.S. Gazzaniga (Ed.), *The cognitive neurosciences* (pp. 721–733). Cambridge, MA: MIT Press.

Duncan, J., Burgess, P., & Emslie, H. (1995). Fluid intelligence after frontal lobe lesions. *Neuropsychologia, 33*, 261–268.

Eysenck, H.J. (1986). The theory of intelligence and the psychophysiology of cognition. In R.J. Sternberg (Ed.), *Advances in the psychology of human intelligence, Vol. 3*. Hillsdale, NJ: Lawrence Erlbaum Associates Inc.

Goel, V., & Grafman, J. (1995). Are the frontal lobes implicated in "planning" function? Interpreting data from the Tower of Hanoi. *Neuropsychologia, 33*(5), 623–642.

Goldman-Rakic, P.S. (1993). Specification of higher cortical functions. *Journal of Head Trauma Rehabilitation, 8*, 13–23.

Goldman-Rakic, P.S., & Brown, R.M. (1981). Regional changes of monoamines in cerebral cortex and subcortical structures of aging rhesus monkeys. *Neuroscience, 6*, 177–187.

Gur, R.C., Gur, R.E., Orbist, W.D., Skolnick, B.E., & Reivich, M. (1987). Age and regional cerebral blood flow at rest and during cognitive activity. *Archives of General Psychiatry, 44*, 617–621.

Hamm, V.P., & Hasher, L. (1992). Age and the availability of inferences. *Psychology and Aging, 7*, 56–64.

Harnishfeger, K.K., & Bjorklund, D.F. (1993). The ontogeny of inhibitory mechanisms: A renewed approach to cognitive development. In M.L. Howe & R. Pasnak (Eds.), *Emerging themes in cognitive development* (pp. 28–49). New York: Springer-Verlag.

Hartman, M., & Hasher, L. (1991). Aging and suppression: Memory for previously relevant information. *Psychology and Aging, 6*, 587–594.

Hasher, L., Quig, M.B., & May, C.P. (1997). Inhibitory control over no-longer relevant information: Adult age differences. *Memory and Cognition, 25*(3), 286–295.

Hasher, L., Stoltzfus, E.R., Zacks, R.T., & Rypma, B. (1991). Age and inhibition. *Journal of Experimental Psychology: Learning, Memory and Cognition, 17,* 163–169.

Hasher, L., & Zacks, R.T. (1988). Working memory, comprehension and aging: A review and a new view. In G.H. Bower (Ed.), *The psychology of learning and motivation* (Vol. 22, pp. 193–225). San Diego: Academic Press.

Haug, H., & Eggers, R. (1991). Morphometry of the human cortex cerebri and cortex striatum during aging. *Neurobiology of Aging, 12,* 336–338.

Heaton, R.K. (1981). *Wisconsin card sorting test manual.* Odessa, FL: Psychological Assessment Resources.

Houx, P.J., Jolles, J., & Vreeling, F.W. (1993). Stroop interference: Aging effects assessed with the Stroop colour–word test. *Experimental Aging Research, 19,* 209–224.

Jensen, A.R. (1982). Reaction time and psychometric "g". In H.J. Eysenck (Ed.), *A model for intelligence, Vol. 1.* Hillsdale, NJ: Lawrence Erlbaum Associates Inc.

Kane, M.J., Hasher, L., Stoltzfus, E.R., Zacks, R.T., & Connelly, S.L. (1994). Inhibitory attentional mechanisms and aging. *Psychology and Aging, 9,* 103–112.

Kausler, D.H., & Hakami, M.K. (1982). Frequency judgements by young and elderly adults for relevant stimuli with simultaneously presented irrelevant stimuli. *Journal of Gerontology, 37,* 438–442.

Kimberg, D., & Farah, M. (1993). A unified account of cognitive impairments following frontal lobe damage: The role of working memory in complex, organized behavior. *Journal of Experimental Psychology: General, 122*(4), 411–438.

Kramer, A.F., Humphrey, D.G., Larish, J.F., Logan, G.D., & Strayer, D.L. (1994). Aging and inhibition: Beyond a unitary view of inhibitory processing in attention. *Psychology and Aging, 9,* 491–512.

Loranger, A.W., & Misiak, H. (1960). The performance of aged females on five nonlanguage tests of intellectual function. *Journal of Clinical Psychology, 16,* 189–191.

Lowe, C. (1998). *An examination of the validity of a "frontal lobe model" of cognitive ageing.* Unpublished PhD thesis, University of Manchester, UK.

Lowe, C., & Rabbitt, P.M.A. (1997). Cognitive models of ageing and frontal lobe deficits. In P.M.A. Rabbitt (Ed.), *Methodology of frontal and executive function.* Hove, UK: Psychology Press.

Lowe, C., & Rabbitt, P.M.A. (1998). Test/retest reliability of the CANTAB and ISPOCD neuropsychological batteries: Theoretical and practical issues. *Neuropsychologia, 36*(9), 915–923.

Lowe, C., Rabbitt, P.M.A., & Shilling, V. (2000). Longitudinal follow up of a cognitive neuropsychological test battery in an aged population. *Manuscript in preparation.*

McDowd, J.M., & Oseas-Kreger, D.M. (1991). Aging, inhibitory processes and negative priming. *Journal of Gerontology, 46,* 340–345.

Mittenberg, W., Seidenberg, M., O'Leary, D.S., & DiGuilio, D.V. (1989). Changes in cerebral functioning associated with normal aging. *Journal of Clinical and Experimental Neuropsychology, 11*(6), 918–932.

Moller, J.T., Cluitmans, P., Rasmussen, L.S., Houx, P., Rasmussen, H., Carnet, J., Rabbitt, P., Jolles, J., Larsen, K., Hanning, C.D., Langeron, O., Johnson, T., Lauven, P.M., Kristensen, P.A., Biedler, A., van Beem, H., Fraidakis, O., Silverstein, J.H., Beneken, J.E.W., & Gravenstein, J.S. (1998). Long-term postoperative cognitive dysfunction in the elderly: ISPOCD1 study. *Lancet, 351* (9106), 857–861.

Navon, D. (1977). Forest before trees: The precedence of global features in visual perception. *Cognitive Psychology, 9,* 353–383.

Nelson, H.E. (1976). A modified card sorting test sensitive to frontal lobe defects. *Cortex, 12,* 313–324.

Neumann, E., & DeSchepper, B.G. (1992). An inhibition-based fan effect: Evidence for an active suppression mechanism for selective attention. *Canadian Journal of Psychology*, *46*, 1–40.

Panek, P.E., Rush, M.C., & Slade, L.A. (1984). Focus of the age–Stroop interference relationship. *Journal of Genetic Psychology*, *145*, 209–216.

Pendleton, M.G., Heaton, R.K., Lehman, R.A., & Hulihan, D. (1982). Diagnostic utility of the Thurstone word fluency test in neuropsychological evaluation. *Journal of Clinical Neuropsychology*, *4*, 307–317.

Perfect, T.J. (1994). What can Brinley plots tell us about cognitive aging? *Journal of Gerontology: Psychological Sciences*, *49*(2), 60–64.

Phillips, L.H. (1998). Do "frontal tests" measure executive function? Issues of assessment and evidence from fluency tests. In P.M.A. Rabbitt (Ed.), *Methodology of frontal and executive function*. Hove, UK: Psychology Press.

Rabbitt, P.M.A. (1996a). Do individual differences in speed reflect "global" or "local" differences in mental abilities? *Intelligence*, *22*, 69–88.

Rabbitt, P.M.A. (1996b). Intelligence is not just mental speed. *Journal of Biosocial Sciences*, *28*, 425–449.

Rabbitt, P.M.A. (1997). Methodologies and models in the study of executive function. In P.M.A. Rabbitt (Ed.), *Methodology of frontal and executive function* (pp. 1–38). Hove, UK: Psychology Press.

Rabbitt, P.M.A., & Goward, L. (1994). Age, information processing speed and intelligence. *Quarterly Journal of Experimental Psychology*, *47A*(3), 741–760.

Rankin, J.L., & Kausler, D.H. (1979). Adult age differences in false recognitions. *Journal of Gerontology*, *34*, 58–65.

Reitan, R.M., & Wolfson, D. (1994). A selective and critical review of neuropsychological deficits and the frontal lobes. *Neuropsychology Review*, *4*(3), 161–198.

Rogers, R.D., & Monsell, S. (1995). Cost of a predictable switch between simple cognitive tasks. *Journal of Experimental Psychology: General*, *124*(2), 207–231.

Sahakian, B.J., & Owen, A.M. (1992). Computerised assessment in neuropsychiatry using CANTAB. *Journal of the Royal Society of Medicine*, *85*, 399–402.

Salthouse, T.A. (1998). Independence of age-related influences on cognitive abilities across the life span. *Developmental Psychology*, *34*(5), 851–864.

Salthouse, T.A., Fristoe, N., & Rhee, S.H. (1996). How localized are age-related effects on neuropsychological measures? *Neuropsychology*, *10*(2), 272–285.

Salthouse, T.A., & Meinz, E.J. (1995). Aging, inhibition, working memory and speed. *Journal of Gerontology: Psychological Sciences*, *50B*(6), 297–306.

Scheibel, M.E., & Scheibel, A.B. (1975). Structural changes in the aging brain. In H. Brody, D. Harmon, & J.M. Ordy (Eds.), *Aging* (Vol. 1, pp. 11–37). New York: Raven Press.

Shaw, R.J. (1991). Age-related increases in the effects of automatic semantic activation. *Psychology and Aging*, *6*, 595–604.

Shaw, T.G., Mortel, K.F., Meyer, J.S., Rogers, R.L., Hardenberg, J., & Cutaia, M.M. (1984). Cerebral blood flow changes in benign aging and cerebrovascular disease. *Neurology*, *34*, 855–862.

Shilling, V. (2000). *An investigation of age-related inhibitory deficits and individual consistency across measures*. Unpublished PhD thesis, University of Manchester, UK.

Shilling, V., Chetwynd, A., & Rabbitt, P.M.A. (2000). The construct validity of inhibition: Individual inconsistency across four measures of Stroop interference. *Manuscript in preparation*.

Shor, R.E. (1970). The processing of conceptual information on spatial directions from pictorial and linguistic symbols. *Acta Psychologica*, *32*, 346–365.

Shor, R.E. (1971). Symbol processing speed differences and symbol interference effects in a variety of concept domains. *Journal of General Psychology*, *85*, 187–205.

Siegler, I.C., & Botwinick, J. (1979). A long-term longitudinal study of intellectual ability of older adults: The matter of selective subject attrition. *Journal of Gerontology, 34,* 242–245.

Spearman, C. (1927). *The abilities of man.* New York: Macmillan.

Stroop, J.R. (1935). Studies of interference in serial verbal reactions. *Journal of Experimental Psychology, 18,* 643–662.

Verhaegen, P., & DeMeersman, L. (1998). Aging and the Stroop effect: A meta-analysis. *Psychology and Aging, 13*(1), 120–126.

Vernon, P.A. (1985). Individual differences in general cognitive ability. In L.C. Hartledge & C.F. Telzrow (Eds.), *The neuropsychology of individual differences: A developmental perspective.* New York: Plenum.

Walker, R., Husain, M., Hodgson, T.L., Harrison, J., & Kennard, C. (1998). Saccadic eye movements and working memory deficits following damage to human prefrontal cortex. *Neuropsychologia, 36*(11), 1141–1159.

Whelihan, W.M., & Lesher, E.L. (1985). Neuropsychological changes in frontal functions with aging. *Developmental Neuropsychology, 1,* 371–380.

Wilson, B.A., Alderman, N., Burgess, P., Emslie, H., & Evans, J. (1996). *Behavioural assessment of the dysexecutive syndrome.* Bury St Edmunds, UK: Thames Valley Test Co.

Xureb, J.H., Brayne, C., Dufoil, C., Gertz, H., Wischik, C., Harrington, C., Mukaetova-Ladinska, E., McGee, M.A., O'Sullivan, A., O'Connor, D., Paykel, E.S., & Huppert, F.A. (2000). Neuropathological findings in the very old: Results from the first 101 brains of a population-based longitudinal study of dementing disorders. *Annals of the New York Academy of Sciences, 903,* 490–496.

Zacks, R.T., Radvansky, G., & Hasher, L. (1996). Studies of directed forgetting in older adults. *Journal of Experimental Psychology: Learning, Memory and Cognition, 22*(1), 143–156.

EUROPEAN JOURNAL OF COGNITIVE PSYCHOLOGY, 2001, *13* (1/2), 29–46

A research strategy for investigating group differences in a cognitive construct: Application to ageing and executive processes

Timothy A. Salthouse

Department of Psychology, University of Virginia, USA

A strategy involving five distinct phases is proposed as a means of obtaining the most informative evidence about group differences in a particular aspect of cognitive functioning. Perhaps because the phases require different types of analytical methods, most prior research has focused on only a few of the proposed phases. This is unfortunate because each phase provides valuable information about the nature of the relevant construct, and its role in group differences in cognition. The strategy is illustrated with research on adult age differences in executive processes.

How can one determine whether a specific cognitive construct is an important contributor to differences in cognitive functioning associated with membership in a particular individual differences category or group? In this paper I describe a strategy that could be used for this purpose, and I illustrate its application with research focused on adult age differences in executive processes. The strategy is designed to incorporate strengths of both experimental and correlational approaches, which have largely been pursued independently in past research on ageing and cognition.

The five phases of the proposed strategy are schematically illustrated in Figure 1. They consist of: (1) construct specification and operationalisation; (2) examination of group-related differences on a variable presumed to reflect the construct; (3) examination of unique group-related influences

Requests for reprints should be addressed to Timothy A. Salthouse, Department of Psychology, University of Virginia, Charlottesville, Virginia 22904–4400, USA.
Email: salthouse@virginia.edu

This research was supported by National Institute on Aging Grant R01 AG06826. I would like to thank Reinhold Kliegl and Dan Spieler for their helpful comments on an earlier version of this manuscript.

http://www.tandf.co.uk/journals/pp/09541446.html   DOI:10.1080/09541440042000205

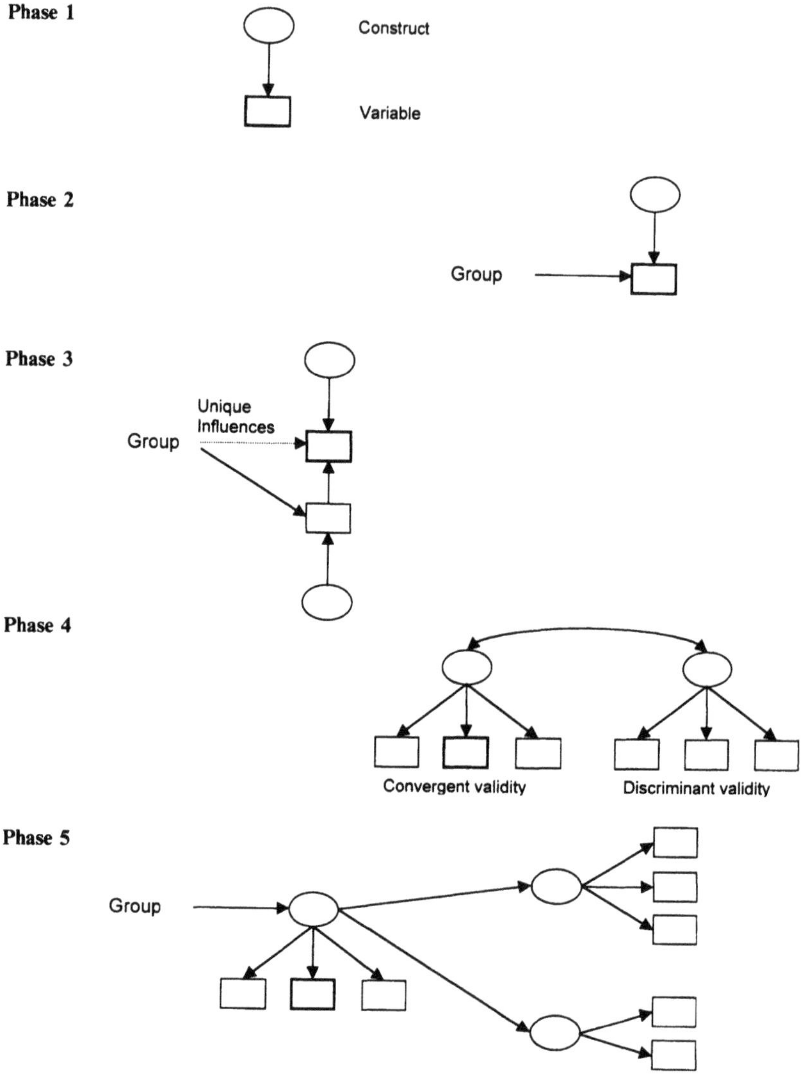

Figure 1. Schematic illustration of the five phases in the proposed strategy. Following convention in structural equation models, the squares represent manifest variables and the circles represent latent variables or constructs.

on the variable or construct; (4) investigation of convergent and discriminant validity of the construct; and (5) evaluation of the centrality of the construct in group differences in cognition. Although the phases are described sequentially, except for the first phase they need not proceed in any particular order and several may be combined in the same stage of data collection. This strategy is obviously not the only possible method of investigating group or between-person differences in cognition, but each of the phases can be justified as providing distinct and valuable information about the existence and nature of group differences in the relevant construct, and its role in other aspects of cognitive functioning.

The first phase consists of the development of theoretical assumptions or speculations about why the construct is important, and how it can be most meaningfully assessed. The primary purpose of this phase is to justify the relevance of the construct, and provide a rationale for a particular operationalisation of it. No data are collected or analysed in this phase, and instead the purpose is to establish a conceptual foundation for the tasks and variables used in subsequent phases.

The second phase in the proposed strategy consists of the collection of evidence that the groups differ in the level of the variable used to operationalise the construct. Several iterations of phases 1 and 2 are often needed to rule out construct-irrelevant influences and optimise the purity of the assessment because assumptions may have to be altered and tasks modified as data are collected. Because it is difficult to interpret the meaning of group differences with coarse variables that are likely to reflect a variety of different constructs, the refinement aspect of phases 1 and 2 is viewed as critical by many researchers. Depending on the theoretical assumptions, a variety of analytical procedures (e.g., subtraction, process dissociation, etc.) and derived measures (e.g., differences, proportions, etc.) could be used to try to achieve process purity. However, in all cases the major goal of phases 1 and 2 is to isolate the purest possible measure of the relevant construct, and then determine whether the groups differ in that measure.

The third phase in the proposed strategy involves obtaining evidence that the group differences in the relevant variable are at least partially independent of the group differences in other variables. Although frequently neglected, this phase is potentially quite important because many variables are often found to exhibit group differences, and it is desirable to establish that at least some of the group-related effects on the relevant variable are unique to that variable. That is, because organismic variables, or pre-existing individual difference categories such as group membership, typically cannot be randomly assigned or manipulated; people who differ on one variable are likely also to differ on other variables. However, if none of the group differences on the relevant variable or construct are independent of the group differences on variables that reflect other constructs, it is possible that the differences on the target variable are merely another manifestation of a more general phenomenon. A variety of statistical control procedures can be used to rule out this possibility, and establish that there are unique group differences on the relevant variable. Each procedure is designed to control the variation on other variables to allow a determination of the extent to which the group-related effects on the target variable are independent of the group-related effects on other variables.

The fourth phase in the proposed strategy consists of investigating construct validity by determining whether different operationalisations of the construct have moderately high correlations with one another, but relatively low correlations with variables presumed to reflect other constructs. Efforts in phases 1 and 2 are designed to maximise the correspondence between the construct and one particular variable, but they are unlikely to be completely successful because almost all constructs are broader than any single variable or else they would be of very limited interest. That is, even if the phase 2 research was successful in yielding a relatively pure assessment of the construct, purity needs to be complemented with breadth in order to ensure that the construct has meaning beyond one specific paradigm.

The idea that the most valid assessment of a construct should be based on several different operationalisations of that construct is similar to the recommendation by Garner, Hake, and Eriksen (1956) that converging operations be used in the investigation of theoretical constructs. The primary modification from the Garner et al. proposal is that in the context of individual differences research convergence is typically assessed with correlations. The rationale is that if two variables represent the same theoretical construct, then they should vary in a systematic fashion, such that individuals high on one variable should be high on the other variable reflecting that same construct. In contrast, much weaker relations should be apparent between variables representing different constructs. Correlations among variables hypothesised to reflect the same construct should therefore be moderately high to establish convergent validity, and substantially greater than the correlations among variables hypothesised to reflect different constructs to establish discriminant validity.

It is instructive to compare the approach to construct assessment in phases 1 and 2 with that in phase 4. As noted previously, phases 1 and 2 typically rely on an isolation approach by attempting to eliminate the contribution of construct-extraneous influences through task manipulations and various types of experimental control. In contrast, the approach in phase 4 relies more on the principle of aggregation by examining several variables that are all presumed to reflect the same construct, and then defining the construct by what is common among them. The two approaches are complementary because subtracting out irrelevant influences can be expected to yield a relatively pure but narrow construct, whereas averaging out irrelevant influences is likely to yield a less precise but broader and potentially more generalisable construct.

Notice that there are two key aspects to the proposed phase 4: (1) examining group differences in several different variables hypothesised to reflect the same construct to determine if the groups differ in the expected direction on each variable, and (2) examining the correlations among the variables to determine whether the variables reflect a distinct and unitary construct with respect to the pattern of individual differences. The first aspect is therefore necessary but not sufficient because group differences could exist in a variety of variables, and yet it cannot be determined whether the variables reflect the same construct or different constructs unless all the variables are available from the same individuals to allow correlations among them to be examined. If the variables reflect the same construct then not only should they all exhibit a similar pattern of group differences, but the correlations among the variables should be high, particularly relative to the correlations with variables hypothesised to reflect different constructs.

The final phase of the proposed strategy involves obtaining evidence that group-related effects on the target construct partially mediate group-related effects on other aspects of cognitive functioning. The rationale for this phase is that variables or constructs are generally of little interest in isolation, but instead are interesting with respect to their interrelations with, and impact on, other types of cognition. In order to establish that the construct is related to important and interesting aspects of cognitive functioning, therefore, empirical linkages need to be established both between group membership and the construct, and between the construct and variables reflecting other types of cognitive functioning.

Phase 2 research is concerned with the first of these linkages, but it is limited to a single indicator of the construct. Because few variables exhaust the meaning of the relevant constructs, and are seldom exclusively influenced by a single construct, the linkages are likely to be most meaningful when each construct is represented by multiple variables or indicators. Furthermore, the construct of interest should be linked not only to group membership, but also to variables representing other aspects of cognitive functioning. The most convincing evidence for this type of linkage is likely to be based on experimental interventions, in which the level of the critical construct is altered and concomitant changes are produced in the group differences in a variety of other cognitive variables. However, because experimental interventions may not always be possible, weaker evidence for the hypothesised linkages can be obtained from correlational data, in the form of structural models of the relations among group membership, the critical construct and other cognitive variables. Correlational data also allow statistical control procedures to be used to investigate implications of the hypothesised linkages. For example, if the construct mediates some of the group-related effects in cognitive functioning, then statistical control of the variation in the construct should lead to an attenuation of the group differences in other cognitive variables.

It is important to emphasise that different analytical methods are required across the five phases of the proposed strategy. Phase 1 is primarily theoretical to establish the conceptual foundation for the construct and its assessment, phase 2 is primarily experimental to refine and purify assessment of the construct, phases 3 and 4 rely on correlational procedures because they are based on the examination of relations among variables, and phase 5 is based on either experimental (strong) or correlational (weak) methods. From the perspective of the proposed strategy, therefore, no particular research method is inherently superior to another. Furthermore, exclusive reliance on a single method of investigation would be inappropriate because experimental control is needed to ensure precise assessment and to provide the strongest evidence for a causal role of the construct in group differences in other aspects of cognition, but correlational procedures are needed to evaluate the degree to which variables are independent of one another.

APPLICATION OF THE PROPOSED STRATEGY TO AGE DIFFERENCES IN EXECUTIVE PROCESSES

A considerable variety of tasks have been claimed to reflect executive processes. For example, within the field of neuropsychology the following tasks have been used to assess executive processes, with the accompanying types of justifications: The Wisconsin Card Sorting Test, because the examinee needs to maintain a task set (i.e., follow a rule to select responses), and exhibit flexibility to change the rule according to feedback and changing contingencies; verbal and figural fluency tests, because the respondent must generate multiple responses that satisfy particular constraints while flexibly using different retrieval strategies; various tower and maze tasks, because they require the planning and execution of a sequence of actions to achieve a goal; random generation tests in which the research participant attempts to produce a novel sequence of responses, and thus must inhibit or suppress stereotyped responses while keeping track of the responses already produced; the Stroop Colour–Word Test, because a prepotent response (reading a word) must be inhibited when making another response (naming a colour); and the Trail Making Test, because the examinee must maintain the position in one sequence while switching attention to a different sequence.

Although at least superficially these tasks appear to have little in common, the idea of executive processes has been appealing because the term refers to control processes that oversee the operation of more specialised processes. In this respect the concept is intended to capture aspects similar to the functioning of a business executive who is not a specialist in any particular area, but instead is responsible for the smooth functioning of an entire organisation. He or she creates and executes plans, establishes priorities, and monitors the execution of action sequences.

A more precise description of the processes often encompassed by the term executive has recently been provided by Smith and Jonides (1999, p. 1659). The five processes in their list are: (1) focusing attention on relevant information and processes, and inhibiting irrelevant ones; (2) scheduling processes in complex tasks, which requires the switching of focused attention between tasks; (3) planning a sequence of subtasks to accomplish some goal; (4) updating and checking the contents of working memory to determine the next step in a sequential task; and (5) coding representations in working memory for time and place of appearance. Subjective decisions are still required with respect to whether these processes are involved in a particular task, but the Smith and Jonides taxonomy is useful as a first step in determining whether a task reflects executive processes.

In the subsequent discussion I will focus on three sets of tasks each containing pairs of similar conditions designed to allow the isolation of a critical executive process: the Stroop Test, the Trail Making Test, and experimental switching tasks. In the familiar Stroop Test, the examinee is instructed to name colours as rapidly as possible when they are in the context of congruent words, incongruent words, or neutral stimuli (i.e., a row of Xs). The additional time in the incongruent condition compared to the neutral condition has been interpreted as a reflection of the failure to inhibit irrelevant information (i.e., Smith & Jonides criterion 1). One study in my laboratory was conducted with the traditional Stroop Colour–Word task (Salthouse, 1996). In another study (Salthouse & Meinz, 1995) three different versions of the Stroop task were administered: the standard version with colour names in different colours, a position version with location names in different positions, and a number version with digits in different quantities.

The stimulus materials in the Trail Making Test consist of a page containing an array of circled targets, and the task for the participant is to connect targets in either numerical order (version A), or in alternating numerical and alphabetical order (version B), as rapidly and accurately as possible. The additional time to complete the alternating sequences compared to the non-alternating sequences has been interpreted as a reflection of inefficient switching (Smith & Jonides criterion 2), and possible difficulty in the updating of working memory to maintain the correct positions in each sequence (Smith & Jonides criterion 4). Two studies in my laboratory were conducted with the standard version of the Trail Making Test (Salthouse, Fristoe, & Rhee, 1996; Salthouse, Toth, Hancock, & Woodard, 1997), one study (Salthouse et al., 2000) was conducted with an alternative paper-and-pencil version (Connections), and another study (Salthouse & Fristoe, 1995) was conducted with a computer-administered version.

In addition to tasks based on these neuropsychological tests, in another study in my laboratory (Salthouse, Fristoe, McGuthry, & Hambrick, 1998) specially created experimental tasks were designed to investigate the task switching process (i.e., Smith & Jonides #2). Three pairs of tasks with reaction time responses were used, and within each pair the tasks had different rules for mapping the stimuli to responses. The rules were: right/left—respond by either typing the digit on the right or on the left; more/odd—respond with one key if the digit is more than 5 and with another key if it is less than 5, or respond with one key if the digit is odd and with another key if it is even; and add/subtract—type the sum of, or the difference between, two digits. The additional time for the response when a switch to a different rule is required compared to when no switch is required can be assumed to reflect processes involved in switching such as redirection of attention, change in task set, reconfiguration of production, rules, etc.

The second phase of the proposed strategy consists of documenting age differences in measures of the relevant executive processes. Because the tasks just described each involve a pair of similar conditions, the differences between the scores in the two conditions can be postulated to reflect a specific executive process. Age differences could be examined by comparing the means of groups of young and old adults, but because all of the studies to be described involved samples with a continuous distribution of age, correlations between age and the difference score are reported. These values are presented in Table 1, where it can be seen that they ranged from .18 to .60. There were between 124 and 259 participants in each study, and thus all of the correlations were significantly different from 0. Because the contributions of other processes are presumably eliminated by subtraction of another similar variable, these results provide clear evidence of age differences in variables that can be hypothesised to reflect relevant executive processes.

The third phase in the proposed strategy involves estimating the unique age-related influences in the target variables. The estimates could be obtained with any of several different methods. For example, one possible method consists of statistically controlling the variance in a similar

TABLE 1
Age correlations in potential measures of executive processes

Variable	Age correlation	Sample size	Source
Stroop Colour Incongruent–neutral	.60	178	Salthouse (1996)
Stroop Colour Incongruent–neutral	.47	242	Salthouse and Meinz (1995)
Stroop Position Incongruent–neutral	.18	242	Salthouse and Meinz (1995)
Stroop Number Incongruent–neutral	.27	242	Salthouse and Meinz (1995)
Trail Making Test B–A	.53	259	Salthouse et al. (1996)
Trail Making Test B–A	.32	124	Salthouse et al. (1997)
Connections B–A	.41	207	Salthouse et al. (2000)
Computer-administered Trail Making B–A	.29	167	Salthouse and Fristoe (1995)
Switching—more/less Switch RT–Pre-switch RT	.38	161	Salthouse et al. (1998)
Switching—right/left Switch RT –Pre-switch RT	.38	161	Salthouse et al. (1998)
Switching—add/subtract Switch RT–Pre-switch RT	.41	161	Salthouse et al. (1998)

Note that the age of correlations are with difference scores created by subtracting the second variable from the first.

variable before examining the age-related effects in the target variable. With the three tasks described earlier, the controlled variable could be the neutral variable in the Stroop Test (i.e., the time to name the colours of Xs), the time in the non-alternating (A) condition in the Trail Making Test, and the reaction time on pre-switch trials in the switching tasks. (It is worth noting that this type of analysis of residuals is often recommended instead of comparisons of difference scores because unlike difference scores, the residual is independent of the original scores [e.g., Cohen & Cohen, 1983].)

A second possible method for estimating the unique age-related effects on a variable involves statistically controlling the variance in a different type of variable before examining the age-related effects on the target variable. Because letter comparison and pattern comparison tasks have been administered in many studies in my laboratory, results will be reported with a composite perceptual speed variable (formed by averaging the two z-scores) as the different type of controlled variable. However, it is important to note that virtually any variable could be used as the control variable because the question of independence of age-related influences could be applied to any combination of variables. A third method that could be used to derive estimates of unique age-related effects involves controlling an estimate of the variance common to many variables before examining the age-related effects on the target variable. Results from this method will not be described here, but it should be noted that several studies using this method have found results consistent with those from the other methods (e.g., Salthouse, 1996; Salthouse et al., 1996, 1997, 1998).

Table 2 summarises the proportions of variance associated with age in the target variable, and in residuals created by partialling either the variance of a similar variable or the variance of a perceptual speed composite. Because when a simple variable is partialled from a complex variable the age-related effects on the residual represent effects on the unique aspects of the complex variable, the purest assessment of the relevant executive processes construct might have been expected when the similar variable was controlled. Because the perceptual speed construct appears to have little in common with the complex Stroop interference or switching variables, the meaning of the residual formed by partialling the composite perceptual speed variable from these complex variables is somewhat ambiguous. Nevertheless, the two columns on the right of Table 2 indicate that there was considerable reduction of the age-related effects in the complex variable after partialling either the similar variable or the perceptual speed composite variable. The average total age-related variance across the 11 variables in Table 2 was .254, but the average unique age-related variance was only .032 both after control of a similar variable, and after control of the composite perceptual speed variable.

These results imply that an average of less than 13% (i.e., .032/.254 = .126) of the total age-related variance on the variables presumed to represent the relevant executive processes construct is unique to those variables. Because most of the age-related effects on the target variables are shared with age-related effects on other variables, these results raise the possibility that age-related effects on variables postulated to reflect executive processes are merely another manifestation of a broader phenomenon. In other words, these data suggest that, at least in terms of age-related influences, there may be very little that is special or unique about the purported executive process variables.

Because there is frequently confusion about the interpretation of statistical control results such as these, several points should be noted. First, it

TABLE 2
Total and unique age-related variance in target variables presumed to include executive processes

| Variables | | Age-related variance | | |
Target	Similar	Total	After similar	After PSpd
Stroop Colour Incongruent	Neutral	.429	.068	.057
Stroop Colour Incongruent	Neutral	.323	.038	.037
Stroop Position Incongruent	Neutral	.234	.009	.007
Stroop Number Incongruent	Neutral	.193	.001	.006
Trail Making Test B	A	.348	.056	.060
Trail Making Test B	A	.182	.033	.013
Connections B	A	.161	.00	.007
Computer-administered Trail Making B	A	.293	.041	.086
Switching—more/less Switch RT	PreSwitch RT	.159	.052	.025
Switching—right/left Switch RT	PreSwitch RT	.265	.016	.045
Switching—add/subtract Switch RT	PreSwitch RT	.202	.033	.012

Note: The sample sizes and sources of these comparisons are the same as those listed in Table 1. PSpd refers to the perceptual speed composite formed by averaging z-scores for the letter comparison and pattern comparison variables.

is important to recognise that proportions of variance are always equal to or greater than zero, and thus some of the residual R^2 values may actually reflect a reversal of the original age relation, and this possibility cannot be detected without inspecting other parameters from the regression analysis such as the beta coefficients. That is, the beta coefficient may change from −.5 to +.2 after statistical control, but the corresponding R^2 values would only change from .25 to .04, which is misleading with respect to the total change in the direction and magnitude of the age relation. Second, both statistical significance and the power to be able to detect an effect as significant need to be considered before interpreting the results. For example, a decrease from a significant R^2 associated with age to a nonsignificant R^2 is not particularly informative unless the research design had sufficient power to have been able to detect medium to small effects as significant. Third, the residual R^2 values should be examined in both relative and absolute terms. Relative comparisons, such as the residual age-related variance versus the initial age-related variance, are informative about the proportional contributions of different types of influences. However, because the residual age-related variance represents the age-related effects that are statistically independent of effects shared with other variables, it can be important regardless of its size relative to the initial age-related variance since it presumably requires a unique explanation. Finally, it should be recognised that results of statistical control analyses are not explanations, but rather are outcomes of methods intended to clarify the nature of the phenomenon that needs to be explained. A discovery that, for example, 87% of the age-related variance on a variable was shared with other variables therefore implies that unique or task-specific explanations are necessary, but that they are likely to contribute to a maximum of about 13% of the total age-related variance on the variable. Other types of explanations are consequently needed to account for the remainder of the age-related effects that are shared across several variables, and to indicate how those effects are manifested in particular variables.

The fourth phase in the proposed strategy focuses on investigating two aspects of construct validity. Convergent validity would be established if different variables hypothesised to represent the same construct have moderate to high correlations with one another, and discriminant validity would be established if those variables have much lower correlations with variables representing different constructs. Ideally, convergent validity would be evaluated with variables from tasks involving different methods, materials, and measures that are all presumed to reflect the same construct. Unfortunately, there is little evidence for this type of convergent validity for the executive processes construct because the correlations among variables from different tasks hypothesised to reflect executive processes are often no higher than the correlations with variables from tasks hypothesised to represent other constructs (e.g., Burgess, Alderman, Evans, Emslie, & Wilson, 1998; Duncan, Johnson, Swales, & Freer, 1997; Kopelman, 1991; Lehto, 1996; Rabbitt, 1997; Robbins et al., 1997; but see Della Sala, Gray, Spinnler, & Trivelli, 1998; and Hanes, Andrews, Smith, & Pantelis, 1996).

The analyses to be described therefore examine a very restricted type of convergent validity based on correlations among variables obtained from parallel versions of the Stroop and switching tasks. These data can be expected to provide upper limit estimates of the true convergent validity because the variables are derived from nearly identical tasks, and hence the resulting constructs are narrow due to the limited variation of methods, materials, or measures. In order to investigate discriminant validity, correlations were also examined with two variables hypothesised to represent a different construct, namely, perceptual speed. This also is not the optimum type of evaluation because the perceptual speed variables involved written responses, whereas the executive process variables were based on either vocal responses (for the Stroop tasks) or manual reaction time responses (for the switching tasks), and thus there is a confounding of theoretical construct and response mode. The confounding is likely to reduce the magnitude of the between-construct correlations, and hence the true degree of discriminant validity for the interference and switching constructs may be over-estimated with these data.

Although convergent and discriminant validity could be examined with raw correlations, or with reliability-adjusted correlations, a more powerful method relies on confirmatory factor analysis or structural equation modeling procedures. Two sets of analyses were therefore conducted on the data from Stroop interference (difference score) measures in three versions of the Stroop task (Salthouse & Meinz, 1995), and on the data from switching cost (difference score) measures in three switching tasks (Salthouse et al., 1998). Although difference scores frequently have low levels of reliability, that was not the case with these variables as the reliability estimates were all greater than .7. The first analysis was a confirmatory factor analysis with a perceptual speed factor represented by the letter comparison and pattern comparison variables, and either a Stroop interference factor or a switching factor each represented by three variables. A two-factor model fit the data in each data set quite well, which established that the constructs had convergent validity because the relevant variables loaded on the same factor, and discriminant validity because the correlation of the executive process factor with the perceptual speed factor was significantly less than 1.0.

The next analysis within each data set was a combination of the proposed phases 3 and 4. That is, this analysis consisted of a structural model with two latent constructs corresponding to perceptual speed and either Stroop interference or switching, and a path from the perceptual speed construct to the hypothesised executive process construct. In an initial model the age variable was related to both the speed and executive process constructs, but neither the path from age to the Stroop interference construct nor from age to the switching construct were significantly different from zero, and thus it was deleted from the model. The second model with each data set is illustrated in Figure 2, along with the fit statistics that indicate that the models provided excellent fits to the data.

Figure 2 provides information relevant to both phases 3 and 4 of the proposed strategy. That is, construct validity (phase 4) is established by the existence of two distinct constructs, but the absence of a direct path between age and either the Stroop interference construct or the switching

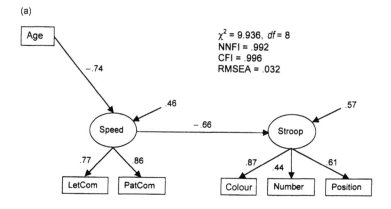

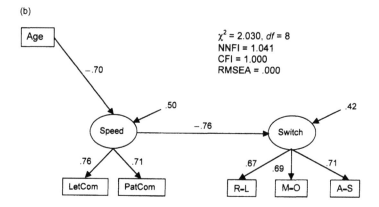

Figure 2. Structural models of the relations of age on perceptual speed and Stroop interference constructs (a), and of age on perceptual speed and switching constructs (b). No path is portrayed between age and the Stroop interference construct or between age and the switching construct because the path coefficient was not significantly different from zero.

construct means that there was no evidence of (statistically significant) unique age-related influences on the hypothesised executive processes constructs (phase 3).

The fifth phase in the proposed strategy consists of examining linkages between age and the construct, and between the construct and variables reflecting other aspects of cognitive functioning. The strongest and most convincing evidence for these linkages would be based on experimental manipulations of the critical construct because that would allow unequivocal conclusions about causal connections among the constructs. Unfortunately, there are not yet any experimental interventions of executive processes, in part because it is not obvious if, and how, constructs such as executive processes, or even more specific aspects such as resistance to interference or switching efficiency, might be altered.

A much weaker form of evidence for the hypothesised linkages is available from structural equation models based on correlations. The primary expectation with respect to the structural models is that executive process variables should function as a statistical mediator of age-cognition relations. That is, when executive process variables are included in the model the direct age-related effects on variables representing other aspects of cognitive functioning should be substantially smaller than the total age-related effects on those variables, because the total effects include both direct effects and effects that are mediated through the executive process constructs. A pattern such as this would be consistent with the hypothesis that the executive process construct may be mediating some of the age-related effects on other aspects of cognitive functioning. Evidence of this type is not definitive because there are many possible configurations of variables with correlational data, and it is well known that correlations by themselves do not imply causality. Nevertheless, correlational data do provide an opportunity to test critical implications of causal hypotheses. Specifically, if the target construct has little relation to age or to the other cognitive variables, or if there is little attenuation of the age-cognition relations when the construct is taken into consideration, then the results would be inconsistent with hypotheses that the construct is an important contributor to age differences in cognitive functioning.

Results from analyses reported in the original studies are consistent with the resistance to interference and switching constructs functioning as partial mediators of the age-related effects on other cognitive variables (Salthouse & Meinz, 1995; Salthouse et al., 1998, 2000). However, it is important to note that similar, and even stronger, patterns of mediation were evident with other potential mediators, such as perceptual speed. The interference and switching constructs are therefore not unique in exhibiting a pattern consistent with the mediation of age-related effects in other measures of cognitive functioning. Furthermore, because there was no evidence of unique age-related influences on the interference or switching constructs in the results summarised in Figure 2, all of the significant age-related effects on the executive process constructs in these studies appear to be mediated through perceptual speed.

CONCLUSION

What conclusion can be reached about age differences in executive processes based on the application of the proposed strategy? Perhaps the best one can say at the current time is that the evidence is still inconclusive. A major problem with respect to phase 1 is that it is not clear how one could determine whether executive processes were actually being assessed with a particular variable when no external criterion is available to validate that the variable truly reflects executive processes (e.g., Burgess, 1997; Tranel, Anderson, & Benton, 1994). In the absence of an explicit validation criterion, construct validity must be investigated with other techniques, such as examining the pattern of correlations with other variables, as in the proposed phase 4. There was clear evidence of age differences in variables hypothesised to reflect executive processes (phase 2), and the correlational evidence is consistent with the existence of Stroop interference and switching constructs distinct from a perceptual speed construct (phase 4), and with the involvement of these executive process constructs in the age differences in other cognitive tasks (phase 5). However, relative to the total age-related effects on these variables the unique age-related effects on the executive process variables were either very small or non-existent (phase 3), and similar or stronger patterns of mediation were evident with other types of variables and constructs.

Few if any phases in the proposed strategy are novel, but several of the phases have been neglected in prior research concerned with individual differences in cognitive functioning. For example, many researchers focus only on phases 1 and 2, and when group differences are found in the target variable it is often claimed that there are group differences in the relevant construct, and that the construct is responsible for at least some of the group differences in other types of cognition. Although evidence of group differences in the relevant variables is a necessary first step, it is insufficient to justify these other inferences. That is, with only data from phase 2 it is impossible to determine if the group-related effects on the relevant variable are unique to that variable or are shared with other variables that also exhibit group differences, the construct is defined very narrowly and can be considered to be confounded with a particular method of assessment, and there is no evidence that the construct is an important factor in group differences in other aspects of cognitive functioning.

Other researchers focus only on phases 4 and 5, and rely exclusively on correlational data. This type of evidence is also valuable, but it is incomplete in several respects. For example, interpretation of constructs may be difficult if none of the variables representing the construct is very precise, and if all are affected by an unknown mixture of different influences. Furthermore, because many alternative structural models are possible with correlational data, the data are often most informative in determining which models are *not* plausible rather than which of many possible models are plausible. Establishing that a particular model of the relations among constructs is the correct model may ultimately require other methods of investigation, such as experimental interventions.

It is not surprising that researchers from different backgrounds would emphasise different types of information or phases, but from the perspective of the proposed strategy this is undesirable because it results in the neglect of valuable information. There is clearly a need for variables that are precise and pure in reflecting the construct (phase 2), but there is also a need for evidence of construct validity in the form of moderately high correlations with other variables representing the same construct and low correlations with variables representing other constructs (phase 4). Moreover, in order to ensure that the relevant construct is both distinct and important with respect to group differences, the variable and construct should be found to have unique group-related effects (phase 3), and to have linkages to other variables and constructs (phase 5). As noted earlier, the order in which these different types of information is acquired is somewhat arbitrary, and in some circumstances it may be more efficient to combine several of the phases. Regardless of how the phases of the strategy are implemented, however, each aspect of the proposed strategy has the potential to contribute important information about the nature and role of group differences in cognitive constructs such as those intended to represent executive processes.

Manuscript received September 2000

REFERENCES

Burgess, P.W. (1997). Theory and methodology in executive function research. In P.M.A. Rabbitt (Ed.), *Methodology of frontal and executive function* (pp. 81–116). Hove, UK: Psychology Press.

Burgess, P.W., Alderman, N., Evans, JH., Emslie, H., & Wilson, B.A. (1998). The ecological validity of tests of executive function. *Journal of the International Neuropsychological Society, 4,* 547–558.

Cohen, J., & Cohen, P. (1983). *Applied multiple regression/correlation analysis for the behavioral sciences.* Hillsdale, NJ: Lawrence Erlbaum Associates Inc.

Della Sala, S., Gray, C., Spinnler, H., & Trivelli, C. (1998). Frontal lobe functioning in man: The riddle revisited. *Archives of Clinical Neuropsychology, 13,* 663–682.

Duncan, J., Johnson, R., Swales, M., & Freer, C. (1997). Frontal lobe deficits after head injury: Unity and diversity of function. *Cognitive Neuropsychology, 14,* 713–741.

Garner, W.R., Hake, H.W., & Eriksen, C.W. (1956). Operationism and the concept of perception. *Psychological Review, 63,* 149–159.

Hanes, K.R., Andrewes, D.G., Smith, D.J., & Pantelis, C. (1996). A brief assessment of executive control dysfunction: Discriminant validity and homogeneity of planning, set shift, and fluency measures. *Archives of Clinical Neuropsychology, 11,* 185–191.

Kopelman, M.D. (1991). Frontal dysfunction and memory deficits in the alcoholic Korsakoff syndrome and Alzheimer-type dementia. *Brain, 114,* 117–137.

Lehto, J. (1996). Are executive function tests dependent on working memory capacity? *Quarterly Journal of Experimental Psychology, 49A,* 29–50.

Rabbitt, P.M.A. (1997). Introduction: Methodologies and models in the study of executive function. In P.M.A. Rabbitt (Ed.), *Methodology of frontal and executive function* (pp. 1–38). Hove, UK: Psychology Press.

Robbins, T.W., James, M., Owen, A.M., Sahakian, B.J., McInnes, L., & Rabbitt, P.M.A. (1997). A neural systems approach to the cognitive psychology of ageing using the CANTAB battery. In P.M.A. Rabbitt (Ed.), *Methodology of frontal and executive function* (pp. 215–238). Hove, UK: Psychology Press.

Salthouse, T.A. (1996). General and specific speed mediation and adult age differences in memory. *Journal of Gerontology: Psychological Sciences, 51B,* P30–P42.

Salthouse, T.A., & Fristoe, N. (1995). Process analysis of adult age effects on a computer-administered trail making test. *Neuropsychology, 9,* 518–528.

Salthouse, T.A., Fristoe, N., McGuthry, K.E., & Hambrick, D.Z. (1998). Relation of task switching to speed, age, and fluid intelligence. *Psychology and Aging, 13,* 445–461.

Salthouse, T.A., Fristoe, N., & Rhee, S.H. (1996). How localized are age-related effects on neuropsychological measures? *Neuropsychology, 10,* 272–285.

Salthouse, T.A., & Meinz, E.J. (1995). Aging, inhibition, working memory, and speed. *Journal of Gerontology: Psychological Sciences, 50B,* P297–P306.

Salthouse, T.A., Toth, J., Daniels, K., Parks, C., Pak, R., Wolbrette, M., & Hocking, K. (2000). Effects of aging on the efficiency of task switching in a variant of the trail making test. *Neuropsychology, 14,* 102–111.

Salthouse, T.A., Toth, J.P., Hancock, H.E., & Woodard, J.L. (1997). Controlled and automatic forms of memory and attention: Process purity and the uniqueness of age-related influences. *Journal of Gerontology: Psychological Sciences, 52B,* P215–P228.

Smith, E.E., & Jonides, J. (1999). Storage and executive processes in the frontal lobes. *Science, 283,* 1657–1661.

Tranel, D., Anderson, S.W., & Benton, A. (1994). Development of the concept of "executive function" and its relationship to the frontal lobes. In F. Boller & J. Grafman (Eds.), *Handbook of neuropsychology* (Vol. 9, pp. 125–148). Amsterdam: Elsevier.

EUROPEAN JOURNAL OF COGNITIVE PSYCHOLOGY, 2001, *13* (1/2), 47–69

Is there an age deficit in the selection of mental sets?

Ulrich Mayr

University of Oregon, USA

Thomas Liebscher

University of Potsdam, Germany

Efficient selection of actions is dependent on higher-level constraints (mental sets) on lower-level selection. This paper explores the hypothesis that ageing leads to specific impairments associated with higher-level selection between mental sets. Indirect evidence for such a deficit comes from occasional findings of age differences in situations with high executive-control demands (e.g., Mayr & Kliegl, 1993) that are not easily explained in terms of other factors, such as general slowing or working memory parameters. More direct evidence comes from recent results with the so-called task-switching paradigm. Specifically, age-sensitive set-selection processes are indicated by age differences in "global selection costs" (i.e., the response-time difference between task-switching blocks and single-task blocks) which seem to be particularly large when demands in terms of "keeping competing mental sets apart" are high. Finally, data from a new variant of the task-switching paradigm (the "fade-out paradigm") are reported which show that age differences in global costs persist substantially beyond a phase in which set-selection is actually necessary. Generally, evidence is consistent with the view that in older age, a costly set-selection mode of processing dominates over the more efficient within-set-selection mode of processing, possibly because of a problem with maintaining distinct representations of what ought to be done in the face of competing representations of what could be done in principle.

Given an infinite number of potential actions to select from at any point in time, goal-directed action is conditional on internal constraints, often referred to as mental sets (e.g., Logan, 1978; Woodworth, 1918). An

---

Requests for reprints should be addressed to Ulrich Mayr, Department of Psychology, University of Oregon, Eugene, OR 97403, USA. Email: mayr@oregon.uoregon.edu

This research was funded through the Deutsche Forschungsgemeinschaft (Grant INK 12, Project C).

---

http://www.tandf.co.uk/journals/pp/09541446.html DOI:10.1080/09541440042000214

implemented mental set has profound effects on the entire cognitive system because it "configures" the system to allow efficient, even automatic selection within a subspace of "allowed" actions. Such efficient within-set selection has sometimes been referred to as a "prepared reflex" (Hommel, 2000; Woodworth, 1918). In the context of a typical choice response-time task, a mental set may constrain selection to occur only between the S–R links specified by the instruction. The flip side of "reflex-like" within-set selection is that there must be a second level of between-set selection processes that supports the preparation part of the "prepared reflex". Generally speaking these processes should be responsible for ensuring that the adequate mental set is in place as long as necessary, but not longer (e.g., Mayr & Keele, 2000). Obviously, such processes are critically involved in all complex thought and action. However, given that lower-level selection is conditional on adequately activated mental sets, set-selection processes may also determine when lower-level selection is efficient and when it is not.

In this paper we explore the hypothesis that set-selection processes may be involved in the emergence of negative effects of ageing on cognitive functioning. There are several reasons why this is an interesting possibility. First, set-selection processes often are associated with the frontal-executive system (e.g., Keele & Rafal, in press; Rogers et al., 1998) and the frontal lobes seem to show particularly strong effects of ageing (e.g., Raz, 2000; West, 1996). Thus, there seems to be some neurological plausibility to the idea that set-selection processes may be a key factor in age-related cognitive decline (see also Meiran & Gotler, this issue). Second, given the critical role of mental sets in enabling efficient within-set selection, there is the interesting possibility that age differences in lower-level selection (i.e., "within-set" selection) may be an indirect consequence of a deficit on the level of "between-set" selection. Finally, as will be discussed in greater detail in the following section, there is a pattern of particularly large age effects in executively demanding tasks that can be interpreted in terms of a set-selection deficit.

INDIRECT EVIDENCE: AGE DIFFERENCES IN EXECUTIVELY DEMANDING SITUATIONS

Our approach to the issue of age differences in executive control was shaped by the finding of very large age-related differences in conditions of what we then called high "coordinative complexity" (e.g., Mayr & Kliegl, 1993). The initial experimental contrast was implemented in the context of an object-comparison task (see Figure 1a and b; Mayr & Kliegl, 1993; Mayr, Kliegl, & Krampe, 1996). In the so-called sequentially complex

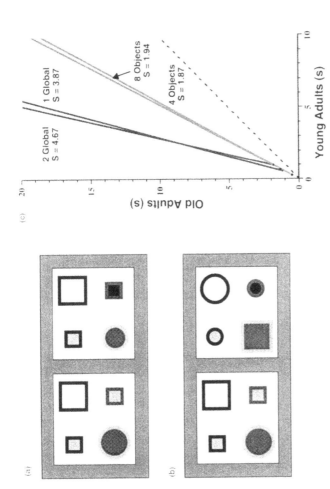

Figure 1. (a) Sample item from the four-object sequentially complex condition. Participants had to press one of four possible keys corresponding to the change affecting one of the objects (in this case "inside colour"). Sequential complexity could be increasing by using eight objects per array. Stimuli are not drawn to scale. (b) Sample item of a one-global condition where, in addition to the to-be-identified single-object change, all objects were also changed in the same dimension (in this case "shape"). Coordinative complexity could be further increased by adding an additional global change (two-global condition). (c) Old–young functions derived from the time–accuracy functions representing performance in four-object, eight-object, one-global, and two-global conditions (after Mayr et al., 1996). The numerical slope difference between the one-global and the two-global conditions was far from reliable.

49

baseline conditions, a difference between two arrays of four or eight objects each had to be identified. In the example shown in Figure 1a the correct response would be "inside colour" (which has changed for the lower-left object); alternative changes could have occurred to the frame colour, the size, or the shape (Figure 1a). What is critical about this condition is that no matter whether four or eight objects have to be checked, a simple progression through a series of independent search steps is required. In the coordinatively complex conditions, participants again had to identify the change that had occurred to one of the objects. However, in addition there was a "global" change in each of the objects in one dimension (in the example shown in Figure 1b the global change affected the objects' shape). In order to identify the single-object change the global change had to be "coordinated" with the search for the single-object change. Or, to put it more in line with the theme of this paper, an online re-specification of the search set had to occur on the basis of the global change.

Figure 1c shows representative results from the two types of conditions in terms of old–young functions (i.e., Brinley Plots). As evident, slowing is much greater in the coordinate conditions than in the sequential conditions. The proportional factor in the sequential conditions with a value around 2.0 is at the higher end of the general range of "general slowing" results (e.g., Cerella, 1990). In contrast, the slowing factor for the coordinative conditions was with a value of around 3.8, nearly 200% larger. It should be noted that the old–young functions shown here were derived from time–accuracy functions. These relate performance accuracy to presentation time, which was experimentally manipulated across each participant's entire functional range (i.e., from chance performance to a symptotic performance). The time–accuracy method not only allows capturing performance accurately across wide ranges of abilities and task difficulty. It is also based on extensive testing (more than 10 sessions). Thus, the processing limitations we observed likely reflect fundamental, practice-resistance constraints rather than more transient phenomena.

The dissociation between sequential and coordinative complexity is not a singular finding. Not only do other ways of producing coordinative demands in the context of the object-comparison task produce similar dissociations (see Mayr & Kliegl, 1993), very similar results have also been obtained when applying the time–accuracy method to the domain of episodic memory (Kliegl, Mayr, & Krampe, 1994). The proportional slowing factor for the episodic memory condition was with 3.6, very similar as in the coordinatively complex object-comparison task. Along with others' results this finding suggests that at least certain aspects of episodic memory are affected by an over-proportional age effect (e.g., Henkel, Johnson, & De Leonardis, 1998; Spencer & Raz, 1995). Whether or not there is a similar processing constraint behind the large age differences in coordinative and episodic-memory conditions is an open question. However, the similarity in slowing functions is at least consistent with the idea that they may be manifestations of a common source of age deficits.

What is the role of general slowing?

Before turning to the possible role of mental sets we need to examine other factors that may be responsible for the large age differences in coordinatively complex conditions. One dominant model of age-related decline holds that many, if not all, age-related changes can be explained in terms of consequences of an unspecific slowing of processing speed (e.g., Cerella, 1990; Salthouse, 1996). The fact that the age differences we obtained in the coordinatively complex tasks were so much larger than those typically obtained in speed-based tasks (e.g., Cerella, 1990) seems to suggest that general slowing is not a viable account. However, there is an important, unresolved issue here. Performance in a complex task may be a non-linear function of basic system parameters (Salthouse, 1996). For example, if every processing step is slowed, the probability of losing intermediately stored information (e.g., about the global change) may increase (e.g., Meyer, Glass, Mueller, Seymour, & Kieras, this issue) so that a slower system not only requires more time to completion but also more frequent reiterations (and, thus even more time).

To examine this possibility it is necessary to look at age differences in the critical conditions after somehow eliminating age differences in control conditions. Under normal situations such empirical constellations are very rare. However, they can be established with adequate selection of control groups or tasks. For example, Mayr et al. (1996) tested in the object-comparison task not only old and young adults, but also a group of 7–9-year-old children. Children of this age typically show a similar type of "slowing" as old adults. In fact, we could put together a group of 7-year-olds that operated on a lower level than old adults in sequentially complex control conditions. Nevertheless, old adults exhibited much larger deficits than children in the coordinatively complex condition. This result suggests that there is no unconditional link between basic speed and "coordinative" deficits (for another successful attempt of demonstrating coordinative-complexity age differences in the face of an "equal-slowing" baseline see Verhaeghen, Kliegl, & Mayr, 1997).

What is the role of working memory capacity?

Another possible factor contributing to the large age differences in coordinatively complex conditions are age differences in working memory capacity. There is ample evidence that functional working-memory capacity is reduced in older age (e.g., Verhaeghen, Marcoen, & Goosens, 1993). Furthermore, in coordinatively complex conditions, information concerning the global transformation has to be maintained and/or retrieved during the flow of processing in order to guide the single-object search (Mayr & Kliegl, 1993). Loss of this information from working memory may have led to additional, time-consuming recovery processes in old adults. To test this account we manipulated storage demands by adding a condition with two global transformations that had to be detected and applied. If storage actually is a critical factor, age differences should have become even larger for two than for one global transformation. However, age differences for both the one-global and the two-global condition were very similar (see Figure 1c). Interestingly, for children the two-global condition did produce marked additional decrements, suggesting that their performance problems actually could be attributed to limited capacity for storage or parallel storage and processing (Mayr et al., 1996).

What is the role of speed of working-memory access?

Possibly, the problem in coordinatively complex conditions is not one of losing information from working memory. Instead, old adults may simply take longer to access information maintained in working memory and to integrate it into the processing flow. In young adults, retrieving information from working memory in the course of an ongoing task has been identified as a major performance limitation (see Wegner & Carlson, 1996). We recently looked at this factor in the context of a task in which arithmetic-chain problems had to be solved (Oberauer, Demmrich, Mayr, & Kliegl, in press; Exp. 2). Specifically, we compared conditions in which half of the numbers to be added or subtracted were replaced by a "X" and participants either had to look up the number represented by the variable from the screen or from a three-item or six-item memory set that was encoded prior to problem presentation. Having to "look up" the number in working memory produced a large RT cost (between 1 and 2 s). Importantly, however, this cost was the same for young and old adults suggesting that speed of working-memory retrieval is not the critical age-related factor.

Of course, these results on the possible role of age differences in working memory capacity or access speed do not imply that there are no age differences in working memory. However, we found little evidence that working memory plays a critical role when processing demands stay within the functional spans for both old and young adults (which probably is the case for coordinatively complex conditions). Also, although age differences in working memory tasks are well-documented there is much less convergence concerning the nature of the underlying deficit (e.g., Zacks, Hasher, & Li, 2000).

THE ROLE OF MENTAL SETS

The results concerning large age differences in conditions with high coordinative demands are suggestive of an age-related processing constraint that cannot easily be attributed to generalised slowing or basic working-memory parameters. The hypothesis of age-related problems with the selection of mental sets does, however, provide a potential account of the observed age deficits. Take for example the coordinatively demanding object-comparison task (Mayr et al., 1996). Here, the "search-set" for identifying the critical single-object change needs continuous respecification within each single trial after identification of the global change, and also across trials. Similarly, in episodic-memory tasks the "set" is the list context that is required during encoding and retrieval. As has been repeatedly shown, age differences in episodic memory are particularly large when reliable representations of list context are critical for performance (e.g., Henkel et al., 1998; Kliegl et al., 1994; Spencer & Raz, 1995).

In the paradigms discussed so far, mental sets may have played an indirect, modulatory role for observable action and therefore any reference to set-selection processes must remain speculative (e.g., Shallice & Burgess, 1998). However, there are paradigms that seem to promise more direct access to set-selection processes. Specifically, in the so-called task-switching paradigm, situations are established in which participants select on a trial-to-trial basis both the responses to be given to a particular stimulus and the mental set that specifies the currently valid stimulus dimension and S–R rules (e.g., Allport, Styles, & Hsieh, 1994; Mayr & Kliegl, 2000b; Meiran, 1996; Rogers & Monsell, 1995). A change of set across successive trials usually leads to a marked RT cost compared to set repetitions, an effect that is usually referred to at the switch cost. Switch costs likely reflect constraints associated with the dynamical change of sets. However, aside from these "local" costs as switch points often also a more "global" cost is obtained (also referred to as "mixing costs", e.g., Meiran & Gotler, this issue): RTs from blocks in which a set switch can occur in principle take longer than RTs from set-homogeneous blocks (e.g., De Jong, this issue; Fagot, 1994; Kray & Lindenberger, 2000; Mayr, in press; Meiran & Gotler, this issue). Global costs may indicate the principal difficulty of having to ensure the adequate set on every given trial, irrespective of whether or not a change is actually necessary. In the next two subsections, we will review critical evidence concerning the age-sensitivity of local and global set-selection costs.

Age differences in local switch costs

A critical difference between coordinatively complex tasks and sequentially complex tasks is that only in the former does the relevant search set need to be switched in the course of processing. Thus, it is possible that a "set-switching operation" causes the observed age-related problems. Interestingly, however, the evidence for an age-related switching problem is mixed, at best. For example, in the first application of the now so widely applied old–young plots, Brinley (1965; see Figure 1c for an example of an old–young plot) demonstrated that age differences in switch RTs fell on the same old–young function as age differences from blocks of trials in which no switching was required.

Another example comes from a recent study by Mayr and Kliegl (2000a) who used what seemed like a particularly demanding switching situation. Participants had to alternate between two different semantic fluency tasks in a word-by-word manner. In addition, the semantic categories used were manipulated in semantic difficulty. Figure 2 shows the relevant data. As can be seen, both semantic difficulty and the switch contrast produced very large general effects (and also a highly significant interaction). For example, the mean switch cost for young adults was 2.8 s and 3.1 s for old adults. However, neither the switch contrast nor the semantic-difficult manipulation produced a general interaction with age. Only for the most difficult semantic categories age effects were slightly increased, both generally and in terms of switch costs. Thus, although in terms of time demands switching between semantic categories seemed to be a very "complex" process, no evidence for a "general switching deficit" was found. Interestingly this result is in clear opposition to recent suggestions that age differences in semantic fluency tasks arise from the need of switching between semantic subcategories (Troyer, Moscovitch, & Winocur, 1997).

Other authors have also failed to find specific age differences in switch costs (e.g., Kray & Lindenberger, 2000; Salthouse, Fristoe, McGuthry, & Hambrick, 1998). Interestingly, the age differences seem to be particularly small when there is little time for preparation (i.e., a small cue–stimulus interval), a case in which switch costs may reflect mainly the actual dynamical "switching process". In contrast, larger age effects have been obtained for the so-called residual costs after long preparatory intervals (De Jong, this issue; Meiran & Gotler, this issue). The lack of a specific age difference in the dynamical switching component is consistent with a recent proposal about the nature of local switch costs by Mayr and Kliegl (2000b). These authors argued that a major component of local costs consists of the time needed for the long-term memory retrieval of upcoming task rules. (Note, that the interaction between the semantic difficulty and the switch contrast present in Figure 2 is consistent with

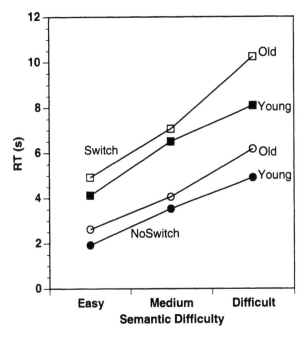

Figure 2. Mean retrieval latencies (averaged across the first nine retrieval positions of each semantic fluency protocol) as a function of semantic category difficulty and the switch contrast for old and young adults (after Mayr & Kliegl, 2000a).

such a hypothesis.) Memory retrieval is not uniformly affected by ageing in a negative manner (Zacks et al., 2000) and there are several examples of only very minor age differences in speed of retrieval (e.g., Mayr & Kliegl, 2000b; Oberauer et al., in press; Wingfield, Lindfield, & Kahana, 1998). From this perspective, it should not be too surprising that clear evidence for age differences in local costs is absent. At the same time, the finding of larger age differences in residual costs after long preparatory intervals (e.g., De Jong, this issue; Meiran & Gotler, this issue) could be interpreted in terms of problems with maintaining a once-retrieved action prescription in the face of stimulus and/or response ambiguity.[1]

---

[1] A complicating factor in the interpretation of local switch costs are response priming effects which usually are positive and large for no-switch transitions but often negative (and smaller) for switch transitions. Age effects in the size of such repetition effects may increase the size of "switch costs" simply because of a particularly large facilitation in case of set-plus-response repetitions. In fact, Mayr (in press) recently found that age differences in residual switch costs could be accounted for almost entirely by much larger positive response-repetition effects in old than in young adults in the case of no-switch transitions.

Age differences in global selection costs

From the perspective of a set-selection hypothesis of age differences in executively demanding situations, results regarding local costs are disappointing. There seems to be little evidence for a genuine switching deficit. However, a sole focus on local switch costs when the goal is to understand set-selection processes would be analogous to looking only at response priming effects when the goal is to understand response selection. In situations in which mental sets vary on a trial-to-trial basis, demands in terms of ensuring unambiguous representations of the currently relevant mental set may be present on every single trial, not only when a switch is necessary.

At first sight, evidence is again mixed. Although there are some studies in which no age effects in global costs were observed there are other studies that did report substantial age effects in this parameter. We will return to the inconsistencies across studies at the end of this section and for now will focus on the evidence in favour of age differences in global costs. A study by Kray and Lindenberger (2000) is particularly important in this respect. These authors assessed local and global switch costs for three different task pairs (from different task domains) across six sessions of practice. Whereas age differences in local switch costs were minor, age differences in global costs were substantial across the entire practice phase. In addition, psychometric analyses revealed that global and local costs could be dissociated factor-analytically into two distinct, albeit related, factors.

The general finding of larger age differences in global (but not in local costs) was recently confirmed in a study by Mayr (in press). In addition, this study contained conditions that eliminated an interpretational ambiguity present in the Kray and Lindenberger study. In their study, participants had to alternate tasks every two trials without external prompting. Thus, the demands of keeping track of the current position in the sequence of tasks in working memory may have been a critical factor. Also, the mere fact that in the critical condition two tasks were principally relevant (instead of only one task in the pure block control condition) may have overtaxed old adults' working memory capacity.

To eliminate these confounds between the set-selection and the single-task situation Mayr (in press) used a set-selection condition in which randomly selected visual task cues indicated which of two tasks (discriminating either colour or form of an object) was currently relevant. Thus, no endogenous sequencing demands were present here. Also, to avoid the contrast between a single-task block and a set-switching block (which entails a number-of-tasks confound), a different control condition was used. Participants had to work on the same two randomly cued tasks as in the experimental condition, except that the stimuli were unambiguous throughout the block (i.e., for the task dimension that was currently irrelevant a value was presented to which no response was assigned). Thus, here S–R rules of two different tasks were relevant, however no endogenous trial-by-trial selection of tasks was necessary because each stimulus uniquely cued its associated task. The fact that large age differences in global selection costs were found even in this condition suggests that working-memory demands are not critical for the emergence of these costs. Instead, global costs seem to be associated with the demands of endogenously selecting mental sets.

This study also contained an additional manipulation that was meant to test the idea that global costs are associated with the principal problem of maintaining clear representations of currently relevant courses of action in the face of competing mental sets. A critical factor in this respect may be the degree to which competing sets share common elements. Interestingly, in task-switching situations often common response specifications (the same two keys) have been used for the tasks to select from. Thus, it is possible that at least part of old adults' problem has to do with arriving at unique representations of mental sets when these converge on the same response alternatives. In such a situation, every use of the overlapping code in the context of one task may lead to the inappropriate reactivation of the other, competing set associated with that code.

To test this idea, a between-subject contrast between three different conditions differing in response specifications was used (see Figure 3). In the first condition, both tasks converged on the same two response keys (complete overlap). In the second condition two different sets of two keys were used, one set for each hand, but with the same left–right arrangement for each of the two sets (conceptual overlap). Finally, in the third condition, also different spatial arrangements were used with a left–right specification in one and an up–down specification in the other task (no overlap). As shown in Figure 3, age differences in global selection costs were much larger in the complete-overlap condition than in the other two conditions (with no difference between the two). Thus, this result is consistent with the hypothesis that age differences in set selection may be driven at least in part by problems with establishing a distinct representation of the currently relevant mental set. Specifically distinct representations should be difficult to select or maintain when the competing sets contain overlapping elements (for more extensive discussion, see Mayr, in press).

This last result may also bring order to the inconsistent pattern age differences in global costs we had mentioned in the beginning of this section. Whereas some (De Jong, this issue; Kray & Lindenberger, 2000;

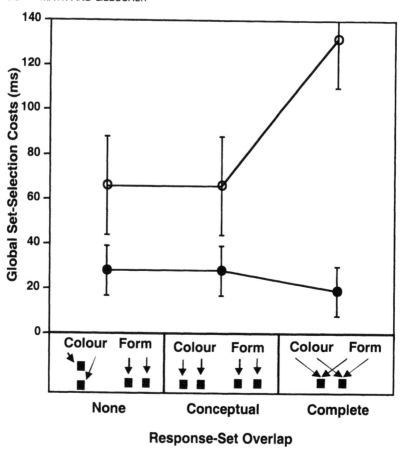

Figure 3. General set-selection costs (i.e., RT difference between ambiguous and non-ambiguous selection RTs) as a function of age and response-set overlap (after Mayr, in press).

Mayr, 2000; Meiran & Gotler, this issue) found age differences in global costs, a number of other studies that either explicitly or implicitly assessed global costs found no such age differences (Brinley, 1965; Mayr & Kliegl, 2000a; Salthouse et al., 1998). A common feature of the studies that did not find global-cost age differences was the use of non-overlapping and/or highly natural response specifications. For example, one of the task pairs used by Brinley (1965) involved reporting antonyms versus synonyms of stimulus words. In each of these two tasks, responses occur in a highly natural manner (i.e., simply speaking the correct word) and the relevant response codes are non-overlapping on the word level. The same argument also holds for the Mayr and Kliegl (2000a) study on alternative fluency tasks where participants also had to make natural, verbal responses. Thus, both the results of our explicit manipulation of response-set overlap and a critical review of the relevant literature suggest that age differences in global costs depend on the degree to which critical elements of competing mental sets overlap. When such overlap is eliminated or when response specifications are so natural (i.e., dominant) that a response set is not required, age differences in global costs disappear.[2]

THE FADE-OUT PARADIGM: DO AGE DIFFERENCES REFLECT PROCESSING CONSTRAINTS OR STRATEGY DIFFERENCES?

There is an important open issue concerning the interpretation of global selection costs that we want to address in the remainder of this paper. So far, global-cost effects were obtained in situations that involved continuous back-and-forth switching between two different tasks. This leaves the possibility that such effects have an intentional, strategic component (De Jong, this issue). Whenever selecting one of two competing tasks, participants know that the alternative task will become relevant again in the very near future. This may induce a strategy of keeping both tasks constantly in a state of readiness at the cost of reducing readiness for each of the two single tasks (for a similar suggestion, see Meiran, 2000). Possibly old and young adults differ in the degree to which they adopt such a "playing-it-safe" strategy.

We therefore tried to come up with a variant of the task-selection paradigm in which keeping both tasks ready was not a rational strategy. Figure 4 shows the task we used and the two critical conditions. Participants saw a two-dimensional stimulus with colour (yellow or blue) and shape (circle or square) as relevant dimensions. In the so-called fade-out condition, participants were cued on a trial-to-trial basis whether to respond to the colour dimension (i.e., press the left key for yellow and the right key for blue) or to the shape dimension (i.e., press the left key for circle and the right key for square) for the first 40 trials of a block. Task sets were cued by "filling" the circle below the corresponding verbal label (Figure 4). The critical phase started in trial 41, where one of the two task sets became irrelevant for the rest of the block in trial 120.

---

[2]The current focus on overlapping response specifications does not imply that stimulus aspects may not be a critical factor in producing age differences in global set-selection costs. For example, Kray and Li (2000) recently reported that age differences in global costs disappeared in a situation in which there were no stimulus repetitions across trials. Automatic retrieval of sets associated with recent stimulus aspects may be one critical factor in producing old adults' problems with arriving at unique set-level representations.

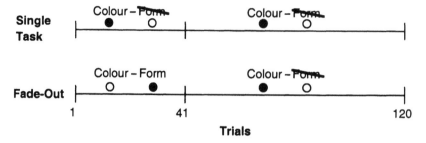

Figure 4. Block structure for the fade-out condition and the single-task baseline condition. Note that the second phase (trials 41–120) is equivalent for both conditions (i.e., single task).

Participants were not only informed prior to the block which task set would drop out, the label of the now irrelevant task set was also crossed out (see Figure 4). The second condition served as a control for this so-called fade-out condition: Participants worked on one task set throughout (i.e., the single-task condition) and the irrelevant task set was "crossed out" from trial 1 onwards. Comparisons between the fade-out condition and the single-task condition for trials 41 to 120 allowed to examine the development of "fade-out costs" across trials and, thus, the process of disengaging from a no-longer relevant task set or from a task-selection mode of processing. Finally, as a third condition a task-switching block was used that allowed us to assess global and local selection costs.

Method

Participants. Twenty-four young adults (M = 18.3 years, SD = .8, 12 females) and 24 old adults (M = 68.7 years, SD = 2.6, 12 females) took part in the experiment. Age groups did not differ in scores of the German version of the Wechsler Adult Intelligence Scale (WAIS) vocabulary test (old adults: M = 23.4, SD = 4.1, young adults: M = 24.8, SD = 3.0, $t(46)$ = 1.33, p > .15). Young adults outperformed old adults in the Digit Symbol subtest of the WAIS (old adults: M = 45.0, SD = 6.9, young adults: M = 59.7, SD = 7.6, $t(46)$ = 7.0, p < .01). Young adults were recruited among last-year students of a local high school (note that last-year students in German high schools are roughly equivalent to American first-year college students). Young adults received the equivalent of about $7 for participation, old adults received the equivalent of about $12.

Apparatus and procedures. Macintosh 7100/66 computers attached to Apple Multisync 17-inch colour monitors were used to display stimuli and collect responses. PsyScope 1.2 (Cohen, MacWhinney, Flatt, &

Provost, 1993) was used for programming the experiment. Stimulus form could be circle or square; stimulus colour could be yellow or blue. Above the stimulus each of the two verbal labels "colour" and "form" were presented together with a small circle that was filled if the associated attribute was currently relevant and otherwise open. The verbal label for the colour task was always shown on the left, the one for the form task was always shown on the right.

Depending on task (i.e., colour or form), participants responded with the left arrow key if stimulus form was circle or the colour was yellow and with the right arrow key if the form was square or the colour was blue. After a response, there was a 100 ms interval in which only the frame surrounding both stimulus and task cues (see Figure 4) was visible. Then, task cues (i.e., words and the filled and open circle) were presented for a cue–stimulus interval (CSI) of either 100 or 1000 ms before the stimulus was presented. Stimuli were visible until the associated response was entered.

Trials were presented in blocks of 120 trials each. Conditions differed in terms of the structure of these blocks. In single-task blocks, one of the two tasks was presented throughout. In this case, the circle under the verbal label was filled and in addition the irrelevant task cue was "crossed out" by a line throughout the entire block (see Figure 4). In task-selection blocks, both tasks could be relevant and on each trial, one of the two tasks was cued via filled circles. The irrelevant task was not crossed out here. Selection of tasks occurred randomly with the constraint that each task should occur equally often within a block. Finally, the structure of fade-out blocks was identical to that of task-selection blocks for the first 40 trials and identical to the single-task block for the last 80 trials (i.e., the fade-out phase). Thus, from trial 41 onwards, one of the two tasks became irrelevant and, accordingly, was crossed out. Participants were validly informed prior to each block per written instruction on the screen what the exact structure of the following block would be. Participants also knew that once a task was "crossed out", it would not become relevant again until the end of the block.

In order to examine the role of the time to prepare for the next task and/or the time to disengage from the preceding task, we also manipulated the cue–stimulus interval (CSI). In different blocks it could either be 100 and 1000 ms. The block-structure factor combined with the CSI-time factor yielded six different block types. Each block type was realised by a pair of blocks, which were identical for the task-selection condition, but differed with respect to relevant task for the single-task condition and the second single-task phase in the fade-out condition. The same-condition pairs of blocks were presented together. Also, each of the six blocks with same CSI were presented together in one of the two halves of the experiment. Within these two constraints, all relevant design aspects were completely counterbalanced.

Prior to the 12 experimental blocks, there was one 80-trial practice block in which both tasks were cued randomly (i.e., task-selection condition). To reduce the possibility of carry-over effects across blocks, a filler task was used between each of two blocks in which participants had to produce exemplars to different semantic categories for 60 s. For each filler task, the semantic category (e.g., animals) was presented on the screen and exemplars had to be written on a sheet of paper as quickly as possible.

Results

Based on correct response times (RTs) below 4000 ms (i.e., eliminating a total of 40 observations for old adults and 7 observations for young adults) mean RTs were computed for each participant and primary design cell. Accuracy was generally high and young adults performed slightly less accurately than old adults (young adults: $M = .978$, SD $= .16$; old adults: $M = .985$, SD $= .09$), a difference that did not reach significance, $F(1, 46) = 2.8$, $MSe = 1.4$, $p > .1$.

We first report results on local and global switch costs, thereby focussing on the no-switch versus switch RTs from the set-selection blocks and the single-task RTs versus the set-selection no-switch RTs. The relevant data are shown in Figure 5. Local switch costs were present for each age group and condition and they generally were smaller for longer cue–stimulus intervals, $F(1, 46) = 130.33$, $p < .01$. However, the local switch contrast was not involved in any significant interaction with age, all $Fs(1, 46) < .3$, $p > .6$. Replicating other results in the literature there was no evidence for age effects in local switch costs. This lack of an age effect in local costs has to be viewed against the background of large age effects in global costs. The difference between single-task and no-switch RTs was highly significantly larger for old than for young adults, $F(1, 46) = 55.0$, $p < .01$, an effect that was also present when log-transformed RTs were analysed, $F(1, 46) = 40.4$, $p < .01$. Thus, consistent with other reports in the literature, global costs seemed sensitive to the effects of ageing.

Next, we looked at fade-out blocks to examine development of set-selection costs after the point where active maintenance of the two task sets could be regarded a rational strategy. We subdivided the 80-trial fade-out phase into eight 10-trial segments (the first segment was only 9 trials long because we omitted the "transition trial" 41). Difference scores between corresponding segments of the fade-out condition and the single-task condition (also starting with trial 42) are presented in Figure 6 for

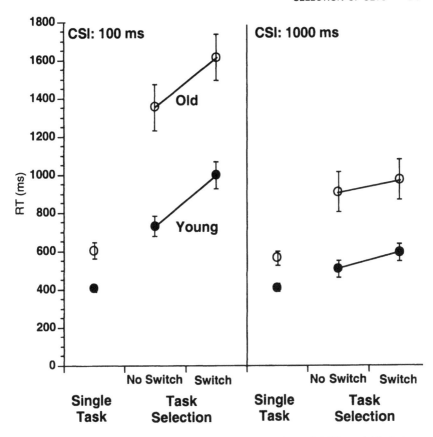

Figure 5. Mean RTs as a function of age, cue–stimulus interval (CSI), and block type. Error bars represent 95% confidence intervals.

the two age groups and the two CSI conditions. Young adults required not more than 10 trials to operate in the fade-out condition as efficiently as in the single-task condition. In contrast, old adults started with huge costs (180 ms to almost 450 ms depending on CSI) and were not able to eliminate these across the entire fade-out phase.

In terms of separate *t*-tests for young and old adults, the difference between the fade-out and the single-task condition was significant in the first segment only for young adults and for both CSI conditions. In contrast, for old adults, differences were significant for each segment except for non-significant trends in segment 7 in the 100 ms and the 1000 ms CSI condition and for segment 8 in the 100 ms CSI condition, $t(23) > 1.6$, $p < .15$. It is important to note that although old adults' problems in the fade-out condition may be initially somewhat reduced for

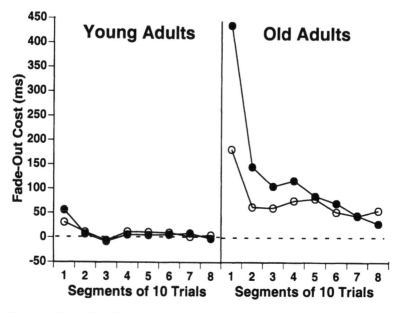

Figure 6. Mean RT differences between the fade-out condition and the single-task condition as a function of age, cue–stimulus interval (CSI) separately for eight 10-trial segments. Filled circles = 100 ms CSI; open circles = 1000 ms CSI.

the 1000 ms CSI condition, the qualitative pattern of costs is present for both CSI conditions.

Discussion

As this new result suggests, age differences in global costs persist into a situation in which there was little reason to suspect that participants might try to keep competing sets in a state of readiness. Rather, the large age differences in fade-out costs obtained here suggest a non-intentional processing constraint that prevents old adults from moving to the level of efficient within-task selection (i.e., the "prepared reflex"), even when this seems to be no problem for young adults. In further experiments we have replicated this phenomenon under a variety of different circumstances suggesting that a slowed transition between set-level selection and within-set selection is a stable characteristic of old adults' executive functioning.

One possible interpretation of the pattern of age effects observed in this experiment is in terms of a problem with disengaging from a mental set that is no longer relevant. This would account for both global costs during set-selection blocks and the fade-out costs. It also would be consistent with theoretical models suggesting an age-related inhibitory deficit (e.g., Lustig, Hasher, & Tonev, this issue). There are, however, a number of results from recent experiments that seem inconsistent with such a view. First, in an attempt to directly assess age differences in inhibition on the level of mental sets using the backward-inhibition paradigm (Mayr & Keele, 2000) we found that, if anything, old adults exhibited stronger inhibition than young adults (Mayr, in press). Second, in a new variant of the fade-out paradigm we had participants work on one of two tasks in an initial phase followed by a single trial in which they had to select which of the two tasks would be relevant for the final trials of that block. Interestingly, this single set-selection trial was sufficient to elicit substantial fade-out costs and these costs did not differ depending on whether the task selected on the set-selection trial was the same or different from the initial selection phase. Thus, fade-out costs seem to arise not so much when participants have to switch away from a no-longer relevant mental set, but rather when they have to switch away from a set-selection mode of processing (even when that was relevant only for a single trial).

Taken together, old adults seem to have problems with maintaining clear representations of the currently relevant set when competing and potentially confusable sets exist in the same context. This assertion is generally consistent with the "goal-neglect" interpretation of age differences in the Stroop task (e.g., West, 1999, this issue) or variants of the anti-saccade task (e.g., De Jong, this issue). What we add here is the suggestion that overlapping elements in competing higher-level control settings may be particularly critical in eliciting set-selection problems (or failures to obey to an implemented goal). Interestingly, this latter aspect is also consistent with the pattern of age-related deficits in episodic memory tasks with high demands on keeping representations with shared elements apart (e.g., Henkel et al., 1998; Kliegl et al., 1994).

The difficulty with maintaining clear prescriptions of what to do in a certain situation may force old adults into a control mode in which time-consuming set-updating operations occur with high frequency. In contrast, young adults may operate with a control mode in which set-updating steps are more limited to those points in time where they are required (e.g., when a new task cue appears). In case of a change in situation (e.g., from a set-selection to a single-task situation), the set-selection mode may persist until gradually superseded by a mode that is better adapted to the new demands. Thus, old adults' fade-out costs may simply be a result of them having to establish a very strong and therefore persistent "set-selection mode" characterised by frequent updating steps during the set-selection phase. Finally, the fact that the age differences in control modes reflect unintentional adaptations does not preclude the possibility that they could be changed more flexibly once participants become aware of them and are explicitly instructed to do so. Evidence from several sources suggests that the quality of high-level representations may be codetermined by a number of different factors, such as experimental context (i.e., West, this issue), attentional resources (Duncan, Emslie, Williams, Johnson, & Freer, 1996), or motivational/intentional settings (De Jong, 2000, this issue). In such a situation it seems possible that the weakening of one factor (e.g., attentional resources) may be compensated by other factors (e.g., explicit, intentional settings). Thus, the current results call for further studies in which global selection costs and fade-out costs are examined while manipulating instructions or incentives emphasising either fast within-task performance or accurate selection of sets.

CONCLUSION AND OUTLOOK

The question raised in the title of this paper was whether there are specific age differences in the selection of mental sets. The answer we can give on the basis of the evidence provided here and also considering results presented by others (e.g., De Jong, this issue; West, this issue) is a cautious "yes". However, an important qualification is necessary: There seems to be no general deficit affecting all set-selection processes. For example, the dynamical switching process, represented by local switch costs, is not generally affected by ageing. This pattern resembled other results on typical indicators of executive functioning, such as the Stroop task (e.g., Spieler, this issue). While generally not subject to specific age-related effects, there seem to be certain conditions where overproportional effects do arise (e.g., West, this issue). Generally, these seem to be conditions in which maintenance of the current task set is for some reason particularly difficult (e.g. De Jong, this issue).

In closing, we want to point out two lines of future research that would follow the work reviewed here in interesting ways. First, we have started off this paper by reviewing evidence for particularly large age differences in coordinatively demanding situations. We also reviewed some of the failures of providing convincing explanations for these age differences on the basis of "obvious" hypotheses in terms of age decrements in speed or working memory. Whether or not the hypothesis of a set-selection deficit provides such an explanation for the observed executive-control demands must remain open at this point. However, note for example the structural similarity between the critical task-selection situations and the object comparison task in that in both cases mental sets need to be selected continuously which share critical elements (response specifications and potential object changes). Nevertheless, there is a considerable empirical gap between the finding of large age differences in coordinatively complex situations (or episodic memory tasks) on the one hand, and the finding of large age differences in set-selection situations on the other. This gap needs to be bridged with paradigms that allow direct tests of the idea that there is a common factor underlying age differences across the different paradigms. One prediction following from this hypothesis is that the age-related sequential-coordinative complexity dissociation should disappear when the need for constant updating of mental sets in coordinatively complex conditions is eliminated.

Second, the data we reported on age differences in fade-out costs also point to a more fundamental issue. There seems to be an often overlooked, general executive control problem that could be characterised as the problem of "selecting between levels of selection". Obviously, it makes a substantial difference whether participants operate optimally (i.e., with as little processing on the costly set-selection level as necessary and with as much processing on the efficient within-set level as possible) or in some suboptimal manner (i.e., with more set-selection processing than "necessary"). Little is known about how transitions between the different levels of selection occur, to what degree between-level transitions are subject to unintentional and intentional influences, and the nature of age differences in relevant transition rules. We believe that variants of the fade-out paradigm introduced here will provide empirical access to the various issues surrounding this important executive control problem (see Mayr, 2000).

Manuscript received September 2000

REFERENCES

Allport, D.A., Styles, E.A., & Hsieh, S. (1994). Switching intentional set: Exploring the dynamic control of tasks. In C. Umiltà & M. Moscovitch (Eds.), *Attention and performance XV: Conscious and unconscious information processing* (pp. 421–452). Hillsdale, NJ: Lawrence Erlbaum Associates Inc.

Brinley, J.F. (1965). Cognitive sets, speed and accuracy of performance in the elderly. In A.T. Welford & J.E. Birren (Eds.), *Behavior, aging, and the nervous system* (pp. 114–149). Springfield, IL: Charles C. Mason.

Cerella, J. (1990). Aging and information-processing rate. In J.E. Birren & K.W. Schaie (Eds.), *Handbook of the psychology of aging* (3rd ed.). San Diego, CA: Academic Press.

Cohen, J.D., MacWhinney, B., Flatt, M., & Provost, J (1993). Psyscope: A new graphic interactive environment for designing psychological experiments. *Behavioral Research Methods, Instruments, & Computers, 25*, 257–271.

De Jong, R. (2000). An intention-activation account of residual switch costs. In S. Monsell & J. Driver (Eds.), *Attention and performance XVIII: Control of cognitive processes* (pp. 337–399). Cambridge, MA: MIT Press.

Duncan, J., Emslie, H., Williams, P., Johnson, R., & Freer, C. (1996). Intelligence and the frontal lobe: The organization of goal-directed behavior. *Cognitive Psychology, 30*, 257–303.

Fagot, C. (1994). *Chronometric investigation of task switching.* Unpublished PhD thesis, University of California, San Diego.

Henkel, L.A., Johnson, M.K., & De Leonardis, D.M. (1998). Aging and source monitoring: Cognitive processes and neuropsychological correlates. *Journal of Experimental Psychology: General, 127,* 251–268.

Hommel, B. (2000). The prepared reflex: Automaticity and control in stimulus-response translation. In S. Monsell & J. Driver (Eds.), *Attention and performance XVIII: Control of cognitive processes* (pp. 247–273). Cambridge, MA: MIT Press.

Keele, S.W., & Rafal, B. (in press). Deficits of attentional set in frontal patients. In S. Monsell & J. Driver (Eds.), *Attention and performance XVIII: Control of cognitive processes.* Cambridge, MA: MIT Press.

Kliegl, R., Mayr, U., & Krampe, R.T. (1994). Time-accuracy functions for determining process and person differences: An application to cognitive aging. *Cognitive Psychology, 26,* 134–164.

Kray, J., & Li, K. (2000, April). *Adult age differences in task-switching components.* Paper presented at the eighth Cognitive Aging conference in Atlanta, GA, USA.

Kray, J., & Lindenberger, U. (2000). Adult age differences in task switching. *Psychology and Aging, 15,* 126–147.

Logan, G.D. (1978). Attention in character-classification tasks: Evidence for the automaticity of component stages. *Journal of Experimental Psychology: General, 107,* 32–63.

Mayr, U. (2000, April). *Is there a specific age deficit in the selection of mental sets?* Invited overview talk at the eighth Cognitive Aging conference in Atlanta, GA, USA.

Mayr, U. (in press). Age differences in the selection of mental sets: The role of inhibition, stimulus ambiguity, and response overlap. *Psychology and Aging.*

Mayr, U., & Keele, S. (2000). Changing internal constraints on action: The role of backward inhibition. *Journal of Experimental Psychology: General, 129,* 4–26.

Mayr, U., & Kliegl, R. (1993). Sequential and coordinative complexity: Age-based processing limitations in figural transformations. *Journal of Experimental Psychology: Learning, Memory, and Cognition, 19,* 1297–1320.

Mayr, U., & Kliegl, R. (2000a). Complex semantic processing in old age: Does it stay or does it go? *Psychology and Aging, 15,* 29–43.

Mayr, U., & Kliegl, R. (2000b). Task-set switching and long-term memory retrieval. *Journal of Experimental Psychology: Learning, Memory, and Cognition, 26,* 1124–1140.

Mayr, U., Kliegl, R., & Krampe, R.T. (1996). Sequential and coordinative processing dynamics in figural transformations across the life span. *Cognition, 59,* 61–90.

Meiran, N. (1996). Reconfiguration of processing mode prior to task performance. *Journal of Experimental Psychology: Learning, Memory, and Cognition, 22,* 1423–1442.

Meiran, N. (2000). Reconfiguration of stimulus task-sets and response task-sets during task-switching. In S. Monsell & J. Driver (Eds.), *Attention and performance XVIII: Control of cognitive processes* (pp. 377–399). Cambridge, MA: MIT Press.

Oberauer, K., Demmrich, A., Mayr, U., & Kliegl, R. (in press). Dissociating retention and access in working memory: An age-comparative study of mental arithmetic. *Memory and Cognition.*

Raz, N. (2000). Aging of the brain and its impact on cognitive performance: An integration of structural and functional findings. In F.I.M. Craik & T.A. Salthouse (Eds.), *The handbook of aging and cognition* (2nd ed.). Mahwah, NJ: Lawrence Erlbaum Associates Inc.

Rogers, R.D., & Monsell, S. (1995). The cost of a predictable switch between simple cognitive tasks. *Journal of Experimental Psychology: General, 124,* 207–231.

Rogers, R.D., Sahakian, B.J., Hodges, J.R., Polkey, C.E., Kennard, C., & Robbins, T.W. (1998). Dissociating executive mechanisms of task control following frontal damage and Parkinson's disease. *Brain, 121,* 815–842.

Salthouse, T.A. (1996) A processing-speed theory of adult age differences in cognition. *Psychological Review*, *103*, 403–428.

Salthouse, T.A., Fristoe, N.M., McGuthry, K.E., & Hambrick, D.Z. (1998). Relation to task switching to speed, age, and fluid intelligence. *Psychology and Aging*, *13*, 445–461.

Shallice, T., & Burgess, P. (1998). The domain of supervisory processes and the temporal organization of behaviour. In A.C. Roberts, T.W. Robbins, & L. Weiskrantz (Eds.), *The prefrontal cortex* (pp. 22–35). Oxford, UK: Oxford University Press.

Spencer, W.D., & Raz, N. (1995). Differential effects of ageing on memory for content and context: A meta-analysis. *Psychology and Aging*, *10*, 527–539.

Troyer, A.K., Moscovitch, M., & Winocur, G. (1997). Clustering and switching as two components of verbal fluency: Evidence from younger and older healthy adults. *Neuropsychology*, *11*, 138–146.

Verhaeghen, P., Kliegl, R., & Mayr, U. (1997). Sequential and coordinative complexity in time-accuracy functions for mental arithmetic. *Psychology and Aging*, *12*, 555–564.

Verhaeghen, P., Marcoen, A., & Goossens, L. (1993). Facts and fiction about memory aging: A quantitative integration of research finding. *Journals of Gerontology*, *48*, P157–P171.

Wegner, J.L., & Carlson, R.A. (1996). Cognitive sequence knowledge: What is learned? *Journal of Experimental Psychology: Learning, Memory, and Cognition*, *22*, 599–619.

West, R. (1999). Age differences in lapses of intention in the Stroop task. *Journal of Gerontology: Psychological Sciences*, *54B*, P34–P43.

West, R.L. (1996). An application of prefrontal cortex functioning theory to cognitive aging. *Psychological Bulletin*, *120*, 272–292.

Wingfield, A., Lindfield, L.C., & Kahana, M.J. (1998). Adult age differences in the temporal characteristics of category free recall. *Psychology and Aging*, *13*, 256–266.

Woodworth, R.S. (1918). *Dynamic psychology*. New York: Columbia University Press.

Zacks, R., Hasher, L., & Li, K.Z.H. (2000). Aging of the brain and its impact on cognitive performance: An integration of structural and functional findings. In F.I.M. Craik & T.A. Salthouse (Eds.), *The handbook of aging and cognition* (2nd ed.). Mahwah, NJ: Lawrence Erlbaum Associates Inc.

EUROPEAN JOURNAL OF COGNITIVE PSYCHOLOGY, 2001, *13* (1/2), 71–89

Adult age differences in goal activation and goal maintenance

Ritske De Jong

University of Groningen, The Netherlands

According to the goal-neglect hypothesis of age-related decrements in cognitive control advocated in this paper, such decrements can be usefully and parsimoniously attributed to a reduced capacity for goal selection and goal maintenance in working memory. A selective review of research findings on age-related differences in exogenous and endogenous control of visual attention and eye movements and on performance in the task-switching paradigm serves to illustrate and clarify this hypothesis. The relative merits and scope of the hypothesis are examined within a broader theoretical perspective on the organisation of the domain of executive functions.

Theoretical considerations regarding the effects of normal ageing on executive control functions are presently dominated by the frontal lobe hypothesis of cognitive ageing, which assumes that major aspects of decline in cognitive functioning are associated with age-based changes in the frontal lobe (Dempster, 1992; West, 1996). As reviewed by West (1996), some fairly specific predictions about which aspects of cognitive functioning should be most prone to ageing can be derived from assumptions about the executive or control functions served by the frontal lobes, and such predictions are moderately well borne out by available evidence. As pointed out by Baddeley (1996), a simple mapping of executive functions onto a neuroanatomical structure may not provide a satisfactory or useful basis for defining and exploring (age-related effects on) cognitive control, and can be no substitute for systematic functional explorations of the domain of executive functions. Nevertheless, the frontal lobe hypothesis of cognitive ageing has considerable heuristic value and it will be used in that sense here.

Requests for reprints should be addressed to R. De Jong, Experimental and Work Psychology, University of Groningen, Grote Kruisstraat 2/1, 9712 TS Groningen, The Netherlands. Email: r.de.jong@ppsw.rug.nl

---

http://www.tandf.co.uk/journals/pp/09541446.html   DOI:10.1080/09541440042000223

The perspective on age-related effects on cognitive control pursued in the present paper draws heavily on a theoretical proposal that has been put forward by Duncan and co-workers (Duncan, Emslie, Williams, Johnson, & Freer, 1996; Duncan, Johnson, Swales, & Freer, 1997). Starting from three relevant phenomena—cognitive impairment in frontal patients, performance decrements in dual-task paradigms, and individual differences in fluid intelligence—they suggested that these phenomena might be closely linked, each concerning a primary function of the frontal lobe: goal selection and goal maintenance under conditions of novelty or weak environmental support. In a similar vein, the ability or capacity to generate and maintain goals or intentions in working memory has been argued to be a primary determinant of performance in tasks that require the organisation and management of a hierarchy of goals (Anderson, Reder, & Lebiere, 1996; Carpenter, Just, & Shell, 1990). The hypothesis to be pursued in this paper states that age-related deficits in cognitive control can be usefully attributed to a reduced capacity for generating and maintaining goals in working memory. Particularly under conditions of novelty or weak environment, this reduction in capacity in the elderly should result in pronounced *goal neglect*, defined as disregard of a task requirement even if it has been understood, resulting in a mismatch between what is known about task requirements and what can be done in principle, and what is actually attempted in behaviour (De Jong, Berendsen, & Cools, 1999; Duncan et al., 1996). Furthermore, the elderly can be predicted to be both more dependent on and more sensitive to means for external support offered by the task environment in order to compensate for a reduced capacity for internal control (e.g., Hultsch, Hertzog, & Dixon, 1987). In the remainder of the paper I will clarify and illustrate this hypothesis. In the next two sections I will consider relevant research findings on age-related effects on exogenous and endogenous direction of visual attention and eye movements and on performance in the task-switching paradigm, respectively. In the final section I will examine the relative merits and scope of the present hypothesis within a broader theoretical perspective on the organisation of the domain of executive functions.

AGEING EFFECTS ON EXOGENOUS AND ENDOGENOUS CONTROL OF VISUAL ATTENTION AND EYE MOVEMENTS

In the prosaccade task subjects are required to make a swift saccade towards a peripherally presented, abrupt-onset stimulus. In the antisaccade task subjects are required to suppress a reflexive saccade towards the presented stimulus and instead produce a swift saccade in the opposite direction (antisaccade). The basic findings in this paradigm are straight-forward and robust (Everling & Fischer, 1998). Saccadic reaction times (SRT) of correct antisaccades are substantially slower than those of correct prosaccades, and reflexive direction errors are quite common in the antisaccade task, whereas errors occur only rarely in the prosaccade task. The relative ease of the prosaccade task can be attributed to the fact that abrupt-onset peripheral stimuli elicit saccades to their location in a highly reflexive manner. Such exogenous saccadic control is generally believed to depend on the integrity of the posterior attentional system without much or any involvement of the anterior attentional system or frontal lobes (Posner, 1992). Accordingly, little or no deficits in prosac-cade performance have been found for frontal-lesioned groups (for review, see Roberts, Hager, & Heron, 1994). The antisaccade task, in contrast, requires subjects to suppress the reflexive prosaccade and to endogenously direct their gaze instead to the opposite location, and may thus be expected to critically involve the frontal lobes. Indeed, pronounced deficits in antisaccade performance have been demonstrated in frontal-lesioned groups and in other syndromes with known or suspected frontal dysfunctioning (Roberts et al., 1994).

Ageing studies that used the pro/anti saccade tasks have produced only modest evidence for age-related differences in performance. Consistent with much other research, older adults are somewhat slower at initiating saccades, but those studies in which subjects were practised and tested extensively have generally found comparable performance by young and old adults both in terms of the percentage of reflexive direction errors in the antisaccade task (Munoz, Broughton, Goldring, & Armstrong, 1998) and in terms of the additional time required to initiate correct antisac-cades compared to prosaccades (Butler, Zacks, & Henderson, 1999; Fischer, Biscaldi, & Gezeck, 1997; Munoz et al., 1998). These results would seem to pose obvious problems for the frontal-lobe hypothesis, an issue to which I will return shortly.

Our original intent in developing the pro/anti cue paradigm was to obtain a paradigm that was logically and functionally isomorphic with the pro/anti saccade paradigm but did not require measurement of eye movements. The tasks in the pro/anti cue paradigm require subjects to judge whether the emotional expression of a schematic face was happy or sad, where the happy and sad face differed only in the shape of the mouth. The mouth is displayed only briefly and then masked, making the judgement a challenging one. At the beginning of each trial, the display consists of a central fixation cross surrounded by four boxes that are symmetrically positioned above and below and to the left and right of the fixation cross; the whole display subtends approximately 8 × 8 degrees of visual angle. After a short period, one of the boxes briefly flickers, providing a clearly perceptible spatial cue. There are two conditions, a procue and an anticue condition. In the procue condition, subjects are informed that the face will appear in the cued box, and in the anticue condition that it will appear in the box opposite to the cued one. The stimulus onset asynchrony (SOA) between the cue and onset of the face is one of eight equiprobable and randomly selected values (100, 200, 300, 400, 600, 800, 1000, or 1500 ms). On one-third of the trials in each condition, a neutral cue is presented that consists of a brief flickering of all four boxes. At the start of the experiment, the time that the mouth should be displayed, before being masked, in order to yield 67% correct responses with the neutral cue is determined for each subject; this duration is subsequently used for that subject throughout the remainder of the experiment. In the first experiment, 16 young adults, all college students (age range 20–27 years; mean age 22.3 years), and 16 old adults, all highly educated, socially active, and in good health (age range 65–82 years; mean age 72.4 years), served as participants. The mean presentation duration of the mouth was 114 ms for the young and 156 ms for the old adults. Subjects were not instructed to maintain fixation on the central fixation point; possible eye movements were not recorded (though later experiments revealed that eye movements usually occur in this version of the paradigm; for further details, see Nieuwenhuis, Broerse, Nielen, & De Jong, 2000).

The results are shown in Figure 1. Accuracy for procues rises quickly to a high asymptote as a function of SOA, and, in accordance with previous studies, the functions for young and old adults are very similar. In contrast, the function for anticues reveals marked differences between the age groups. For young adults, the function briefly dips below the control level for the neutral cue but then rises quickly to the same asymptotic level as for procues. For old adults, however, accuracy for anticues remains well, and highly significantly so, below the neutral control level for at least 300 ms, reflecting a much stronger tendency for the cue to pull attention to the wrong location. Also, unlike for young adults, the asymptotic level of accuracy for anticues is significantly lower than that for procues, indicating that old adults had difficulty redirecting attention (and/or gaze) to the opposite location even if they were given ample time to do so.

These results provide clear evidence for specific deleterious effects of normal ageing on performance in the anticue condition, and in that respect contrast markedly with results from ageing studies that used the pro/anti saccade paradigm. How can these radically different outcomes for two paradigms that we assumed to be logically and functionally isomorphic, be explained? A closer analysis of the two paradigms may

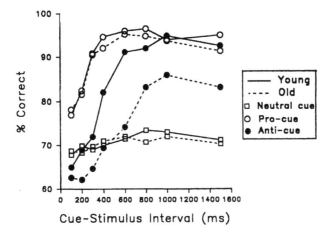

Figure 1. Average percentage correct perceptual judgements in the pro/anti cue paradigm, as a function of age group, cue–stimulus interval, and type of cue.

suggest an answer. In the pro/anti saccade paradigm, the explicit and only goal is to make a swift and correct saccade. In the pro/anti cue paradigm, in contrast, the main goal is to correctly judge the emotional expression of the face stimulus; in this paradigm, an attentional shift or saccade is only instrumental in enhancing the likelihood of achieving that goal. Put differently, the goal to make a saccade is the primary goal in the pro/anti saccade paradigm but only a subordinate goal in the pro/anti cue paradigm. According to the hypothesis pursued in this paper, normal ageing brings about a reduced capacity for endogenous goal selection and goal maintenance. It seems reasonable to assume that this reduced capacity might not be severely taxed when, as in the pro/anti saccade paradigm, there is only one relevant and simple goal, but may become significant when, as in the pro/anti cue paradigm, subordinate goals need to be set and maintained as well. In the procue condition, a reduced capacity for endogenously activating the subordinate goal of executing an instrumental saccade should be amply compensated, and thus masked, by the exogenous triggering of such a saccade by the cue itself. In the anticue condition, however, it should result in a diminished effectiveness of inhibitory control of reflexive glances and cause the endogenous triggering of the antisaccade to be greatly slowed, which would explain age-related differences at short SOAs, or to fail altogether on some proportion of trials, which would explain the finding that, for old adults only, the asymptotic level of accuracy for anticues was significantly lower than that for procues. Interestingly, the only other published study we know of that also found age-related deficits in an antisaccade task, in terms of direction errors but not in terms of saccade latency, also employed a perceptual identification task "to provide motivation for the participants to move their eyes as quickly as possible" (Butler et al., 1999, p. 586; for further discussion of their results, see Nieuwenhuis, Ridderinkhof, De Jong, Kok, & van der Molen, in press). Clearly, this account of the different results in the pro/anti saccade and pro/anti cue paradigms must be considered speculative, and we therefore decided to pursue it further in a series of follow-up experiments.

If the previous account is approximately correct, it should be possible to replicate the results found for the pro/anti saccade paradigm in ageing studies with the pro/anti cue paradigm by using manipulations that enhance the saliency or prominence of the subordinate goal of making instrumental saccades. In the first experiment to be reviewed next (Nieuwenhuis et al., Exp. 1, in press), we attempted to achieve this by enhancing the distance between fixation point and the location of the cue and stimulus (from 4 to 9 degrees of visual angle) and by including explicit instructions to make eye movements; eye movements were also recorded. In all other respects, this experiment was virtually identical to the previous one. The results were very similar to those of the previous experiment, with one important exception: The substantial difference in asymptotic level of accuracy between procues and anticues that was found for old adults in the previous experiment, was now entirely absent. Thus, our manipulations were successful in the sense that they remedied the purported occasional failures by the older adults to initiate an instrumental antisaccade, but they did not seem to have affected the speed with which older adults were able to initiate antisaccades. Close inspection of the eye movement recordings suggested a reason for this latter result. These recordings clearly indicated that many older adults used a strategy in the anticue condition of waiting briefly after the cue had been presented before endogenously initiating the antisaccade if, at long SOAs, the face stimulus did not appear promptly after the cue. Put differently, many older subjects appeared to have adopted a strategy in which they attempted to exploit the onset of the stimulus itself to trigger the antisaccade; none of the younger subjects used such a strategy. At first sight, this strategy would seem pointless and counterproductive; in order to maximise their chances of correctly perceiving the facial expression, subjects should initiate the requisite saccade without delay. However, the perceptual impression of the facial expression at short SOAs, and especially in the anticue condition, was quite dim at best, resulting in the subjective experience of having to guess. Subjectively, therefore, the deleterious effects on the quality of perceptual judgement of briefly delaying the endogenous initiation of the antisaccade in wait of the face stimulus may not have been obvious. With respect to the other, and in this experiment also prominent, goal, of making a correct antisaccade, the strategy must be deemed adaptive and clever, with older subjects apparently exploiting the external support provided by the triggering properties of the face stimulus itself to help them achieve that goal with greatly reduced effort.

In order to test these conjectures, we devised an experiment that was identical to the previous one, with one important exception. Whereas in the previous versions of the pro/anti cue paradigm the stimulus consisted of a single face presented at the cued location, now at stimulus onset a face appeared at each of the four possible locations, with only the face at the cued location containing a (smiling or frowning) mouth (Nieuwenhuis et al., Exp. 2, in press). In this way we sought to ensure that the requisite saccade in the anticue condition had to be initiated by fully endogenous means. The results of this experiment were very clear in showing, analogous to results obtained with the pro/anti saccade paradigm, no differences in performance between young and old adults in either the procue or in the anticue condition.

I will finish this section by summarising the relevant results and the conclusions that these results suggest. First, when task requirements emphasise the need for swift saccades and when external support for initiating such saccades is minimised, similar ageing effects are obtained for prosaccades and antisaccades. Thus, the basic mechanism needed for inhibitory control of reflexive eye movements and for endogenous initiation of voluntary eye movements would seem little affected in older age. Second, when task requirements do not emphasise the need for swift saccades or when external support can be exploited to help trigger antisaccades, clear and specific age-related effects are obtained for antisaccades. Thus, in situations where antisaccades are instrumental actions to achieve some higher goal, i.e., when the goal to make swift antisaccades is subordinate to that higher goal, older adults would seem to have considerable difficulty in maintaining that goal at a level of activation sufficient to ensure swift and reliable endogenous triggering of antisaccades. Also, older adults appear prone to detect and exploit means for external support in order to circumvent or compensate for such internal goal-maintenance problems. Thus, the available evidence on ageing effects on exogenous and endogenous control of visual attention and saccades would seem to be quite consistent with the notion that ageing effects on cognitive control can be largely and coherently accounted for in terms of a reduced capacity to generate and maintain goals in working memory. An important corollary of this notion is that age-related reductions in the effectiveness of inhibitory control that become manifest in some variants of the antisaccade paradigm (present experiments; Butler et al., 1999), should not be attributed to a fundamental decline in inhibitory capabilities (Butler et al., 1999) but rather to failures, due to goal neglect, to fully or consistently utilise such capabilities (De Jong et al., 1999).

AGEING EFFECTS IN TASK SWITCHING

The task-switching paradigm has recently become a popular tool for investigating important aspects of cognitive control. Before turning to ageing effects in task switching, some background regarding the paradigm and relevant theoretical proposals will be provided.

In the task-switching paradigm, the task to be performed on each trial is selected from a set of alternative tasks, usually choice RT tasks. In one version of the paradigm, tasks are presented in an unpredictable order and each trial begins with the presentation of a cue, or instruction signal, that signals the task to be performed (e.g., Meiran, 1996). The cue is followed after a fixed or random delay, called the preparation interval, by the presentation of the imperative stimulus. In another version, the tasks are presented in a predictable order, either in a simple alternating order (e.g., Allport, Styles, & Hsieh, 1994) or according to a more complex pattern (e.g., Rogers & Monsell, 1995), with the response–stimulus interval serving as the preparation interval. Typically, the imperative stimulus is ambiguous as to which task is to be performed, rendering it necessary to process the cue or to keep track of the task sequence.

There are three basic types of trials to be distinguished in the task-switching paradigm. On *pure-task trials*, that constitute control blocks, the task remains constant throughout a block of trials. The other two trial types constitute switch blocks. On *non-switch trials* the task to be performed is the same as that on the previous trial, so that the task set used in the previous trial can remain in place. On *switch trials* the task changes and the task set needs to be reconfigured. For reasons that will become clear shortly, we distinguish between two types of switch costs. *Type 1 switch costs* are defined as differences in performance between switch and non-switch trials (called switching costs by Meiran and Gotler, this issue). *Type 2 costs* are defined as differences in performance between nonswitch and pure-task trials (called mixing costs by Meiran and Gotler, this issue).

At short preparation intervals, the imperative stimulus is assumed to arrive at a time when preparation for the assigned task, i.e., the selection and implementation of the proper task set, is still underway. In such cases, the response can be expected to be slow or inaccurate, either because preparation, i.e., reconfiguration of the task set, needs to be completed before task performance can proceed or because performance is hampered by a weak or incomplete task set. As the preparation interval is prolonged, providing more time for preparation, responses are expected to become progressively faster and more accurate. Thus, type 1 switch costs are expected to diminish gradually as the preparation interval is prolonged. With few exceptions, such beneficial effects of longer preparation intervals have been found, indicating that subjects are generally quite capable of using advance information to prepare in advance for an upcoming task. Type 2 switch costs will be further addressed later on.

Recently, some theoretical controversy has been sparked by the phenomenon of *residual switch costs*, defined as type 1 switch costs at long preparation intervals that should have provided ample time for advance preparation to be completed. Many task-switching studies have yielded residual switch costs, but the magnitude of such costs, relative to initial switch costs, varies widely across studies, ranging from very large (e.g., Allport et al., 1994; Rogers & Monsell, 1995, Exp. 2) to very small (e.g., De Jong, Emans, Eenshuistra, & Wagenmakers, 2000, Exp. 3; Meiran, 1996).

Two basic accounts of residual switch costs have been proposed. The first one is best exemplified by Rogers and Monsell's (1995) distinction between an endogenous and an exogenous component of task set reconfiguration. The endogenous component, they proposed, can be carried out during the preparation interval but cannot attain a completely reconfigured task set. Completion of the reconfiguration process must await triggering by a task-relevant stimulus, which constitutes the exogenous component. According to this perspective, residual switch costs represent the duration of the latter exogenous component. I will refer to this as the additional-process (AP) hypothesis. The second account starts from the notion that advance preparation is optional (De Jong, 2000; De Jong et al., 1999). Advance preparation is useful because it promotes fast responding to the imperative stimulus, but postponing task set reconfiguration until the arrival of the imperative stimulus still suffices to ensure an accurate, albeit slow, response. According to this perspective, residual switch costs are due to intermittent failures to engage in advance preparation, rather than to a fundamental inability to attain a complete reconfiguration of task set during the preparation interval (i.e., by fully endogenous means). I will refer to this as the failure-to-engage (FTE) hypothesis.

Of course, both proposals may have merit and both proposed factors may contribute to residual switch costs. I developed a modelling technique that enables the estimation of the relative contributions of these two factors to observed residual switch costs (De Jong, 2000). According to the FTE hypothesis, performance on switch trials with a long preparation interval results from a probabilistic mixture of trials on which the subject prepared in advance during the preparation interval and trials on which preparation failed to get underway during the preparation interval and thus still needed to be performed after onset of the imperative stimulus. Performance on switch trials with a long preparation interval, on which advance preparation was carried out and completed, should be very similar to that on non-switch trials. Performance on switch trials with a long preparation interval on which advance preparation failed to get underway, should be very similar to that on switch trials with a short preparation interval that provides very little time for advance preparation. Thus, the distribution of RTs on switch trials with a long preparation interval should be well fitted by a mixture of RTs from two other conditions: non-switch trials and switch trials with a short preparation interval. The AP hypothesis holds that even when advance preparation is carried out on switch trials, the additional exogenous component of task-set reconfiguration will prolong the RT, by the duration of that component, on such trials, relative to the RT on non-switch trials. Combining the two hypotheses, it follows that the distribution of RTs on switch trials with a long preparation interval should be well fit by a mixture of RTs from switch trials with a short preparation interval and RTs from non-switch trials, with these latter RTs augmented by the duration of the exogenous component. The fitting technique employs two free parameters in order to optimise the fit: the first parameter (that assumes a value between 0 and 1) representing the probability that advance preparation was successfully triggered during the preparation interval on switch trials (its complement indicating the probability of failures to engage in advance preparation), and the second parameter representing the average duration (in ms) of the purported exogenous component of the AP hypothesis. As discussed in detail by De Jong (2000), application of this technique to results from task-switching studies using young adults as subjects and relative simple component tasks has consistently established that residual switch costs in these cases could be solely attributed to intermittent failures to take advantage of opportunities for advance preparation, and has not provided any evidence for the presence of fundamental preparatory limitations of the type assumed by the AP hypothesis.

De Jong (2000) proposed an intention–activation account of failures to engage in advance preparation in task switching. According to this account effective use of opportunities for advance preparation requires: (1) an explicit goal or intention to be added to the basic goal structure that governs performance in the task-switching paradigm, and (2) retrieval and carrying out of this intention at the proper time, that is, at the start of the preparation interval. Degree of success in intention retrieval is assumed to depend on the joint influence of two factors: the activation level of the intention and the characteristics or triggering power of the retrieval cue. Thus, frequent failures to engage in advance preparation may be due to low levels of intention activation (in which case such failures reflect goal neglect), to weak retrieval cues (as in the case of weak environmental support), or to a combination of these factors. Evidence in support of this theoretical account is discussed by De Jong (2000).

With this background, we can now turn to the issue of possible age-related differences in task-switching performance.

Age-related differences in type 1 switch costs

One important question, addressed in various recent studies, concerns the degree to which young and old adults might differ in the degree to which they are able to benefit from opportunities for advance preparation. This question can be addressed by comparing young and old adults with respect to the beneficial effects of prolonged preparation times on Type 1 switch costs. Figure 2 presents representative data from an as yet unpublished experiment that was recently conducted in my lab by Mark Dekker. The stimuli in the experiment were red or blue vowels or consonants. The alternative tasks involved the same two response alternatives; in one task the correct key press response was determined by the colour of the letter and in the other task by its category. In switch blocks the two tasks regularly alternated across trials according to a fixed AABAABB... scheme. Sixteen young college students and sixteen high functioning old adults (mean age

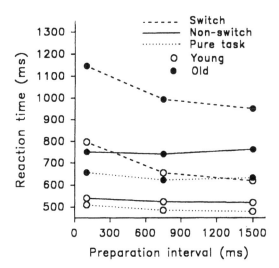

Figure 2. Mean correct reaction time as a function of age group, preparation interval, and type of trial.

73.6 years) served as participants. Initial Type 1 switch costs at the shortest preparation interval (100 ms) averaged 260 ms for young adults and 399 ms for old adults. At the longest preparation interval, these switch costs had declined to 98 ms and 192 ms for young and old adults, respectively; these are considered residual switch costs.

These results resemble those obtained in several related studies (Eenshuistra, Wagenmakers, & De Jong, 2000; Hartley, Kieley, & Slabach, 1990; Kramer, Hahn, & Gopher, 1999; Kray & Lindenberger, 2000; Mayr & Liebscher, this issue; Meiran, Gotler, & Perlman, 2000). They clearly indicate that, although older adults are slower to switch between two simple tasks than younger adults, they are quite capable of making effective use of opportunities for advance preparation. In fact, these results would seem to be in line with recent suggestions that age-based limitations in the latter ability are often small or absent (Hartley et al., 1990; Kramer et al., 1999; Mayr & Liebscher, this issue; Salthouse, Fristoe, McGuthry, & Hambrick, 1998). However, the more detailed analysis afforded by the mixture modelling technique suggests a somewhat different interpretation of the present results. Figure 3 shows for young and older subjects the cumulative distribution functions for reaction times in the three relevant conditions: non-switch trials, switch trials with a short preparation interval, and switch trials with a long preparation interval. Also shown are the best fits of the distribution function for switch trials with a long preparation interval, as produced by the mixture model; for both young and older subjects the mixture model produced an excellent fit. Average estimated probabilities of failures to

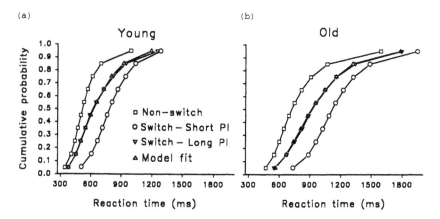

Figure 3. Vincentised cumulative distribution functions for reaction times on non-switch trials and switch trials with a short or long preparation interval (PI). Also shown is the fit of the distribution function for switch trials with a long preparation interval, as produced by the mixture model. (a) young adults; (b) old adults.

engage in advance preparation were .38 and .33 for young and old adults, respectively. Average estimated durations of the exogenous component of the AP account were a non-significant 8 ms and a highly significant 84 ms for young and old adults, respectively. This latter difference can be appreciated by observing in Figure 3 that for young subjects relatively fast responses on switch-long preparation interval (PI) trials were about as fast as relatively fast responses on non-switch trials, suggesting fully adequate advance preparation on a subset of switch-long PI trials. In contrast, for older subjects relatively fast responses on switch-long PI trials remained substantially slower than relatively fast responses on non-switch trials, which suggests that a fully adequate or complete reconfiguration of task set could not be attained by means of advance preparation.

Very similar results have been obtained in several other related experiments (Eenshuistra et al., 2000). These results indicate that old adults are not more prone than young adults to exhibit failures to engage in advance preparation in the task-switching paradigm. Given that the intention–activation account of residual switch costs proposed by De Jong (2000; De Jong et al., 1999) attributes such failures to goal neglect and that the central hypothesis pursued in this paper assumes that old adults are likely to exhibit goal neglect, these results would seem to cause problems for one or both of these hypotheses; I will return to this issue later. The results also indicate that old adults, unlike young adults, do exhibit limitations in their ability to attain a complete reconfiguration of task set during the preparation interval (i.e., by fully endogenous means).

Age-related differences in type 2 switch costs

Figure 2 reveals another, and quite striking, difference between young and old adults. Whereas type 2 switch costs were quite small for young adults, these costs were very considerable for old adults. The same phenomenon has been reported and extensively analysed by Kray and Lindenberger (2000). As suggested by Rogers and Monsell (1995), type 2 switch costs might be due to the additional requirement in switch blocks, not present in pure-task blocks, to efficiently maintain and coordinate two alternating task sets in working memory. Accordingly, Kray and Lindenberger (2000) suggested that age-related increments in type 2 switch costs might reflect a reduced ability in the elderly to maintain and coordinate multiple task sets in working memory. Their suggestion shows some resemblance to the central hypothesis pursued in this paper. However, there are other possible interpretations of type 2 switch costs. De Jong (2000) suggested that a switch between tasks may require not only activating the now relevant task set but also actively disengaging the prior task set (see also Mayr & Keele, 2000). Even though perhaps capable of completely disengaging prior task sets, subjects might opt not to fully exercise this capability when, as in switch blocks, these sets may need to be reinstalled shortly. The effort requirements for executive control would be reduced by such a conservative control strategy, but at the expense of suboptimal task performance and potential interference effects in switch blocks. Thus, the presence of type 2 switch costs might reflect a somewhat conservative compromise between minimising control effort and maximising task performance. Some initial evidence in support of this hypothesis was discussed by De Jong (2000). Several studies have provided evidence that older adults tend to adopt conservative response strategies in reaction-time tasks (Botwinick, 1984; Strayer, Wickens, & Braune, 1987). Thus, it seems possible that the much larger type 2 switch costs for older adults might have a largely strategic basis, rather than being due to a reduced ability in the elderly to maintain and coordinate multiple task sets in memory.

To further investigate this issue, we conducted an experiment in which we employed a time-band procedure (Wickelgren, 1977) to force subjects, all older adults, to respond very quickly and within a narrow time band (Eenshuistra et al., 2000, Exp. 3). The purpose of this extreme time pressure was to force the older adults to drop any possible conservative control strategy and to fully bring to bear their capabilities for executive control. Only a single preparation interval of 1500 ms was used and the same time band was used for pure-task and switch blocks, thus equating response speed for the different trial types and making response accuracy the dependent variable. Response accuracy was found to be very similar on pure-task and non-switch trials and substantially lower on switch trials. Put differently, the original and substantive type 2 switch costs in reaction time found in the standard task-switching paradigm were not transformed into type 2 switch costs in accuracy by the time-band procedure. This outcome is entirely consistent with the notion that type 2 switch costs in reaction time have a largely strategic origin. In contrast, and significantly, residual type 1 switch costs in reaction time were transformed into substantial and significant residual type 1 switch costs in accuracy by the time-band procedure. This outcome is fully consistent with the evidence, discussed earlier, that residual switch costs in reaction times in older adults are partially due to fundamental preparatory limitations, limitations that should not have been mitigated by the time-band procedure.

Discussion

The previous limited review of ageing studies of task switching focused on possible age-related effects on type 1 and type 2 switch costs. One clear and consistent finding is that older adults exhibit disproportionately larger type 2 switch costs than younger adults. On the basis of evidence that type 2 switch costs can be eliminated by straightforward speed manipulations, I suggested that this difference should probably be attributed to older adults employing a more conservative or cautious strategy when internally switching between task sets. It is possible that the adoption of such a conservative strategy represents a conscious decision by our older subjects to "take it easy" in switch blocks; such an account would seem unlikely, however, as older volunteers are typically highly motivated and cooperative subjects. More likely then, as this conservative "strategy" would seem to represent a failure to fully and consistently engage and utilise available control capabilities in order to optimise performance, it should be viewed as an instance of goal neglect.

A second consistent finding is that, unlike young adults, old adults exhibit limitations in the degree to which they can prepare for an upcoming simple task by fully endogenous means. This limitation does not appear to be attributable to goal neglect but to represent a veridical limitation in set shifting ability in the elderly; possibly it might represent a specific inhibitory problem that limits the ability to disengage prior task sets in the elderly, although the evidence on this issue is still scant. Preliminary results from a collaborative study with Art Kramer and Sowon Hahn suggests that this limitation may be greatly ameliorated by extended practice in task switching (see also, Kramer et al., 1999).

The third consistent finding is that old adults are not more prone than young adults to intermittent failures to take advantage of opportunities for advance preparation in task switching. The intention–activation account of residual switch costs holds that the probability of failures to engage in advance preparation depends jointly on the level of activation at which the associated (subordinate) goal is maintained and on the triggering power of the cue. Because it would seem unlikely that the triggering power of the cue could have been higher for old than for young adults, the conclusion must be that old and young adults did not differ with respect to their ability to maintain the goal to engage in advance preparation at a high level of activation. At first sight, this conclusion would appear to be at odds with the goal-neglect hypothesis of cognitive ageing. However, there are two aspects of the typical versions of the task-switching paradigm that might suggest otherwise. First, the requirement to prepare in advance occurred very frequently, on average every other trial. This high frequency of occurrence represents a strong source of external support to help keep the goal highly activated. It is noteworthy in this regard that prospective memory performance, for which models very similar to the intention-activation account of residual switch costs have been proposed (Mäntylä, 1996), and in which critical events occur at much wider intervals, have yielded significant age-related differences, especially so in time-based prospective memory tasks that offer less environmental support than event-based tasks (Einstein & McDaniel, 1990; West & Craik, 1999). Also, there is some evidence that old adults may exhibit deficits in advance preparation when the frequency of set shifting is reduced (Kramer et al., 1999). Second, although engaging in advance preparation is optional, failing to do so would seem to offer few advantages in terms of reduced effort. Because the stimulus is ambiguous with respect to the relevant task, shifting task set will need to be done by fully endogenous means, whether it is done during the preparation interval or after the stimulus has been presented. Taken together, these considerations suggest that the regular task-switching paradigm provides ample external support for keeping the goal to engage in advance preparation properly activated and does not provide opportunities to reduce effort requirement of internal control by taking advantage of external aids. As the results in the previous section suggested, these are exactly the conditions under which manifestations of goal neglect in the elderly should be minimised. From this perspective, the absence of age-related effects on the incidence of failures of anticipatory preparation in the prototypical task-switching paradigm might be considered to be quite consistent with the goal-neglect hypothesis of cognitive ageing.

If these considerations are approximately correct, they should also suggest how the task-switching paradigm might be amended in order to produce a higher prevalence of preparatory failures in the elderly. One such amendment would be to reduce the frequency of set shifts (Kramer et al., 1999). Another would be to provide opportunities for strategic use of external aids in order to reduce effort requirements of internal control; this could be done by employing univalent stimuli, i.e., stimuli that afford only the cued task (e.g., Rogers & Monsell, 1995), or a random mixture of bivalent, task-ambiguous and univalent stimuli (Kantowitz & Sanders, 1972). According to the goal-neglect hypothesis, especially a combination of these two amendments should produce substantial age-related differences in the probability and extent to which opportunities for advance preparation will be effectively utilised.

CONCLUSION

In this paper, I suggested that age-related effects on cognitive control might be usefully attributed to a reduced capacity for goal generation and goal maintenance in old age. I reviewed findings from two lines of research that were argued to be in general agreement with this hypothesis. I should stress that while the necessarily limited scope of the review may serve to suggest the viability and potential of this hypothesis on cognitive ageing, it must fall far short of establishing its relative merits or correctness. Indeed, concepts such as goal selection, goal maintenance, internal control, and environmental support are presently so poorly defined that it is on one hand often difficult to derive precise predictions from the goal-neglect hypothesis of cognitive ageing, while on the other hand it is often relatively easy to provide some reasonable post hoc account for findings that would at first sight seem to fit uncomfortably with the hypothesis. Many of these conceptual problems have been eloquently addressed by Rabbitt (1997).

Although several taxonomies of executive functions have been proposed in the literature, three major functions are frequently distinguished (for review, see Miyake, Friedman, Emerson, Witzki, Howerter & Wager, 2000): (1) shifting between tasks or mental sets, (2) updating and monitoring of representations in working memory, and (3) inhibition of dominant or prepotent responses. Not surprisingly, there are now several proposals in the literature that normal ageing may affect all or a specific subset of these functions (this issue). The present hypothesis does not deny the possibility that specific control functions may be impaired in normal ageing, but it focuses on one superordinate control function, the selection and active maintenance of goals in working memory, that will, to a greater or lesser degree, be involved in almost any task, regardless of its specifics. In a related vein, Engle, Kane, and Tuholski (1999) proposed that a crucial component of working memory is "controlled attention", which is a domain-free attentional capacity to actively maintain, or in some cases suppress, working memory representations. In their account, any situation that involves controlled processes—goal maintenance, conflict resolution, resistance to or suppression of distracting information, error monitoring, and effortful memory search—would require this "controlled attention" capacity, regardless of the specifics of the tasks to be performed (for similar suggestions, see De Jong et al., 1999; Duncan et al., 1996). The core of the present hypothesis is that age-related decrements in such a superordinate capacity may account for the majority of age-related deficits in cognitive control, and although it does not deny the possibility of deficits in more specific control functions it holds that, once decrements in this more general capacity are taken into account, there may be little need and explanatory room left for such more specific proposals.

Manuscript received September 2000

REFERENCES

Allport, D.A., Styles, E.A., & Hsieh, S. (1994). Shifting attentional set: Exploring the dynamic control of tasks. In C. Umiltà & M. Moscovitch (Eds.), *Attention and perfor-*

mance XV: Conscious and unconscious information processing (pp. 421–452). Cambridge, MA: MIT Press.

Anderson, J.R., Reder, L.M., & Lebiere, C. (1996). Working memory: Activation limitations on retrieval. *Cognitive Psychology, 30,* 221–256.

Baddeley, A. (1996). Exploring the central executive. *Quarterly Journal of Experimental Psychology, 49A,* 5–28.

Botwinick, J. (1984). *Aging and behavior: A comprehensive integration of research findings* (3rd ed.). New York: Springer-Verlag.

Butler, K.M., Zacks, R.T., & Henderson, J.M. (1999). Suppression of reflexive saccades in younger and older adults: Age comparisons on an antisaccade task. *Journal of Memory and Cognition, 27,* 584–591.

Carpenter, P.A., Just, M.A., & Shell, P. (1990). What one intelligence test measures: A theoretical account of the processing in the Raven Progressive Matrices Test. *Psychological Review, 97,* 404–431.

De Jong, R. (2000). An intention-activation account of residual switch costs. In S. Monsell & J. Driver (Eds.), *Attention and performance XVIII: Control & cognitive processes.* Cambridge, MA: MIT Press.

De Jong, R., Berendsen, E., & Cools, R. (1999). Goal neglect and inhibitory limitations: Dissociable causes of interference effects in conflict situations. *Acta Psychologica, 101,* 379–394.

De Jong, R., Emans, B., Eenshuistra, R., & Wagenmakers, E.J. (2000). Strategies and inhibitory limitations in intentional task control. *Manuscript submitted for publication.*

Dempster, F.N. (1992). The rise and fall of the inhibitory mechanism: Toward a unified theory of cognitive development and aging. *Developmental Review, 12,* 45–75.

Duncan, J., Emslie, H., Williams, P., Johnson, R., & Freer, C. (1996). Intelligence and the frontal lobe: The organization of goal-directed behavior. *Cognitive Psychology, 30,* 257–303.

Duncan, J., Johnson, R., Swales, M., & Freer, C. (1997). Frontal lobe deficits after head injury: Unity and diversity of function. *Cognitive Neuropsychology, 14*(5), 713–741.

Eenshuistra, R., Wagenmakers, E.J., & De Jong, R. (2000). Age-related strategy differences in task switching. *Manuscript in preparation.*

Einstein, G.O., & McDaniel, M.A. (1990). Normal aging and prospective memory. *Journal of Experimental Psychology: Learning, Memory, and Cognition, 16,* 717–726.

Engle, R.W., Kane, M.J., & Tuholski, S.W. (1999). Individual differences in working memory and what they tell us about controlled attention, general fluid intelligence, and functions of the prefrontal cortex. In A. Miyake & P. Shah (Eds.), *Models of working memory: Mechanisms of active maintenance and executive control* (pp. 102–134). New York: Cambridge University Press.

Everling, S., & Fischer, B. (1998). The antisaccade: A review of basic research and clinical studies. *Neuropsychologia, 36,* 885–899.

Fischer, B., Biscaldi, M., & Gezeck, S. (1997). On the development of voluntary and reflexive components in human saccade generation. *Brain Research, 754,* 285–297.

Hartley, A.A., Kieley, J.M., & Slabach, E.H. (1990). Age differences and similarities in the effects of cues and prompts. *Journal of Experimental Psychology: Human Perception and Performance, 16,* 523–537.

Hultsch, D.F., Hertzog, C., & Dixon, R.A. (1987). Memory self-knowledge and self-efficacy in the aged. In N.L. Lowe & C.J. Brainerd (Eds.), *Cognitive development in adulthood: Progress in cognitive developmental research* (pp. 65–92). New York: Springer-Verlag.

Kantowitz, B.H., & Sanders, M.S. (1972). Partial advance information and stimulus dimensionality. *Journal of Experimental Psychology, 92,* 412–418.

Kramer, A.F., Hahn, S., & Gopher, D. (1999). Task coordination and aging: Explorations of executive control processes in the task switching paradigm. *Acta Psychologica, 101,* 339–378.

Kray, J., & Lindenberger, U. (2000). Adult age differences in task switching. *Psychology and Aging, 15,* 126–147.

Mäntylä, T. (1996). Activating actions and interrupting intentions: Mechanisms of retrieval sensitization in prospective memory. In M.A. Brandimonte, G.O. Einstein, & M.A. McDaniel (Eds.), *Prospective memory: Theory and application.* Hillsdale, NJ: Lawrence Erlbaum Associates Inc.

Mayr, U., & Keele, S.W. (2000). Changing internal constraints on action: The role of backward inhibition. *Journal of Experimental Psychology: General, 129,* 4–26.

Meiran, N. (1996). Reconfiguration of processing mode prior to task performance. *Journal of Experimental Psychology: Learning, Memory, and Cognition, 22,* 1423–1442.

Meiran, N., Gotler, A., & Perlman, A. (2000). Old age is associated with a pattern of relatively intact and relatively impaired task set switching abilities. *Manuscript submitted.*

Miyake, A., Friedman, N.P., Emerson, M.J., Witzki, A.H., Howerter, A, & Wager, T.D. (2000). The unity and diversity of executive functions and their contributions to complex frontal lobe tasks: A latent variable analysis. *Cognitive Psychology, 41,* 49–100.

Munoz, D.P., Broughton, J.R., Goldring, J.E., & Armstrong, I.T. (1998). Age-related performance of human subjects on saccadic eye movement tasks. *Experimental Brain Research, 121,* 391–400.

Nieuwenhuis, S., Broerse, A., Nielen, M., & De Jong, R. (2000). A goal activation approach to the study of executive function: An application to antisaccade tasks. *Manuscript in preparation.*

Nieuwenhuis, S., Ridderinkhof, K.R., De Jong, R., Kok, A., & van der Molen, M.W. (in press). Inhibitory inefficiency and failures of intention-activation: Age-related decline in the control of saccadic eye movements. *Psychology and Aging.*

Posner, M. (1992). Attention as a cognitive and neural system. *Current Directions in Psychological Science, 1,* 11–15.

Rabbitt, P. (1997). Introduction: Methodologies and models in the study of executive function. In P. Rabbitt (Ed.), *Methodology of frontal and executive functions* (pp. 1–38). Hove, UK: Psychology Press.

Roberts, R.J., Hager, L.D., & Heron, C. (1994). Prefrontal cognitive processes: Working memory and inhibition in the antisaccade task. *Journal of Experimental Psychology: General, 123,* 374–393.

Rogers, R.D., & Monsell, S. (1995). Costs of a predictable switch between simple cognitive tasks. *Journal of Experimental Psychology: General, 124,* 207–231.

Salthouse, T.A., Fristoe, N.M., McGuthry, K.E., & Hambrick, D.Z. (1998). Relation of task switching to speed, age, and fluid intelligence. *Psychology and Aging, 13,* 445–461.

Strayer, D.L., Wickens, C.D., & Braune, R. (1987). Adult age differences in the speed and capacity of information processing: 2. An electrophysiological approach. *Psychology and Aging, 2,* 99–110.

West, R., & Craik, F.I.M. (1999). Age-related decline in prospective memory: The roles of cue accessibility and cue sensitivity. *Psychology and Aging, 14*(2), 264–272.

West, R.J. (1996). An application of prefrontal cortex function theory to cognitive aging. *Psychological Bulletin, 120,* 272–292.

Wickelgren, W.A. (1977). Speed–accuracy tradeoff and information processing dynamics. *Acta Psychologica, 41,* 67–85.

EUROPEAN JOURNAL OF COGNITIVE PSYCHOLOGY, 2001, *13* (1/2), 91–105

The transient nature of executive control processes in younger and older adults

Robert West

University of Notre Dame, IN, USA

In this paper I review data from recent studies supporting the hypothesis that executive control processes fluctuate in efficiency over time and that these fluctuations are more pervasive in older than younger adults. Patterns of response accuracy in tasks requiring selective attention and prospective memory reveal that lapses of intention are often preceded and followed by periods of goal-directed action. Analysis of response time distributions reveals that increased performance variability in older adults for task conditions requiring executive control results from an increase in the degree of positive skewing of the distribution. Together, these findings lead to the suggestion that disruptions of executive control processes supporting performance in demanding tasks are temporally limited in nature. Data from recent neurophysiological studies indicates a possible role of the prefrontal cortex in maintaining optimal levels of executive control.

The ability to maintain a high level of sustained executive control in the face of distracting environmental information or prolonged task performance has been of interest to psychologists in the areas of cognition, human factors, and neuropsychology for some time. Evidence from across these domains indicates that executive control is easily disrupted in novel task conditions and when information inconsistent with task demands is present in the environment (West, 1999b), that disruptions of executive control processes can result in human errors leading to costly disasters (Reason, 1979), and that damage to the prefrontal cortex and related neural structures can result in the reduced efficiency of executive control processes (Stuss, Shallice, Alexander, & Picton, 1995). Researchers

Requests for reprints should be addressed to R. West, Department of Psychology, University of Notre Dame, Notre Dame, IN 46556, USA. Email: west.19@nd.edu

The research described in this article was conducted while the author was a postdoctoral fellow at the Rotman Research Institute in Toronto supported by grant RO1AG13845-01 from the National Institute on Aging.

http://www.tandf.co.uk/journals/pp/09541446.html   DOI:10.1080/09541440042000232

in the area of cognitive gerontology have reported age-related performance declines in a variety of situations demanding high levels of executive control including tasks requiring sustained attention (Parasuraman & Giambra, 1991), selective attention (Spieler, Balota, & Faust, 1996), and executive aspects of working memory (West, Ergis, Winocur, & Saint-Cyr, 1998).

An interesting characteristic of executive control is that it seems to fluctuate in efficiency over time, with periods of optimal and non-optimal executive control being interwoven over time, creating a dynamic ebb and flow of performance on tasks requiring controlled attention. It has been proposed that there is an age-related increase in the frequency of fluctuations of executive control observed in continuous performance (Bunce, Warr, & Cochrane, 1993) and selective attention (West, 1999a) tasks. In the present review I consider findings from my own and others' recent work that are related to this proposal. My guiding hypothesis is that there is an age-related increase in the tendency for executive control processes to fluctuate in efficiency over time that is revealed in patterns of response accuracy, response latency, and performance variability when comparing younger and older adults. I also present data from recent neurophysiological studies using event-related brain potentials (ERPs) indicating a possible role of the prefrontal cortex in maintaining optimal levels of executive control over time.

RESPONSE ACCURACY AND FLUCTUATIONS OF EXECUTIVE CONTROL

My interest in the hypothesis that executive control processes fluctuate in efficiency over time was inspired by the findings of two studies designed to explore age-related increases in lapses of intention (Craik & Kerr, 1996) in tasks measuring prospective memory (PM; West & Craik, 1999) and selective attention (West, 1999a). Lapses of intention reflect those curious and often frustrating occasions in daily life when our actions become dissociated from our intentions (Reason, 1979). For instance, failing to give an important message to a friend at the appropriate time (a lapse of intention) or putting salt instead of sugar into our morning coffee (an action slip).

In laboratory-based PM tasks individuals are often asked to make a select response to some particular PM cue embedded in a more or less engaging on-going activity (e.g., press the b key each time the word shoe is encountered while performing a semantic classification task). Many studies include only one or two PM cues making the retrospective demands of the task minimal. However, age-related decline in the detection of and/or response to PM cues is often observed when using these tasks (Maylor, 1996; West & Craik, 1999). When the pattern of PM failures has been examined in these studies the efficiency of PM reflects a dynamic process, with individuals often failing to respond to a PM cue that elicited a prospective response only a few minutes ago, and responding to a PM cue that failed to elicit a prospective response in the recent past. Maylor (1996) proposed that these characteristics of PM can be quantified in indices of forgetting (i.e., the probability of failing to respond to a PM cue given a correct response to the preceding PM cue) and recovery (i.e., the probability of responding to a PM cue given that the preceding PM cue failed to elicit a prospective response). In Maylor's study, older adults were more likely than middle-aged adults to forget and less likely to recover. These data are consistent with the suggestion that age-related differences in PM failure result from moments where the intention fails to guide behaviour and not from the intention being forgotten (Craik & Kerr, 1996), as a forgotten intention would result in a failure to recover resulting in a ratio of zero.

West and Craik (1999) also provide evidence consistent with the proposal that lapses of intention contribute to age-related differences in failures of PM. In this study, levels of forgetting were comparable to those reported by Maylor (1996). An examination of the data for trials where a PM cue failed to elicit a prospective response (i.e., a response appropriate to the on-going task was made) revealed that response latency for these trials was slower than for on-going task trials preceding the presentation of a missed PM cue (West & Craik, 1999). Furthermore, response latency for trials following missed PM cues was elevated relative to trials preceding the presentation of the missed cues possibly resulting from the awareness that an error had been made.

In a study examining lapses of intention in selection attention younger and older adults performed the Stroop task, and lapses of intention were defined as intrusion errors reflecting those trials where the individual read the word instead of making the goal-directed response of naming the colour (West, 1999a). Across three experiments the frequency of intrusion errors was greater for older than younger adults, while the number of non-intrusion errors was similar between these groups of individuals, suggesting that there was an age-related increase in lapses of intention. Examination of the intrusion error data from Experiment 1 of this study revealed that older adults were more likely than younger adults to experience pairs of intrusion errors on consecutive incongruent trials and that the frequency of pairs of intrusion errors was greater than would be expected by change in older adults. This finding led me to wonder whether lapses were actually more frequent in older adults or whether lapses simply lasted longer in older adults than younger adults. These alternatives were considered in a second experiment including only incongruent trials, permitting the independent calculation of the number of lapses and the duration of each lapse. This analysis revealed that the number of distinct lapses was greater for older than younger adults, suggesting that lapses of intention were more frequent for older than younger adults (see Figure 1). Also, longer duration lapses were more frequent in older than younger adults, where 15% of lapses lasted two or more trials in duration for older adults, whereas only 6% of lapses lasted two or more trials in duration for younger adults.

In Experiment 1 of this study there was a significant decrease in the number of intrusion errors across the course of the task for older adults, consistent with other data indicating that lapses or goal-neglect are most likely to occur when a task is relatively novel (Duncan, Emslie, Williams, Johnson, & Freer, 1996; Reason, 1979). However, it is unclear whether the decrease in the number of intrusion errors resulted from a decrease in the number or duration of lapses of intention over the course of task performance. To consider these alternatives the number of lapses lasting a single trial or two or more trials in duration were examined across quarters of the task in Experiment 2 of this study (West, 1999a). The number of lapses lasting a single trial in duration did not decrease across

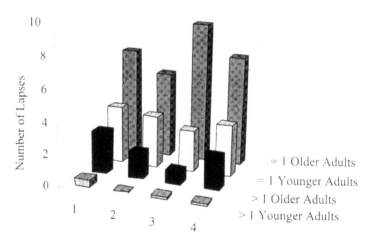

Figure 1. The number of lapses of intention lasting a single trial (i.e., = 1) or more than one trial in duration (i.e., > 1) for younger and older adults in the Stroop task during the first to fourth quarters of the task (adapted from West, 1999a). Notice that the number of lapses lasting a single trial in duration is generally stable for younger and older adults over time, whereas the number of lapses lasting more than a single trial decreases from the first to third quarters of the task and then increases in the fourth quarter of the task.

the course of the task for younger or older adults (see Figure 1). In contrast, the number of lapses lasting two or more trials in duration decreased from the first to third quarters of the task for both older and younger adults and then increased slightly from the third to fourth quarters of the task. Based upon this data it seems that task experience leads to a decrease in the duration of lapse and has relatively little impact on their overall frequency. The stable distribution of lapses lasting a single trial in duration across task performance leads to the proposal that fluctuations in efficiency are an intrinsic property of executive control processes that serve to maintain goal-directed responding in the Stroop task (West, 1999a), whereas processes that serve to restore goal-directed responding in the midst of a lapse of intention are sensitive to the effects of task experience and possibly fatigue.

Other data consistent with the idea that lapses result from fluctuations in the efficiency of executive control emerged from a consideration of the response time data for trials preceding intrusion errors. For these trials there was a systematic slowing of response time on trials preceding an intrusion error relative to trials in the experiment that were temporally distant from intrusion errors (West, 1999a). This slowing may be thought to result from a gradual waning in the efficiency of executive control giving rise to intrusion errors once the system crosses some critical boundary required to maintain goal-directed action.

RESPONSE LATENCY AND FLUCTUATIONS OF EXECUTIVE CONTROL

In recent years there has been a growing interest in moving away from analyses of response latency data based solely upon measures of central tendency such as the mean or median to analytic strategies that allow the investigator to more fully characterise the entire shape of the response time distribution (Heathcote, Popiel, & Mewhort, 1991; Miller, 1988). One such approach is to fit the ex-Gaussian function to the response latency distribution (Hohle, 1965; Ratcliff, 1979). The ex-Gaussian function represents the convolution of an exponential and Gaussian (normal) distribution characterised in a three parameter model (μ, σ, τ). Mu and σ provide estimates of the mean and standard deviation of a Gaussian distribution that is assumed to characterise the leading edge of the response time distribution; while τ provides an estimate (i.e., mean and standard deviation) of the tail of the response time distribution that is often positively skewed. By considering conditional and group differences in the three parameters of the ex-Gaussian function one can gain insight into the degree to which effects are pervasive in nature, operating across the entire range of the response time distribution, or are more limited in nature influencing one but not the other parameters.

The ex-Gaussian analysis has been used to explore the nature of age-related differences in executive control processes in the areas of selective attention and working memory. In one study, Spieler et al. (1996) found that the magnitude of the Stroop interference effect was similar in younger adults and young–old adults for the μ parameter, whereas the magnitude of the interference effect was greater for older than younger adults in the τ performance. Based upon these findings one could suggest that the operational efficiency of an inhibitory mechanism supporting performance of the Stroop task was similar for older and younger adults on the majority of trials, reflected in the μ parameter, and that fluctuations in the efficiency of this executive control process (reflected in the τ parameter) have a more profound impact on the performance of older adults than that of younger adults (but see Spieler, this issue).

The ex-Gaussian analysis has also been used to explore the nature of age-related differences in response latency observed in a continuous working memory task (i.e., 1-back; West, 1999b). In this study, younger and older adults performed a task where they were required to identify in which of four spatial locations a stimulus appeared (i.e., immediate condition), or to identify the spatial location of the stimulus presented in the previous display (i.e., 1-back condition). As might be expected, mean response latency was greater for older than younger adults and this difference was greater in the 1-back condition than the immediate condition. Decomposition of these data using the ex-Gaussian analysis revealed that for younger adults the response latency costs associated with the 1-back condition were essentially limited to the τ parameter, suggesting that fluctuations of executive control processes supporting working memory contributed to the increased response latency observed for younger adults in this condition. For older adults the latency costs associated with the 1-back condition for the τ parameter were greater than for the younger adults, consistent with the idea that fluctuations in the efficiency of executive control processes are more detrimental to the performance of older adults than to that of younger adults. There were also substantial response latency costs associated with the 1-back conditions for older adults in the μ parameter, suggesting that, in addition to the increased susceptibility to fluctuations in the efficiency of executive control processes, older adults also experienced a pervasive decline in the ability to manage the demands of the 1-back condition.

PERFORMANCE VARIABILITY AND FLUCTUATIONS
OF EXECUTIVE CONTROL

If ageing results in an increased tendency for executive control processes to fluctuate in efficiency over time, this could be expected to result in an increase in intra- and possibly inter-subject variability in tasks requiring the recruitment of executive processes. In a recent study designed to test this prediction a group of younger and older adults performed a task including non-executive (i.e., choice RT) and executive (i.e., 1-back) conditions on four consecutive days. Participants were asked to press one of four keys to identify which of four digits was presented on a computer monitor for a given trial (choice RT) or to report the identity of the digit presented in the previous display (1-back; West, Murphy, Armilio, Craik, & Stuss, 2000). The effects of ageing and non-executive/executive task demands on three measures of performance variability were considered: (1) *diversity* or inter-subject variability, (2) *dispersion* or intra-subject variability, and (3) *consistency* of performance over days of testing. The relevant data from this study are presented in Figure 2. For the choice RT condition there were robust age-related differences in mean response time on all four days of testing. In comparison, there were no significant differences between younger and older adults in diversity, dispersion, or consistency for this condition across the four days of testing. For the 1-back condition there were also robust age-related differences in mean response time across the four days of testing. Consideration of the performance variability measures revealed that the degree of diversity was greater for older than younger adults on only the first day of testing (see Figure 2a), whereas age-related differences in dispersion were significant across the four days of testing (see Figure 2b). There was also an age-related difference in consistency of performance across days of testing.

In an effort to further characterise the age-related difference in dispersion the data from this study were submitted to an ex-Gaussian analysis to determine the degree to which the increase in dispersion was pervasive, influencing both the σ and τ parameters, or resulted from skewing of the responses time distribution in the 1-back condition, influencing only the τ parameter. This analysis revealed significant age-related differences in the σ parameter on only the first day of testing (see Figure 2c), whereas age-related differences in the τ parameter were maintained across the four days of testing (see Figure 2d). These findings indicate that age-related differences in dispersion in a task requiring executive control primarily resulted from an increase in the degree of positive skewing of the response time distribution in older adults. This finding is consistent with the proposal that older adults are more susceptible to fluctuations in the efficiency of executive control processes than are younger adults.

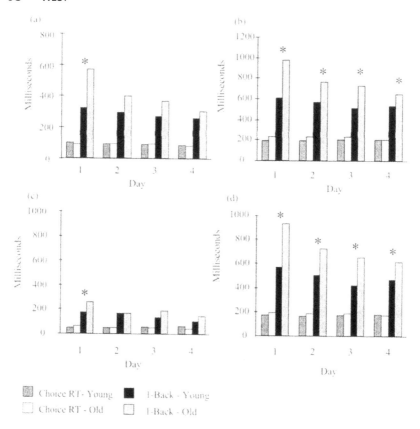

Figure 2. Estimates of (a) diversity, (b) dispersion, (c) the σ parameter, and (d) the τ parameter for younger and older adults in a choice RT and 1-back task requiring identification of the identity of a digit. The * marks significant differences between younger and older adults for the 1-back task.

NEURAL CORRELATES OF FLUCTUATIONS IN EXECUTIVE CONTROL

In addition to examining the transient nature of executive control processes in younger and older adults using behavioural methods I have also been engaged in a line of research designed to explore the neural correlates of fluctuations in executive control using event-related brain potentials (ERPs) in collaboration with Claude Alain of the Rotman Research Institute in Toronto. Our first study was designed to determine whether or not we could identify a pattern of neural activity associated with the waning of executive control giving rise to intrusion errors in the

Stroop task that would parallel the slowing of response latency preceding intrusion errors (West, 1999a). In this study we reasoned that if intrusion errors result from the transient disruption of a neural system supporting executive control there should be a pattern of neural activity that would differentiate trials where an intrusion error was committed from trials where a goal directed response was made that would precede the intrusion error (West & Alain, 2000b). Consistent with this prediction we observed a slow wave that reversed polarity from the fronto-central to fronto-polar regions that preceded stimulus onset by 400 ms to 800 ms for those trials where an intrusion error was made relative to trials where a correct colour naming or word reading response was made (see Figure 3). This finding indicates that lapses of intention, which give rise to intrusion errors, are associated with a transient change in neural activity that was not related to the nature of the stimulus presented—since the stimuli were identical for incongruent trials eliciting a correct response or an intrusion error—or the response made—since the response was the same for incongruent trials eliciting an intrusion error and trials where the goal-directed response was to identify the word. In a second experiment we found that the amplitude of this slow wave was highly sensitive to the contextual demands of the Stroop task, being greater when trials were mostly congruent relative to when trials were mostly incongruent. This finding is consistent with behavioural data indicating that lapses of inten-

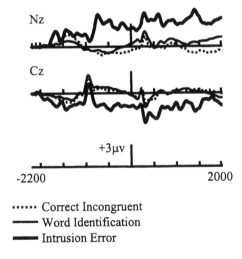

Figure 3. Grand averaged ERPs at fronto-polar (Nz) and central (Cz) electrode locations demonstrating the slow wave preceding the occurrence of an intrusion error in the Stroop task that is differentiated from incongruent and word reading trials where the colour or word were correctly identified, respectively. The tall bar represents stimulus onset.

tion are more frequent when individuals are in a task context where few demands are placed upon executive control processes (West, 1999a; West & Baylis, 1998). Interestingly, the transient disruption of the neural system which guards against lapses of intention does not appear to extend to neural systems supporting other executive control processes as the amplitude of ERP components reflecting inhibitory control and error monitoring were intact on trials where an intrusion error occurred (West & Alain, 2000b).

In a related study we sought to determine the degree to which neural mechanisms supporting performance of the Stroop task were susceptible to fluctuations in efficiency (West & Alain, 2000a). This study was inspired by my earlier work (West & Baylis, 1998) where manipulating the proportion of congruent and incongruent trials in the Stroop task modulated the magnitude of the interference effect for the μ parameter of the ex-Gaussian distribution and not the τ parameter. For this study we reasoned that one source of variability in the response time distribution was variation in the efficiency of executive control processes with faster responses reflecting optimal executive control and slower responses reflecting sub-optimal executive control (West & Alain, 2000b). Based upon this assumption we predicted that the N450 (an index of inhibition) would be modulated by the proportion of congruent and incongruent trials for faster trials, but not slower trials. The interference effect was not significant for faster trials in the mostly incongruent condition and was significant for faster trials in the mostly congruent condition, consistent with the findings of West and Baylis (1998). The interference effect was similar in magnitude for slower trials in both the mostly congruent and mostly incongruent conditions. Consistent with our predictions, the amplitude of the N450 was greater for faster trials in the mostly congruent condition than the mostly incongruent condition and equal in amplitude for slower trials in these two conditions. These data lead to the suggestion that fluctuations in the efficiency of executive control processes give rise to the interference effect observed in the mostly incongruent condition when there is a high demand placed upon neurocognitive mechanisms supporting the suppression of word information in the Stroop task (West & Alain, 1999; West & Alain, 2000a).

The data from these two studies indicate that the neural mechanisms supporting executive control in the Stroop task are dynamic in nature, tending to fluctuate in efficiency over the course of task performance; both the slow wave preceding intrusion errors and the N450 reverse polarity from the fronto-central to the fronto-polar and lateral fronto-polar regions, respectively. This inversion pattern suggests that the neural generators of these ERP components lie within the polar and lateral prefrontal cortical regions. The role of the prefrontal cortex in maintaining the optimal efficiency of executive control processes is consistent with data from a number of other sources. Studies of individuals sustaining a traumatic brain injury (TBI)—often resulting in damage to the prefrontal cortex—demonstrate increased performance variability both within and between testing sessions relative to matched controls (Stuss, Pogue, Buckle, & Bonder, 1994). TBI has also been associated with an increased susceptibility to goal neglect (Duncan et al., 1996), a decreased ability to maintain a high level of sustained attention (Robertson, Manly, Andrade, Baddeley, & Yiend, 1997), and an increased susceptibility to prospective memory failure (Shum, Valentine, & Cutmore, 1999). Neuroimaging studies have revealed that the prefrontal cortex is activated in tasks requiring both sustained attention (Pardo, Fox, & Raichle, 1991) and sustained intention (Bench et al., 1993).

AGEING, PREFRONTAL CORTEX, AND FLUCTUATIONS OF EXECUTIVE CONTROL

There is mounting evidence indicating that the prefrontal cortex is more susceptible to the effect of the ageing process than some other cortical and subcortical neural structure (see Phillips & Della Sala, 1999; West, 1996), although this position is not universally accepted (Greenwood, 2000). Age-related declines in the functional integrity of the prefrontal cortex have been revealed in studies reporting declines in frontal grey matter in older adults (Raz et al., 1997), declines in resting levels of cerebral blood flow and irregularities in patterns of blood flow in cognitive activation studies using PET (Cabeza, in press).

Given these data, it seems reasonable to propose that the age-related increase in the tendency for executive control processes to fluctuate in efficiency over time demonstrated by the increased number of intrusion errors in the Stroop task (West, 1999a), the greater positive skewing of the response time distribution for older adults (West, 1999b), and increased performance variability (West et al., 2000) results from a decline in the functional integrity of the prefrontal cortex. What is not apparent at this time is whether there is a single neurocognitive mechanism that serves to maintain the optimal efficiency of executive control processes or whether the efficiency of various executive control processes becomes more transient in nature in later adulthood, in the absence of a higher order process. Li and Lindenberger (1999) have recently argued that dedifferentiation of cognitive abilities and increased performance variability in older adults results from an age-related decline of the catecholaminergic system, consistent with the idea that there is a common neurobiological locus for the increased sensitivity of older adults to fluctuations in the efficiency of executive control processes and relatively general age-related declines in cognition. In contrast, there is both behavioural and neurophysiological evidence indicating that the transient disruption of one executive control process does not necessarily accompany the disruption of other executive control processes. For instance, West and Alain (2000b) demonstrated that ERPs indices of inhibitory control and error detection were intact on trials where an intrusion error occurred, presumably resulting from the transient disruption of a neural system supporting goal-directed action. Also, behavioural evidence for both younger and older adults indicates that error-related slowing of response latency is observed following intrusion errors in the Stroop and 1-back tasks, indicating that executive control processes supporting performance monitoring are active during lapses of intention (West, 1999a).

DISCUSSION

In the previous pages I have reviewed evidence from a number of studies consistent with the proposal that older adults experience an increased tendency for executive control processes to fluctuate in efficiency over time, giving rise to age-related declines in tasks requiring selective attention, working and prospective memory. These fluctuations in efficiency appear to be an intrinsic property of executive control processes, being relatively immune to task experience or fatigue (West, 1999a; West et al., 2000).

Consistent with the work of Salthouse (1993), age-related increases in fluctuations of executive control cannot fully account for age-related differences in task performance. Robust age-related differences in the Stroop interference effect (West & Baylis, 1998) and the response latency costs associated with a 1-back task were observed across the full range of the response time distribution, indicating a pervasive effect of age (West, 1999b). These findings indicate that it will be necessary to consider the contribution of both transient and pervasive disruptions in the efficiency of executive control processes when trying to understand the nature of age-related declines in cognition.

Analysis of measures of performance variability (i.e., diversity, dispersion, and consistency) in non-executive (i.e., choice RT) and executive (i.e., 1-back) task conditions revealed that levels of dispersion or within-subject variability were greater for older than younger adults in an executive and not non-executive task condition, and that this difference was not eliminated with practice. Additionally, the decomposition of this effect in an ex-Gaussian analysis revealed that the age-related increase in dispersion resulted almost entirely from an increase in the degree of positive skewing of the response time distribution. These findings lead to the suggestion that age-related increases in fluctuations of efficiency are limited to those cognitive processes that are executive in nature. This degree of selectivity may arise from differences in sensitivity to the effects of ageing for those neural structures that support executive control processes (i.e., the prefrontal cortex and related structures) more so than those less involved in executive control.

In conclusion, an age-related increase in the tendency for executive control processes to fluctuate in efficiency over time contributes to the poor performance observed for older adults in a variety of tasks. These fluctuations are an intrinsic property of executive control processes and may be related to the moment-to-moment operational efficiency of the prefrontal cortex. Future research efforts should: (1) be devoted to examining the degree to which transient and/or pervasive disruptions of executive control processes contribute to age-related declines in cognition, and (2) focus on determining the neural mechanisms responsible for fluctuations in the efficiency of executive control in younger and older adults.

Manuscript received September 2000

REFERENCES

Bench, C.J., Frith, C.D., Grasby, P.M., Friston, K.J., Paulesu, E., Frackowiak, R.S.J., & Dolan, R.J. (1993). Investigations of the functional anatomy of attention using the Stroop task. *Neuropsychologica, 31*, 907–922.

Bunce, D.J., Warr, P.B., & Cochrane, T. (1993). Blocks in choice responding as a function of age and physical fitness. *Psychology and Aging, 8*, 26–33.

Cabeza, R. (in press). Functional neuroimaging of cognitive aging. In R. Cabeza & A. Kingstone (Eds.), *Handbook of functional neuroimaging of cognition*. Cambridge, MA: MIT Press.

Craik, F.I.M., & Kerr, S.A. (1996). Commentary: Prospective memory, aging, and lapses of intention. In M. Brandimonte, G.O. Einstein, & M.A. McDaniel (Eds.), *Prospective memory: Theory and applications* (pp. 227–238). Mahwah, NJ: Lawrence Erlbaum Associates Inc.

Duncan, J., Emslie, H., Williams, P., Johnson, R., & Freer, C. (1996). Intelligence and the frontal lobe: The organization of goal-directed behavior. *Cognitive Psychology, 30*, 257–303.

Greenwood, P.M. (2000). The frontal lobe hypothesis evaluated. *Journal of the International Neuropsychological Society, 6*, 705–726.

Heathcote, A., Popiel, S.J., & Mewhort, D.J.K. (1991). Analysis of response time distributions: An example using the Stroop task. *Psychological Bulletin, 109*, 340–347.

Hohle, R.H. (1965). Inferred components of reaction times as functions of foreperiod duration. *Journal of Experimental Psychology, 69*, 382–386.

Li, S.-C., & Lindenberger, U. (1999). Cross-level unification: A computational exploration of the link between deterioration of neurotransmitter systems and dedifferentiation of cognitive abilities in old age. In L.-G. Nilsson & H.J. Markowitsch (Eds.), *Cognitive neuroscience of memory* (pp. 103–146). Seattle: Hogrefe & Huber.

Maylor, E.A. (1996). Age-related impairment in an event-based prospective memory task. *Psychology and Aging, 11,* 74–78.

Miller, J. (1988). A warning about median reaction time. *Journal of Experimental Psychology: Human Perception and Performance, 14,* 539–543.

Parasuraman, R., & Giambra, L. (1991). Skill development in vigilance: Effects of event rate and age. *Psychology and Aging, 6,* 155–169.

Pardo, J.V., Fox, P.T., & Raichle, M.E. (1991). Localization of a human system for sustained attention by positron emission tomography. *Nature, 349,* 61–64.

Phillips, L.H., & Della Sala, S. (1999). Aging, intelligence, and anatomical segregation in the frontal lobes. *Learning and Individual Differences, 10,* 217–243.

Ratcliff, R. (1979). Group reaction time distributions and an analysis of distribution statistics. *Psychological Bulletin, 86,* 446–461.

Raz, N., Gunning, F.M., Head, D., Dupuis, J.H., McQuain, J., Briggs, S.D., Loken, W.J., Thornton, A.E., & Acker, J.D. (1997). Selective aging of the human cerebral cortex observed *in vivo*: Differential vulnerability of the prefrontal gray matter. *Cerebral Cortex, 7,* 268–282.

Reason, J. (1979). Actions not as planned: The price of automatization. In G. Underwood & R. Stevens (Eds.), *Aspects of consciousness* (pp. 67–89). London: Academic Press.

Robertson, I.H., Manly, T., Andrade, J., Baddeley, B.T., & Yiend, J. (1997). "Oops!": Performance correlates of everyday attentional failures in traumatic brain injured and normal subjects. *Neuropsychologia, 35,* 747–758.

Salthouse, T.A. (1993). Attentional blocks are not responsible for age-related slowing. *Journal of Gerontology: Psychological Sciences, 48,* P263–P270.

Shum, D., Valentine, M., & Cutmore, T. (1999). Performance of individuals with severe long-term traumatic brain injury on time-, event-, and activity-based prospective memory tasks. *Journal of Clinical and Experimental Neuropsychology, 2,* 49–58.

Spieler, D.H., Balota, D.A., & Faust, M.E. (1996). Stroop performance in healthy younger and older adults and in individuals with dementia of the Alzheimer's type. *Journal of Experimental Psychology: Human Perception and Performance, 22,* 461–479.

Stuss, D.T., Pogue, J., Buckle, L., & Bonder, J. (1994). Characterization of variability of performance in patients with traumatic brain injury: Variability and consistency on reaction time tests. *Neuropsychology, 8,* 316–324.

Stuss, D.T., Shallice, T., Alexander, M.P., & Picton, T.W. (1995). A multidisciplinary approach to anterior attentional functions. *Annals of the New York Academy of Science, 769,* 191–211.

West, R. (1999a). Age differences in lapses of intention in the Stroop task. *Journal of Gerontology: Psychological Sciences, 54B,* P34–P43.

West, R. (1999b). Visual distraction, working memory, and aging. *Memory and Cognition, 27,* 1064–1072.

West, R., & Alain, C. (1999). Event-related neural activity associated with the Stroop task. *Cognitive Brain Research, 8,* 157–164.

West, R., & Alain, C. (2000a). Effect of task context and fluctuations of attention on neural activity supporting performance of the Stroop task. *Brain Research, 873,* 102–111.

West, R., & Alain, C. (2000b). Evidence for the transient nature of a neural system supporting goal-directed action. *Cerebral Cortex, 8,* 748–752.

West, R., & Baylis, G.C. (1998). Effects of increased response dominance and contextual disintegration on the Stroop interference effect in older adults. *Psychology and Aging, 13,* 206–217.

West, R., & Craik, F.I.M. (1999). Age-related decline in prospective memory: The roles of cue accessibility and cue sensitivity. *Psychology and Aging, 14*, 264–272.

West, R., Ergis, A.-M., Winocur, G., & Saint-Cyr, J. (1998). The contribution of impaired working memory monitoring to performance of the self-ordered pointing task in normal aging and Parkinson's disease. *Neuropsychology, 12*, 546–554.

West, R., Murphy, K.J., Armilio, M.L., Craik, F.I.M., & Stuss, D.T. (2000). Lapses of intention and performance variability reveal age-related increases in fluctuations of executive control. *Manuscript submitted for publication.*

West, R.L. (1996). An application of prefrontal cortex function theory to cognitive aging. *Psychological Bulletin, 120*, 272–292.

EUROPEAN JOURNAL OF COGNITIVE PSYCHOLOGY, 2001, *13* (1/2), 107–122

Inhibitory control over the present and the past

Cindy Lustig
Duke University, NC, USA

Lynn Hasher
University of Toronto, Canada

Simon T. Tonev
Duke University, NC, USA

From the perspective of the Hasher, Zacks, and May (1999) inhibitory framework, optimal performance occurs only when there is control over nonrelevant information. Relative to a current, goal-directed task, there are at least two potential sources of nonrelevant information that need to be controlled. The first is no longer relevant information. Such information would include, for example, a previous topic of conversation, or, in our work, a previous list of materials presented for study and recall. The second source of nonrelevant information is currently present (in thought or in the world) stimuli that are not relevant to the task at hand. Inhibitory processes are critical to the effective control of both sources of information—the no longer relevant past and the irrelevant present. If inhibitory processes are inefficient, irrelevant information from both the past and the present will disrupt performance on the current task. We illustrate this with studies showing the role of irrelevant information in reducing the working memory capacity of older adults and in slowing them down as they do even reasonably simple tasks.

"Oops! My mind wandered for a second—could you repeat that, please?"

We've all had occasion to say something like this during a conversation, even one that we were interested in and motivated to attend to. Perhaps

---

Requests for reprints should be addressed to L. Hasher, Department of Psychology, University of Toronto, 100 St George St., Toronto, Ontario, Canada, M5S 3G3. Email: hasher@psych.utoronto.ca

The research reported here was supported by the National Institute on Aging grants AG 2753 and 4306. We thank Ulrich Mayr and Jason M. Watson for comments on a previous version of this manuscript.

---

http://www.tandf.co.uk/journals/pp/09541446.html   DOI:10.1080/09541440042000241

the mention of a mutual friend's name sparked a memory for the entertaining dinner you had with her last weekend, and you spent a moment too long reminiscing; perhaps an interesting person across the street caught your eye and distracted you from the conversation. These examples show how extraneous information—either from the environment or one's own mind—can divert one's attention from the task at hand.

Our theoretical framework (Hasher et al., 1999) emphasises the importance of inhibiting this extraneous information for controlling goal-directed behaviour. By this framework, keeping attention focused on the information important for current activities via the suppression of irrelevant information plays a critical role in the successful performance of many tasks, both current and future (e.g., remembering). We further suggest that many of the difficulties older adults face on laboratory tests and in everyday life stem from an age-related reduction in inhibitory control. Other views of cognitive ageing emphasise age changes in the capacity or speed of information processing (e.g., Craik, 1986; Salthouse, 1996), our view focuses the importance of *efficient* processing, such that attention is occupied only by information relevant to accomplishing current goals. Failures to keep attention free from irrelevant information can disrupt both present performance and memory.[1]

In this paper, we concentrate on how the failure to inhibit memories that have become irrelevant can hamper the retrieval of currently important memories, and how distraction from irrelevant information in the environment can impair performance even on simple and well-practised tasks.[2] To this end, we describe studies using both young adults, who are relatively good at inhibiting irrelevant information (at least at their optimal time of day; see Yoon, May, & Hasher, 2000), and older adults, who often have difficulty inhibiting irrelevant information and thus are very vulnerable to its effects.

IRRELEVANT INFORMATION FROM THE PAST: ITS IMPACT ON RETRIEVAL

In an earlier example, memories for a previous outing with a friend served as distraction from a current conversation. Irrelevant information

---

[1] Although we will not further explore this issue here, neuroimaging and neuropsychological evidence suggests that age-related declines in attentional control may be related to age-related changes in the frontal lobes of the brain (see Moscovitch & Winocur, 1995; Shimamura & Jurica, 1994; West, 2000).

[2] These concerns relate to the *deletion* and *access* functions of inhibitory control, respectively. The full framework (see Hasher et al., 1999) includes a third function for inhibition, the *restraint* of dominant but currently inappropriate behaviours.

from the past can also hamper the ability to correctly remember new information. For example, suppose that this friend has recently moved, leading to a change in address and phone number. When calling your friend to arrange another outing, you may find it difficult at first to remember her new phone number because the memory for the old number "gets in the way of", or interferes with, its retrieval.

Laboratory studies of the detrimental effects of previous information often use paired-associate list procedures in a proactive interference design. In the paired-associate procedure, the participant is presented with, say, 10 pairs of items to be learned and recalled on a later memory test. One item in each pair is designated the "stimulus" or "cue". The other item is the "response". The participant's task is to learn to give the correct response to each stimulus item. In a proactive interference design, participants next learn a second list of paired-associates, in which each stimulus word from the first list is paired with a new response word (e.g., List 1: SHIRT–WINDOW; List 2: SHIRT–FINGER). After learning the second list, participants are then given the stimulus words as cues, and their memory for the second-list response terms is compared to that of a control group, who either learned only the second, critical list or whose first list used different stimulus items (e.g., List 1: ENERGY–WINDOW; List 2: SHIRT–FINGER). Participants in the proactive interference condition reliably show worse memory for the second-list responses than do control participants (for reviews see Anderson & Neely, 1996; Crowder, 1976; Keppel, 1968; Postman & Underwood, 1973; Underwood, 1945).

For participants in the proactive interference condition, inhibition of irrelevant information from the past (i.e., the first list) may be important both for learning the second, critical list and for producing the second-list response terms on the memory test. Learning the second-list response terms will be easier if the first-list responses are suppressed, so that they do not compete with the second-list response terms and disrupt their learning. Likewise, for the memory test, participants in the proactive interference condition must limit the retrieval of the now-irrelevant first-list items in order to successfully remember the critical, second-list items. Thus, the successful learning and remembering of the critical second-list items depends on the inhibition of the now-irrelevant items from the first list. Older adults are less likely to inhibit these irrelevant items from the past and thus are more likely to retrieve them (e.g., Hamm & Hasher, 1992; Hartman & Dusek, 1994; Hartman & Hasher, 1991; May & Hasher, 1998; May, Zacks, Hasher, & Multhaup, 1999), and older adults often show larger proactive interference effects than do young adults (Kane & Hasher, 1995; Lustig & Hasher, in press; Winocur & Moscovitch, 1983).

Irrelevant information from the past can also hurt performance on tasks with much shorter lists than are commonly used in paired-associate tasks (e.g., Keppel & Underwood, 1962). An important modern example is the impact of interference on the span tasks commonly used to measure working memory capacity, or the amount of information that can be simultaneously processed and stored (e.g., Baddeley, 1986; Baddeley & Hitch, 1974; Daneman & Carpenter, 1980, 1983; Just & Carpenter, 1980, 1992). Working memory capacity is thought to be an important determinant of performance on many tasks, especially language and reading comprehension (see Daneman & Merikle, 1996 for a review). Consistent with this idea, working memory span performance predicts performance on numerous tasks, including reading, problem solving, writing, and prose recall (e.g., Daneman & Carpenter, 1980; Dempster & Corkill, 1999; Gernsbacher, 1997; Kyllonen & Christal, 1990; Logie, Gilhooly, & Wynn, 1994; MacDonald, Just, & Carpenter, 1992; Stine & Wingfield, 1990). Young children, older adults, poor readers, and various patient groups typically obtain lower working memory span scores than do healthy college students (e.g., Brebion, Amador, Smith, & Gorman, 1998; Frisk & Milner, 1990; Gabrieli, Singh, Stebbins, & Goetz, 1996; Gernsbacher, 1997; Gick, Craik, & Morris, 1988; Light & Anderson, 1985; Salthouse & Babcock, 1991; Siegel, 1994; Swanson, 1993). Presumed group and individual differences in capacity, as measured by working memory span tasks, are thought to lead to differences in many areas of cognitive performance.

However, a close examination of many working memory span tasks reveals that their design actually encourages the build-up of proactive interference. For example, in the most commonly used span task, the reading span task (Daneman & Carpenter, 1980), each trial consists of a short series of sentences, at the end of which participants are asked to recall the final word of each sentence in the series. After completing five series of two sentences, participants are given five series of three sentences, then four sentences, and so on until they can no longer reliably produce the final words for all the sentences in the series. The largest series at which a person can reliably produce all the sentence-final words is used as the measure of his or her working memory capacity. Although working memory span tasks are used as measures of capacity, their structure strongly encourages the build-up of proactive interference. Many words are learned and recalled as the person proceeds through the span task. As a result, now-irrelevant words from previous series may interfere with the retrieval of words from a current series. This proactive interference will have an especially large impact on the ability to remember words from the longer, later series that are important for obtaining a high span score.

Based on this observation, as well as on evidence that individuals and groups thought to be very vulnerable to interference typically have low span scores (e.g., Butters, Delis, & Lucas, 1995; Chiappe, Hasher, & Siegel, 2000; Dempster, 1991, 1992; Gernsbacher, 1997), May, Hasher, and Kane (1999a) tested the effects of interference-reducing manipulations on the span performance of younger and older adults. The first of these manipulations simply reversed the order in which the series of sentences was presented. In this reversed administration, the largest series appeared first, rather than last. Because the large series appeared early in the task, before numerous other words had been learned and recalled, the impact of proactive interference on these trials was greatly reduced relative to the usual version of the task, in which the large series occur last, not first.[3]

When tested using this interference-reducing, reversed administration, the span scores of older adults were much higher than in the standard, interference-heavy administration. In fact, older adults tested in the interference-reducing condition performed as well as young adults, in stark contrast to the usual finding of age-related reductions in working memory span (e.g., Gick et al., 1988; Salthouse & Babcock, 1991; Zacks & Hasher, 1988). The addition of a second interference-reducing manipulation, breaks between each series that increased their distinctiveness, also raised the span scores of young adults (May et al., 1999a). These results strongly suggest that proactive interference impacts working memory span scores, that young adults are less sensitive to proactive interference than are older adults, and that age differences in working memory span may be the result of older adults' greater vulnerability to proactive interference from now-irrelevant past information, rather than age-related reductions in the capacity to store and process information overall.

Working memory span tasks are so commonly used because they are highly predictive of performance on tasks that are thought to be determined primarily by capacity to store and process information, such as reading and language comprehension (see Daneman & Merikle, 1996 for review). The ability to simultaneously store and process information may be especially important in such tasks, since comprehension typically involves integrating the information from a current sentence or phrase with the relevant previous information that will facilitate its interpretation (see Daneman & Carpenter, 1980; Daneman & Merikle, 1996). However, if *irrelevant* information is not deleted from working memory, it may

---

[3]Of course, proactive interference also builds up as participants progress through the trials in the descending condition. However, it will not have as great an impact on span scores as in the standard condition, since in the descending condition proactive interference will be greatest on the smallest, easiest trials that are least important for obtaining a high span score (rather than the largest, hardest trials that are most important for obtaining a high span score, as in the standard condition).

impair this integration of the *relevant* past and current information, leading to reduced speed and increased errors (see Hasher & Zacks, 1988; Hasher et al., 1999). Thus, a critical question is the degree to which the interference present in working memory span tasks contributes to their ability to predict performance on other cognitive tasks.

To address this question, we asked younger and older adults to read and recall a short story after completing the span task in either the standard or interference-reducing conditions (Lustig, Hasher, & May, in press). The results of this study replicated those of May et al. (1999a): Reducing the influence of proactive interference on the span task raised span scores, and older adults performed as well as young adults in the interference-reducing reversed condition. More importantly, for each age group, the same interference-reducing manipulations that increased span scores eliminated the span task's ability to predict story recall perfor-mance (see Table 1). These results fit well with other findings suggesting that individual and group differences on many language tasks are greatly influenced by differences in vulnerability to interference (e.g., Gernsba-cher, 1997; Gernsbacher & Faust, 1991; Light & Capps, 1986; Zacks & Hasher, 1988; see Dempster & Corkill, 1999 and Kemper, 1992 for reviews). In combination, these findings strongly suggest that not only are the span tasks that are supposed to measure capacity heavily influenced by interference, but span tasks' ability to predict performance on other cognitive tasks depends upon a shared influence of interference.

Thus, there are (at least) two interpretations of the widespread indivi-dual and group differences in working memory span and the ability of working memory span to predict performance on other cognitive tasks.

TABLE 1

Means and standard deviations (in parentheses) of span scores, prose recall scores, and correlation between span and prose recall for older and younger adults (from Lustig et al., in press. Used with the permission of the American Psychological Association)

| | Older adults | | Younger adults | | |
	Ascending	*Descending*	*Ascending*	*Descending*	*Descending-breaks*
Span score	20.10	23.56	26.20	25.52	30.72
	(8.07)	(6.05)	(8.86)	(7.21)	(7.61)
Prose recall	12.43	12.88	14.69	14.72	14.93
	(3.26)	(3.56)	(4.32)	(3.65)	(3.94)
Correlation	.29	.08	.27	.33	.02

By the dominant view, working memory span tasks measure the capacity to simultaneously store and process information (e.g., Baddeley, 1986; Baddeley & Hitch, 1974; Daneman & Carpenter, 1980, 1983; Just & Carpenter, 1980, 1992). This capacity is further thought to be a stable trait (though decreasing with age) of fundamental importance in many areas of cognition, especially reading and language and comprehension (e.g., Daneman & Merikle, 1996; Engle, Kane, & Tuholski, 1999). An alternative view calls attention to the heavy influence of interference on both working memory span tasks and the measures they predict, as well as noting that the same people that typically obtain low span scores have been shown in other contexts to be very sensitive to interference (Chiappe et al., 2000; Hasher et al., 1999; Lustig et al., in press; May et al., 1999a; see also Dempster & Corkill, 1999; Gernsbacher, 1997). By this alternative view, individual and group differences (particularly age differences) in working memory span reflect individual and group differences in interference vulnerability, and the ability of span performance to predict performance on other tasks rests on a shared influence of interference. In turn, the present view suggests that what underlies interference effects is the ability (or lack thereof) to suppress no-longer-relevant or never-relevant information. To the degree that people are able to do so, their spans will be large and their performance on any other test containing a memory component, including reading comprehension, will be improved.

In summary, information learned in the past that is no longer relevant can impair performance on a current task. This is true for both laboratory measures of memory, such as the paired-associates and working memory span tests, and for more "real-world" activities such as reading and language. Older adults' greater vulnerability to the detrimental effects of now-irrelevant past information plays an important role in producing age differences on these measures. In some cases, reducing the opportunity for interference from past information can eliminate age differences, such that older adults perform as well as young adults (e.g., Lustig, et al., in press; May et al., 1999a). Age differences in the ability to resist interference from previously learned information, as well as individual differences within an age group, may be responsible for differences on many cognitive tasks that have been previously ascribed to other cognitive constructs such as capacity.

IRRELEVANT INFORMATION FROM THE ENVIRONMENT: THE IMPACT OF DISTRACTION

Extraneous information can also come from the surrounding environment, slowing performance and leading to mistakes. For example, we usually slow down when driving through road construction full of various distractions such as warning cones, machinery, and highway workers. We may attempt to reduce distraction from other sources in order to compensate, turning down the radio and quieting rowdy children in the back seat. Environmental distraction even affects performance on relatively simple, well-practised tasks, such as reading. This consideration has taken on new importance because of increased Internet usage, with web page designers exhorted to avoid crowded text, blinking ads, and other forms of clutter that make extracting the desired information a slow and painful process.[4]

Older adults are less able to ignore environmental distractors than are young adults, as demonstrated by age differences on simple visual attention tasks as well as more complex tasks such as reading and problem-solving in the face of distraction. For example, the presence of distractors in a visual display disrupts older adults' ability to find a target item more than it disrupts young adults' ability (e.g., Cremer & Zeef, 1987; Lepage, Stuss, & Richer, 1999; Rabbitt, 1965; but see Kotary & Hoyer, 1995). As the number of distractors increases, so do age differences in errors and speed, unless the distractors are easily distinguished from the target or unless they occur in predictable locations (Scialfa, Esau, & Joffe, 1998; Zeef, Sonke, Kok, Buiten, & Kenemans, 1996; see Madden & Plude, 1993 for a discussion of sparing factors).

The similarity of environmental distractors to target information also influences age differences in distraction on reading tasks. Both younger and older adults are slower to read a passage of text that has distracting words scattered throughout it than they are to read a control passage without such distraction. However, older adults are more impaired by the distractors than are young adults, and older but not younger adults are further slowed if the distractor words are related to the passage (Carlson, Hasher, Connelly, & Zacks, 1995; Connelly, Hasher, & Zacks, 1991; Duchek, Balota, & Thessing, 1998; Dywan & Murphy, 1996; Li, Hasher, Jonas, Rahhal, & May, 1999) (see Figure 1). As with the target–search tasks described earlier, age differences on the reading-with-distraction task are greatly reduced if the distractors appear in fixed or predictable locations (Carlson et al., 1995).

In other cases, strongly related environmental distractors can lead to age differences even if distractors appear in predictable locations. Furthermore, even young adults can be affected by strongly related environmental distractors, if they are tested at nonoptimal times of day. For example, each trial of the classic Remote Associations Test (RAT; Mednick, 1962) presents participants with three cue words (e.g., ship, outer, crawl), and

---

[4]For a dramatic illustration, visit www.webpagesthatsuck.com/badtext.htm

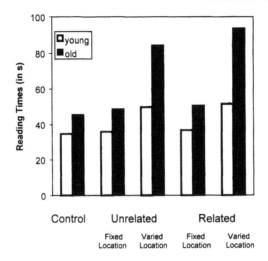

Figure 1. Reading times (in seconds) for younger and older adults in the reading-with-distraction task (from Carlson et al., 1995. Used with the permission of the American Psychological Association).

asks them to find the word that connects them (e.g., SPACE). May (1999) examined how younger and older adults' ability to solve the RAT problems was affected by distractor words presented immediately below the cue words. Two types of distractors were used. "Leading" distractor words (e.g., rocket, atmosphere, attic) had meanings that would help link the cue words with the target. "Misleading" distractors (e.g., ocean, inner, floor) had meanings that would link the cue words with meanings other than the target.

May (1999) hypothesised that, in general, older adults would be less able to ignore the distracting words than would young adults, and thus would show both greater costs from the misleading distractors and greater benefits from the leading distractors. In addition, recent evidence suggests that the ability to control attention fluctuates over the course of the day, with younger and older adults at opposing ends of the circadian cycle (e.g., May & Hasher, 1998; May, Hasher, & Stoltzfus, 1993; see Yoon et al., 2000 for a review). Young adults' inhibitory abilities are at their lowest in the morning and reach a maximum in the late afternoon; older adults' inhibitory abilities are at their highest in the morning and wane throughout the day. Thus, May hypothesised that young adults tested in the morning (their nonoptimal time) would resemble older adults in being affected by distraction, and that older adults tested in the afternoon (their nonoptimal time) would show very large costs and benefits from the misleading and leading distractor words.

May (1999) found that younger and older adults completed an equal number of control problems (i.e., those presented with no distractor words), and that the ability to solve control problems did not change with the time (optimal or nonoptimal) of testing. In contrast, the ability to solve problems presented with misleading or leading distractor words was clearly affected by both age and testing time. Figure 2 illustrates the costs of misleading distractor words and the benefits of leading distractor words, relative to control problems presented without distractors.

Overall, older adults completed more of the problems presented with leading distractors than young adults did, and fewer of the problems presented with misleading distractors. Older adults were less able than young adults to ignore the distractor words, and thus showed both greater costs benefits from distractors. However, for both younger and older adults, the ability to ignore the distractors varied according to whether they were tested at their "good" or "bad" times of day. Young adults tested in the morning showed distraction effects much like those of older adults; in fact, there were no statistically significant age differences in either costs or benefits for participants tested in the morning. For older adults, distraction effects were much greater for participants tested in the afternoon (older adults' nonoptimal time of day) than for participants tested in the morning (older adults' optimal time). Thus, circadian influences on inhibitory control can have dramatic effects on the size of age differences in performance, and even on whether age differences in performance occur (May, 1999).

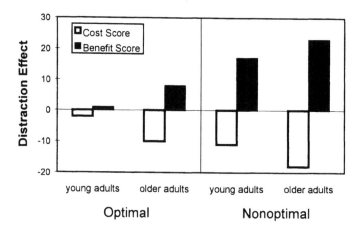

Figure 2. Costs and benefits of distractor words in the Remote Associations Test for younger and older adults tested at optimal and nonoptimal times of day (from May, 1999. Used with the permission of Cynthia P. May and the Psychonomic Society).

For both younger and older adults, extraneous information in the environment can make it difficult to locate, identify, and use target information. This concurrent distraction leads to slowing and errors on a wide range of tasks, from very simple visual attention tasks such as target location to more complex tasks such as solving word problems. Even very well-practised activities, such as reading and driving, are not immune to the effects of distraction, especially at one's "down" time of day. Environmental distractors can have an especially large impact on the performance of older adults, who are less able than young adults to control their attention and keep it away from these distracting, irrelevant stimuli. Older adults' ability to resist distraction can be improved if the distractors are very distinct from the targets or occur in predictable locations, but older adults are particularly vulnerable to distractors that are highly related to the target.

INHIBITORY CONTROL: ITS IMPLICATIONS FOR LIFE IN AND OUT OF THE LAB

Interacting with the world is a complex proposition, with many sources of information simultaneously competing for our attention. In addition to the incoming streams of stimulation from radios, televisions, and mobile phones, internal thoughts and memories may also occupy our minds as we go through the day. The ability to control our attention, keeping it away from irrelevant information so that we can focus on what *is* important, is thus a critical factor for successful performance in many situations.

In this paper, we have for the most part restricted our discussion to the importance of inhibitory control for performance on standard laboratory measures of cognitive function. Older adults' reduced ability to control attention away from irrelevant information plays an important role in determining age differences on many laboratory tasks. Older adults are less able than young adults to avoid keeping thoughts of previous, now irrelevant experience from coming to mind, making it more difficult for them to retrieve the memories that are current and correct for the present situation (e.g., Lustig et al., in press; May et al., 1999a; Winocur & Moscovitch, 1983). Older adults are also more likely than young adults to attend to distracting information present in the environment, which leads to slower performance and an increase in errors (e.g., Carlson et al., 1995; May, 1999; Scialfa et al., 1998).

Inhibitory control—and age differences in inhibition—thus plays an important role in theoretical considerations of attention and memory and how they change with increased age (e.g., Dempster & Corkill, 1999; Gernsbacher & Faust, 1991; Hasher & Zacks, 1988; Hasher et al., 1999; Kuhl, 1992; McDowd, Oseas-Kreger, & Filion, 1995). Indeed, recent evidence

(Lustig et al., in press; May et al., 1999a) suggests that laboratory tasks thought to measure working memory's capacity to simultaneously store and process current information are in fact heavily influenced by participants' ability to avoid the adverse effects of past information. This influence seems to play a critical role in both age differences on these working memory tests and in their ability to predict performance on other cognitive measures. Such a pattern suggests that at least some of the individual and group differences in cognition previously ascribed to differences in working memory capacity may be due to differences in inhibitory control.

The ability to keep attention away from irrelevant thoughts and distraction is also important for everyday life. Memory changes are a major concern for many older adults, and older adults' reduced ability to keep previous, now-irrelevant information out of active consideration impairs their retrieval of the currently desired information (e.g., Lustig et al., in press; May et al., 1999a; Winocur & Moscovitch, 1983). Older adults' difficulty in ignoring environmental distraction can also lead to driving impairments, particularly when they are navigating in a complicated environment or attempting to simultaneously perform other tasks such as using a car phone and carrying on a conversation (e.g., Ball & Rebok, 1994; McKnight & McKnight, 1993; Sekuler, Bennett, & Mamelak, 2000).

These findings have important implications for the ability of older adults to maintain their optimal performance at home and in the workplace. Noisy or visually cluttered environments may be fine for young adults—think of a teenager doing homework in his or her bedroom with the stereo blaring—but older adults may be disrupted by such distraction. This will particularly be the case in the afternoon, when older adults' inhibitory abilities are especially low and those of young adults are at a high point (Yoon et al., 2000).

In short, our perspective is that performance is best when attention is focused on the current task and away from extraneous information. This extraneous information may come either from external sources or from currently irrelevant internal thoughts and memories. Optimal performance depends on the ability to keep this information out of the focus of attention, and age differences in many situations may stem from age-related reductions in inhibitory control.

Manuscript received September 2000

REFERENCES

Anderson, M.C., & Neely, J.H. (1996). Interference and inhibition in memory retrieval. In E.L. Bjork & R.A. Bjork (Eds.), *Memory* (pp. 237–313). San Diego, CA: Academic Press.

Baddeley, A.D. (1986). *Working memory*. Oxford, UK: Clarendon Press.

Baddeley, A.D., & Hitch, G.J. (1974). Working memory. In G.A. Bower (Ed.), *The psychology of learning and motivation* (Vol. 8, pp. 47–89). New York: Academic Press.

Ball, K., & Rebok, G.W. (1994). Evaluating the driving ability of older adults. *Journal of Applied Gerontology, 13*, 20–38.

Brebion, G., Amador, X., Smith, M.J., & Gorman, J.M. (1998). Memory impairment in schizophrenia: The role of processing speed. *Schizophrenia Research, 30*, 31–39.

Butters, N., Delis, D.C., & Lucas, J.A. (1995). Clinical assessment of memory disorders in amnesia and dementia. *Annual Review of Psychology, 46*, 493–523.

Carlson, M.C., Hasher, L., Connelly, L.S., & Zacks, R.T. (1995). Aging, distraction, and the benefits of predictable location. *Psychology and Aging, 10*, 427–436.

Chiappe, P., Hasher, L., & Siegel, L.S. (2000). Working memory, inhibitory control, and reading disability. *Memory and Cognition, 28*, 8–17.

Connelly, S.L., Hasher, L., & Zacks, R.T. (1991). Age and reading: The impact of distraction. *Psychology and Aging, 7*, 56–64.

Craik, F.I.M. (1986). A functional account of age differences in memory. In F. Klix & H. Hagendorf (Eds.), *Human memory and cognitive capabilities* (pp. 409–422). Amsterdam: Elsevier.

Cremer, R., & Zeef, E.J. (1987). What kind of noise increases with age? *Journal of Gerontology, 42*, 515–518.

Crowder, R.G. (1976). *Principles of learning and memory*. Hillsdale, NJ: Lawrence Erlbaum Associates Inc.

Daneman, M., & Carpenter, P.A. (1980). Individual differences in working memory and reading. *Journal of Verbal Learning and Verbal Behavior, 19*, 450–466.

Daneman, M., & Carpenter, P.A. (1983). Individual differences in integrating information between and within sentences. *Journal of Experimental Psychology: Learning, Memory, and Cognition, 9*, 561–584.

Daneman, M., & Merikle, P.M. (1996). Working memory and language comprehension: A meta-analysis. *Psychonomic Bulletin and Review, 3*, 422–433.

Dempster, F.N. (1991). Inhibitory processes: A neglected dimension of intelligence. *Intelligence, 15*, 157–173.

Dempster, F.N. (1992). The rise and fall of the inhibitory mechanism: Toward a unified theory of cognitive development and aging. *Developmental Review, 12*, 45–75.

Dempster, F.N., & Corkill, A.J. (1999). Interference and inhibition in cognition and behavior: Unifying themes for educational psychology. *Educational Psychology Review, 11*, 1–88.

Duchek, J.M., Balota, D.A., & Thessing, V.C. (1998). Inhibition of visual and conceptual information during reading in healthy aging and Alzheimer's disease. *Aging, Neuropsychology, and Cognition, 5*, 169–181.

Dywan, J., & Murphy, W. (1996). Aging and inhibitory control in text comprehension. *Psychology and Aging, 11*, 199–206.

Engle, R.W., Kane, M.J., & Tuholski, S.W. (1999). Individual differences in working memory capacity and what they tell us about controlled attention, general fluid intelligence, and functions of the prefrontal cortex. In A. Miyake & P. Shah (Eds.), *Models of working memory: Mechanisms of active maintenance and executive control* (pp. 102–134). New York: Cambridge University Press.

Frisk, V., & Milner, B. (1990). The relationship of working memory to the immediate recall of stories following unilateral temporal or frontal lobectomy. *Neuropsychologia, 28*, 121–135.

Gabrieli, J.D.E., Singh, J., Stebbins, G.T., & Goetz, C.G. (1996). Reduced working memory span in Parkinson's disease: Evidence for the role of frontostriatal system in working and strategic memory. *Neuropsychology, 10*, 321–332.

Gernsbacher, M.A. (1997). Group differences in suppression skill. *Aging, Neuropsychology, and Cognition, 4*, 175–184.

Gernsbacher, M.A., & Faust, M.E. (1991). The mechanism of suppression: A component of general comprehension skill. *Journal of Experimental Psychology: Learning, Memory, and Cognition, 17*, 245–262.

Gick, M.L., Craik, F.I.M., & Morris, R.G. (1988). Task complexity and age differences in working memory. *Memory and Cognition, 16*, 353–361.

Hamm, V.P., & Hasher, L. (1992). Age and the availability of inferences. *Psychology and Aging, 7*, 56–64.

Hartman, M., & Dusek, J. (1994). Direct and indirect memory tests: What they reveal about age differences in interference. *Aging and Cognition, 1*, 292–309.

Hartman, M., & Hasher, L. (1991). Aging and suppression: Memory for previously relevant information. *Psychology and Aging, 6*, 587–594.

Hasher, L., & Zacks, R.T. (1988). Working memory, comprehension, and aging: A review and a new view. In G.H. Bower (Ed.), *The psychology of learning and motivation* (Vol. 22, pp. 193–225). San Diego, CA: Academic Press.

Hasher, L., Zacks, R.T., & May, C.P. (1999). Inhibitory control, circadian arousal, and age. In D. Gopher & A. Koriat (Eds.), *Attention and performance XVII* (pp. 653–675). Cambridge, MA: MIT Press.

Just, M.A., & Carpenter, P.A. (1980). A theory of reading: From eye fixations to comprehension. *Psychological Review, 87*, 329–354.

Just, M.A., & Carpenter, P.A. (1992). A capacity theory of comprehension: Individual differences in working memory. *Psychological Review, 99*, 122–149.

Kane, M.J., & Hasher, L. (1995). Interference. In G. Maddox (Ed.), *Encyclopedia of aging* (2nd ed., pp. 514–516). New York: Springer.

Kemper, S. (1992). Language and aging. In F.I.M. Craik & T.A. Salthouse (Eds.), *The handbook of aging and cognition* (pp. 213–270). Hillsdale, NJ: Lawrence Erlbaum Associates Inc.

Keppel, G. (1968). Retroactive and proactive inhibition. In T.R. Dixon & D.L. Horton (Eds.), *Verbal behavior and general behavior theory* (pp. 172–213). Englewood Cliffs, NJ: Prentice-Hall.

Keppel, G., & Underwood, B.J. (1962). Proactive inhibition in short-term retention of single items. *Journal of Verbal Learning and Verbal Behavior, 1*, 153–161.

Kotary, L., & Hoyer, W.J. (1995). Age and the ability to inhibit distractor information in visual selective attention. *Experimental Aging Research, 21*, 159–171.

Kuhl, J.K. (1992). A theory of self-regulation: Action versus state orientation, self-discrimination, and some applications. *Applied Psychology: An International Review, 41*, 97–129.

Kyllonen, P.C., & Christal, R.E. (1990). Reasoning ability is (little more than) working memory capacity?! *Intelligence, 14*, 389–433.

Lepage, M., Stuss, D.T., & Richer, F. (1999). Attention and the frontal lobes: A comparison between normal aging and lesion effects. *Brain and Cognition, 39*, 63–66.

Li, K.Z.H., Hasher, L., Jonas, D., Rahhal, T.A., & May, C.P. (1999). Distractibility, circadian arousal, and aging: A boundary condition? *Psychology and Aging, 13*, 574–583.

Light, L.L., & Anderson, P.A. (1985). Working-memory capacity, age, and memory for discourse. *Journal of Gerontology, 40*, 737–747.

Light, L.L., & Capps, J.L. (1986). Comprehension of pronouns in young and older adults. *Developmental Psychology, 22*, 580–585.

Logie, R.H., Gilhooly, K.J., & Wynn, V. (1994). Counting on working memory in arithmetic problem solving. *Memory and Cognition, 22*, 395–410.

Lustig, C., & Hasher, L. (in press). Interference. In G. Maddox (Ed.), *Encyclopedia of aging* (3rd ed.). New York: Springer-Verlag.

Lustig, C., Hasher, L., & May, C.P. (in press). Working memory span and the role of proactive interference. *Journal of Experimental Psychology: General.*

MacDonald, M.C., Just, M.A., & Carpenter, P.A. (1992). Working memory constraints on the processing of syntactic ambiguity. *Cognitive Psychology, 24*, 56–98.

Madden, D., & Plude, D.J. (1993). Selective preservation of selective attention. In J. Cerella, J.M. Rybash, W. Hoyer, & M.L. Commons (Eds.), *Adult information processing: Limits on loss* (pp. 273–300). San Diego, CA: Academic Press.

May, C.P. (1999). Synchrony effects in cognition: The costs and a benefit. *Psychonomic Bulletin and Review, 6*, 142–147.

May, C.P., & Hasher, L. (1998). Synchrony effects in inhibitory control over thought and action. *Journal of Experimental Psychology: Human Perception and Performance, 24*, 363–379.

May, C.P., Hasher, L., & Kane, M.J. (1999a). The role of interference in memory span. *Memory and Cognition, 27*, 759–767.

May, C.P., Hasher, L., & Stolzfus, E.R. (1993). Optimal time of day and the magnitude of age differences in memory. *Psychological Science, 4*, 326–330.

May, C.P., Zacks, R.T., Hasher, L., & Multhaup, K.S. (1999). Inhibition in the processing of garden-path sentences. *Psychology and Aging, 14*, 304–313.

McDowd, J.M., Oseas-Kreger, D.M., & Filion, D.L. (1995). Inhibitory processes in cognition and aging. In F.N. Dempster & C.J. Brainerd (Eds.), *Interference and inhibition in cognition* (pp. 363–400). San Diego, CA: Academic Press.

McKnight, J.A., & McKnight, S.A. (1993). The effect of cellular phone use on driver attention. *Accident Analysis and Prevention, 25*, 259–265.

Mednick, S. (1962). The associative basis of the creative process. *Psychological Review, 69*, 220–232.

Moscovitch, M., & Winocur, G. (1995). Frontal lobes, memory, and aging. *Annals of the New York Academy of Sciences, 769*, 119–150.

Postman, L., & Underwood, B.J. (1973). Critical issues in interference theory. *Memory and Cognition, 1*, 19–40.

Rabbitt, P.M. (1965). An age decrement in the ability to ignore irrelevant information. *Journal of Gerontology, 20*, 233–238.

Salthouse, T.A. (1996). The processing-speed theory of adult age differences in cognition. *Psychological Review, 103*, 403–428.

Salthouse, T.A., & Babcock, R.L. (1991). Decomposing adult age differences in working memory. *Developmental Psychology, 27*, 763–776.

Scialfa, C.T., Esau, S.P., & Joffe, K.M. (1998). Age, target–distractor similarity, and visual search. *Experimental Aging Research, 24*, 337–358.

Sekuler, A.B., Bennett, B.J., & Mamelak, M. (2000). Effects of aging on the useful field of view. *Experimental Aging Research, 26*, 103–120.

Shimamura, A.P., & Jurica, P.J. (1994). Memory interference effects and aging: Findings from a test of frontal lobe function. *Neuropsychology, 8*, 408–412.

Siegel, L.S. (1994). Working memory and reading: A lifetime perspective. *International Journal of Behavioral Development, 17*, 109–124.

Stine, E.A., & Wingfield, A. (1990). How much do working memory deficits contribute to age differences in discourse memory? *European Journal of Cognitive Psychology, 2*, 289–304.

Swanson, H.L. (1993). Individual differences in working memory: A model testing and subgroup analysis of learning-disabled and skilled readers. *Intelligence, 17*, 285–332.

Underwood, B.J. (1945). The effect of successive interpolations on retroactive and proactive inhibition. *Psychological Monographs, 59*.

West, R. (2000). In defense of the frontal lobe hypothesis of cognitive aging. *Journal of the International Neuropsychological Society, 6*, 727–729.

Winocur, G., & Moscovitch, M. (1983). Paired-associate learning in institutionalized and noninstitutionalized old people: An analysis of interference and context effects. *Journal of Gerontology, 38,* 455–464.

Yoon, C., May, C.P., & Hasher, L. (2000). Aging, circadian arousal patterns, and cognition. In N. Schwartz, D. Park, B. Knauper, & S. Sudman (Eds.), *Aging, cognition, and self reports* (pp. 151–171). Washington, DC: Psychological Press.

Zacks, R., & Hasher, L. (1988). Capacity theory and the processing of inferences. In L.L. Light and D.M. Burke (Eds.), *Language, memory, and aging* (pp. 155–169). New York: Cambridge University Press.

Zeef, E.J., Sonke, C.J., Kok, A., Buiten, M.M., & Kenemans, J.L. (1996). Perceptual factors affecting age-related differences in focused attention: Performance and psychophysiological analyses. *Psychophysiology, 33,* 555–565.

EUROPEAN JOURNAL OF COGNITIVE PSYCHOLOGY, 2001, *13* (1/2), 123–164

Executive-process interactive control: A unified computational theory for answering 20 questions (and more) about cognitive ageing

David E. Meyer, Jennifer M. Glass, Shane T. Mueller, Travis L. Seymour, and David E. Kieras

University of Michigan, USA

Although the effects of ageing on human information processing and performance have been studied extensively, many fundamental questions about cognitive ageing remain to be answered definitively. For example, what are the sources of age-related slowing? How much is working-memory capacity reduced in older adults? Is time-sharing ability lost with age? Answering such questions requires a unified computational theory that characterises the interactive operations of many component mental processes and integrates diverse data on cognitive ageing. Toward fulfilling this requirement, an executive-process interactive control (EPIC) architecture has been extended to model performance of both young and older adults. EPIC models yield accurate accounts of ageing effects on reaction times and accuracy in basic dual-task and working-memory paradigms. From these accounts, it appears that time-sharing ability and working-memory capacity decrease relatively little until after 70 years of age. Before age 70, at least some apparent performance decrements may be attributable to conservative executive processes and inefficient task procedures rather than decreased "hardware" functionality. By clarifying and deepening such insights, unified computational theories like EPIC will help answer many questions about cognitive ageing.

Requests for reprints should be addressed to D.E. Meyer, Cognition and Perception Program, Department of Psychology, University of Michigan, 525 East University, Ann Arbor, MI 48109-1109, USA. Email: demeyer@umich.edu

This paper is based on research supported in part by grant N00014-92-J-1173 from the United States Office of Naval Research to the University of Michigan, David E. Kieras, and David E. Meyer, Principal Investigators. We thank Ulrich Mayr, Reinhold Kliegl, Steven Keele, Trey Hedden, and participants of the Potsdam Conference on Aging and Executive Control for helpful suggestions and criticisms. Contributions by members of the Brain, Cognition, and Action Laboratory (David Fencsik, Leon Gmeindl, Cerita Jones, Ryan Kettler, Erick Lauber, Eric Schumacher, Molly Schweppe, and Eileen Zurbriggen) at the University of Michigan are also gratefully acknowledged.

---

http://www.tandf.co.uk/journals/pp/09541446.html   DOI:10.1080/09541440042000250

INTRODUCTION

The effects of ageing on cognition are pervasive and complex (Craik & Salthouse, 2000). Within the human information-processing system, many interconnected components mediate perception, attention, memory, decision, and other mental processes. Ageing may affect the capabilities of each component, but the magnitudes of these effects may differ from one component to the next, and their contributions to the performance of particular tasks may depend on various contextual factors. Thus, to characterise cognitive ageing thoroughly and veridically requires answering many fundamental questions about the nature of age-related changes in information processing and task performance.

During the 20th century, few of these questions were answered definitively by theories of cognitive ageing. In our opinion, several related factors contributed to this slow progress:

(1) Definitions of basic concepts such as *mental energy, processing resource, memory capacity, task complexity,* and *executive control* have not been sufficiently rigorous (Salthouse, 1988).
(2) Too little consideration has been given to how complicated interactions between perceptual-motor and cognitive mechanisms change with age.
(3) Explicit distinctions between the information-processing system's "hardware" and "software", which are both affected by ageing, have remained mostly unarticulated.
(4) Contributions of alternative strategies for performing various tasks have yet to be modelled in detail and used for interpreting age-related declines in ability.
(5) Retarded skill acquisition has received relatively little emphasis in assessments of decreased information-processing capacities and task performance due to ageing.

Because of these limitations, controversies still exist over the answers to many questions about cognitive ageing. For example, is there a principal processing resource whose declining capacity mediates age-related slowing? Do older adults have substantially less working-memory capacity than young adults? Are older adults' mechanisms of selective attention and inhibitory control significantly impaired? Is time-sharing ability lost with age? Regarding each of these questions, some researchers have answered positively, and others negatively.

To make progress toward the correct answers, further theoretical developments are required. One way of satisfying this requirement has been suggested by Newell (1973, 1990). He argued that to win the game of 20

Questions with Mother Nature, cognitive psychology needs general unified computational theories. These theories must include both an "architecture" that embodies the components of the information-processing system's "hardware", and a set of heuristic guidelines for how the system's "software" should be programmed to perform various tasks.

Such a unified theory may have great benefits (Newell, 1990). On the basis of it, diverse results from research on cognition and action can be integrated. This integration may reveal strong constraints that these results impose. By incorporating these constraints, models of performance in many tasks can be constructed and tested quantitatively against empirical data. Insofar as these models account well for observed dependent variables, this will facilitate the analysis of underlying mental and physical processes, leading to new predictions about them. Also, the models' failures can guide improvements to the theory's assumptions. Through this activity, cumulative scientific progress is more likely than if an informal piecemeal approach to theorising were taken.

Given these considerations, this paper outlines a unified computational theory, *executive-process interactive control* (EPIC), which has been formulated for modelling human multiple-task performance (Kieras & Meyer, 1997; Meyer & Kieras, 1997a, b, 1999). Here we describe how models based on EPIC can help answer fundamental questions about ageing and cognition. Two major phenomena, age-related slowing and reduced working memory, will be discussed specifically for this purpose. With respect to these phenomena, it will be shown that EPIC yields precise analytic accounts of ageing effects on various components of information processing. By taking the essence of these accounts seriously, a clearer and more accurate picture of cognitive ageing may be developed, and promising directions for future research on ageing and cognition may be identified. Also, novel perspectives on issues raised by other papers in this issue may be reached.

THE EPIC ARCHITECTURE

The architecture of EPIC extends previous theories about the structures and functions of the human information-processing system (e.g., Anderson, 1983; Card, Moran, & Newell, 1983; Newell, 1990). With computational models based on EPIC, interactions among perceptual, cognitive, and motor processes can be described precisely in terms of executive control and task scheduling strategies. Thus, EPIC models are potentially well suited for characterising how speed of processing, working-memory capacity, dual-task performance, and other cognitive abilities change with age.

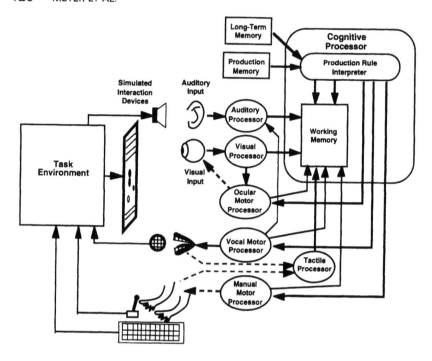

Figure 1. Overview of the EPIC architecture (adapted from Kieras, Meyer, Mueller, & Seymour, 1999).

Architectural components

EPIC has a cognitive processor with a production-rule interpreter and working memory (WM) connected to modality-specific sensors, perceptual processors, motor processors, and effectors (Figure 1). These components constitute EPIC's "hardware" and operate in parallel with each other. The perceptual and motor processors serve as limited-capacity input and output channels. We model task performance by programming the cognitive processor with production rules that manipulate the contents of WM to make decisions and produce responses to stimuli (e.g., see Appendix). Details of EPIC's perceptual and motor processors appear elsewhere (e.g., Kieras & Meyer, 1997). For now, EPIC's WM and cognitive processor are especially relevant to models of cognitive ageing.

Working memory

EPIC's WM has several complementary parts (Kieras et al., 1999).

- *Modal stores.* Three parts of WM are the visual, auditory, and tactile stores that contain coded information from the modality-specific perceptual processors.

- *Control store.* Another part of WM is the control store. It contains (1) *goals*, which appear in the conditions of production rules that help perform particular tasks, (2) *steps*, which cause rules to fire in specified sequences, (3) *strategy notes*, which enable or disable rules for alternative task strategies, and (4) *status notes*, which indicate the current states of various processes.
- *Tag store.* The tag store contains labels that assign specific roles to modal-store items. For example, such a label might designate an object in visual WM to be "the stimulus".
- *Storage capacity.* Items in the various parts of WM may decay after random amounts of time unless they are refreshed. However, there are no preset limits on the numbers of stored items. Thus, the capacity of EPIC's WM depends on the decay times and refresh rates during task performance.

Cognitive processor

EPIC's cognitive processor operates in cycles. On each cycle, the conditions of all rules in procedural memory are tested, and the actions of all rules whose conditions match the contents of WM are executed. We assume that for young adults, the mean time taken by a cognitive-processor cycle is 50 ms, in accord with periodicities of human information processing (Kristofferson, 1967).

In EPIC, the cognitive-processor cycle time does not depend on how many rule conditions have to be tested or how many actions have to be executed, nor is there a set limit on how many rules can be applied during each cycle. Thus, EPIC has no cognitive hardware decision or response-selection bottleneck. This contrasts with the classic response-selection bottleneck hypothesis (Pashler, 1994), which assumes that if two choice-reaction tasks have to be performed concurrently, then response selection for one task must wait until response selection for the other task has finished.

EPIC's unlimited parallel application of production rules helps avoid the vagueness and circularity that plague resource and single-channel theories (cf. Allport, 1987). This is crucial for research on cognitive ageing. By tentatively assuming ample cognitive processing capacity, we are led to take careful account of limits in peripheral perceptual-motor mechanisms, which can cause performance decrements that might otherwise be misattributed to immutable cognitive decision or response-selection bottlenecks. Also, because EPIC has no such bottlenecks, it strongly encourages understanding human performance in terms of adaptive executive control and flexible task strategies, to which studies of cognitive ageing should devote due consideration.

EPIC MODELLING OF COGNITIVE AGEING

Using EPIC, performance by young and older adults in many tasks can be modelled. Given results from a particular task, two computational models—one that fits the young adults' data closely, and another that fits the older adults' data—may be formulated.[1] By determining how the models must differ to fit all of the data, we can infer where and in what amounts cognitive ageing affects individual components of the adult information-processing system. Also, after formulating potentially veridical EPIC models, we can continue refining them and testing new predictions about additional effects of ageing that should be observable if the models are indeed worthy.

There are two types of components, *hardware* and *software*, wherein EPIC models might incorporate effects of cognitive ageing (Table 1). Hardware components are modules of the architecture that stay the same across task environments and implement various types of information processing. Software components are sets of task and executive production rules that instantiate procedural knowledge and change from one task to the next. Both the parameters of the hardware and the contents of the software might change with the age of the adults whose performance is being modelled. A major goal of our research is to discover what age-related changes are essential to include as part of EPIC models that account well for performance of important perceptual-motor and cognitive tasks over the life span. Not all of our discoveries will seem surprising in light of prior knowledge about cognitive ageing. Nevertheless, through the rigorous theoretical approach that EPIC enables, deeper insights into the effects of ageing on cognition may be achieved.

Of course, we also assume that some aspects of EPIC may stay the same for young and older adults. At present, these age-invariant aspects include the types of processing components in the architecture, the established connections among them, and their qualitative properties (e.g., stimulus feature coding, parallel production-rule firing, movement feature coding). This then raises issues about what other aspects of the hardware and software components are likely to change with age.

---

[1]Of course, many EPIC models will not fit the data closely for either age group. Because EPIC has limited "free" parameters, we can often reject models based on it when they are unveridical (Kieras, Meyer, Ballas, & Lauber, 2000; Meyer & Kieras, 1997a).

TABLE 1
Components of EPIC models that incorporate potential effects of cognitive ageing

Type of component	Locus of ageing effect	Nature of age-related changes
Hardware	Perceptual processors	Decreased acuity of sensory interfaces
		Increased stimulus detection times
		Increased stimulus identification times
	Motor processors	Increased movement-preparation times
		Increased movement-initiation times
		Increased movement-execution times
		Increased movement variability
		Increased feedback-transmission times
	Cognitive processor	Increased cycle times
	Working memory	Decreased decay times
	Skill-acquisition mechanisms	Decreased efficiency of compiled rules
		Decreased rate of rule refinement
Software	Task production rules	Decreased algorithmic efficiency
		Increased conservatism
		Increased number of rule steps
	Executive production rules	Decreased algorithmic efficiency
		Increased conservatism
		Increased number of rule steps

Potential ageing effects in EPIC's hardware

EPIC's hardware includes its perceptual, cognitive, and motor processors. Models of young and older adults' performance may incorporate effects of ageing in each of these components.

Perceptual-processor parameters. For example, EPIC's perceptual processors implement stimulus detection and identification. Associated with them are parameters that determine their fidelity (e.g., retinal sensitivity) and duration (e.g., identification time). Close fits of EPIC models to empirical data from young and older adults could involve different parameter values, manifesting how perceptual processing changes with age.

Motor-processor parameters. Similarly, EPIC's motor processors implement movement preparation, initiation, and execution. Associated with them are parameters that determine their fidelity (e.g., spatial movement variability) and duration (e.g., movement-feature preparation times). Again, close fits of EPIC models to data from young and older adults could involve different parameter values manifesting how motor processing changes with age.

Working-memory parameters.   The capacity of WM in EPIC is limited because stored items may decay unless they are refreshed periodically. Consequently, EPIC models of performance may incorporate effects of ageing on WM through shorter decay times and/or slower refresh rates. We would attribute shorter decay times to changes in underlying hardware, whereas slower refresh rates could be attributable to changes in either the hardware or software used for the refreshing processes.

Cognitive-processor parameters.   The rate of processing in EPIC is constrained by the cognitive processor's mean cycle time. For young adults, we assume that this parameter equals 50 ms. Our assumption is supported by both behavioural and psychophysiological data (e.g., Kristofferson, 1967). It conforms well with the mean period between zero crossings in the brain's alpha rhythm, which equals about 50 ms for young adults and correlates positively with their mean simple RTs (Callaway & Yeager, 1960; Surwillo, 1963; Woodruff, 1975). It appears that alpha-rhythm zero crossings perhaps correspond to the onsets of cognitive-processor cycles.

In contrast, for older adults around 70 years of age, the mean zero-crossing period of the alpha rhythm is about 10–15% longer than for young adults (Marsh & Thompson, 1977; Obrist & Busse, 1965; Surwillo, 1963), and older adults' mean simple RTs are also about 10–15% longer (Cerella, 1985; Somberg & Salthouse, 1982). These results lead us to make the following strong but at least somewhat plausible assumption: *In EPIC models for older adults (circa 70 years of age), the mean cognitive-processor cycle time should be set to 56.5 ms, about 13% longer than the mean cycle time in models for young adults (circa 20 years of age).* This assumption is consistent with Kail and Salthouse (1994), who claimed that ageing affects "a fundamental component of the architecture of human cognition" which functions like the CPU clock of a microcomputer whose "clock speed" determines the rate of information processing.

Our assumption also agrees with Madden (1992), who claimed that in visual word-recognition tasks, mean RTs increase by roughly 4–10 ms per decade of age. Under EPIC, such tasks usually require about 3–8 cognitive-processor cycles to be completed. Moreover, ageing would involve roughly a 1.3 ms increase per decade in the mean cycle time. The latter factor, multiplied by 3–8 cycles, yields a range close to Madden's 4–10 ms per decade.

Furthermore, another key parameter that presumably mediates RTs and age-related slowing under EPIC is the number of cycles taken to complete a task, which depends on what production rules are used for task performance (Kieras & Meyer, 2000). Insofar as older adults use less efficient rules and so take more cognitive-processor cycles than young adults, age-related RT differences may be larger than if only the mean time per cycle differs between groups.[2] Such inefficiency might occur either because older adults prefer more conservative performance strategies (Botwinick, 1966), or because their rate of skill acquisition is lower than that of young adults (Strayer & Kramer, 1994).

Skill-acquisition parameters. Currently, EPIC has no mechanisms of skill acquisition. However, we plan to implement them soon (Kieras et al., 2000), and this may help assess the extent to which older adults learn new procedures less quickly than young adults do.

Potential ageing effects in EPIC's software

There are two ways that effects of ageing might be incorporated in EPIC's software.

Task rule sets. Older adults may use less efficient sets of production rules for individual tasks. When this happens, especially salient slowing of performance should result. By fitting EPIC models to RT data, it is possible to quantify how much age-related slowing stems from such software differences above and beyond increases in the mean cognitive-processor cycle time.

Executive rule sets. Also relevant are potential ageing effects in executive production rules, which coordinate operations during concurrent tasks. Like task rules, the executive rules of older adults may be less efficient than those of the young (Mayr & Kliegl, 1993). We can assess this possibility precisely by formulating EPIC models of dual-task performance for each age group. As a result, the extent to which older adults have impaired time-sharing abilities can be quantified.

APPLICATION OF EPIC TO DUAL-TASK PERFORMANCE AND COGNITIVE AGEING

To illustrate how fundamental questions about cognitive ageing may be answered on the basis of EPIC, we (Glass et al., 2000; Meyer & Kieras, 1997a, b) have formulated computational models of performance by young and older adults in a basic dual-task paradigm, the psychological

---

[2]An inefficient set of production rules is one that takes more than the minimum number of algorithmic steps (and cognitive-processor cycles) required to perform a task properly. The extent to which a rule set is more or less efficient depends on the content and organisation of the rules' conditions and actions. If the conditions and actions are not configured optimally, then a rule set will fail to exploit the full parallel-processing capabilities of EPIC's cognitive processor (Kieras et al., 2000).

refractory period (PRP) procedure. From doing so, we learn more about the sources of age-related slowing, and we show that older adults have better preserved time-sharing abilities than has sometimes been claimed before (cf. Allen, Smith, Vires-Collins, & Sperry, 1998; Craik & Byrd, 1982; Hartley & Little, 1999).

PRP procedure

On each trial of the PRP procedure, a primary Task 1 stimulus is followed by a secondary Task 2 stimulus with a short (e.g., ≤ 1 sec) stimulus-onset asynchrony (SOA). Participants have to give Task 1 higher priority, and they are encouraged to make the Task 1 response first. RTs and response accuracy are measured as a function of the SOA and other task factors. The difference between mean Task 2 RTs at the shortest and longest SOAs is called the *PRP effect*. Because shorter SOAs typically yield longer Task 2 RTs, the PRP effect has been interpreted as a measure of interference caused by limited processing capacity in dual-task performance (Pashler, 1994).

PRP effects in young and older adults

Glass et al. (2000) measured PRP effects in young (age = 18–26 years) and older (age = 60–70 years) adults who performed an auditory-manual primary task and an "easy" or "hard" visual-manual secondary task. Task 1 involved two alternative stimulus–response (S-R) pairs and required keypresses with left-hand fingers to tones. Task 2 required keypresses with right-hand fingers to digits. For the easy and hard Task 2, respectively, there were two and eight alternative S-R pairs, which affected the difficulty of response selection in Task 2 (Schumacher et al., 1999).

For young adults, Glass et al. (2000, Exp. 1) found that mean Task 1 RTs were short and not affected reliably by the SOA (Figure 2a). The young adult's mean Task 2 RTs increased as the SOA decreased. There was also a Task 2 difficulty effect, which interacted reliably with the SOA; the difference between mean RTs for the hard and easy Task 2 decreased as the SOA decreased.

For older adults, mean Task 1 RTs were longer than those of young adults (490 vs. 300 ms), but SOA affected them relatively little (Figure 2b). Also, mean Task 2 RTs of older adults were longer and more affected by SOA, yielding greater PRP effects than those of young adults (300 vs. 130 ms for the easy Task 2, and 250 vs. 85 ms for the hard Task 2). The older adults' PRP effects were larger when divided by their mean Task 2 RTs at the longest SOA, which yields a normalised measure of dual-task interference (i.e., for the easy and hard Task 2, older adults'

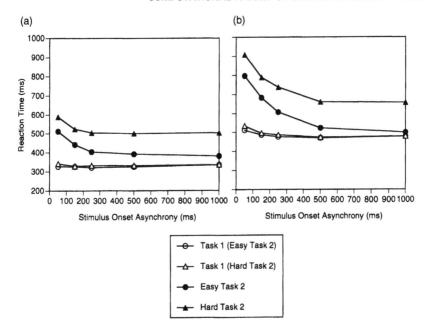

Figure 2. Mean reaction times (RTs) of young (a) and older (b) adults for Tasks 1 and 2 as a function of Task 2 difficulty (easy or hard) and stimulus onset asynchrony (SOA) in Glass et al. (2000, Exp. 1).

normalised dual-task interference = 0.60 and 0.38; young adults' normalised dual-task interference = 0.34 and 0.17).

In other respects, however, mean RTs for the two age groups were similar.[3] Most important, older as well as young adults had reliable interactions between the SOA and task-difficulty effects on mean Task 2 RTs. As SOA decreased, the difficulty effect decreased by about 50 ms regardless of age. This is crucial for interpreting the overall pattern of results from the two age groups.

Theoretical interpretation of RT data

At first glance, Glass et al.'s (2000) results might be interpreted as showing that older adults have impaired time-sharing ability. This seems

---

[3]For both age groups, error rates were low (<5%) and revealed no major speed–accuracy tradeoffs. Like young adults, older adults produced extremely few (<0.1%) out-of-order responses in which, contrary to instructions of the PRP procedure, a Task 2 response occurred before the accompanying Task 1 response. Ageing did not disrupt older adults' control over the serial order of their responses.

consistent with their PRP effects and normalised dual-task interference, which were larger than those of young adults. Indeed, such enlarged costs have led some researchers to conclude that older adults are seriously hampered in dual-task performance, perhaps because of an "elongated" response-selection bottleneck (e.g., Allen et al., 1998).

Nevertheless, further aspects of Glass et al.'s (2000) results suggest otherwise. Older adults had a significant underadditive interaction between the effects of SOA and task difficulty on mean Task 2 RTs, just like the young adults. This interaction may stem from concurrent response-selection processes for Tasks 1 and 2 (Meyer & Kieras, 1997a, b). If so, then perhaps older adults can time-share about as well as the young, despite age-related slowing in the performance of each task. To test this hypothesis further, we have used EPIC to formulate adaptive executive-control (AEC) models that fit the data from both young and older adults in Glass et al.'s (2000) study.

Adaptive executive-control models

According to our AEC models, dual-task performance progresses through stages of stimulus identification, response selection, and movement production (Figure 3). We assume that an executive process coordinates this progress by postponing some Task 2 processes until Task 1 has finished, satisfying priorities of the PRP procedure. The functions of the executive process include: (a) enabling Task 1 and Task 2 processes to start on each trial; (b) specifying a Task 2 lockout point; (c) specifying a Task 1 unlocking event; (d) waiting for the Task 1 unlocking event to occur; and (e) unlocking the Task 2 processes so that they may be completed.[4]

Task 2 lockout points. By definition, the Task 2 lockout point occurs during the course of Task 2. When it is reached, further processing for Task 2 is postponed until Task 1 is "completed". Our AEC models have three possible lockout points (Figure 3, lower small ovals), located respectively before the onsets of stimulus identification, response selection, and movement production for Task 2. After short SOAs, Task 2 processes would overlap more or less with Task 1 processes, depending on whether the executive process uses a pre-movement-production, pre-response-selection, or pre-stimulus-identification lockout point.

---

[4]Representative sets of production rules that illustrate how executive and task processes have been implemented with EPIC for the PRP procedure appear in Meyer and Kieras (1997a).

Task 1 Processes

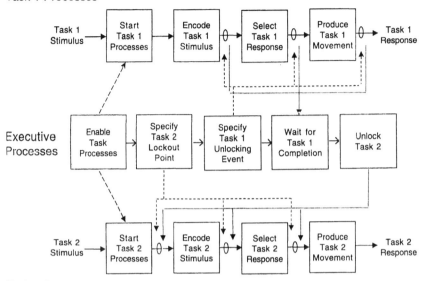

Figure 3. Component processes of adaptive executive-control (AEC) models for flexible scheduling of dual-task performance in the psychological refractory period (PRP) procedure. The top, middle, and bottom rows of the diagram depict Task 1, executive, and Task 2 processes, respectively. Downward arrows from the executive process that specifies the Task 2 lockout points indicate alternative sites (lower small ovals) at which progress on Task 2 may be suspended until Task 1 is deemed to be "completed". Upward arrows from the executive process that specifies the Task 1 unlocking events indicate alternative sites (upper small ovals) at which Task 1 processes may signal the executive processes to treat Task 1 as "completed" and to resume Task 2 by unlocking it. (From "Concurrent response-selection processes in dual-task performance: Evidence for adaptive executive control over task-scheduling strategies", E.H. Schumacher, E.J. Lauber, J.M. Glass, E.L. Zurbriggen, L. Gmeindl, D.E. Kieras, and D.E. Meyer, 1999, *Journal of Experimental Psychology: Human Perception and Performance*, 25, p. 793. Copyright 1999 by the American Psychological Association. Reprinted with permission of the author.)

Task 1 unlocking events.   The overlap between Task 1 and Task 2 processes also depends on which Task 1 unlocking event is used. This event determines when Task 1 is "completed", allowing the executive process to resume processing for Task 2. There are three possible Task 1 unlocking events (Figure 3, upper small ovals), which occur after stimulus identification, response selection, and movement production for Task 1. After short SOAs, Task 2 processes would overlap more or less with Task 1 processes, depending on whether the executive process uses a post-stimulus-identification, post-response-selection, or post-movement-production unlocking event.

Specific AEC models. Overall, our AEC models include various specific cases. For each possible combination of the Task 2 lockout point and Task 1 unlocking event, there is a set of executive production rules that implements them. Consequently, some AEC models can mimic a response-selection bottleneck with a post-stimulus-identification/pre-response-selection lockout point for Task 2 (cf. Pashler, 1994). This constitutes *cautious task scheduling* because it precludes much overlap between stages of processing for the two tasks, thereby decreasing the likelihood that responses occur out of order. Other AEC models may mimic a movement-initiation bottleneck with a post-response-selection/pre-movement-production lockout point for Task 2 (cf. Keele, 1973). This constitutes *daring task scheduling* because it allows more overlap between processing stages, increasing the likelihood of out-of-order responses. Task instructions, perceptual-motor requirements, prior practice, and cognitive style may influence which type of scheduling is used.

Young and older adults' AEC models

We have identified two AEC models that account respectively for quantitative results from the young and older adults in Glass et al. (2000).

TABLE 2
Mean values of parameters in the adaptive executive-control models of dual-task performance for young and older adults in Glass et al. (2000)

Component	Parameter type	Task 1		Easy Task 2		Hard Task 2	
		Young	Old	Young	Old	Young	Old
Perceptual processors	Stimulus identification time	120	254	121	205	121	205
Motor processors	Number of movement features	1	1	2	2	2	2
	Movement production time	100	113	150	169	150	169
Cognitive processor	Cycle time	50	56.5	50	56.5	50	56.5
Task rules	Number of selection steps	1.5	1.5	1.5	1.5	4.0	4.5
	Response-selection time	75	85	75	85	200	254
Executive rules	Task 1 unlocking event	PME	PME				
	Task 2 lockout point			PRS	PRS	PRS	PRS
	Unlocking duration			80	224	80	224

PME = pre-movement-execution in Task 1; PRS = post-response-selection in Task 2.

Table 2 shows the similarities and differences between these models in terms of their hardware parameters, task processes, and executive processes.[5]

Differences between hardware parameters.   There are several age-related differences between the hardware parameters of the young and older adults' models. Consistent with our previous assumptions, the mean cognitive-processor cycle time is 13% longer (56.5 vs. 50 ms) for the older adults.[6] Supplementing this increase, stimulus identification by the visual and auditory perceptual processors take about 70% and 110% longer, respectively, in the young and older adults' models. That these latter increases are so large may be attributable at least partly to deficits from ageing in peripheral sensory mechanisms (Glass, 2000; Scialfa, 2000). For example, ageing in parts of the inner ear could cause the identification and discrimination of tone stimuli to be especially slow (cf. van Boxtel et al., 2000).

Differences between task processes.   Also, to fit Glass et al.'s (2000) data, the older adults' AEC model uses less efficient rules for response selection in the hard Task 2, which cause its response-selection times to be longer than those of the young adults' model.[7] This feature is essential because the difficulty effect on older adults' mean Task 2 RTs at the longest SOA exceeded what could stem simply from their 13% longer mean cognitive-processor cycle times.

Differences between executive processes.   Furthermore, there is one difference between the executive processes of the two models that has been incorporated to fit the data in Figure 2. It involves the *unlocking duration* (i.e., the amount of time taken to resume Task 2 after the Task 1 unlocking event occurs). The older adults' model has executive processes that take almost three times longer to unlock Task 2 than do those of the young adults' model. This may be needed here because older adults are sometimes rather cautious in avoiding out-of-order Task 2 responses. However, their unlocking durations are not always much longer than young adults'; instead, they appear to depend on relevant contextual factors (Glass et al., 2000). Such context dependence implies that age-related

---

[5]For more details about how we arrived at these models and their parameter values, see Glass et al. (2000).

[6]Models in which the mean cognitive-processor cycle time substantially exceeded 56.5 ms for the older adults did not fit their mean RTs very well (Glass et al., 2000).

[7]Examples of how such inefficiency might be embodied in sets of task production rules appear in Meyer and Kieras (1997a).

changes in the unlocking durations probably stem from adjustable soft-ware characteristics rather than chronic hardware deficiencies.

Similarities between executive processes.   Most important, in two major respects, the executive processes of the present older adults' model are essentially like those of the young adults' model. First, both models involve a post-response-selection Task 2 lockout point, which enables concurrent response selection for Tasks 1 and 2, unlike what would happen if there were a response-selection bottleneck. Second, both models involve a pre-movement-execution Task 1 unlocking event, which enables unlocking of Task 2 to start relatively early. These features are hallmarks of "daring" task scheduling, and they suggest that older adults have well preserved time-sharing abilities.

Fits of the AEC models to RT data.   Supporting this latter suggestion, Figure 4 shows fits between empirical mean RTs from Glass et al. (2000, Exp. 1) and theoretical mean RTs from the young and older adults' AEC models. Here we focus on RTs at the shortest and longest SOAs, which embody the PRP and task difficulty effects for the two age groups.

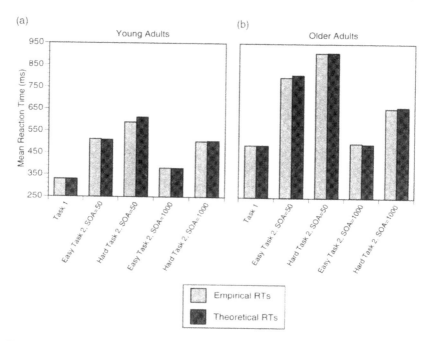

Figure 4.   Theoretical mean reaction times (RTs) from best-fitting adaptive-executive control (AEC) models paired with corresponding empirical mean reaction times from Glass et al. (2000, Exp. 1). (a) RTs for young adults. (b) RTs for older adults.

Clearly, the theoretical RTs approximate the empirical RTs closely, accounting well for the magnitudes of observed factor effects on them.

Theoretical conclusions

From this application of EPIC to cognitive ageing and dual-task performance, several theoretical conclusions follow. First, we conclude that computational modelling based on a principled architecture helps resolve ambiguities created by merely evaluating empirical data qualitatively. Second, we conclude that under conditions like Glass et al.'s (2000), cognitive ageing has selective effects on hardware and software components whose proportional magnitudes are task-dependent and differ across various stages of processing. Third, the good fits of our AEC models suggest that, in some dual-task paradigms, older adults exhibit well-preserved time-sharing abilities.[8]

APPLICATION OF EPIC TO VERBAL WORKING MEMORY AND COGNITIVE AGEING

A second application of EPIC involves verbal working memory (WM) and cognitive ageing. Here again, our work distinguishes precisely between contributions by hardware and software components of processing. To appreciate the importance of this, more background is in order.

Some evidence shows that older adults perform less well than young adults in tasks that impose heavy loads on WM (Craik & Jennings, 1992). This decline has been revealed by complex memory-span tasks in which participants must integrate and retain successive bits of information (e.g., words, numbers, pictures) while executing other operations (e.g., sentence comprehension, arithmetic calculations) related to the input. During such tasks, final serial recall of the retained information has sometimes been much lower in older adults, and older adults' relative declines have increased with task complexity (e.g., Foos, 1989; Gick, Craik, & Morris, 1988; Park et al., 1996; Wingfield, Stine, Lahar, & Aberdeen, 1988).

---

[8]This last conclusion is not contradicted by the relatively long unlocking durations for Task 2 of the older adults' AEC model in Table 2. As mentioned previously, older adults do not always take especially long times to unlock secondary tasks of the PRP procedure, and their unlocking durations appear to be adjustable through adaptive executive control (Glass et al., 2000). Also consistent with this conclusion are the quite small age-related effects on switching-time costs that have been observed in some studies of task switching (e.g., Brinley, 1965; Mayr & Kliegl, 2000).

Nevertheless, some aspects of WM—as revealed by putatively "simpler" tasks—appear rather well-preserved with age. A large recency effect on immediate free recall occurs for older adults (Craik, 1968; Raymond, 1971). In the Brown-Peterson procedure, the memory traces of older adults are about as durable as young adults' (Charness, 1981; Puckett & Stockburger, 1988; Talland, 1967). Also, older adults often have very small (e.g., ≤5%) deficits in forward memory span (Botwinick & Storandt, 1974; Bromley, 1958; Clark & Knowles, 1973). One interpretation of these results is that the storage component of verbal WM remains intact for older adults, but their executive processes that update and manipulate the contents of WM in more complex tasks may be deficient (D'Esposito & Postle, 1999; Salthouse, Babcock, & Shaw, 1991; Smith & Jonides, 1999).

Yet other results raise doubts about this interpretation. From a meta-analysis of studies that involved various WM tasks, Babcock & Salthouse (1990) found multiple cases in which older adults performed almost as well on complex tasks as on simpler ones, and there were only small age-related differences (e.g., Baddeley, Logie, Bressi, Della Salla, & Spinnler, 1986; Burke & Yee, 1984; Dobbs & Rule, 1989; Ferris, Crook, Clark, McCarthy, & Rae, 1980; Hooper, Hooper, & Colbert, 1984; Light & Anderson, 1985). These prominent "islands of preservation" raise intriguing issues about when and in what ways WM becomes impaired with age.

To help resolve such issues, we have formulated EPIC models of age-related effects on coding, storage, maintenance, updating, manipulation, and coordinative operations in verbal WM. For example, one of our models describes performance by young and older adults in basic serial memory-span tasks, which are prototypical WM paradigms (Baddeley, 1986). This description extends past research that has modelled age-related declines of WM (e.g., Byrne, 1998; Maylor, Vousden, & Brown, 1999). From doing so, more may be learned about the effects of ageing on WM functions.

Basic serial memory-span tasks

The memory-span tasks with which we deal here are basic ones as used in the WAIS-R battery (Wechsler, 1981) and many studies of verbal WM (e.g., Baddeley, Thomson, & Buchanan, 1975; Drewnowski, 1980; Longoni, Richardson, & Aiello, 1993; Standing, Bond, Smith, & Isely, 1980). On each trial, a sequence of verbal items (digits, letters, words, or pseudowords) is presented auditorily at a constant moderate rate (1–2 s per item). At the end of the sequence, which typically contains two to ten items, there is a recall signal, and the participant tries to recall the items either in their original forward order, or in backward order. The presented items are sampled randomly from a small set whose members occur repeatedly across trials but no more than once per trial.[9]

An EPIC model for verbal serial memory span

Our model has some similarities to the phonological-loop model of Baddeley (1986) and others (e.g., Schweickert & Boruff, 1986). We assume that when a sequence of items is presented auditorily, the auditory perceptual processor codes each item as a packet of phonological features with pointers that let the packet be linked to ones for preceding and following items. The coded items are stored in auditory WM, where they decay after some time. Such coding and storage are also assumed to occur when the vocal motor processor produces a sequence of items through covert articulation, which sends them to the auditory perceptual processor as if they had been presented auditorily.[10] By having EPIC's cognitive processor pass stored items from auditory WM to the vocal motor processor repeatedly, a cyclic rehearsal process that maintains the items for final serial recall is implemented in our model (Kieras et al., 1999; Meyer, Mueller, Seymour, & Kieras, 2000; Mueller, Seymour, Glass, Kieras, & Meyer, 2000).

However, this implementation is not like an automatic tape loop that passively records and replays item sequences. Instead, we have found that the basic memory-span task requires much more than just "pure storage" (cf. D'Esposito & Postle, 1999). To account for both forward and backward memory spans, the auditory perceptual processor, WM, and vocal motor processor must be controlled by intricate supraordinate executive and subordinate task processes, which interactively coordinate and accomplish the mental construction, storage, maintenance, and recall of presented item sequences. This is because processing of successive new items has to overlap in a complementary manner with continued cyclic rehearsal of prior stored items (Figure 5).

Chain-construction processes. As part of our model, there is a process that constructs an "add-chain" with new coded items from the external stimulus source (Figure 5, upper left). The add-chain construction process

---

[9]This procedure helps ensure that performance of the memory-span task is based on phonological codes in WM rather than graded levels of activation in long-term semantic memory.

[10]EPIC's vocal motor processor can produce either overt or covert utterances in response to commands from the cognitive processor, which provides symbolic information about the utterances' required style and content. In EPIC, overt and covert utterances are produced at essentially equivalent rates, consistent with reported empirical data (Landauer, 1962).

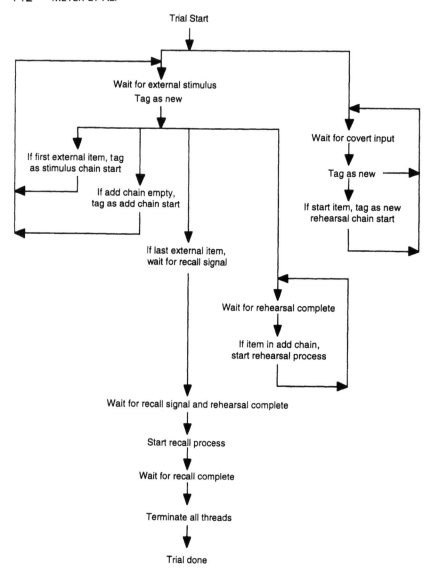

Figure 5. Flowchart of supraordinate executive control and subordinate task processes (item chain-construction, rehearsal, and recall procedures) in the present EPIC model for performing the verbal serial memory-span task. (Adapted from Kieras et al., 1999.)

is implemented by production rules that wait for each item to arrive initially in auditory WM and then tag it as a "new" one for the add-chain. Another related process (Figure 5, upper right) constructs a "rehearsal-chain" with covert verbal items produced by subvocal rehearsal. The rules of this rehearsal-chain construction process wait for each covert item and tag it as a "new" one to be included in the next cycle of rehearsal. During successive rehearsal cycles, multiple evolving chains of stored items are constructed. The most recent copy of the rehearsal chain and the current add-chain are used for the next rehearsal cycle.

Rehearsal process.   The rehearsal process is implemented by another set of rules. A cycle of rehearsal starts whenever the first external stimulus item arrives in auditory WM, or a preceding rehearsal cycle has been completed and the current add-chain contains items that have not been rehearsed yet (Figure 5, middle right). Thereafter, the current rehearsal cycle proceeds as shown in Figure 6. Along its way, the pointers associated with individual items of the current rehearsal-chain and add-chain are used to determine the order of subvocalisation. For the next cycle of

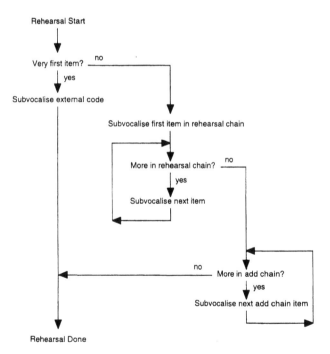

Figure 6.   Steps in one cycle of the rehearsal process used by the present EPIC model for performing the verbal serial memory-span task. A rehearsal cycle includes consecutive phases that, when need be, subvocalise the first external stimulus item on a trial, subvocalise each item of the current rehearsal-chain in auditory working memory, and then subvocalise each item of the current add-chain. (Adapted from Kieras et al., 1999.)

rehearsal, the chain-construction processes designate the new rehearsal chain in auditory WM, tagging its starting item as "new" so that it can be accessed when needed. Chains of items from previous cycles are tagged as "old" but remain in auditory WM, decaying haphazardly as time passes.[11]

Recall process.   The recall process starts after the last external stimulus item has been received, a recall signal has been detected, and the most recent rehearsal cycle has been completed. During recall, additional production rules enable attempts to vocalise every item in the last rehearsal-chain. This entails having the cognitive processor send rehearsal-chain items one-by-one from auditory WM to the vocal motor processor for overt output, conforming insofar as possible to the required forward or backward order of recall.[12] If serial-order pointers or phonological features for an item have decayed before its recall occurs, then the recall process makes sophisticated guesses about the item's identity. Errors in recall occur when these guesses are either incorrect or impossible to make.

Other ancillary assumptions.   Finally, so our model is specified fully, it includes other ancillary assumptions: (1) No preset limit exists on the number of items in auditory WM. (2) Phonologically similar items have more features in common than do dissimilar items. (3) Individual phonological features and serial-order pointers decay according to independent, discrete, all-or-none stochastic processes. (4) The decay times have log-normal distributions with two parameters, the median (M) and "spread" (s) of the distribution.[13] (5) The values of M and s may differ for phonological features and serial-order pointers. (6) These values also depend on whether the features and pointers come from external stimulus presentation or internal subvocal articulation.

---

[11]A difficulty caused by haphazard decay of items is that the rehearsal process may fail occasionally and unpredictably. Such failures can occur during a rehearsal cycle if an item in the current rehearsal-chain or add-chain disappears from auditory WM before it has been subvocalised. Graceful recovery and continuation after this requires intervention by appropriate executive control that is implemented as part of our model.

[12]When the memory-span task is performed with articulatory suppression during presentation of an item sequence (Baddeley, 1986), we assume that no subvocal rehearsal occurs, and our model's recall process bases its output instead on the initial stimulus-chain sent by the auditory perceptual processor to auditory WM (Kieras et al., 1999).

[13]The log-normal distribution is unimodal and positively skewed over the non-negative real numbers (Hastings & Peacock, 1975). Distributions of real decay times presumably have these features. Parameterisation with M and s helps implement and interpret effects caused by changes in the log-normal distribution's central tendency and dispersion.

Previous tests of the model.   On the basis of these assumptions, we have tested our model by using it to account for data from studies that measured young adults' memory spans (e.g., Baddeley et al., 1975; Drewnowski, 1980; Longoni et al., 1993). These studies have shown that memory spans are affected by the numbers of items in the sequences, the items' articulatory durations, phonological similarity, serial position, and articulatory suppression. Our model has yielded close fits to percentages of correct recall and effects of these factors, using minimal "free" parameters. The model's successes suggest that it may help understand age-related changes in verbal WM.

Modelling of memory span in young and older adults

Pursuing the latter prospect further, we have applied our EPIC model of memory span to analyse changes in verbal WM across the life span.

Gregoire and Van der Linden's study.   For now, our analysis focuses on a study by Gregoire and Van der Linden (1997). They measured memory spans of adults from 20 to 80 years old with WAIS-R digit-span tests (Wechsler, 1981). Between 20 and 70 years of age, quite gradual declines occurred in both forward and backward memory spans, but the declines became steeper thereafter (Figure 7). Also, backward spans were less than forward spans, but they declined at about the same rate. Similar results have been reported by others (Burke & Yee, 1984; Dobbs & Rule, 1989; Ferris et al., 1980; Hooper et al., 1984; Light & Anderson, 1985; Orsini et al., 1986; Park et al., 1996).

Theoretical account.   Our EPIC model provides a theoretical account for these age-related changes of memory span. Simulated spans produced by the model closely approximate observed spans (Figure 7). For 20–70 years of age, the declines of forward and backward spans are well predicted by the gradual increase of the cognitive-processor cycle time assumed before (Table 2). The increase that yields a good fit to the data is about 1.3 ms per decade, rising from a mean of 50 to 56.5 ms over the 20- to 70-year range. Thus, for this age range, there appears to be no change in verbal WM capacity other than what stems from modest cognitive slowing (cf. Salthouse, 1996).

However, according to our model, the steeper declines of memory spans from 70 to 80 years stem from one or more changes in other WM components. Such changes may involve (1) shorter decay times of phonological codes in WM, (2) longer speech production times of the vocal motor processor, or (3) decreased success rates of executive control

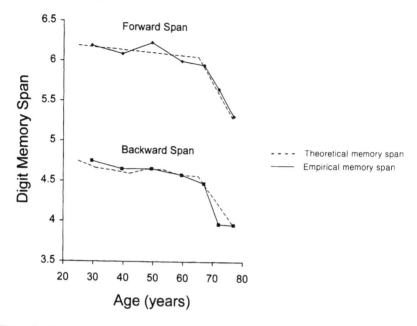

Figure 7. Theoretical memory spans from the present EPIC model compared to corresponding empirical memory spans as a function of age in Gregoire and Van der Linden (1997). Upper and lower pairs of curves show results for forward and backward memory-span tasks, respectively. Over the 20- to 70-year age range, the changes in theoretical memory spans were obtained simply by increasing the mean cycle time of EPIC's cognitive processor by 1.3 ms per decade, starting with 50 ms at 20 years and reaching 56.5 ms at 70 years. Over the 70- to 80-year age range, additional adjustments in components of the model (Table 3) were made to account as best possible for steeper declines in the empirical memory spans. The empirical memory spans shown here have been recalculated from the original reported ones so that subgroups of adults having different levels of education contribute the same proportional amounts of data for each age group.

processes.[14] Table 3 shows how large each such change would have to be by itself to account for the data over the 70–80 year range.

Effects of old age on the model's parameters. From Table 3, we see that effects of old age on verbal WM may produce various percentages of change, depending on which component is involved. Relatively small (15%) decreases of decay times may yield the steep declines of memory span from 70 to 80 years. Alternatively, these declines may stem from

---

[14]In this context, "success" means completing the trial without suffering any catastrophic disruptions during it.

TABLE 3
Age-related changes in parameters of the EPIC model for serial memory spans from
Gregoire and Van der Linden (1997)

Component	Parameter	Age	Value
Cognitive processor	Mean cycle time	20	50.0 ms
		70	56.5 ms
		80	57.8 ms
Auditory working memory	Median decay time	20	4800 ms
		70	4800 ms
		80	4050 ms
Vocal motor processor	Mean digit-articulation time	20	250 ms
		70	250 ms
		80	360 ms
Executive control process	Mean success rate	20	100%
		70	100%
		80	75%

larger ($\geqslant 40\%$) increases in speech production times, or intermediate (25%) decreases in the success rates of executive processes.[15]

Theoretical conclusions

Our application of EPIC to verbal WM suggests that across much of the life span, the components of WM remain well-preserved. We have discovered that basic memory-span tasks require intricate executive control to be performed successfully; they are not merely "pure storage" tasks. Yet before adults reach about 70 years old, their memory spans are almost as great as those of 20-year-olds. Thus, unlike what some researchers have suggested, it appears to us that adults do not lose much capacity for "coordinative" information processing until relatively late in life (cf. Mayr & Kliegl, 1993).[16] This insight is enabled because EPIC allows the

---

[15]Apparent declines in verbal WM may also stem from impairments of peripheral hearing mechanisms (van Boxtel et al., 2000). Such impairments could have especially large deleterious effects on performance of complex WM tasks, because these tasks often entail elaborate and unfamiliar sequences of auditory stimuli.

[16]Some readers may wonder whether measures of basic forward and backward memory spans are sensitive to large increases in the durations of executive processes that mediate them (Steven Keele, personal communication). The answer is "yes". For example, if the times taken by the executive processes of our EPIC model to perform the memory-span tasks had been lengthened by much more than the age-related increase of 13% in the mean cognitive-processor cycle time over the 20- to 70-year age range, then the model could not have fit Gregoire and Van der Linden's (1997) reported memory spans closely.

information-processing requirements of memory-span tasks to be specified thoroughly and precisely.

20 QUESTIONS AND ANSWERS ABOUT COGNITIVE AGEING

On the basis of our preceding discourse, we can now use EPIC's premises to accept Newell's (1973) challenge and tentatively answer 20 fundamental questions about cognitive ageing.

Question 1: What are the sources of age-related slowing?

Answer: According to EPIC, age-related slowing stems from changes in various "hardware" and "software" components of the information-processing system. Like some others (e.g., Bashore, Osman, & Heffley, 1989; Fisher & Glaser, 1996; Fisk, Fisher, & Rogers, 1992; Madden, 1992; Sliwinski, 1997), we endorse specialised-slowing hypotheses about selective effects of ageing on distinct processing stages. Yet in one key respect, our theoretical position abides by the generalised-slowing hypothesis (cf. Birren, Woods, & Williams, 1980; Cerella, 1985; Salthouse, 1978b, 1985). For every task, an age-related increase of the mean cycle time in EPIC's cognitive processor presumably contributes to longer RTs.

Question 2: Why does perceptual speed account for so much age-related variance in performance?

Answer: Perceptual speed has been measured with tasks like digit-symbol substitution and alphanumeric-string comparison (Salthouse, 1996). However, when analysed in terms of EPIC, these tasks are not simple; they presumably evoke a whole microcosm of complex cognition. Performing them requires assorted hardware (visual, ocular, manual, cognitive processors) and software (executive control, search, judgement, response selection, rechecking). The speed of this performance may embody effects of ageing on all of these components, so it can account for much age-related variance in performance of other tasks to which some of these same components contribute. Our research has revealed that virtually no task is truly simple. This pervasive complexity must be understood in detail to characterise cognitive ageing.

Question 3: How much does perceptual-motor hardware contribute to age-related slowing?

Answer: Time increments contributed by "peripheral" perceptual-motor hardware to lengthened RTs sometimes seem to embody relatively small

(<20%) ageing effects (e.g., Bashore, 1994; Cerella, 1985). Nevertheless, our EPIC models reveal that such increments may increase by much larger percentages with age. In accounting for Gregoire and Van der Linden's (1997) memory spans, estimated mean durations of speech production by older adults were over 40% longer than those of the young (Table 3). In accounting for Glass et al.'s (2000) dual-task RTs, estimated mean durations of auditory stimulus identification by older adults were over 100% longer (Table 2). Thus, age-related changes of perceptual-motor hardware should be taken seriously even when older adults have to perform tasks that are mainly "cognitive" (cf. Baltes & Lindenberger, 1997; Welford, 1977).

Question 4: How much does central cognitive hardware contribute to age-related slowing?

Answer: Our modelling shows that ageing from 20 to 70 years increases the mean cycle time of the cognitive processor by about 13%, which may contribute more or less to age-related differences between RTs, depending on how many processing cycles are taken to complete a task (cf. Cerella, 1985; Cerella, Poon, & Williams, 1980). Other hardware changes associated with ageing may also affect these RT differences indirectly. For example, because of shorter WM decay times, elderly adults may need more elaborate procedures to perform some tasks correctly (Mayr & Kliegl, 1993; Salthouse, 1996). This requirement, along with increased cycle times, can lengthen RTs significantly.

Question 5: How much does central cognitive software contribute to age-related slowing?

Answer: Old/young time ratios are sometimes between 1.1 and 1.2 (Cerella, 1985). When this occurs, it may stem entirely from the increase of about 13% in the mean cognitive-processor cycle time, implying that less efficient cognitive software has not contributed to older adults' slowing. Nevertheless, old/young time ratios are sometimes much greater than 1.2 (Cerella, 1985; Mayr & Kliegl, 1993). Then one may infer that older adults have used cognitive software whose execution takes more processor cycles than that of the young. The proportional amount by which an old/young time ratio exceeds 1.13 quantifies how much a software difference has contributed to age-related slowing in terms of proportionally more cycles being taken. For example, a 2.26 ratio relative to 1.13 would imply that older adults have taken twice as many cycles as young adults. Such increases are manifested in both the unlocking durations of the executive process and the response-selection times of the hard Task 2 process for our AEC model of dual-task performance by older adults (Table 2).

Question 6: Why are some Brinley plots linear?

Answer: Brinley (1965) plots are graphs that depict mean RTs of older adults paired with mean RTs of young adults for each of several tasks (e.g., Figure 8). According to EPIC, these plots will be linear when increased task complexity leads older adults to use either the same number of additional cognitive-processor cycles as the young do, or proportionally more cycles. This prediction, which is supported by some data of Mayr and Kliegl (1993), agrees with the classic complexity hypothesis (Birren, 1965) and results from some meta-analyses of age-related slowing (e.g., Cerella, 1985).

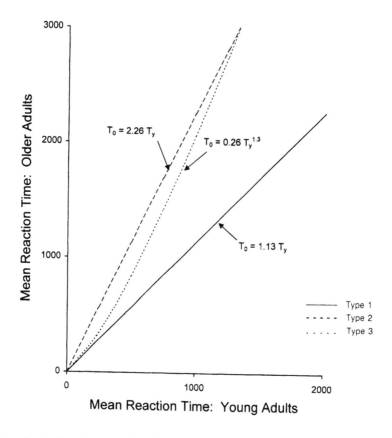

Figure 8. Idealised Brinley plots of alternative quantitative relationships between mean reaction times (RTs) of young and older adults for tasks whose complexity varies. Type 1: Linear old/young RT function with shallow 1.13 slope. Type 2: Linear old/young RT function with steep 2.26 slope. Type 3: Positively accelerated old/young RT function.

Question 7: Why are slopes of some linear Brinley plots very shallow?

Answer: Some linear Brinley plots (e.g., Figure 8, solid line) have very shallow slopes because they include a proportional age-related increase of 13% in the mean cognitive-processor cycle time, with no accompanying differences between young and older adults' cognitive software. Such shallowness is most likely when basic RT tasks are involved. For them, both age groups may use identical or very similar rule sets whose execution takes the same numbers of cycles.

Question 8: Why are slopes of some linear Brinley plots much steeper?

Answer: Some linear Brinley plots have steeper slopes (e.g., Figure 8, dashed line) because as task complexity increases, older adults may use rule sets whose execution takes proportionally more cognitive-processor cycles than the young. This could stem from effects of ageing on skill acquisition. For example, within EPIC, skill acquisition involves at least three phases (Kieras et al., 2000). First, declarative knowledge about how to perform a given task is acquired. Second, production rules are compiled from this knowledge to create executable task procedures. Third, these rules are refined through practice to enhance their efficiency. For some complex tasks, perhaps older adults initially compile inefficient rule sets whose execution takes proportionally more processor cycles than those of the young (cf. Mayr & Kliegl, 1993). This inefficiency, combined with certain learning functions for rule refinement, would yield linear Brinley plots whose slopes exceed 1.13.[17]

---

[17]To be precise, suppose that for each of J tasks whose complexity varies, $n_{oj1} = g(n_{yj1})$, where n_{yj1} is the number of processor cycles taken by young adults' production rules on the first trial of practice for the jth task $(1 \leqslant j \leqslant J)$, n_{oj1} is the number of cycles taken by older adults' rules on the first trial, and g is a function that relates n_{oj1} to n_{yj1}. Also suppose that $n_{yjm} = f_y(m)$ and $n_{ojm} = f_o(m)$, where n_{yjm} is the number of cycles taken by the young adults' rules on the mth trial $(m \geqslant 1)$, n_{ojm} is the number of cycles taken by the older adults' rules on the mth trial, f_y is a learning function for young adults, f_o is a learning function for older adults, and $f_o(m) = g[f_y(m)]$. Then the Brinley plot of mean RTs for these tasks would have the same type of form as g. For example, if $g(n_{yj1}) = kn_{yj1}$, so that n_{oj1} is larger than n_{yj1} $(1 \leqslant j \leqslant J)$ by a proportional constant $(k > 1)$, then the Brinley plot would be linear with a slope of $1.13k$, where 1.13 is the proportional amount by which the mean cognitive-processor cycle time of older adults exceeds the young adults' mean cycle time. Also, if the young adults' learning function, $f_y(m)$, conforms to the power law of practice (Anderson, 1983; Newell, 1990) such that $n_{yjm} = a + bm^{-r}$, where $a \geqslant 0$, $b > 0$, and $r > 0$, then the older adults' learning function, $f_o(m)$, would conform to the power law of practice with $f_o(m) = k(a + bm^{-r})$. Alternatively, if g makes n_{oj1} be disproportionally larger than n_{yj1} $(1 \leqslant j \leqslant J)$, this different relationship—combined with the other previous assumptions—would yield a positively accelerated Brinley plot, and the older adults' learning function would not necessarily conform to the power law of practice when that of the young adults does.

Question 9: Why are some Brinley plots nonlinear?

Answer: Nonlinear Brinley plots (e.g., Figure 8, dotted curve) can occur for two reasons. First, they may come from conjoining segments of linear old/young RT functions whose slopes subtly differ (Mayr & Kliegl, 1993). Second, for some complex tasks, older adults may compile inefficient rule sets whose execution takes disproportionately more cycles than those of the young. This inefficiency, combined with certain learning functions (see footnote 17), would yield positively accelerated Brinley plots (e.g., Hale, Myerson, & Wagstaff, 1987). Our claim here differs from Cerella's (1990) overhead and Myerson, Hale, Wagstaff, Poon, and Smith's (1990) information-loss hypotheses, which assume a *correspondence axiom* that young and older adults use the same sequence of algorithmic steps for performing a given task.

Question 10: Is the correspondence axiom correct?

Answer: Perhaps sometimes, but not often. When a set of tasks yields a linear Brinley plot whose slope is about 1.13 (e.g., Figure 8, solid line), it is plausible to conclude that young and older adults have used the same algorithmic steps, consistent with the correspondence axiom. However, when Brinley plots have steeper linear or positively accelerated RT functions, another plausible conclusion is that the two age groups have compiled rule sets whose execution takes different numbers of algorithmic steps, contrary to this axiom. In fact, there are probably many circumstances where the correspondence axiom does not hold when complex tasks have to be performed.

Question 11: Are there qualitatively different types of task complexity?

Answer: Perhaps, but more research is needed to understand what the complexities are. For example, Mayr & Kliegl (1993, p. 1298) distinguished between sequential and coordinative complexity. *Sequential complexity* involves "a variation in the number of independent processing steps that does not increase the amount of information exchange between single steps", whereas *coordinative complexity* involves a variation in "the amount of processing required to regulate and monitor the flow of information between interrelated processing steps". Supporting this distinction,

Mayr and Kliegl obtained linear Brinley plots with steeper slopes for manipulation of coordinative complexity. However, others (e.g., Brinley, 1965; McDowd & Craik, 1988) have not obtained such results. Nor does our research show that moderately older adults (60 ≤ age ≤ 70 years) are always impaired at coordinative information processing. Instead ageing effects on coordinative information processing may stem from malleable differences between strategies adopted to manage performance when both WM and perceptual-motor loads are heavy. Taking these strategy differences fully into account will be crucial for aptly distinguishing alternative types of task complexity.

Question 12: Why do some measures of WM capacity decrease very little with age?

Answer: Modelling with EPIC has yielded three results that, in combination, explain why older adults perform almost as well as the young on basic WM tasks. First, from 20 to 70 years of age, the mean cognitive-processor cycle time increases by only 13%. Second, decay times of phonological codes in verbal WM remain essentially constant until at least 70 years of age. Third, over a broad age range, concurrent threads of information processing can be executed for multiple tasks. These abilities, when exploited by efficient task procedures, can yield rather stable measures of WM capacity across much of the life span. For example, this accounts for the well-preserved forward, backward, and *n*-back memory spans reported in studies of ageing and verbal WM (e.g., Dobbs & Rule, 1989; Gregoire & Van der Linden, 1997).

Question 13: Why do some measures of WM capacity decrease much more than others with age?

Answer: Larger age-related decreases in measures of WM capacity have been obtained with reading-span, calculation-span, and other relatively complex tasks (e.g., Foos, 1989; Gick et al., 1988; Wingfield et al., 1988). One possible explanation for this is that studies with such tasks have included many very old adults, whose WM components are more impaired than those in moderately old adults. A second important possibility is that as adults grow older, they tend to adopt cautious strategies for performing complex WM tasks, thereby neglecting to exploit their available cognitive capacities. However, from our research, it appears that, before 70 years of age, older adults retain great potential for coordinative and executive information processing. If so, then training that improves their strategies could enable them to manifest high capacity even for complex WM tasks.

Question 14: Is inhibitory control impaired with age?

Answer: We have obtained no compelling evidence that inhibitory control is impaired with age. EPIC models of memory span suggest that older adults are not especially distracted by discarded information in WM. Similarly, in our PRP experiments (Glass et al., 2000), older adults were not more distracted than the young by secondary-task stimuli during primary-task performance. Their mean primary-task RTs were essentially independent of SOA, and out-of-order secondary-task responses were extremely rare, yet older adults identified stimuli and selected responses concurrently for the two tasks. These results suggest that inhibitory control has been preserved. This is consistent with a variety of data on ageing and Stroop colour-word interference (Salthouse & Meinz, 1995; Verhaeghen & De Meersman, 1998), inhibition of return (Faust & Balota, 1997; Hartley & Kieley, 1995), visual marking (Kramer & Atchley, 2000), and negative priming (Sullivan & Faust, 1993).[18]

Nevertheless, some researchers (e.g., Dempster, 1992; Hasher & Zacks, 1988; Rabbitt, 1965) have hypothesised that ageing impairs inhibitory control. Consistent with this, older adults are disproportionately slower when reading text that contains irrelevant information at unpredictable locations (Connelly, Hasher, & Zacks, 1991), and older adults' negative priming is sometimes less than that of the young (Hasher, Stoltzfus, Zacks, & Rypma, 1991; Kane, Hasher, Stoltzfus, Zacks, & Connelly, 1994; McDowd & Oseas-Kreger, 1991; Stolzfus, Hasher, Zacks, Ulivi, & Goldstein, 1993; Tipper, 1991). However, these results may stem at least partly from ageing effects on peripheral perceptual-motor mechanisms rather than central inhibition (Murphy, McDowd, & Wilcox, 1999; Scialfa, Hamaluk, Skaloud, & Pratt, 1999). Also, inhibitory control may seem impaired if older adults adopt visual inspection strategies that expose them to more irrelevant information but have other compensatory benefits.[19]

---

[18]For a thorough review of relevant studies like these, see Kramer, Humphrey, Larish, Logan, and Strayer (1994).

[19]For example, inspection strategies with more closely spaced and redundant visual fixation points might make it harder to ignore irrelevant information but help compensate for age-related random noise in the perceptual and motor systems (cf. Scialfa et al., 1999; Welford, 1977).

Question 15: Have older adults lost their ability to time-share during dual-task performance?

Answer: Standard wisdom about cognitive ageing proclaims that older adults lose their ability to time-share during dual-task performance (McDowd, Vercruyssen, & Birren, 1991). "One of the clearest results in the experimental psychology of aging is that older subjects are more penalized when they must divide their attention" (Craik, 1977, p. 391). Lost time-sharing ability seems apparent from many studies in which disproportionate dual-task costs occurred with age (e.g., Allen et al., 1998; Crossley & Hiscock, 1992; Guttentag & Madden, 1987; Hawkins, Kramer, & Capaldi, 1992; Korteling, 1991; Lorsbach & Simpson, 1988; Ponds, Brouwer, & van Volfelaar, 1988). However, close perusal reveals that these studies perhaps should be discounted somewhat because of how their data were collected and analysed. Our work with the PRP procedure suggests that older adults still time-share efficiently when encouraged to do so.

Question 16: Do older adults suffer from goal neglect?

Answer: Because the brain's frontal lobes deteriorate with age (Raz, 2000; West, 1996), older adults may suffer goal neglect, a symptom of "dysexecutive syndrome" (Baddeley, 1986; Duncan, 1986, 1995; West & Baylis, 1998). Goal neglect involves inadequate readiness or "set" for tasks. This could occur if items like "GOAL: DO TASK A" and "GOAL: DO TASK B" are not inserted and maintained in WM. Nevertheless, we have evidence that adults may be spared from goal neglect before 70 years of age. If goal neglect affected them, then our EPIC models—which assume intact usage of goals—would have failed to fit older adults' dual-task RTs and memory spans. Beyond age 70, however, other results from our models suggest that task goals in WM may become less resilient.

Question 17: How are age-related slowing and skill acquisition associated?

Answer: Like some researchers (e.g., Fisk & Rogers, 1991; Kramer, Larish, Weber, & Bardell, 1999; Strayer & Kramer, 1994), we believe skill acquisition and age-related slowing are closely associated. Many tasks used to measure RTs and time-sharing costs are initially novel to participants. Strategies that older adults adopt to cope with this novelty, and the mechanisms that they use to modify their strategies, determine response speed and accuracy. Taking these matters seriously enables EPIC to account for steeply sloped linear and positively accelerated

Brinley plots. Other researchers have provided such accounts for both single-task (e.g., Fisk & Rogers, 1991; Strayer & Kramer, 1994) and dual-task (e.g., Kramer et al., 1999) performance. In particular, the extent to which older adults time-share well between dual-tasks is affected by the type of training they receive. This is what we expect based on EPIC's emphasis of adaptive executive control and flexible task management.

Question 18: What strategies can and should older adults adopt to cope with cognitive ageing?

Answer: Much evidence shows that older adults tend to adopt conservative strategies for performing speeded tasks (e.g., Baron & Matilla, 1989; Botwinick, 1966; Okun & Di Vesta, 1976; Rabbitt, 1979; Salthouse, 1978a; Salthouse & Somberg, 1982; Strayer, Wickens, & Braune, 1987). Three factors could underlie this tendency. First, mechanisms for compiling procedural knowledge may become less optimal with age and generate initial inefficient sets of production rules. Second, older adults' cautiousness may be warranted because of their reduced processing capacities. Third, older adults may prefer conservative strategies because they do not fully appreciate their preserved capacities. From our EPIC models, it appears that the first and second factors perhaps prevail after age 70. Before then, the third factor may be more important because, until age 70, relatively little is lost in terms of cognitive-processor speed, WM trace durability, and some other hardware parameters. Thus, adults under 70 should be encouraged to exploit the capacities that they still have.

Question 19: Is cognitive ageing a gradual uniform process?

Answer: Cognitive ageing is not gradual and uniform in all respects. Some "hardware" parameters like the mean cognitive-processor cycle time change modestly over the life span. Other parameters, such as WM decay times, remain almost constant until 70 years of age, but change more rapidly thereafter. Meanwhile, cognitive software for performing tasks may vary greatly, depending on task priorities, personal predilections, training, and other contextual factors. This pattern implies that although meritorious, hypotheses about specific age-related effects may not hold for all adult subgroups. Special care is needed to interpret results from each subgroup. Characterising their performance requires models that accommodate complex interactions between the more or less functional and ever-changing components of the adult information-processing system.

Question 20: Where should future research on cognitive ageing go from here?

Answer: Future research on cognitive ageing may take several promising paths. Steps toward unified computational theories of cognitive ageing should continue. More work is needed to identify ageing effects on hardware and software components of information processing. Changes in perceptual-motor hardware mechanisms and their interactions with central cognitive software must be better understood. Closer attention must be directed to the different types of executive-control strategies and task procedures adopted by young and older adults. Also, it will be important to credit contributions of skill acquisition more fully in assessing the ultimate performance levels that older adults can achieve. From so doing, far more than 20 questions about cognitive ageing will be answered during the 21st century.

Manuscript received September 2000

REFERENCES

Allen, P.A., Smith, A.F., Vires-Collins, H., & Sperry, S. (1998). The psychological refractory period: Evidence for age differences in attentional time-sharing. *Psychology and Aging*, *13*, 218–229.

Allport, D.A. (1987). Selection-for-action: Some behavioral and neurophysiological considerations of attention and action. In H. Heuer & A.F. Sanders (Eds.), *Perspectives on perception and action* (pp. 395–419). Hillsdale, NJ: Lawrence Erlbaum Associates Inc.

Anderson, J.R. (1983). *The architecture of cognition*. Cambridge, MA: Harvard University Press.

Babcock, R.L., & Salthouse, T.A. (1990). Effects of increased processing demands on age differences in working memory. *Psychology and Aging*, *5*, 421–428.

Baddeley, A.D. (1986). *Working memory*. New York: Oxford University Press.

Baddeley, A.D., Logie, R., Bressi, S., Della Sala, S., & Spinnler, H. (1986). Dementia and working memory. *Quarterly Journal of Experimental Psychology*, *38A*, 603–618.

Baddeley, A.D., Thomson, N., & Buchanan, M. (1975). Word length and the structure of short-term memory. *Journal of Verbal Learning and Verbal Behavior*, *14*, 575–589.

Baltes, P.B., & Lindenberger, U. (1997). Emergence of a powerful connection between sensory and cognitive functions across the adult life span: A new window to the study of cognitive aging? *Psychology and Aging*, *12*, 12–21.

Baron, A., & Matilla, W.R. (1989). Response slowing of older adults: Effects of time-limit contingencies on single- and dual-task performance. *Psychology and Aging*, *4*, 66–72.

Bashore, T.R. (1994). Some thoughts on neurocognitive slowing. *Acta Psychologica*, *86*, 295–325.

Bashore, T.R., Osman, A.M., & Heffley, E.F. (1989). Mental slowing in elderly adults: A cognitive psychophysiological analysis. *Psychology and Aging*, *4*, 235–244.

Birren, J.E. (1965). Age changes in speed of behavior: Its central nature and physiological correlates. In A.T. Welford & J.E. Birren (Eds.), *Behavior, aging, and the nervous system* (pp. 191–216). Springfield, IL: Thomas.

Birren, J.E., Woods, A.M., & Williams, M.V. (1980). Behavioral slowing with age: Causes, organization, and consequences. In L.W. Poon (Ed.), *Aging in the 1980s* (pp. 293–308). Washington, DC: American Psychological Association.

Botwinick, J. (1996). Cautiousness in old age. *Journal of Gerontology, 21*, 347–353.

Botwinick, J., & Storandt, M. (1974). *Memory, related functions and age.* Springfield, IL: Charles C. Thomas.

Brinley, J.F. (1965). Cognitive sets, speed and accuracy of performance in the elderly. In A.T. Welford & J.E. Birren (Eds.), *Behavior, aging, and the nervous system* (pp. 114–149). Springfield, IL: Thomas.

Bromley, D.B. (1958). Some effects of age on short-term learning and remembering. *Journal of Gerontology, 12*, 398–406.

Burke, D.M., & Yee, P.L. (1984). Semantic priming during sentence processing by young and older adults. *Developmental Psychology, 20*, 903–910.

Byrne, M.D. (1998). Taking a computational approach to aging: The SPAN theory of working memory. *Psychology and Aging, 13*, 309–322.

Callaway, E., & Yeager, C.L. (1960). Relationship between reaction time and electro-encephalographic alpha base. *Science, 132*, 1765–1766.

Card, S.K., Moran, T.P., & Newell, A. (1983). *The psychology of human–computer interaction.* Hillsdale, NJ: Lawrence Erlbaum Associates Inc.

Cerella, J. (1985). Information processing rates in the elderly. *Psychological Bulletin, 98*, 67–83.

Cerella, J. (1990). Aging and information-processing rate. In J.E. Birren & K.W. Schaie (Eds.), *Handbook of the psychology of aging* (3rd ed., pp. 201–221). New York: Academic Press.

Cerella, J., Poon, L.W., & Williams, D.M. (1980). Age and the complexity hypothesis. In L.W. Poon (Ed.), *Aging in the 1980s* (pp. 332–340). Washington, DC: American Psychological Association.

Charness, N. (1981). Visual short-term memory and aging in chess players. *Journal of Gerontology, 36*, 615–619.

Clark, L.E., & Knowles, J.B. (1973). Age differences in dichotic listening performance. *Journal of Gerontology, 28*, 173–178.

Connelly, S.L., Hasher, L., & Zacks, R.T. (1991). Age and reading: The impact of distraction. *Psychology and Aging, 6*, 533–541.

Craik, F.I.M. (1968). Two components in free recall. *Journal of Verbal Learning and Verbal Behavior, 7*, 996–1004.

Craik, F.I.M. (1977). Age differences in human memory. In J.E. Birren & K.W. Schaie (Eds.), *Handbook of the psychology of aging* (pp. 384–420). New York: Van Nostrand Reinhold.

Craik, F.I.M., & Byrd, M. (1982). Aging and cognitive deficits: The role of attentional resources. In F.I.M. Craik & A.S. Trehub (Eds.), *Aging and cognitive processes* (pp. 191–211). New York: Plenum.

Craik, F.I.M., & Jennings, J.M. (1992). Human memory. In F.I.M. Craik & T.A. Salthouse (Eds.), *The handbook of aging and cognition* (pp. 51–110). Hillsdale, NJ: Lawrence Erlbaum Associates Inc.

Craik, F.I.M., & Salthouse, T.A. (Eds.). (2000). *The handbook of aging and cognition* (2nd ed.). Mahwah, NJ: Lawrence Erlbaum Associates Inc.

Crossley, M., & Hiscock, M. (1992). Age-related differences in concurrent-task performance of normal adults: Evidence for a decline in processing resources. *Psychology and Aging, 7*, 499–506.

Dempster, F.N. (1992). The rise and fall of the inhibitory mechanism: Toward a unified theory of cognitive development and aging. *Developmental Review, 12*, 45–75.

D'Esposito, M., & Postle, B.R. (1999). The dependence of span and delayed response performance on prefrontal cortex. *Neuropsychologia, 37*, 1303–1315.

Dobbs, A.R., & Rule, B.G. (1989). Adult age differences in working memory. *Psychology and Aging, 4*, 500–503.

Drewnowski, A. (1980). Attributes and priorities in short-term recall: A new model of memory span. *Journal of Experimental Psychology: General, 109*, 208–250.

Duncan, J. (1986). Disorganization of behaviour after frontal-lobe damage. *Cognitive Neuropsychology, 3*, 271–290.

Duncan, J. (1995). Attention, intelligence, and the frontal lobes. In M.S. Gazzaniga (Ed.), *The cognitive neurosciences* (pp. 721–733). Cambridge, MA: MIT Press.

Faust, M.E., & Balota, D.A. (1997). Inhibition of return and visuospatial attention in healthy older adults and individuals with dementia of the Alzheimer types. *Neuropsychology, 11*, 13–29.

Ferris, S.H., Crook, T., Clark, E., McCarthy, M., & Rae, D. (1980). Facial recognition memory deficits in normal aging and senile dementia. *Journal of Gerontology, 35*, 707–714.

Fisher, D.L., & Glaser, R.A. (1996). Molar and latent models of cognitive slowing: Implications for aging, dementia, depression, development, and intelligence. *Psychonomic Bulletin and Review, 3*, 458–480.

Fisk, A.D., Fisher, D.L., & Rogers, W. (1992). General slowing alone cannot explain age-related search effects: Reply to Cerella (1991). *Journal of Experimental Psychology: General, 121*, 73–78.

Fisk, A.D., & Rogers, W. (1991). Toward an understanding of age-related memory and visual search effects. *Journal of Experimental Psychology: General, 120*, 131–149.

Foos, P.W. (1989). Adult age differences in working memory. *Psychology and Aging, 4*, 269–275.

Gick, M.L., Craik, F.I.M., & Morris, R.G. (1988). Task complexity and age differences in working memory. *Memory & Cognition, 16*, 353–361.

Glass, J.M. (2000, April). *Visual function and cognitive aging: Differential role of contrast sensitivity in verbal versus spatial tasks.* Paper presented at the Cognitive Aging Conference, Atlanta, GA.

Glass, J.M., Schumacher, E.H., Lauber, E.J., Zurbriggen, E.L., Gmeindl, L., Kieras, D.E., & Meyer, D.E. (2000). Aging and the psychological refractory period: Task-coordination strategies in young and old adults. *Psychology and Aging, 15*, 571–595.

Gregoire, J., & Van der Linden, M. (1997). Effects of age on forward and backward digit spans. *Aging, Neuropsychology, and Cognition, 4*, 140–149.

Guttentag, R.E., & Madden, D.J. (1987). Adult age differences in the attentional capacity demands of letter matching. *Experimental Aging Research, 13*, 93–98.

Hale, S., Myerson, J., & Wagstaff, D. (1987). General slowing of nonverbal information processing: Evidence for a power law. *Journal of Gerontology, 42*, 131–136.

Hartley, A.A., & Kieley, J.M. (1995). Adult age differences in the inhibition of return of visual attention. *Psychology and Aging, 10*, 670–683.

Hartley, A.A., & Little, D.M. (1999). Age-related differences and similarities in dual-task interference. *Journal of Experimental Psychology: General, 128*, 416–449.

Hasher, L., Stoltzfus, E.R., Zacks, R.T., & Rypma, B. (1991). Age and inhibition. *Journal of Experimental Psychology: Learning, Memory, and Cognition, 17*, 163–169.

Hasher, L., & Zacks, R.T. (1988). Working memory, comprehension, and aging: A review and a new view. In G.H. Bower (Ed.), *The psychology of learning and motivation* (Vol. 22, pp. 193–225). San Diego, CA: Academic Press.

Hastings, N.A.J., & Peacock, J.B. (1975). *Statistical distributions.* London: Butterworth.

Hawkins, H.L., Kramer, A.F., & Capaldi, D. (1992). Aging, exercise, and attention. *Psychology and Aging*, 7, 643–653.

Hooper, F.H., Hooper, J.O., & Colbert, K.C. (1984). *Personality and memory correlates of intellectual functioning: Young adulthood to old age*. Basel, Switzerland: Karger.

Kail, R., & Salthouse, T.A. (1994). Processing speed as mental capacity. *Acta Psychologica*, 86, 199–226.

Kane, M.J., Hasher, L., Stoltzfus, E.R., Zacks, R.T., & Connelly, S.L. (1994). Inhibitory attentional mechanisms and aging. *Psychology and Aging*, 9, 103–112.

Keele, S.W. (1973). *Attention and human performance*. Pacific Palisades, CA: Goodyear.

Kieras, D.E., & Meyer, D.E. (1997). An overview of the EPIC architecture for cognition and performance with application to human–computer interaction. *Human–Computer Interaction*. 12, 391–438.

Kieras, D.E., & Meyer, D.E. (2000). The role of cognitive task analysis in the application of predictive models of human performance. In J.M. Schraagen, S.F. Chipman, & V.L. Shalin (Eds.), *Cognitive task analysis* (pp. 237–260). Mahwah, NJ: Lawrence Erlbaum Associates Inc.

Kieras, D.E., Meyer, D.E., Ballas, J.A., & Lauber, E.J. (2000). Modern computational perspectives on executive mental control: Where to from here? In S. Monsell & J. Driver (Eds.), *Attention and performance XVIII: Control of cognitive processes* (pp. 681–712). Cambridge, MA: MIT Press.

Kieras, D.E., Meyer, D.E., Mueller, S., & Seymour, T. (1999) Insights into working memory from the perspective of the EPIC architecture for modeling skilled perceptual-motor and cognitive human performance. In A. Miyake & P. Shah (Eds.), *Models of working memory: Mechanisms of active maintenance and executive control* (pp. 183–223). New York: Cambridge University Press.

Korteling, J. (1991). Effects of skill integration and perceptual competition on age-related differences in dual-task performance. *Human Factors*, 33, 35–44.

Kramer, A.F., & Atchley, P. (2000). Age-related effects in the marking of old objects in visual search. *Psychology and Aging*, 15, 286–296.

Kramer, A.F., Humphrey, D.G., Larish, J.F., Logan, G.D., & Strayer, D.L. (1994). Aging and inhibition: Beyond a unitary view of inhibitory processing in attention. *Psychology and Aging*, 9, 491–512.

Kramer, A.F., Larish, J.L., Weber, T.A., & Bardell, L. (1999). Training for executive control: Task coordination strategies and aging. In D. Gopher & A. Koriat (Eds.), *Attention and performance XVII* (pp. 617–652). Cambridge, MA: MIT Press.

Kristofferson, A.B. (1967). Attention and psychophysical time. In A.F. Sanders (Ed.), *Attention and performance* (pp. 93–100). Amsterdam: North-Holland Publishing Co.

Landauer, T.K. (1962). The rate of implicit speech. *Perceptual and Motor Skills*, 15, 646.

Light, L.L., & Anderson, P.A. (1985). Working-memory capacity, age, and memory for discourse. *Journal of Gerontology*, 40, 737–747.

Longoni, A.M., Richardson, A.T.E., & Aiello, A. (1993). Articulatory rehearsal and phonological storage in working memory. *Memory & Cognition*, 21, 11–22.

Lorsbach, T., & Simpson, G. (1988). Dual-task performance as a function of adult age and task complexity. *Psychology and Aging*, 243, 210–212.

Madden, D.J. (1992). Four to ten milliseconds per year: Age-related slowing of visual word identification. *Journal of Gerontology: Psychological Sciences*, 47, P59–P68.

Marsh, G.R., & Thompson, L.W. (1977). Psychophysiology of aging. In J.E. Birren & K.W. Schaie (Eds.), *Handbook of the psychology of aging* (pp. 219–248). New York: Van Nostrand Reinhold.

Maylor, E.A., Vousden, J.I., & Brown, G.D.A. (1999). Adult age differences in short-term memory for serial order: Data and a model. *Psychology and Aging*, 14, 572–594.

Mayr, U., & Kliegl, R. (1993). Sequential and coordinative complexity: Age-based processing limitations in figural transformations. *Journal of Experimental Psychology: Learning, Memory, and Cognition, 19*, 1297–1320.

Mayr, U., & Kliegl, R. (2000). Complex semantic processing in old age: Does it stay or does it go? *Psychology and Aging, 15*, 29–43.

McDowd, J.M., & Craik, F.I.M. (1988). Effects of aging and task difficulty on divided attention performance. *Journal of Experimental Psychology: Human Perception and Performance, 14*, 267–280.

McDowd, J.M., & Oseas-Kreger, D.M. (1991). Aging, inhibitory processes, and negative priming. *Journal of Gerontology: Psychological Sciences, 46*, P340–P345.

McDowd, J.M., Vercruyssen, M., & Birren, J.E. (1991). Aging, divided attention, and dual-task performance. In D.L. Damos (Ed.), *Multiple task performance* (pp. 387–414). Bristol, PA: Taylor & Francis.

Meyer, D.E., & Kieras, D.E. (1997a). A computational theory of executive cognitive processes and multiple-task performance: Part 1. Basic mechanisms. *Psychological Review, 104*, 3–65.

Meyer, D.E., & Kieras, D.E. (1997b). A computational theory of executive cognitive processes and multiple-task performance: Part 2. Accounts of psychological refractory-period phenomena. *Psychological Review, 104*, 749–791.

Meyer, D.E., & Kieras, D.E. (1999). Précis to a practical unified theory of cognition and action: Some lessons from computational modeling of human multiple-task performance. In D. Gopher & A. Koriat (Eds.), *Attention and performance XVII* (pp. 17–88). Cambridge, MA: MIT Press.

Meyer, D.E., Mueller, S.T., Seymour, T.L., & Kieras, D.E. (2000, April). *Brain loci of temporal coding and serial-order control for verbal working memory revealed by computational modeling and focal lesion analysis of memory-span performance.* Poster presented at the meeting of the Cognitive Neuroscience Society, San Francisco, CA.

Mueller, S.T., Seymour, T.L., Glass, J.M., Kieras, D.E., & Meyer, D.E. (2000, April). *Components of cognitive aging in verbal working memory revealed by computational modeling with the executive-process interactive control (EPIC) architecture.* Poster presented at the Cognitive Aging Conference, Atlanta, GA.

Murphy, D.R., McDowd, J.M., & Wilcox, K.A. (1999). Inhibition and aging: Similarities between younger and older adults revealed by the processing of unattended auditory information. *Psychology and Aging, 14*, 44–59.

Myerson, J., Hale, S., Wagstaff, D., Poon, L.W., & Smith, G.A. (1990). The information-loss model: A mathematical theory of age-related cognitive slowing. *Psychological Review, 97*, 475–487.

Newell, A. (1973). You can't play 20 questions with nature and win. In W.G. Chase (Ed.), *Visual information processing* (pp. 283–308). New York: Academic Press.

Newell, A. (1990). *Unified theories of cognition.* Cambridge, MA: Harvard University Press.

Obrist, W.D., & Busse, E.W. (1965). The electroencephalogram in old age. In W.W. Wilson (Ed.), *Applications of electroencephalography in psychiatry: A symposium* (pp. 185–205). Durham, NC: Duke University Press.

Okun, M.A., & Di Vesta, F.J. (1976). Cautiousness in adulthood as a function of age and instructions. *Journal of Gerontology, 31*, 571–576.

Orsini, A.L., Chiacchio, L., Cinque, M., Cocchiaro, C., Schiappa, O., & Grossi, D. (1986). Effects of age, education and sex on two tests of immediate memory: A study of normal subjects from 20 to 99 years of age. *Perceptual and Motor Skills, 63*, 727–732.

Park, D.C., Smith, A.D., Lautenschlager, G., Earles, J., Frieske, D., Zwahr, M., & Gaines, C.L. (1996). Mediators of long-term memory performance across the life span. *Psychology and Aging, 11*, 621–637.

Pashler, H. (1994). Dual-task interference in simple tasks: Data and theory. *Psychological Bulletin, 116*, 220–244.

Ponds, R.W., Brouwer, W.H., & van Volfelaar, P.C. (1988). Age differences in divided attention in a simulated driving task. *Journal of Gerontology, 43*, P151–P156.

Puckett, J.M., & Stockburger, D.W. (1988). Absence of age-related proneness to short-term retroactive interference in the absence of rehearsal. *Psychology and Aging, 3*, 342–347.

Rabbitt, P.M.A. (1965). An age-decrement in the ability to ignore irrelevant information. *Journal of Gerontology, 20*, 233–238.

Rabbitt, P.M.A. (1979). How old and young subjects monitor and control responses for accuracy and speed. *British Journal of Psychology, 70*, 305–311.

Raymond, B.J. (1971). Free recall among the aged. *Psychological Reports, 29*, 1179–1182.

Raz, N. (2000). Aging of the brain and its impact on cognitive performance: Integration of structural and functional findings. In F.I.M. Craik & T.A. Salthouse (Eds.), *The handbook of aging and cognition* (2nd ed., pp. 1–90). Mahwah, NJ: Lawrence Erlbaum Associates Inc.

Salthouse, T.A. (1978a). Adult age and the speed–accuracy trade-off. *Ergonomics, 22*, 811–812.

Salthouse, T.A. (1978b). *Age and speed: The nature of the relationship.* Unpublished manuscript, Department of Psychology, University of Missouri, Columbia, MO.

Salthouse, T.A. (1985). Speed of behavior and its implications for cognition. In J.E. Birren & K.W. Schaie (Eds.), *Handbook of the psychology of aging* (2nd ed., pp. 400–426). New York: Van Nostrand Reinhold.

Salthouse, T.A. (1988). Initiating the formalization of theories of cognitive aging. *Psychology and Aging, 3*, 3–16.

Salthouse, T.A. (1996). The processing-speed theory of adult age differences in cognition. *Psychological Review, 103*, 403–428.

Salthouse, T.A., Babcock, R.J., & Shaw, R.J. (1991). Effects of adult age on structural and operational capacities in working memory. *Psychology and Aging, 6*, 118–127.

Salthouse, T.A., & Meinz, E.J. (1995). Aging, inhibition, working memory, and speed. *Journal of Gerontology: Psychological Sciences, 50*, P297–P306.

Salthouse, T.A., & Somberg, B.L. (1982). Time–accuracy relationships in young and old adults. *Journal of Gerontology, 37*, 349–353.

Schumacher, E.H., Lauber, E.J., Glass, J.M., Zurbriggen, E.L., Gmeindl, L., Kieras, D.E., & Meyer, D.E. (1999). Concurrent response selection processes in dual-task performance: Evidence for adaptive executive control over task-scheduling strategies. *Journal of Experimental Psychology: Human Perception and Performance, 25*, 791–814.

Schweickert, R., & Boruff, B. (1986). Short-term capacity: Magic number or magic spell? *Journal of Experimental Psychology: Learning, Memory, and Cognition, 12*, 419–425.

Scialfa, C.T. (2000, April). *Relations between sensceptual and cognitive aging.* Paper presented at the Cognitive Aging Conference, Atlanta, GA.

Scialfa, C.T., Hamaluk, W., Skaloud, P., & Pratt, J. (1999). Age differences in saccadic averaging. *Psychology and Aging, 14*, 695–799.

Sliwinski, M.J. (1997). Aging and counting speed: Evidence for process-specific slowing. *Psychology and Aging, 12*, 38–49.

Smith, E.E., & Jonides, J. (1999). Storage and executive processes in the frontal lobes. *Science, 283*, 1657–1661.

Somberg, B.L., & Salthouse, T.A. (1982). Divided attention abilities in young and old adults. *Journal of Experimental Psychology: Human Perception and Performance, 8*, 651–663.

Standing, L., Bond, B., Smith, P., & Isely, C. (1980). Is the immediate memory span determined by subvocalization rate? *British Journal of Psychology, 71*, 525–539.

Stolzfus, E., Hasher, L., Zacks, R., Ulivi, M., & Goldstein, D. (1993). Investigation of inhibition and interference in younger and older adults. *Journal of Gerontology: Psychological Sciences, 48,* 179–188.

Strayer, D.L., & Kramer, A.F. (1994). Aging and skill acquisition: Learning-performance distinctions. *Psychology and Aging, 9,* 589–605.

Strayer, D.L., Wickens, C.D., & Braune, R. (1987). Adult age differences in the speed and capacity of information processing: II. An electrophysiological approach. *Psychology and Aging, 2,* 99–110.

Sullivan, M.P., & Faust, M.E. (1993). Evidence for identity inhibition during selective attention in old adults. *Psychology and Aging, 8,* 589–598.

Surwillo, W.W. (1963). The relation of simple response times to brain wave frequency and the effects of age. *Electroencephalography and Clinical Neurophysiology, 15,* 105–114.

Talland, G.A. (1967). Age and the immediate memory span. *The Gerontologist, 7,* 4–9.

Tipper, S.P. (1991). Less attentional selectivity as a result of declining inhibition in older adults. *Bulletin of the Psychonomic Society, 29,* 45–47.

Van Boxtel, M.P.J., van Beijsterveldt, C.E.M., Houx, P.J., Anteunis, L.J.C., Metsemakers, J.F.M., & Jolles, J. (2000). Mild hearing impairment can reduce verbal memory performance in a healthy adult population. *Journal of Clinical and Experimental Neuropsychology, 22,* 147–154.

Verhaeghen, P., & De Meersman, L. (1998). Aging and the Stroop effect: A meta-analysis. *Psychology and Aging, 13,* 120–126.

Wechsler, D. (1981). *Manual for the Wechsler Adult Intelligence Scale—revised.* New York: The Psychological Corporation.

Welford, A.T. (1977). Motor performance. In J.E. Birren, & K.W. Schaie (Eds.), *Handbook of the psychology of ageing* (pp. 450–496). New York: Van Nostrand Reinhold.

West, R.L. (1996). An application of prefrontal cortex function theory to cognitive aging. *Psychological Bulletin, 120,* 272–292.

West, R., & Baylis, G.C. (1998). Effects of increased response dominance and contextual disintegration on the Stroop interference effect in older adults. *Psychology and Aging, 13,* 206–217.

Wingfield, A., Stine, E.L., Lahar, C.J., & Aberdeen, J.S. (1988). Does the capacity of working memory change with age? *Experimental Aging Research, 14,* 103–107.

Woodruff, D.S. (1975). Relationships among EEG alpha frequency, reaction time, and age: A biofeedback study. *Psychophysiology, 12,* 673–681.

APPENDIX

AN ILLUSTRATIVE EPIC PRODUCTION RULE

This production rule illustrates possible WM items, rule conditions, and actions in EPIC:

```
IF
((GOAL DESIGNATE TARGET)
 (STRATEGY MAKE POKE IMMEDIATELY)
 (STEP MAKE POKE-RESPONSE)
 (TAG ?OBJECT IS STIMULUS)
 (VISUAL ?OBJECT COLOR RED)
 (NOT (VISUAL ??? SIZE LARGE))
 (STATUS PERF-TACTICAL RESPONSE-PROCESS HAS EYE)
 (MOTOR MANUAL PROCESSOR FREE))
THEN
((SEND-TO-MOTOR MANUAL PERFORM POKE (LEFT INDEX) ?OBJECT)
 (ADDDB (GOAL WATCH-FOR DESIGNATION-EFFECT))
 (DELDB (STEP MAKE POKE-RESPONSE))
 (ADDDB (STEP WAIT-FOR WATCHING-DONE))))
```

The function of this rule is to touch a small red object on a display screen, designating it as a target by poking it with the left index finger. Embedded in the rule's conditions are multiple expressions that must be true conjunctively with respect to the contents of WM: Here, the goal (control-store item) is to designate a target; the strategy (control-store item) is to make the poke movement immediately; the current procedural step (control-store item) calls for making a poke movement; a certain visual object has been tagged as "the stimulus" (tag-store item); the tagged stimulus object (visual WM item) is red; no large object is in view (i.e., visual WM lacks any items about "large" objects); the process responsible for making the poke has a status (control-store item) that enables it to move EPIC's eye; and the state of the manual motor processor (control-store item) indicates that it is free to accept movement commands. If and when EPIC's various WM stores contain all requisite items for matching this rule's conditions, then one of the rule's actions will command the manual motor processor to make a poke movement with the left index finger at the stimulus object. Also, the rule's other actions will establish a new subgoal (control-store item) to be accomplished next, delete the current step item, and add an item for the next step.

EUROPEAN JOURNAL OF COGNITIVE PSYCHOLOGY, 2001, *13* (1/2), 165–186

Modelling cognitive control in task switching and ageing

Nachshon Meiran and Alex Gotler

Ben-Gurion University of Negev, Beer-Sheva, Israel

In an attempt to better understand the reasons for old-age effects on task switching performance, we fitted a quantitative model (Meiran, 2000a) to results from an experiment comparing young and elderly participants. Modelling results indicate that the most pronounced effect of old age was in what can be broadly defined as the duration of the response selection. In addition, compared to young participants, the elderly tended to rely on learning from the preceding trial, which improved their performance in single-task conditions but impaired it when the tasks switched frequently. Relatively modest effects of old age were found in the ability to selectively attend to the task relevant stimulus dimension and on the duration of processing stages preceding or following response selection.

Old age is known to affect cognitive functioning. Physiological evidence (e.g., Raz, Gunning-Dixon, Head, Dupuis, & Acker, 1998) and neuropsychological evidence (e.g., West, 1996) suggest that old age most strongly affects the frontal lobes. Since the frontal lobes are commonly believed to be involved in cognitive control, a reasonable conjecture is that old age has an especially large influence on cognitive control functioning. Along this line, we examined the influence of age on task-switching performance, which is commonly believed to reflect control functioning. Specifically, we applied a model of task switching we have developed (Meiran, 2000a, b; Meiran, Chorev, & Shapir, 2000a; Meiran, Levine, Meiran, & Henik, 2000b) in an effort to interpret old-age effects on task-switching performance. The model has two aspects. The first aspect refers to the fractio-

Requests for reprints should be addressed to N. Meiran, Department of Behavioral Sciences and Zlotowski Center for Neuroscience, Ben-Gurion University of the Negev, Beer-Sheva, Israel. Email: nmeiran@bgumail.bgu.ac.il

This research was supported by a research grant from the Israeli Science Foundation to the first author.

http://www.tandf.co.uk/journals/pp/09541446.html   DOI:10.1080/09541440042000269

nation of task-alternation cost into components. In this paper, we provide only a short description of this aspect of the model. A more complete treatment of the literature on the differential effects of old age on the various components may be found in Meiran, Gotler, and Perlman (in press). The second aspect is more central here and refers to a processing model, which describes the underlying processes involved in task switching performance and enables one to estimate the relevant process parameters based on empirical results. In the present paper we used this model in an attempt to gain a better understanding of the pattern of old-age effects in task switching performance.

A MODEL OF TASK SWITCHING: STUDIES ON NORMAL YOUNG ADULTS

Components of alternation cost

Task switching often produces a sizeable decrement in performance (e.g., Allport, Styles, & Hsieh, 1994; De Jong, 2000; Gopher, Armony, & Greenshpan, 2000; Jersild, 1927; Los, 1999; Mayr & Keele, 2000; Meiran, 1996, 2000a, b; Meiran, Chorev, & Sapir, in press; Rogers & Monsell, 1995). Following Goschke (2000), Los (1999), and Rogers and Monsell (1995), we argue that task switching affects several component processes. One approach to identifying the component processes involved in task switching was suggested by Fagot (1994). In order to identify the components, Fagot distinguished between three experimental conditions. In explaining these conditions, we will mark each trial in a sequence by the task being performed, Task A (e.g., colour discrimination) or Task B (e.g., shape discrimination). The first condition is (1) *single task* (AAA ..., BBB ...); the second condition involves trials immediately following a task switch in mixed-tasks blocks (*switch trials*, e.g., AB**B**AB); and the third condition involves task repetition trials in mixed task blocks (*nonswitch trials*, e.g., AB**B**AB). Usually, the best performance is found in the single-task condition; the worst performance is found in switch trials. Thus, the difference between reaction time (RT) in single task conditions versus switch trials reflects the joint contribution of all component processes and is termed *alternation cost*. Alternation cost is decomposed into two large components: *mixing cost* (nonswitch RT minus single task RT) and *switching cost* (switch RT minus nonswitch RT).

Fagot (1994) decomposed switching cost into two subcomponents that are similar to what we call preparatory cost and residual cost (see later). Later, we (Meiran, Chorev, & Sapir, 2000) identified a third subcomponent, dissipating cost. To do so, we employed the cueing version of the task-switching paradigm. In that paradigm, trials involving the various tasks are ordered randomly, and each trial begins with instructions telling participants which task to execute. Instructions are conveyed by means of symbolic cues. Using instructional cues allowed us to manipulate two intervals. One, the response–cue interval (RCI), is the interval following the response in Trial N–1, when the participant waits for the instructional cue in Trial N. RCI is unlikely to be used for active preparation because the participant has not yet received the information regarding the next task to perform (see Meiran, Chorev, & Sapir, for supporting evidence). Nonetheless, extending the RCI resulted in a significant reduction in switching cost. We also manipulated task preparation time, the cue–target interval (CTI). CTI represents a period during which participants already know which task comes next and can prepare for that task. Accordingly, we found that increasingly the CTI strongly reduced switching cost. Finally, even when given plenty of time to prepare, participants seem to have been unable to eliminate switching cost. Based on these results, we decomposed switching cost into (1) *dissipation component*, related to cost that is reduced by increasing RCI; (2) *preparatory component*, reflecting cost reduced by increasing CTI; and (3) *residual component* (see Figure 1).

At a somewhat less technical level, mixing cost may be interpreted as reflecting performance decrement due to the mere relevance of several tasks rather than a single task. Switching cost represents performance decrement due to having just switched tasks. Its dissipating component

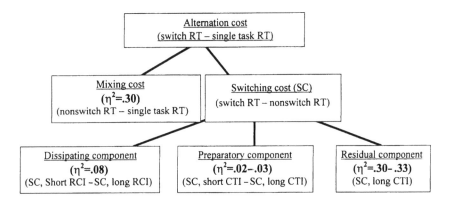

Figure 1. Components of alternation cost.* (η^2 values represent the proportion of aging-related variance in the specific component in Meiran, Gotler, & Perlman's, in press, experiments).

may be interpreted as set disengagement/forgetting and its preparatory component may be interpreted as resulting from set engagement.

Aside from these apparent differences, there is empirical evidence showing that the various components of alternation cost reflect different underlying processes or different combinations of underlying processes. The evidence is based on empirical dissociations, namely, variables that affect the components differentially (see Fagot, 1994, and Meiran, 2000b, for a partial list of these dissociations). The results concerning ageing constitute one of these dissociations, since old age is associated with a pattern of both relatively impaired and relatively intact components. In Figure 1, we present the proportion of old-age related variance (η^2) in each component of alternation cost in Meiran, Gotler, and Perlman's (in press) study. As may be seen, the proportion of old-age related variance was large for mixing cost (see also Hartley, Kieley, & Slabach, 1990; Kray & Lindenberger, 2000) and residual cost (especially De Jong, Emans, Eenshuistra, & Wagenmakers, 2000, but see also Salthouse, Fristoe, McGurthy, & Hambrick, 1998). In contrast, the effect of old age on preparatory cost was negligible (see De Jong et al., 2000; Hartley, et al., 1990; Kramer, Hahn, & Gopher, 1999; Kray & Lindenberger, 2000; and Mayr & Liebscher, this issue). There is an alternative explanation to this finding, suggesting that because the elderly are generally slower, this results in larger switching cost. If preparation was normal among the elderly, it should have resulted in larger reduction in switching cost than among young participants. The fact that preparatory cost was numerically similar in the two age groups suggests, according to this line of reasoning, that preparation was, in fact, less efficient among the elderly. The reason being that the proportional reduction in switching cost was smaller among the elderly, for whom the total switching cost was larger. However, we argue that the normal preparatory cost cannot be the result of general slowing, because the elderly exhibit switching costs in conditions in which young participants usually show zero residual costs (Meiran, Gotler, & Perlman, in press, Exp. 2). Put differently, general slowing may be interpreted as suggesting that all RTs are proportionally slowed. Accordingly, multiplying an effect with a size of zero by a proportional-slowing factor would result in zero, and we have found otherwise. To summarise, the performance of the elderly suffered relatively substantially from the mere presence of trials involving an alternative task (mixing cost), and from immediate switching (residual cost). However, the elderly were nearly as efficient as young participants in preparing for a task switch (preparatory cost).

Processing model

The second stage in our research involves identifying the processes that underlie the components (Meiran, 2000a, b). We suggest that the context in which the tasks are intermixed makes some task elements multivalent. An example of a multivalent task element is a bivalent target stimulus such as *red-X* in a context where participants switch between colour discrimination and letter discrimination. It is bivalent because it is relevant for both tasks. Note that the same target stimulus would have been considered univalent if either colour or letter, but not both, were the only relevant dimensions.

To enable responding according to task requirements, task sets are activated whenever a given task element is multivalent. Each task set is responsible for one multivalent task element, (e.g., the target stimulus, the response, which arithmetic operation to perform, "–5" or "+3", etc.). Moreover, task sets may be activated at different points in time. Some sets are activated by the instructional cues prior to task execution proper. This phenomenon, jointly termed "advanced reconfiguration", is reflected in the reduction in switching cost by preparation (i.e., the preparatory component). Other task sets are activated later. One possibility is to activate the task set only after the presentation of a target stimulus, a phenomenon termed "stimulus cued completion [of reconfiguration]" (Rogers & Monsell, 1995). The other possibility, "retroactive adjustment" is to activate the task set after responding. This reflects learning from experience. Stimulus-cued completion and retroactive adjustment produce residual cost, which is cost that is unaffected by advanced preparation.

In the paradigm we used (Figure 2), participants were asked to perform two tasks involving position discrimination: RIGHT–LEFT, where the vertical dimension is to be ignored, and UP–DOWN, where the horizontal dimension is to be ignored. Thus, in this particular paradigm, the target stimuli as well as the responses were bivalent. Target positions were bivalent because one aspect of target position was relevant for the task at hand (and irrelevant for the alternative task) while another aspect was irrelevant for the task at hand but relevant for the alternative task. An example is the upper-left location, where the UP feature is relevant in the context of the UP–DOWN task but irrelevant in the context of the RIGHT–LEFT task. Similarly, LEFT is irrelevant in the context of the UP–DOWN task but relevant in the context of the RIGHT–LEFT task. Moreover, both of the physical responses (key presses) were used to indicate two nominal responses. For example, a given key press indicated both UP and LEFT, depending on the task. Therefore, the responses were also bivalent. Because the target stimuli as well as the responses were bivalent, two types of task set needed to be employed, a *stimulus task set* (S-Set), that deals with stimulus ambiguity, and *response task sets* (R-Sets), that deal with response ambiguity. The two types of set operate in a similar manner (although the sets themselves are adjusted differently). The S-Set and R-Sets act on low level representations in which relevant

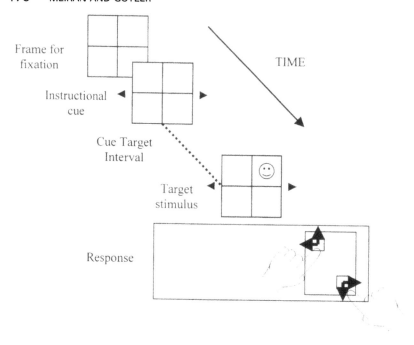

Figure 2. The experimental paradigm used by Meiran, Gotler, and Perlman (in press).

and irrelevant features are equally weighted. As a result of applying the task sets, more abstract representations are generated in which one feature is emphasised while the other feature is de-emphasised. For example, the application of the S-Set may result in representing a target stimulus positioned in the upper-left corner as mostly UP, with the feature LEFT being relatively de-emphasised or ignored. At present we cannot determine if emphasis is achieved by activating the relevant feature, inhibiting the irrelevant feature, or both. However, recent evidence suggests an important role of inhibitory influences (Mayr & Keele, 2000).

According to our model, switching costs arise in two separate processing stages (Figure 3). First, task-switching entails an added processing stage associated with advanced reconfiguration of the S-Set. Advanced reconfiguration involves the biasing of the S-Set such that features that correspond to the task-relevant dimension are strongly emphasised relative to irrelevant features. Second, because the R-Sets are adjusted after responding in Trial N–1, when a task-switch occurs in Trial N, these sets are inappropriately biased in favour of the wrong task. As will

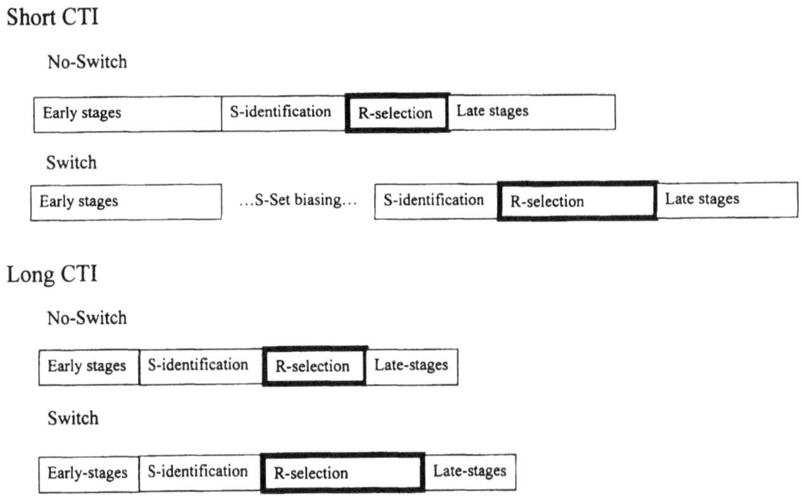

Short CTI

No-Switch

| Early stages | S-identification | **R-selection** | Late stages |

Switch

| Early stages | ...S-Set biasing... | S-identification | **R-selection** | Late stages |

Long CTI

No-Switch

| Early stages | S-identification | **R-selection** | Late-stages |

Switch

| Early-stages | S-identification | **R-selection** | Late-stages |

Figure 3. Processing stages affected by task switching (from Meiran, 2000a. Reproduced with kind permission of Springer-Verlag from Figures 2 and 3 in 'Modeling cognitive control in task-switching', *Psychological Research*, *63*, 234–249).

become clearer soon, these inappropriate biases prolong response selection. Furthermore, since R-Set adjustment takes place after responding to Trial N–1, it is insensitive to the CTI in Trial N, which results in residual cost. In other words, we argue that residual cost is reflected in the prolongation of the response selection stage.

We have modelled response selection by a pattern-matching process, based on an interaction between abstract stimulus and response representations. The task sets act as filters, which block some parts of the information while emphasising other parts of that information (see Figure 4). Put differently, the S-Set is believed to reflect selective attention to a particular dimension in the target stimulus, while the R-Sets reflect selective attention to a particular dimension of the physical response. The dimensions of the physical responses (key presses) refer to the nominal responses which they indicate, e.g. "LEFT" for the RIGHT–LEFT task and "UP" for the UP–DOWN task.

An important difference between the S-Set and the R-Sets refers to the point in time in which these sets are being adjusted. The S-Set is adjusted prior to response selection, and this adjustment can take place during the CTI in response to the instructional cue. Therefore, the S-Set that is used in Trial N is adjusted according to the task-relevant dimension in Trial N.

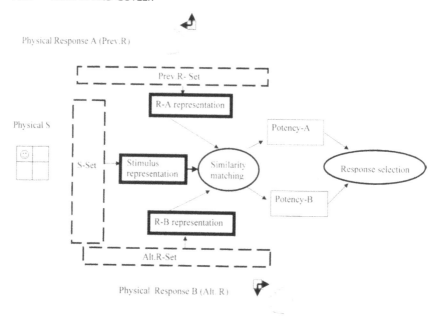

Figure 4. Outline of the processing model (from Meiran, 2000a. Reproduced with kind permission of Springer-Verlag from Figures 2 and 3 in 'Modeling cognitive control in task-switching', *Psychological Research, 63*, 234–249).

In contrast, R-Sets are adjusted, at least partly, by an incremental learning process taking place after responding. Therefore, the R-Sets used in Trial N were adjusted in Trial N–1, implying that the R-Sets are adjusted according to the task-relevant dimension in Trial N–1. In the case of a task repetition, the R-Sets are properly adjusted, because the task relevant dimension in Trial N happens to be the same as that in Trial N–1. However, in switch trials, the R-Sets are adjusted according to the wrong task. Given these features of response task sets, flexible intentional control over performance *in the given task-switching situation* is based primarily on control over the S-Set.

With respect to R-Set adjustment, we suggest that this process is based on labelling the physical responses (key presses) according to the nominal responses they indicate. For example, pressing a key to indicate the nominal response, "UP", presumably results in representing the key press as indicating UP more than LEFT. This learning process probably applies more strongly to the response that had just been emitted as compared to the one which has not been emitted. Thus, the model includes a separate R-Set for each physical response.

Response selection in the model is based on determining the similarity between the abstract stimulus code and the abstract response codes. Consequently, each physical response gains *potency*, representing its "similarity" to the target stimulus, with the most potent response being selected. RT is determined by the relative potency of the responses, and thus reflects response competition. This description translates into a series of equations as explained later. Readers can skip the mathematical description and go directly to "Modeling task switching performance" but before they do so, we should explain the three most important parameters of the model. These include parameters representing the degree of bias (in proportions, with .50 representing no bias) in the task sets *during response selection*. Note that the task sets change their values dynamically, but these dynamics are *not* captured in the task-set parameters. The dynamics of S-Set adjustment are represented in another parameter, W_{CTI-S}, representing the duration, in ms, of the S-Set adjustment process preceding response selection (Figure 3).

W_S represents the S-Set bias in favour of the task-relevant stimulus dimension. If $W_S > .5$, this implies that the task-relevant stimulus dimension in Trial N is more heavily emphasised than the irrelevant dimension. $W_{Prev.R}$ and $W_{Alt.R}$ represent the bias of the R-Sets. This bias is in favour of the relevant dimension *in Trial N–1*. If $W_{Prev.R} > .5$ and/or $W_{Alt.R} > .5$, this implies that the task-relevant response dimension in Trial N–1 is more heavily emphasised than the irrelevant dimension in Trial N–1. An optimally biased S-Set would be associated with $W_S = 1$, reflecting perfect filtering of the irrelevant target-stimulus dimension. In task switching situations, an optimal value for both R-Sets would be .50, representing zero counter-productive post-response adjustment of the R-Sets. Adjusting R-Sets retroactively is productive in single-task conditions where the task in Trial N–1 is the same as the task in Trial N.

Two additional parameters are of interest. These parameters are related to the fact that the model does not yield true RT, but instead yields an analogue of RT*. The model is fit to experimental results by a search algorithm but changes the values of the parameters so that the Pearson correlation between RT and RT* is maximised. This correlation is related to a linear regression, whose two parameters, slope and intercept, are important in comparing age groups. Slope differences between groups reflect the relative speed of what may be broadly defined as response selection processes. The reason is that the slope parameter represents that variation in ms per one unit variation in RT*. Moreover, the variation in RT* is entirely due to the effect of response repetition, congruency, and task-switch, variables whose effects are being modelled. These variables are believed to affect response selection—broadly defined, differences in the slope parameter represent the relative length of response selection. Along a similar line of argument, the (corrected) intercept represents the total duration of processes preceding or coming after response selection, namely stages that are unaffected by congruency task-switch, and response-repetition.

The mathematical description of the model

Formal description of stimuli and responses. Physical target-stimuli and physical responses are represented in the model as a quadruple of zeros and ones. The first two numbers describe the vertical dimension (UP and DOWN, respectively). The last two numbers describe the horizontal dimension (RIGHT, and LEFT, respectively). For example, the pattern "1,0,0,1", represents UP-LEFT. When the pattern refers to a target stimulus, it describes a location, such as the upper-left location. When it represents a physical response, it describes the nominal responses that are indicated by committing that physical response. For example, the previous list describes the physical Response A in Figure 4 because this physical response indicates two nominal responses, UP and LEFT.

Abstract mental codes of stimuli and the responses are quadruples of positive fractions, determined by multiplying the elements in the physical stimulus/response (1 or 0) by the appropriate weights. The weights serve as task-sets. S-Set is related to w_S ($0 \leqslant W_s \leqslant 1$), representing the bias in favour of the task-relevant dimension in the current trial (Trial N). Accordingly, $1-W_s$ is the weight assigned to the task-irrelevant dimension. How the S-Set is applied may be clearer when we consider the example where the task is UP–DOWN, making the relevant stimulus dimension the vertical dimension. In this case, W_s may equal .95, which implies that the (task-relevant) vertical dimension is much more heavily weighted than the horizontal dimension, that is, the irrelevant dimension receives a weight of $1-W_s = .05$. Continuing the example, the abstract representation of the upper-left target stimulus ("1,0,0,1") would be "W_s, 0, 0, $1-W_s$", or ".95, 0, 0, .05".

Unlike the S-Set, where the weight represents the bias in favour of the task-relevant dimension in Trial N, *in the R-Sets, the weights represent the bias in favour of the dimension that was task-relevant in Trial N–1.* Accordingly, $W_{Prev.R}$ represents the bias in Prev.R, and $W_{Alt.R}$ represents the bias in Alt.R ($0 \leqslant W_{Prev.R}, W_{Alt.R} \leqslant 1$). The application of the R-Sets is strictly analogous to the application of the S-Set.

Response selection. Response selection has three separable aspects: Similarity matching, response decision, and RT modelling.

Similarity matching. This process determines which response is "most similar" to the target stimulus, so that a greater degree of similarity results in a relatively potent response. Equation (1) is used to calculate the potency of Response 1, where 1 stands for A (Response A) or B (Response B).

$$(1) \quad P1 = \sum_{i=1}^{k} SiRli \quad (1 = A,B)$$

(k being the number of elements in a list. In the present case k = 4).

Response decision and reaction time. Using response potencies, response strength (Str.) is computed as follows:

$$(2) \quad Str. = P_A - P_B$$

Equation 2 serves two functions: Determining which response is selected, and calculating RT*. The sign of Str. determines which response was more potent, and hence, selected, while |Str.| is related to the quickness of the response, hence:

$$(3) \quad RT^* = 1/|Str.|$$

With RT* being an analogue of RT. Note that the response that was not selected still affects the value of Str. and consequently, affects RT*. This fact reflects the role of response competition, so that a strong competing response results in slower RT.

Model fitting. Note that the equations do not relate the experimental conditions to RT, but to an analogue of it, RT*. In order to fit the model to experimental results, it was assumed for simplicity's sake that RT* is linearly related to RT. Thus, we used a search algorithm to change parameter values in order to maximise the Pearson correlation between RT* and RT. Since the Pearson correlation reflects the strength of the linear between RT and RT*, we also report the parameters in the linear regression relating RT to RT*.

Modelling task switching performance

In this section, we fitted our model to results of Experiment 1 from Meiran, Gotler, and Perlman (in press). The experiment was run in a Kibbutz in the southern part of Israel. An advantage of testing this population is that these people live in a relatively closed community and are relatively homogenous in educational and occupational background. Therefore, the samples of 16 elderly (ages 64–76, mean = 68.3) and 16 young participants (ages 20–29, mean = 24.1) were matched quite closely on these variables (4 additional elderly participants were excluded from the analysis because of making more than 50% errors in the incongruent condition). We used a health questionnaire to exclude participants with a past or present psychiatric diagnosis, and conditions that are likely to affect the brain functioning including hypertension, diabetes, tumours, head trauma, and so forth. The elderly participants were high functioning at the time of the test. There were no significant differences between the groups in vocabulary scores (means, out of 40 were 30.6 and 33.5 for the young and the elderly, respectively), years of education (12.4 and 12.9), or sex distribution (8/8 and 6/10 males/females). In the single-task condition, half of the participants performed the UP–DOWN task and half performed the RIGHT–LEFT task.

The experiment was run as a single session. Participants were first tested in the mixed tasks condition (20 warm-up trials followed by 4 identical blocks, 80 trials each) followed by the single-task condition (1 block of 80 trials). The reason for including the single-task condition at the end of the experiment was that we did not wish to change the relative difficulty of the two tasks when they were mixed. Each trial consisted of: (1) an empty grid presented for a constant RCI of 2032 ms; (2) the presentation of the instructional cue for a variable CTI (116 and 1016 ms); and (3) the presentation of the target stimulus until the response. 400 Hz beeps for 100 ms signalled errors. The instructional cues changed in the mixed-task condition, and were constant in the single-task condition. Participants were explicitly informed regarding the transition to a single task block.

Unlike Meiran, Gotler, and Perlman's (in press) study, we included response-repetition as an independent variable, which is necessary for modelling purposes. Specifically, response-repetition is the variable differentiating $W_{Prev.R}$ from $W_{Alt.R}$. Trials following an error or following a RT exceeding 5 s were excluded. RT in the remaining trials was not analysed if it exceeded 5 s or the response was erroneous. In order to save space we shall restrict the report to the effects involving the added independent variable, response repetition. Alpha was .05. In the analysis of the mixed-tasks condition we found the usual significant interaction between response-repetition and task-switch (e.g., Fagot, 1994; Meiran, 1996, 2000a; Rogers & Monsell, 1995), $F(1, 30) = 22.96$, $MSE = 26658$. Specifically, response-repetition speeded nonswitch RT but slowed switch RT. The triple interaction involving response-repetition, task-switch, and age was nonsignificant. This result indicates that the size of the two-way interaction between response-repetition and task-switch was similar in the two age groups. In our model, the interaction between task-switch and response-repetition is explained by the difference in retroactive-adjustment between the executed response (reflected in the parameter $W_{Prev.R}$), and the response, which has not been executed ($W_{Alt.R}$). Thus, one would expect that the difference between these parameters would be similar in the two age groups, as we have found (see later). In other words, the young participants and the elderly tended to adjust the R-Set of the executed response more than the response that has not been executed.

In the analysis of single-task performance, we excluded the first eight trials in which RT was relatively long. There was a just significant interaction between CTI and response-repetition, $F(1, 30) = 4.14$, $MSe = 2213$, $p = .051$. It indicated that response repetition was facilitatory only when CTI was long (628 vs 610 ms), whereas a weak trend in the opposite direction was found when CTI was short (654 vs 659 ms), for non-repeated and repeated responses, respectively. Our model has little to say about this interaction.

Modelling results

Since the participants were elderly volunteers, we could not test them for very long periods, which resulted in a relatively small number of observations per condition. In order to increase the stability of the results, we modelled group means.

Mixed tasks. We modelled the results including 32 mean RTs. These reflected conditions formed by crossing task-switch, CTI (short/long), congruency (whether the same physical response is indicated as the correct response in the two tasks—*congruent*, or whether the two tasks indicate different correct physical response—*incongruent*), Block (1–2 vs 3–4), and response-repetition. Modelling was performed in each age group, separately (Table 1). The free parameters included the three parameters representing the task-sets (given in proportions), and four additional parameters (given in ms). The additional parameters were (a) W_{CTI}, representing the reduction in RT in the nonswitch condition due to increasing CTI, and (b) W_{CTI-S}, representing the additional reduction in RT in the switch condition. W_{CTI} represents general preparation processes, such as phasic alertness and the prediction of target onset (see Meiran, Chorev, & Sapir, 2000a). In contrast, W_{CTI-S} represents the size of the preparatory component, which, according to our model, reflects the time it takes to bias the S-Set (Figure 3). (c) W_{Block} and (d) $W_{Block-S}$ representing the effect of Block (practice) in the nonswitch condition and the additional effect of Block in the switch condition, respectively. All of the four additional parameters represent differences between means, and as such, the

TABLE 1
Modelling results: Mixed tasks performance

	Young	Old	Proportional age-related decrement
W_S	.955	.934	.46**
$W_{Prev.R}$	.539	.546	.17***
$W_{Alt.R}$	.518	.534	.89***
$W_{Prev.R} - W_{Alt.R}$	.021	.012	
W_{CTI} (ms)	105	181	
W_{CTI-S} (ms)	87	140	
W_{Block} (ms)	99	201	
$W_{Block-S}$ (ms)	47	97	
RT*–RT slope	465	922	.98
RT*–RT intercept	−200	−608	
Corrected intercept	265	314	.18
R^2	.960	.967	

Because the minimal RT = 1, the minimal predicted RT, or the corrected intercept, equals Slope + Intercept.

**Because perfect selectivity implies W_S = 1, the decrement was calculated in terms of the difference between the actual selectivity and perfect selectivity, which was .045 for the young participants and .066 for the elderly.

***Because the best strategy is an unbiased response set (.5), age-related decrement in performance was computed based on the difference between actual biasing and the perfect strategy.

respective effects could have been detected in an ANOVA. In this respect, the model contributes little to our understanding over more standard methods of analysis. The main contribution of the model is in estimation of the three task-set parameters (those represented in proportions).

Features common to both groups. The results indicated a reasonable degree of fit, with R^2 values .960 and .967. This suggests that, as far as we can tell, the model described the strategy of the participants reasonably well. Moreover, if this conclusion is valid, the results also indicate that the strategies adopted by the young and elderly subjects were similar. w_S values indicate that, *when response selection took place*, the task relevant stimulus dimension was strongly emphasised/attended relative to the irrelevant dimension. Note that, according to the model, W_S does not depend on CTI. The reason is that participants are assumed to take as long as needed to bias the S-Set before allowing for the next processing stages to take place (Figure 3). Thus, CTI presumably affects the time it takes to accomplish S-Set biasing (W_{CTI-S}) but CTI does not affect the degree of bias which has been achieved (W_S).

$W_{Prev.R}$ was always larger than $W_{Alt.R}$, a feature that explains the reversal of the response repetition effect in the switch condition (Meiran, 2000a). In explaining this interaction we will use an example. Consider a sequence of trials where Trial N–1 involved the UP–DOWN task and the participant pressed the upper-left key to indicate UP. Consequently, the code for the upper-left response key was adjusted, giving more emphasis to UP (e.g., 6) than to LEFT (e.g., 4). Since the lower-right key was not pressed in Trial N–1, its code was either adjusted more moderately than that of the upper-left key (e.g., .55 and .45) or was not adjusted at all (.5 and .5).

After switching to the RIGHT–LEFT task in Trial N, repeated selection of the upper-left response key would be relatively difficult as compared to selecting the lower-right key press. This is because LEFT is more strongly de-emphasising in the response code corresponding to the upper-left key (.4 in the example) than RIGHT is in the code of the lower-right key (.45 or .5). This explains why response repetition in the context of task switching is associated with response slowing. If, however, Trial N involves task repetition, repeating the response would lead to facilitation, since the relevant interpretation is emphasised in the response. Using the previous example, repeated pressing of the upper-left key to indicate UP would be facilitatory, since UP is relatively strongly emphasised in the mental representation of the response.

Global group differences. An interesting question is to what degree do the differences in the task sets explain the effects of old age on task-switching performance. In an attempt to answer this question, we predicted RT while using the parameters obtained among the young participants, excluding the three task-set parameters. This combination of parameters, when put into the model, simulates the pattern of RTs of a participant who is like the typical young participant in every respect, except for having task-set parameters that are like those obtained by a typical old participant. As a result, we could compare the predicted RT from a typical young participant to that of the simulated participant. This analytic strategy allowed us to examine the changes in RT that are purely due to the change in task-set parameters. Changing the task-set parameters resulted in the following changes in the predicted RT: There was an increase of 28% in switching cost (from 92 to 117 ms), an increase of 27% in congruency effect (from 94 to 119 ms), and a small (4%) increase in mean RT (795 vs. 767). In other words, the fact that the elderly were slower in general is not explained by the differential parameter values, as would be expected, because changing the parameters resulted in only a tiny increase in mean RT. General slowing is explained by the RT–RT* regression parameters, as explained later. Given that, the differential parameter values may be taken as reflecting effects not due to general slowing. These include the increased (residual) switching cost and congruency effects. Put differently, when general slowing is accounted for by the remaining parameters, a change in the task-set parameters alone resulted in a considerable increase in switching cost and in congruency effects.

Focal group differences.   Another way to examine the results is to look at the proportional change in each parameter due to old age. Two parameters were strongly affected by old age. The deviation of $W_{Alt.R}$ from .5 was almost doubled, reflecting the fact that, among the elderly, the difference between the two R-Sets was rather small. This finding indicates that older participants adjusted both response sets retroactively, not only the one associated with the response in Trial N−1. The adjustment of both R-Sets is another expression of the nonsignificant triple interaction between age, response-repetition, and task-switch (see earlier). With respect to the difference between the two R-Sets, Meiran (2000a, b) suggested that the retroactive adjustment of the R-Sets is partly due to response coding (Hommel, 1997), whereas the cognitive representation of the response is linked to its outcome. In the present case, the outcome of a key press was the expression of a nominal response (e.g., "UP"). Because this process applies only or mostly to the response which has just been emitted and not to the alternative response, it is reflected in the difference between $W_{Prev.R}$ and $W_{Alt.R}$. Given the fact that the difference was similar in the two age groups, one may conclude that response coding is not strongly affected by old age.

If response coding does not differentiate between the age groups, then what explains the enlarged residual switching costs among the elderly? In order to answer this question we need to return to the characteristics of the model. In the model, residual cost results from an interaction of two factors. The most important factor is the retroactive adjustment of the R-Sets. However, this factor interacts with the degree of bias in the S-Set. Note that the S-Set is not influenced by the preceding trial, and thus, by itself could not generate switch cost. However, lesser emphasis given to the relevant target-stimulus dimension implies greater emphasis given to the *irrelevant* dimension. More attention to the irrelevant dimension accentuates the effects due to the fact that the irrelevant dimension is emphasised in the R-Sets after a task switch.

Returning to the question regarding residual switching costs in the elderly, the critical factor seems to be the fact that both R-Sets are adjusted retroactively and not only the R-Set of the executed response. One possibility is that, for some reason, the elderly tend to treat the two responses as a group, or an S-R mapping (see Duncan, 1977; Shaffer, 1965).

There were two parameters in the RT–RT* regression: slope and intercept. Before explaining group differences we need to clarify an important point. Given the fact that minimal RT* was 1, the minimal predicted RT equals intercept + slope, which is what we computed as the corrected intercept. The corrected intercept reflects the duration of processing stages that are not modelled (thus not affecting RT*). Returning to the results, we found interesting between-group differences in the RT–RT* slope. The RT–RT* slope was nearly doubled among the elderly, while the (corrected) RT–RT* intercept increased by only 18%. Thus, the regression parameters indicate that old-age related slowing is not general. Old age has a strong influence on the duration of processes related to task switching, response repetition, congruency, and CTI, which we modelled and may be broadly labelled "response selection/preliminary response preparation". In contrast, the RT–RT* intercept represents the duration of low-level perceptual analysis and relatively advanced response preparation processes but were only mildly affected by old age. Such a pattern accords with the neuropsychological evidence, showing greater old-age related damage to the prefrontal cortex than to other brain regions (e.g., West, 1996).

Single task. Because only eight means were modelled (formed by crossing CTI, congruency, and response-repetition), the analysis should be regarded as tentative. In the present analysis, we forced the intercept and slope parameters to equal the values in Table 1 (which is why RT–RT* regression parameters are not included in Table 2). With these values we could predict RT and compare the predicted RT to actual RT. Thus, instead of maximising the Pearson correlation between RT and RT*, we minimised the sum of squared differences between the actual RT and the predicted RT. The results are presented in Table 2 and indicate a poorer degree of fit among the elderly participants as compared to the young ones. While w_S dropped slightly compared to mixed task performance (which should result in a slightly poorer performance), the parameters representing the R-Sets increased appreciably, and more so among the elderly than among the young participants. The somewhat less strongly biased S-Set makes sense since a strongly biased S-Set is required in mixed task performance to ensure correct responding which, in turn, is dependent upon a strongly biased S-Set relative to the R-Sets (see Meiran, 2000a, for an elaboration of this point). In single-task conditions, where the R-Sets are correctly biased (because the task in Trial N–1 is the same as the task in Trial N), such a strongly biased S-Set is no longer required. Note that strongly biased R-Sets represent a reasonable strategy in a single-task condition. Presumably, a strongly biased R-Set reflects the strong (and accumulated) effects of R-Set adjustment, which makes sense given the fact that the physical responses would be consistently mapped

TABLE 2
Modelling results: Single task performance

	Young	Old*	Proportional age-related decrement
W_S	.944	.924	.36**
$W_{Prev.R}$	.686	.753	.36***
$W_{Alt.R}$	.686	.753	.36***
W_{CTI}(ms)	36	39	
R^2	.895	.964	

*The fitting process did not result in successful convergence in this case.
**Because perfect selectivity implies $w_S = 1$, the decrement was calculated in terms of the difference between the actual selectivity and perfect selectivity.
***The proportions represent an advantage of the elderly over the young participants. The estimates were computed by subtracting .50 (unbiased) from the estimates, thus representing the (productive) bias, which was .253 for the elderly and .186 for the young participants.

to their meanings. Learning response meaning makes little sense in mixed-tasks conditions where response meaning changes from trial to trial. For example, a given key press may indicate LEFT in Trial N–1 but it would indicate UP in Trial N. Interestingly, the elderly exhibited an advantage over young participants in their gain from single-task conditions.

The present analysis suggests R-Set adjustment as a common mechanism underlying the enlarged residual costs and mixing costs in old age. Specifically, the elderly exhibited stronger retroactive adjustment of R-Sets in single task conditions, where such adjustment is adaptive, but also in mixed-tasks performance, where such adjustment is counterproductive. The fact that the two R-Set parameters were equal suggests that the incremental retroactive adjustment process reached asymptote, so that the very last update (reflected in $W_{Prev.R}$) did not make a difference compared to less recent updates (represented by $W_{Alt.R}$). As in the analysis of mixed-task performance, we estimated the global effects of the task-set parameters by simulating the performance of a typical young participant. We compared the simulated performance to that of a simulated participant who was similar in every respect except for the task-set parameters, which were like those of a typical old participant. This time, the parameter replacement did not increase congruency effects. Actually, the predicted congruency effect *dropped* from 39 to 36 ms. This result is another expression of the fact that, while there were large old-age influences on congruency effects in mixed tasks conditions (the proportion of old-age related variance was $\eta^2 = .18$), these effects were much smaller (η^2 = .07) and nonsignificant in the single-task condition. According to our model, congruency effects result from less than perfectly and correctly biased S-Set and R-Set. Given the stronger bias of the R-Sets in the single task condition, a bias which is even greater among the elderly than among the younger participants, congruency effects and age differences in these effects should become smaller, as we have found.

DISCUSSION

The present study represents an attempt to characterise task-switching performance in old age in terms of our model. The model has two aspects: describing which components are affected by old age, and estimating model parameters. The results from our laboratory (summarised in Figure 1), agree with most of the literature (Meiran, Gotler, & Perlman, in press, for a review) and indicate a substantial influence of old age on mixing cost and on residual cost (with age group accounting for roughly 30% of the variance in these components). Old age has a smaller influence on congruency effects (roughly 18%) and the rate of set dissipation (roughly 8%). However, old age has a negligible influence on preparatory cost (2–3%).

At the functional level, the modelling results point to four loci of old-age effects, including: (1) the intercept parameter in the regression of RT on RT*, (2) slope parameters in the same regression equation, (3) the task-set parameters, and (4) the duration of S-Set biasing. We will deal with each of them in turn.

The smallest influence of old age was found in the intercept parameter, representing processes preceding response selection and S-Set biasing and processes following response selection. These include low-level perceptual analysis, and relatively advanced response preparation processes. The largest influence of old age was on the slope parameter, suggesting that old age is associated with general slowing in processes related to response selection and initiation. This conclusion concurs with results in the literature showing that ageing has an especially pronounced effect on these processing stages (e.g., Allen, Madden, & Weber, & Groth, 1993; Allen, Smith, Vires-Collins, & Sperry, 1998; Hartley & Little, 1999). In this respect, the present results constitute an important converging operation.

With respect to task-set parameters, the most noteworthy influence of old age was on the R-Sets, illustrating the fact that the elderly had an increased tendency to adjust their performance based on their experience in the preceding trial. This result is completely novel and emphasises the potential of using an explicit modelling approach. For some reason, it appears that the elderly have treated the two responses as a group or mapping. Regardless of this peculiarity, their tendency to learn from the preceding trial caused an advantage in the single-task conditions, but created a disadvantage in the mixed-task conditions. According to the present analysis, the reason why young participants were faster in single-task conditions was mainly due to their generally faster response selection processes, which (over)compensated for their lesser R-Set learning.

Counterproductive effects from the preceding trial, such as those found in the mixed-task conditions, are conceptually analogous to "internal noise", a term used to explain old-age effects in cognitive functioning (e.g., Allen, Weber, & May, 1993; Krueger & Allen, 1987). Thus, our results suggest that (a specific form of) cognitive noise may be an important factor in age-related deterioration in cognitive functioning. Unlike the R-Sets, old-age effects on the S-Set and on W_{CTI-S} were relatively modest. These parameters reflect selective efficiency, and the time it takes to adjust the attentional focus, respectively. Thus, our results support the hypothesis concerning selective attention deficits in old age (e.g., Hasher, Stoltzfus, Zacks, & Rypma, 1991). However, in the present case, the effect of ageing on internal noise (represented by the R-Sets) was much more pronounced than its effect upon attentional selection (the S-Set and W_{CTI-S}). This comparison, made possible by modelling, is yet another advantage of this approach.

To conclude, we used a modelling approach to clarify the reasons underlying age-related differences in task-switching performance. This approach has proven insightful and resulted in a rich and detailed description of performance. Our results led us to conclude that old age had a pronounced effect on the duration of response selection and resulted in an increased tendency to learn from the immediate past experience in the preceding trial. In contrast, old age was associated with relatively minor deficits in selective attention to the task-relevant stimulus dimension and processes preceding or following response selection. These characteristics were true for switching situations and single-task performance alike. The model we applied is still in its infancy, and future research should extend it, making it possible to explore a wide variety of switching paradigms. This is essential in order to examine the generality of the conclusions, as well as for testing their implications.

Manuscript received September 2000

REFERENCES

Allen, P.A., Madden, D.J., Weber, T.A., & Groth, K.E. (1993). Influence of age and processing stage on visual word recognition, *Psychology and Aging, 8*, 274–282.

Allen, P.A., Smith, A.F., Vires-Collins, H., & Sperry, S. (1998). The psychological refractory period: Evidence for age differences in attentional time-sharing. *Psychology and Aging*, *13*, 218–229.

Allen, P.A., Weber, T.A., & May, N. (1993). Age differences in letter and color matching: Selective attention or internal noise. *Journal of Gerontology: Psychological Sciences*, *48*, 69–77.

Allport, D.A., Styles, E.A., & Hsieh, S. (1994). Switching intentional set: Exploring the dynamic control of tasks. In C. Umiltà & M. Moscovitch (Eds.), *Attention and performance XV: Conscious and unconscious processing* (pp. 421–452). Cambridge, MA: MIT Press.

De Jong, R. (2000). Residual switch costs and cognitive control. In S. Monsell & J. Driver (Eds.), *Attention and performance: Control of cognitive processes XVIII*. Cambridge, MA: MIT Press.

De Jong, R., Emans, B., Eenshuistra, R., & Wagenmakers, E.-J. (2000). *Strategies and intrinsic limitations in intentional task control. Manuscript submitted for publication.*

Duncan, J. (1977). Response selection rules in spatial choice reaction tasks. In S. Dornič (Ed.), *Attention and performance VI* (pp. 49–61). Hillsdale, NJ: Lawrence Erlbaum Associates Inc.

Fagot, C. (1994). *Chronometric investigations of task switching.* Unpublished PhD thesis, University of California, San Diego.

Gopher, D., Armony, L., & Greenshpan, Y. (2000). Switching tasks and attention policies. *Journal of Experimental Psychology: General*, *129*, 308–339.

Goschke, T. (2000). Decomposing the central executive: Persistence, deactivation, and reconfiguration of voluntary task set. In S. Monsell & J. Driver (Eds.), *Attention and Performance XVIII: Control of cognitive processes.* Cambridge, MA: MIT Press.

Hartley, A.A., Kieley, J.M., & Slabach, E.H. (1990). Age differences and similarities in the effects of cues and prompts. *Journal of Experimental Psychology: Human Perception and Performance*, *16*, 523–537.

Hartley, A.A., & Little, D.M. (1999). Age-related differences and similarities in dual-task interference. *Journal of Experimental Psychology: General*, *128*, 416–449.

Hasher, L., Stoltzfus, E.R., Zacks, R.T., & Rypma, B. (1991). Age and inhibition. *Journal of Experimental Psychology: Learning, Memory, and Cognition*, 17, 163–169.

Hommel, B. (1997). Toward an action-concept model of stimulus–response compatibility. In B. Hommel & W. Prinz (Eds.), *Theoretical issues in stimulus-response compatibility* (pp. 281–320). Amsterdam: North-Holland.

Jersild, A.T. (1927). Mental set and shift. *Archives of Psychology*, *14*, Whole No. 89.

Kramer, A.F., Hahn, S. & Gopher, D. (1999). Task coordination and aging: Explorations of executive control processes in the task switching paradigm. *Acta Psychologica*, *101*, 339–378.

Kray, J., & Lindenberger, U. (2000). Adult age differences in task-switching. *Psychology and Aging*, *15*, 126–147.

Krueger, L.E., & Allen, P.A. (1987). Same–different judgements of foveal and parafoveal letter pairs by older adults. *Perception and Psychophysics*, *41*, 329–334.

Los, S.A. (1999). Identifying stimuli of different perceptual categories in mixed blocks of trials: Evidence for cost in switching between computational processes. *Journal of Experimental Psychology: Human Perception and Performance*, *25*, 3–23.

Mayr, U., & Keele, S.W. (2000). Changing internal constraints on action: The role of backward inhibition. *Journal of Experimental Psychology: General*, *129*, 4–26.

Meiran, N. (1996). Reconfiguration of processing mode prior to task performance. *Journal of Experimental Psychology: Learning, Memory and Cognition*, *22*, 1423–1442.

Meiran, N. (2000a). Modelling cognitive control in task-switching. *Psychological Research*, *63*, 234–249.

Meiran, N. (2000b). The reconfiguration of the stimulus task-set and the response task set during task switching. In S. Monsell & J. Driver (Eds.), *Attention and performance XVIII: Control of cognitive processes*. Cambridge, MA: MIT Press.

Meiran, N., Chorev, Z., & Sapir, A. (2000a). Component processes in task switching. *Cognitive Psychology, 41*, 211–253.

Meiran, N., Gotler, A., & Perlman, A. (in press). Old age is associated with a pattern of relatively-intact and relatively-impaired task set switching abilities. *Journal of Gerontology: Psychological Sciences*.

Meiran, N., Levine, J., Meiran, N., & Henik, A. (2000b). Task-set switching in schizophrenia. *Neuropsychology, 14*, 471–482.

Raz, N., Gunning-Dixon, F.M., Head, D., Dupuis, J.H., & Acker, J.D. (1998). Neuroanatomical correlates of cognitive aging: Evidence from structural magnetic resonance imaging. *Neuropsychology, 12*, 95–114.

Rogers, R.D., & Monsell, S. (1995). Costs of a predictable switch between simple cognitive tasks. *Journal of Experimental Psychology: General, 124*, 207–231.

Salthouse, T.A., Fristoe, N., McGurthy, K.E., & Hambrick, D.Z. (1998). Relation of task switching to speed, age, and fluid intelligence. *Psychology and Aging, 13*, 445–461.

Shaffer, L.H. (1965). Choice reaction with variable S-R mapping. *Journal of Experimental Psychology, 70*, 284–288.

West, R.J. (1996). An application of prefrontal cortex function theory to cognitive aging. *Psychological Bulletin, 120*, 272–292.

EUROPEAN JOURNAL OF COGNITIVE PSYCHOLOGY, 2001, *13* (1/2), 187–215

Beyond resources: Formal models of complexity effects and age differences in working memory

Klaus Oberauer and Reinhold Kliegl

University of Potsdam, Germany

We explore several alternative formal models of working memory capacity limits and of the effect of ageing on these capacity limits. Three models test variations of resource accounts, one assumes a fixed number of free slots in working memory, one is based on decay and processing speed, one attributes capacity limits to interference, and one to crosstalk between associations of content and context representations. The models are evaluated by fitting them to time–accuracy functions of 16 young and 17 old adults working on a numerical memory-updating task under varied memory-load conditions. With increasing complexity (i.e., memory load), both asymptotic accuracy and the rate of approach to the asymptote decreased. Old adults reached lower asymptotes with the more complex tasks, and had generally slower rates. The interference model and the decay model fit the individual time–accuracy functions reasonably well, whereas the other models failed to account for the data. Within the interference model, age effects could be attributed to the older adults' higher susceptibility to interference. Within the decay model, old adults differed from young adults by a higher degree of variability in the activation of working memory contents.

A well-documented finding in cognitive ageing research is that old adults perform considerably worse than young adults in tasks that require high amounts of working memory capacity (e.g., Babcock, 1994; Mayr & Kliegl, 1993; Salthouse, 1994). Research on individual differences as well as on cognitive development and ageing has shown that working memory

Requests for reprints should be addressed to K. Oberauer, Department of Psychology, University of Potsdam, PO Box 60 15 53, 14415 Potsdam, Germany.
Email: ko@rz.uni-potsdam.de

This research was funded through Deutsche Forschungsgemeinschaft (Grant INK 12, Project C). We thank Petra Grüttner, Hannelore Gensel, Anke Demmrich, and Alexandra Engst for research assistance. Thanks to Stephan Lewandowsky, Ulrich Mayr, David Meyer, and Dan Spieler for thoughtful comments on earlier versions of the paper.

http://www.tandf.co.uk/journals/pp/09541446.html   DOI:10.1080/09541440042000278

capacity is a crucial limiting factor for human performance on a broad range of reasoning tasks (e.g., Case, 1985; Kyllonen & Christal, 1990; Salthouse, 1991). To understand the growth and decline of reasoning ability over the life span, therefore, it seems particularly important to understand the factors that limit working memory capacity in the first place. The purpose of this paper is to explore a number of hypotheses about the nature of capacity limits in working memory. We will propose a formal framework for modelling performance in working memory tasks, and pit a number of mathematical models incorporating different assumptions about the nature of capacity limits against each other within this framework. These models will be tested with data from young and old adults on a representative working memory task. Our goal is to narrow down a set of simple, plausible models of capacity limits in working memory to one or two promising candidates, and to identify the parameters of the viable models that carry age differences.

THE NATURE OF CAPACITY LIMITS IN WORKING MEMORY

We will discuss five potential sources of capacity limits in working memory: (1) limited cognitive resources, (2) a fixed capacity to hold a certain number of information elements simultaneously available, sometimes referred to as a "magical number", (3) a speed account based on the race between decay of memory traces and rehearsal, (4) similarity-based interference, and (5) crosstalk between elements in a memory set.

Limited resources

One common account of working memory capacity limits is that the cognitive system has limited resources for simultaneous storage and processing. Resource theories assume that resources are general (although they may be confined to broad domains like verbal or spatial contents); resources can be allocated to tasks and processes flexibly; and the amount of resources a person can spend at any moment is roughly constant during short periods of time. Two well elaborated models addressing capacity limits in cognition, ACT-R (Anderson, Reder, & Lebiere, 1996) and CAPS (Just & Carpenter, 1992), are based on the idea of limited resources. Resource theories have been criticised for being too vague and unconstrained (e.g., Meyer & Kieras, 1997; Navon, 1984). The theoretical precision of resource theories can be improved by fleshing them out as formal models, as was done with ACT-R and CAPS. Our own attempts to model working memory performance borrow many basic assumptions from these two approaches.

Magical numbers

The idea of a "magical number" of information elements or chunks that can be held in short-term memory was first discussed by Miller (1956) in his famous paper on the "magical number seven". Recently, the idea of a maximum number of chunks to be held in working memory was revived by Halford, Wilson, and Phillips (1998) and by Cowan (in press), who argued for a "magical number" around four. Apparently larger capacities of short-term or working memory in some tasks arise, so they argue, from chunking or rehearsal strategies or long-term memory contributions that increase recall performance over and above the basic capacity. To measure the "magical number", one therefore must use a task that rules out additional help from strategies, long-term memory, and other sources as much as possible.

Decay and rehearsal

Research on verbal short-term memory has produced serious doubts about a constant number of chunks that can be immediately recalled independent of material. One important finding was the word-length effect, a linear relationship between pronunciation time for a class of words and memory span for the same words (Baddeley, Thomson, & Buchanan, 1975). It led researchers to the conclusion that the limiting factor for immediate serial recall of verbal material is not a "magical number" of chunks, but a certain maximum articulation time—what Schweickert and Boruff (1986) called the "magic spell". One way to understand this finding is to assume a constant decay rate for memory traces, which can be refreshed by rehearsal with a speed that roughly corresponds the time to articulate the words. If traces decay below retrieval threshold within a certain time, the maximum span will equal the number of words that can be articulated in this time. The capacity limit results from a race between decay and rehearsal.

This model was first applied to the phonological loop, a short-term retention system for verbal material (Baddeley, 1986). It can be extended, however, to working memory in general. Many working memory tasks require the retention of information while the same or different information is manipulated. If we assume that memory traces decay by a constant rate, then the probability that a given information element is still available when it is needed for a processing step depends on the speed of earlier processing steps during which it had to be remembered. Working memory performance then is a function of the race between decay and processing speed. This may explain why working memory and processing speed measures share a large part of their age-related variance (Salthouse, 1996).

Similarity-based interference and crosstalk

Interference and crosstalk are two strongly related concepts, which are rarely distinguished in the literature; we distinguish them here because they lead to different formalisations of capacity limits. Both concepts rest on the assumption that working memory for some material is impaired by the presence of other, similar, material. We define interference as mutual degradation of memory traces that are held in working memory simultaneously. For example, the representation of a new word might overwrite all features of an old word that are shared among the two (Nairne, 1990), or features belonging to different words might mix up to new, spurious representations (Tehan & Humphreys, 1998).

We define crosstalk as the confusion between two elements that are held simultaneously in working memory. Like interference, crosstalk is a function of similarity between memory elements. Different from interference, which has an effect on the memory traces themselves, crosstalk arises at the selection of one out of several elements in working memory. Crosstalk is the basic mechanism that limits memory span in recent models of serial recall that are based on Hebbian associations between list items and contextual cues (Brown, Preece, & Hulme, 2000; Burgess & Hitch, 1999; Henson, 1998). At retrieval, a context representation coding a given ordinal list position cues the corresponding item at this position. Due to overlap between neighbouring ordinal positions, however, neighbouring list items are also cued, and occasionally a wrong item is activated highest and is selected for output. Note that through this mechanism the representation of the correct item is not degraded, so that there is a high probability that it will be recalled on another position (cf. Henson, Norris, Page, & Baddeley, 1996).

Old age and inhibition

Each of these hypothetical sources of capacity limits is compatible with the inhibition account of working memory deficits in old age as proposed by Hasher and Zacks (1988; Hasher, Zacks, & May, 1999). The general idea is that old adults have less efficient inhibitory processes that eliminate no-longer relevant contents from working memory and prevent irrelevant material from entering working memory. This leaves old adults with more irrelevant information in working memory. Irrelevant material can take away resources or free slots from the relevant material. Irrelevant material can overwrite relevant working memory contents or become confused with them. Irrelevant information can also distract people from rehearsing the relevant material and thereby lead to more forgetting. Therefore, we regard the inhibition-deficit hypothesis not as a further genuine source of capacity limits, but as a hypothesis about why capacity limits, whatever their cause may be, are exaggerated in old age.

A FRAMEWORK FOR MODELLING WORKING MEMORY CAPACITY

Our strategy is to compare different assumptions about the source of capacity limits by building them into a common formal framework. This section will develop such a framework that should be applicable to many, if not all working memory tasks.

We assume that the function of working memory is to hold a number of distinct information elements (e.g., numbers, words, objects, spatial positions) available for ongoing processes. This means that elements in working memory can be retrieved efficiently and selectively as inputs for cognitive operations. This function can be fulfilled by a system that links episodic representations of content elements (i.e., tokens of numbers, words, etc.) to context representations (i.e., temporal contexts, list positions, spatial positions, syntactic roles in parse trees, etc.). The links between content and context representations must be built and dissolved quickly, because usually there is not much time to encode new information into working memory or to update its contents. According to this framework, working memory is more than just a subset of highly activated representations in long-term memory, as was proposed in some models (Anderson, 1983; Cantor & Engle, 1993). Working memory contents must be both activated and flexibly linked to contexts.

We further assume that errors in working memory tasks arise mainly (as an idealisation in the models: exclusively) at retrieval. That is, we assume that the elementary processing steps by which information is manipulated are error free. This assumption is justified for working memory tasks that require only trivial processes like, for example, single-digit addition and subtraction and other tasks where participants usually perform close to ceiling when the memory load is minimal. Conway and Engle (1996) have shown that the difficulty of the processes involved in a working memory task does not play a role for its validity as a measure of working memory. Süß, Oberauer, Wittmann, Wilhelm, and Schulze (2000) provide evidence that working memory tasks with trivial elementary operations are good predictors of reasoning ability. Working memory tasks are difficult, and they tap capacity limits, because of their complexity and not because of the difficulty of the elementary cognitive processes they require. The complexity of a working memory task can be defined as the number of independent elements that must be kept available simultaneously (i.e., the memory load).

The probability of retrieving a single element i from working memory is modelled as a function of this element's activation level at the time of retrieval, A_i. An element in working memory is successfully retrieved as input for a cognitive operation if its activation value surpasses a threshold τ. In its deterministic form, the performance function that transforms activation into retrieval accuracy is a step function. We assume, however, that the activation level of an element, and therefore its availability, is affected by Gaussian noise. The probability of successful retrieval, therefore, follows the cumulative probability of a normal distribution with mean A_i and standard deviation σ, which can be approximated by the logistic function (cf. Anderson & Matessa, 1997):

$$p = \frac{1}{1 + \exp(-(A_i - \tau)/s)} \tag{1}$$

with $s = \mathrm{sqrt}(3)\sigma/\pi$. The logistic function is shown in Figure 1a. Most of the models discussed in this paper will use the logistic function to relate activation to retrieval accuracy. Only the crosstalk model will use a variant of this function to capture the competition between target and distractor elements during retrieval.

Processes in working memory take time, and the most important dependent variable in cognitive psychology besides accuracy is latency. A model of working memory capacity should specify the duration of information processing steps. For the family of models explored here, we

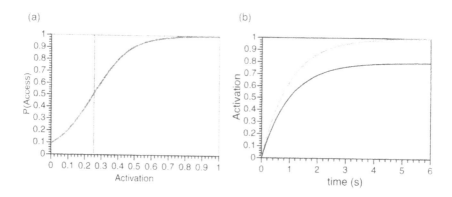

Figure 1. (a) Logistic performance function relating an element's availability to the probability of successful access. The threshold parameter is set to 0.25 and σ to 0.2. (b) Exponential functions for activation accumulation with an asymptote of 1 (dotted line) and with an asymptote of 0.8 (solid line), the rate parameter is set to 1.

assume that information is manipulated by cognitive operations that generate a new element in working memory and gradually increase its activation. The increase of activation is assumed to follow a negatively accelerated exponential function with the general form:

$$A_i = \alpha_i \, (1 - \exp(-t/r_i)), \tag{2}$$

where t is the time since the new element was created, r_i is the rate of activation for the new element, and α_i is the asymptote of activation for the new element i (see Figure 1b). The assumption of processing by gradually activating new elements is incorporated in several models, among them CAPS (Just & Carpenter, 1992) and the cascade model (McClelland, 1979). For one variant of a resource model, we will deviate from this equation to introduce a latency function directly borrowed from ACT-R (Anderson & Lebiere, 1998).

Differences between individuals and groups are assumed to arise from differences in parameter values. In modelling working memory performance for young and old adults, we hope to identify a subset of parameters on which age differences are pronounced. Provided that a viable model can be identified, this will help us to characterise the source of age-related cognitive deficits in complex cognition. Our working hypothesis is that the same parameter that drives the decline in performance with increasing memory load (i.e., the complexity effect) also carries the largest part of the age-related variance. This hypothesis directly implies the Age × Complexity interaction found with many cognitive tasks (e.g., Salthouse, 1992): The complexity effect will be stronger for old adults.

To summarise, we propose to build formal models of working memory capacity from three building blocks:

(1) A processing model for the specific task for which performance is modelled, which specifies the number of independent memory elements required at each time during task solution and the sequence of processing steps required for a solution.
(2) A complexity function that expresses the activation of each content element A_i as a function of task complexity (i.e., the number of content elements that are held in memory at the same time).
(3) Performance functions that express accuracy of retrieval for an element i and latency of processing element i as a function of this element's current activation level A_i.

Taken together, these three building blocks should suffice to make exact predictions for task solution accuracies and latencies of a person working on a task if the person's parameter values are known: The process model determines how many representation elements and processing steps are needed for task solution. The complexity function then determines the activation level of the elements that need to be retrieved at any step. The expected performance scores (accuracy and speed) can be computed by applying the performance functions to this information.

An unknown number of free parameters is hidden in the task-specific process model: Researchers have considerable freedom in specifying how a task is done. In particular, the information required for task solution and the transformations that must be performed on it can be segmented into elementary units in many different ways, yielding quite different complexity values for a task. Does a proposition, for example, count as a single element in working memory, or should we count the number of concepts linked by it? We propose, therefore, to develop a capacity model with as simple tasks as possible in order to limit the space of plausible processing models. We will present our process model together with the first resource model later, after introducing the memory-updating task in the next section.

THE EXPERIMENT

Method

Participants. Eighteen young adults (eight men and ten women; mean age 19.1 years, SD: 0.68) and eighteen old adults (nine women and nine men; mean age 68.8, SD: 3.55) were recruited from the Potsdam participant pool. The young group consisted of high school students, the old participants had responded to newspaper advertisements or were friends or relatives of other participants. The two groups were roughly equivalent in years of formal schooling (young: 11.67 years, SD: .69, old: 10.59 years, SD: 1.62) and a vocabulary test (young: 22.1, SD: 3.92, old: 23.3, SD: 4.55). Young adults performed better on the digit symbol test than old adults (young: 63.1, SD: 9.4, old: 45.4, SD: 8.0). Groups did not differ in their ratings of subjective health as "good". Thus, the two groups were comparable to typical samples of young and healthy old adults in the literature with respect to standard indicators of cognitive status. Participants were paid 15 DM (i.e., about $8) for each one-hour session.

Seventeen old and sixteen young adults from the first part of the experiment could be recruited for a second part. We present only data from the 33 participants who completed the whole experiment.

Materials and procedure.   We chose a numerical memory-updating task introduced by Salthouse, Babcock, and Shaw (1991) to generate a data set for testing our models. Each trial began with simultaneous presentation of *n* digits, where *n* represents the working memory load. Each digit was presented in a separate rectangular frame; the frames were arranged on a virtual circle on the screen. After the initial numbers disappeared, arithmetic operations (e.g., " + 2" or "–5") appeared in individual frames, one at a time. Participants had to apply the operation to the number in the respective frame, thereby updating it in their memory. Eight operations were presented in a regular sequence, always starting with the same frame and moving clockwise through the circular arrangement of frames. After eight arithmetic operations, all frames were probed by question marks in a random order, and participants were required to type the final results of the probed frames on the computer keyboard. An example task is illustrated in Figure 2.

This task has several advantages. First, it was shown to have high loadings on a working memory factor in a comprehensive individual-differences study (Oberauer, Süß, Schulze, Wilhelm, & Wittmann, 2000). Second, it uses only very simple elementary operations (single-digit addition and subtraction). Third, the memory load, as well as the number

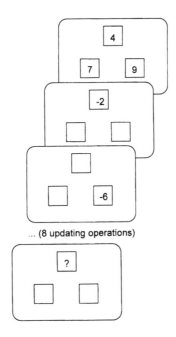

... (8 updating operations)

Figure 2.   Example trials for memory updating with a memory demand of three digits.

of successive operations, can be varied flexibly over a large range. Fourth, the task is not amenable to obvious strategies to surpass a hypothetical capacity limit; e.g., chunking the elements is of little use because they must be updated individually. Finally, the experimenter has control over the available processing time for each updating step by manipulating the presentation time for individual arithmetic operations. We used an adaptive algorithm (Kaernbach, 1991) to vary presentation times for the updating operations over the whole range from chance to nearly asymptotic performance within each memory load condition. This allowed us to determine time-accuracy functions for each participant and each memory load condition.

Participants were informed that final results, as well as all intermediate values, always were numbers between 1 and 9. A time limit of 3000 ms (young) or 5000 ms (old) was set for each response; responses surpassing this limit elicited the feedback message "too slow" instead of "correct" or "false". These responses were nevertheless registered and treated as valid data because the time limit served only to prevent extensive computations after the last operation had been presented.[1] We also instructed participants that only trials with correct responses on all probes counted as passed to discourage the strategy of ignoring some frames from the beginning. Percentage of correct responses was used as score for each trial.

The experiment had two parts. In the first part, old and young adults worked on the memory-updating task with memory loads of one, two, three, and four. In the second part, we extended the range of memory loads, testing the same participants with loads of four, five, and six digits. The load factor was varied between blocks of 13 trials, and counterbalanced within each part of the experiment. For each memory load condition, 234 trials were presented.[2]

Results

A convenient way to summarise the results is to present parameter estimates from descriptive time–accuracy functions. Based on experience

---

[1]Reaction times for keying in the first results were 1232 ms (SD = 1025) for young adults and 1868 ms (SD = 1717) for old adults. This leaves little time for additional computations after the end of the presentation time. If response times were used for computations, this should be the case more often with short than with very long presentation times. The reaction times for the shortest and the longest presentation times, however, differed by only 272 ms for young adults and not at all for old adults.

[2]Details about the adaptive algorithm and the models described only briefly here can be inspected in a technical report at our webpage: http://www.psych.uni-potsdam.de/people/ oberauer/working-e.html

with similar data (Kliegl, Mayr, & Krampe, 1994; Mayr, Kliegl, & Krampe, 1996; Verhaeghen, Kliegl, & Mayr, 1997), we used negatively accelerated exponential functions of the form

$$p = d + (c - d)(1 - \exp(-(t - a)/b)),$$ (3)

where d is a parameter for chance performance, c represents asymptotic performance, b is the rate of approaching asymptote, and a the point in time (t) where accuracy (p) rises above chance. For the present purpose, we fixed d to 1/9, because participants knew that each result must be a number between 1 and 9, leaving three free parameters for each participant and condition. Parameter estimation was done with the CLNR module of SPSS with a Maximum Likelihood loss function called G^2, which can be interpreted like a Chi^2 measure of deviation. Eight functions were fit for each participant simultaneously, five for the memory load conditions in the first part of the experiment, and three for the conditions in the second part.[3]

The descriptive functions yielded an excellent fit with G^2 values for individual data ranging from 28.13 to 97.78. Overall G^2 was 1702.8. Subtracting the free parameters for 33 subjects from the total of 3173 data points yields 2381 degrees of freedom, so that this value is far from significant.

Two summary indicators of performance were extracted from the time-accuracy functions. First, parameter c from equation 3 reflects the asymptotic accuracy reached when processing time is not externally limited. Second, we computed criterion-referenced presentation times (CPTs) relative to the asymptotes. CPTs can be derived from equation 3 by setting p to the desired relative criterion k (e.g., 80% of asymptote) and solving for t:

$$CPT = a + b\left[\ln\left(\frac{c - d}{c}\right) - \ln(1 - k)\right]$$ (4)

Relative CPTs represent the time a participant needs to reach a given proportion of her or his asymptote in a condition. Thus, CPTs reflect processing speed conditional on asymptotic accuracy. Figure 3 shows mean asymptotic accuracies for young and old adults (a) and CPTs for 80% of the asymptotes (b).

---

[3]The memory demand one condition was realised in two slightly different ways, which did not differ significantly in any respect and therefore were aggregated for all further analyses.

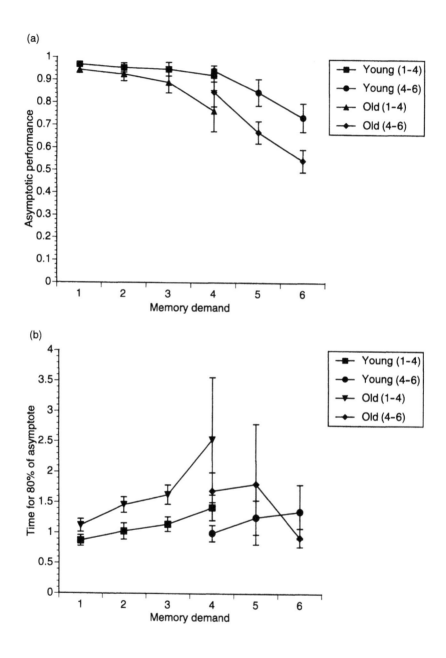

Figure 3. Parameters from exponential time–accuracy functions for young and old adults. (a) asymptotic accuracy. (b) relative criterion-referenced presentation time for 80% of the asymptote. Error bars represent two standard errors.

The data yielded four basic facts that a model should capture.

(1) Asymptotic performance declined with increasing memory load, $F(7, 217) = 77.2$, $MSe = 0.01$. The effect was clearly nonlinear with a highly significant quadratic trend, $F(1, 31) = 39.19$, $MSe = 0.01$, indicating a positively accelerated decline of the performance asymptote with increasing memory load.

(2) The decline in asymptotic accuracy was more pronounced in old adults, leading to an interaction of age and memory load, $F(2, 217) = 7.85$, $MSe = 0.01$.

(3) Processing time, as reflected by the CPTs, increased with memory load, $F(7, 217) = 18.76$, $MSe = 0.59$.

(4) Old adults were slower than young adults ($F = 11.28$, $MSe = 1.12$), and age interacted with memory load ($F = 2.72$, $MSe = 0.59$). In general, age differences increased with higher memory load, as can be expected when old adults are slowed by a constant proportion relative to young adults (Cerella, 1985).

There is a notable exception to the fourth observation for memory load condition 6, where old adults apparently needed less time than young adults to reach 80% of their asymptote. This anomaly in the data pattern was most likely due to strategic influences. If one decides to concentrate on only part of the memory set from the beginning, for example focus on three out of six elements, then a subset of operations can also be ignored. The time for these operations can in effect be used to process the remaining operations. As a result, the actual processing time for each attempted operation is much more than the presentation time controlled by the programme. This leads to an underestimation of processing time needed to reach a relative criterion. In a post-experimental debriefing session, a majority of the old adults confirmed that they used this strategy in the most demanding condition, despite being instructed not to do so, because they felt unable to do the task in any other way.

There was a clear effect of practice from the first to the second part of the experiment, evident in the improvement on memory load level 4. Both asymptotic accuracy ($F = 5.73$, $MSe = 0.01$) and log-transformed CPT values ($F = 10.41$, $MSe = 0.13$) were significantly better in the second part. Practice effects did not interact with age.

THE MODELS

We will first discuss a resource model for the memory-updating task. This model will also serve to explain our processing model for the memory-updating task and how the assumptions of each working memory model are linked to the processing model. Next we will briefly discuss two alternative resource models, and show that a magical number model makes predictions equivalent to one of these resource models. We will then test a model based on a race between decay and rehearsal, and finally turn to models incorporating interference and crosstalk, respectively.

Resource models

A resource sharing model. The most straightforward way to flesh out the notion of limited resources is to postulate a constant quantity of activation that is shared among the elements held in working memory at any time. This leads to a simple complexity function:

$$A_i = W/n \tag{5}$$

where W is the available activation and n is the memory load. Each initial number receives activation according to equation 5 before it is first updated. The task begins with an attempt to retrieve the number in the frame where the first arithmetic operation appears. The success of this attempt can be computed by the logistic function given in equation 1. If retrieval succeeds, the arithmetic operation is applied and the result is gradually activated according to the negative exponential (equation 2) until the presentation time for the operation is over. Since the new element must share the total activation resource with all other elements in working memory plus the arithmetic operand presented on the screen, its asymptote will be A_i as computed by equation 5, but with n = memory load + 1. The rate of activation is a function of the source activation, that is the activation of the elements that serve as input for the cognitive operation, and the connection weights linking the source elements to the resulting element. This is an assumption borrowed directly from CAPS (Just & Carpenter, 1992), but also incorporated in many other models based on spread of activation in semantic or connectionist networks. In the memory-updating task, the source activation comes from the two addends, one retrieved from memory and one presented on the screen:

$$r_i = w_{ji} A_j + w_{ki} A_k \tag{6}$$

Here, w_{ji} is the connection weight from source item j to target item i and w_{ki} is the weight connecting source k to target i. For simplicity, we assume that all addends have equal association weights with the result they generate. This allows us to reduce the individual association weights to a common parameter w. This parameter captures the speed with which activation is transmitted to the new element i, and therefore can be interpreted as a processing speed parameter for a person working on a specific task like addition or subtraction. The parameter w can vary with the type of operation, thereby reflecting mean latency differences between various operations, and with persons or groups of persons, thereby reflecting individual differences in processing speed.

At the first updating step, both addends will have an activation value close to A_i as computed by equation 6. At later steps, the activation of the element retrieved from memory can be considerably lower, because new elements gain activation only gradually according to equation 2, and with short presentation times, the results of earlier computations will not have been activated to asymptote. As a consequence, they will be less likely to be retrieved later, and if they are retrieved, they contribute less source activation to the next updating step in which they serve as an addend.

The models discussed here treat an updating step as a single operation, although it can certainly be broken down into distinct components like activation of the operand, retrieval of the required arithmetic fact, replacement of the old element by the new one, gradual activation of the new element, and maybe rehearsal of all the elements in working memory. The present data, however, do not allow us to distinguish these components, so we summarise them all in the accumulation of activation for a new element. Further research should try to disentangle the contributions of distinct processing components to the overall time demand for an updating step.

Because activation of the memory elements changes over the eight updating steps, the model must be computed iteratively. The model for a single trial consists of eight successive operation cycles, followed by n cycles with the attempt to recall the final values in each frame. For each cycle, the probability of retrieving the element and an activation value for the new element is computed. At the end of all the cycles, the probability of recalling each final element correctly is computed as

$$P_i = 1/9 + 8/9 \prod_c p_{ic} \qquad (7)$$

where p_{ic} is the success probability for retrieving element i in cycle c. The multiplication runs over all cycles where i was updated plus the final recall (e.g., four plus one cycles for each element at memory load level two); 1/9 is added for guessing probability.

The effect of practice between the first and the second part of the experiment was captured by a learning parameter h. We assumed that practice affects primarily the speed with which new elements can be activated because practice with the memory-updating task strengthens the weights between source and target elements used in arithmetic. Thus, the w parameters in equation 6 are multiplied with h in the three conditions from the second part of the experiment. The learning parameter was restricted to be larger than one to reflect positive gains from practice.

Finally, we introduced a strategic parameter specifically for the memory demand of six elements. We assumed that some participants (mostly from the old group) ignored a subset k of the six elements from the beginning, thereby effectively reducing n to $6-k$ and increasing their mean processing time per operation to t times $6/(6-k)$.

To summarise, the first model has six free parameters: The total activation resource W, the speed parameter w, the standard deviation of activation σ, the access threshold τ, the learning parameter h, and the strategy parameter k. Most of the assumptions and parameters outlined in this section are common to all (or at least most) of the models discussed here, only the complexity function expressed in equation 5 is a distinctive feature of the first resource model.

We fit this model to the data from 33 participants, leaving all six parameters free to vary among individuals. This implies that the model has $33 \times 6 = 198$ free parameters overall. They were subtracted from the total number of observations, yielding 2975 degrees of freedom (ranging from 81 to 96 for individual participants). The best fit we were able to produce with model 1 by trying various starting values yielded G^2 values from 49.99 to 250.85 for individual participants, the total G^2 was 4891. This indicates a highly significant deviation from the data.

For comparability, the predicted accuracy values computed by the model were submitted to the same treatment as the observed ones. This means that we estimated exponential time–accuracy functions for each participant and condition according to equation 3 and extracted asymptotic accuracy and the CPTs for 80% of the asymptote as performance indicators. Inspection of these predictions showed that the model captured the asymptotes quite well, but did poorly on the CPTs (space restrictions do not allow us to show the predictions here—see footnote 2). Since model 1 obviously does not fit the present data, we will not present further analyses of parameter estimates.

Resource models inspired by ACT-R and CAPS. There are several ways a resource model could be specified within our general framework. In addition to the one presented earlier, we tried two other variants, one inspired by ACT-R (Anderson et al., 1996) and one motivated by CAPS (Just & Carpenter, 1992). In ACT-R, processing time is not modelled as the gradual increase of activation for a new element. Instead, new elements receive their activation instantaneously, and a time demand for processing arises at retrieval. The time to retrieve an element is a function of this element's activation. We designed a model that incorporates the relevant equations from ACT-R. Since many assumptions of our framework common to all the models were also inspired by ACT-R, we believe that this variant of a resource model comes very close to the way the memory-updating task would be specified in ACT-R. This model had an overall G^2 of 3995.4 (range 60.72 to 163.83), which is better than the original resource model, but again deviates significantly from the data. Panels A and B of Figure 4 show the predictions.

The model inspired by CAPS differs from the previous models by its resource allocation policy. In the previous two resource models, the available activation is always distributed completely among the elements in working memory. An alternative allocation scheme is to provide each element with the activation it demands as long as there are sufficient resources, and cut down on activation proportionally when the sum of all demands surpasses the available resources. This scheme is incorporated in CAPS (Just & Carpenter, 1992) and can be formalised by a modified complexity function:

$$A_i = d_i \qquad \text{if } \sum_{j=1}^{n} d_j \leqslant W \tag{8}$$

$$A_i = d_i \, \frac{W}{n} \qquad \text{if } \sum_{j=1}^{n} d_j > W$$

With this modification, the resource model yielded an overall G^2 of 3193.7 (range 40.6–216.9), which is much better than the previous two models, but still indicates a significant deviation from the data with 2975 degrees of freedom ($p = .003$).

Why did the resource models fail? To sum up, all three resource models did not fit the data well. Why did these models fail? Consider the complexity function of the first and second model (equation 5), which is plotted in Figure 5 for a typical high capacity person ($W = 1$) and a typical low capacity person ($W = 0.7$). With increasing memory load, there is a steep drop in the activation allocated to a single element at the beginning of the complexity scale, which becomes much shallower at the higher end. Moreover, the differences between high and low capacity persons diminish with increasing complexity. The empirical asymptotic accuracies, however, remained stable over the first part of the complexity scale and decreased at higher complexity with positive acceleration. And the accuracy of young and old adults diverged with increasing complexity.

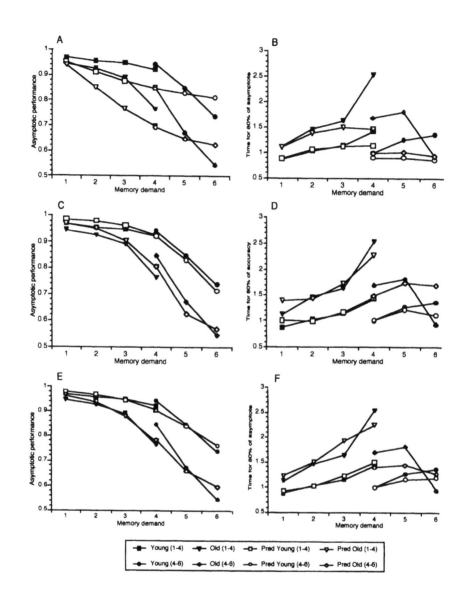

Figure 4. Data and model predictions for parameters of time–accuracy functions for the three models. A: Asymptotic accuracies for the second resource model (with equations from ACT-R). B: Relative criterion-referenced presentation times for 80% of asymptote, second resource model. C: Asymptotic accuracies for the decay model. D: Relative criterion referenced presentation times for the decay model. E: Asymptotic accuracies for the interference model. F: Relative criterion referenced presentation times for the interference model.

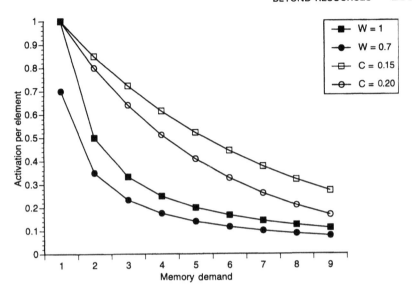

Figure 5. Mean activation of a single item as a function of complexity. Complexity functions are plotted for one high-capacity and one low-capacity individual. Solid squares and circles represent activation functions for resource sharing (with a resource pool W); open squares and circles are activation functions for the interference model (with an interference parameter C).

Likewise, the CPTs increased in an approximately linear way (disturbed by the effects of practice and strategy) and show no sign of convergence of young and old with increasing complexity. A model with a complexity function that behaves opposite to the data will obviously have difficulty reproducing these data. The logistic performance function (equation 1) helps to compensate the inconvenient form of the complexity function, but not enough to reach a good fit. This becomes manifest, for example, in the predictions for asymptotic accuracies derived from the second resource model (Figure 4, panel A), which decline in a negatively accelerated fashion, contrary to the data (Figure 3).

A "magical number" model

Models that assume a capacity for a fixed number of elements can be formalised by the same complexity function as was introduced for the earlier CAPS-oriented model (equation 8). Let us assume that each element that manages to enter working memory receives an activation level of one, and each element that does not find a slot receives zero activation. As long as the memory demand is less than or equal to the "magical number", all elements receive the full activation with a probability of one. If memory demand surpasses the "magical number", each element receives an activation of 1 with probability W/n, where W is the "magical number". Over many trials, the statistical expected value of activation for each element will then equal W/n. Hence, the complexity function of a "magical number" model can be expressed as equation 8. It turns out that a "magical number" model will make the same predictions that would be made by a resource model incorporating the complexity function of CAPS. As a consequence, the "magical number" model will also fail to give a satisfactory account of the data.

A decay-based model

Another plausible idea used to explain the limits of short term or working memory is time-based decay (e.g., Anderson & Matessa, 1997; Byrne, 1998). In this subsection, we discuss a model variant that incorporates the idea that working memory capacity is limited by the interplay of decay and reactivation.

The rationale of the decay model is as follows: The asymptote for the gradual activation of working memory elements is always one, independent of memory load. Each element in working memory decays according to a logarithmic decay rate (cf. Anderson & Matessa, 1997). The rate of decay δ is a free parameter:

$$A_t = A_0 - \delta \ln(t) \tag{9}$$

Decay can be counteracted by reactivation, e.g., through rehearsal. Rehearsal is modelled by equation 2, but with a specific rate parameter for rehearsal. All processes, including reactivation of working memory elements, are performed serially and therefore must share the available processing time. When confronted with a task that requires both manipulation and retention of information, the cognitive system must decide on what proportion of the total processing time is allocated to the manipulation task. This proportion is expressed by the parameter T. The time available for the arithmetic operation in the memory-updating task therefore is T times the presentation time t, and the time available for the reactivation of each of the remaining elements in working memory equals $(t-T)/(n-1)$, assuming that the rehearsal time is distributed evenly among the elements in memory. Thus, with increasing memory demand n the amount of reactivation for each element decreases, and this explains the decrease of asymptotic accuracy and the increase of time demand with memory load. The decay model has eight free parameters for each person, two more than model 1. We had to introduce three new parameters—T, δ, and the rate parameter for rehearsal—in return for the one saved (the resource parameter W).

Our decay model fit the data remarkably well. Overall G^2 was 2741.9 (range 49.3–140.8), which was not significant with 2909 degrees of freedom. Only two out of 33 individual data sets showed a deviation from the model significant at the 5% level. Figure 4 (panels C and D) shows that the predictions traced the asymptotic accuracies and criterion-referenced presentation times with only minor deviations (except for the drop in time demands at memory demand six for old adults, which was underestimated despite of the extra parameter k introduced for it).

Since the decay model gives a satisfactory account for the data, we can use it to investigate age differences in its parameters. The mean parameters of both age groups are summarised in Table 1. Significant age differences emerged for the standard deviation of activation and for the strategy parameter. Old adults' activation of working memory elements seems to be noisier, and they decided more frequently than young adults to drop some elements from the beginning when their capacity was overloaded. There was a nonsignificant trend for slower processing in old adults, but the estimated rehearsal rates were essentially the same for both age groups.

An interference model

Our interference model starts from the assumption that each element is represented in working memory by a set of features. The activation of an element i is the sum of the activation of its features. Any two elements i and j share a proportion C_{ij} of features. When two elements are held in working memory simultaneously, the features they have in common are

TABLE 1
Parameter estimates for decay model, young and old adults

Parameter	Young	Old	t (diff)	p (diff)
r (rehearsal rate)	3.06 (2.70)	3.0 (2.83)	0.05	.96
T (time split)	0.86 (0.15)	0.88 (0.15)	0.40	.69
δ (decay rate)	0.05 (0.01)	0.06 (0.01)	1.86	.07
w (speed)	1.22 (0.39)	0.99 (0.44)	1.57	.13
σ (stdev)	0.19 (0.03)	0.23 (0.07)	2.42	.02
τ (threshold)	0.26 (0.15)	0.23 (0.15)	0.65	.52
h (learning)	1.31 (0.16)	1.34 (0.19)	0.44	.66
k (strategy)	0.65 (0.68)	1.67 (1.33)	2.83	< .01

lost for these representations. One reson why this might happen is because features recruited by two different content elements that are linked to different context representations cannot be bound unambiguously to a specific context. Another reason could be that features included in a vector representing one element are overwritten when a new element including the same feature enters working memory.

Let us assume that an element receives a total activation of one if all its features become fully activated. The activation of an element in the context of other elements can then be expressed as the proportion of the element's features that are not lost through interference. When C_{ij} is the proportion of features that two elements i and j have in common, the proportion of their features that is still active when i and j interfere with each other is $1-C_{ij}$. For more than two elements in working memory, we assume that the sets of overlapping elements are independent of each other. Thus, the proportion of active features of element i can be expressed as

$$A_i = \prod_{j=1}^{n-1} (1 - C_{ij}) \tag{10}$$

with n as the number of elements in working memory. When the degree of overlap among all elements is the same, as can be assumed for a homogeneous set of elements spaced evenly in their respective coordinate system (i.e., no grouping), this reduces to

$$A_i = (1 - C)^{(n-1)} \tag{11}$$

with C as a common interference parameter for a given class of elements (e.g., digits). This provides the complexity function for the interference model. When applied to the memory-updating task, n equals the memory demand plus one, because the arithmetic operation adds one more digit to the set of elements in working memory that interfere with each other. Except for the new complexity function, the interference model is exactly like the first resource model developed earlier.

The interference model had an excellent fit with G^2 values ranging from 40.59 to 130.76 for individual participants. Only one out of 33 individual models was rejected with an alpha level of .05. The overall G^2 was 2524.87 with 2975 degrees of freedom, which is not significant. The predicted asymptotic accuracies and CPT values are plotted in panels E and F of Figure 4. The predictions are generally close to the data, except for the CPT values at higher memory demand levels for old adults. Like the decay model, the interference model underestimates the size of the drop in CPT between memory demands five and six. The data points where the model deviates from the observations, however, have large interindividual variability (see Figure 3), and since the model was fit to individual data, the group aggregates might not reflect the degree of fit on an individual level.

Table 2 presents the means and standard deviations of the six parameters for the two age groups. Separate comparisons revealed significant age differences only in the interference parameter C. This is compatible with the notion that young and old adults differ in their working memory capacity, defined as the capacity to resist interference in working memory. Presumably as a consequence of their reduced capacity, old adults showed a tendency to focus more frequently than young adults on only a subset of elements in the most complex condition. Age differences in several other parameters were marginally significant, so we cannot rule out the hypothesis that additional factors besides working memory differ between young and old adults.

Figure 5 shows the complexity functions of the interference model for a typical young adult ($C = 0.15$) and a typical old adult ($C = 0.2$). In comparison to the complexity functions of the resource models, these functions exhibit a less dramatic negative acceleration, which makes it easier for the interference model to fit the positively accelerated drop of asymptotic performance with increasing memory load. Perhaps more important, the two curves diverge with increasing memory load, so that the interference model can explain the Age × Complexity interaction much better than the resource models.

A crosstalk model

The crosstalk model differs from all other models in that memory load has no effect at all on the activation level of elements in working memory. Memory load effects arise only from the increased chance of

TABLE 2
Parameter estimates for interference model, young and old adults

Parameter	Young	Old	t(diff)	p(diff)
C (interference)	0.14 (0.03)	0.17 (0.05)	2.69	.01
w (speed)	1.67 (0.31)	1.46 (0.43)	1.57	.13
σ (stdev)	0.19 (0.03)	0.21 (0.05)	1.29	.21
τ (threshold)	0.22 (0.12)	0.20 (0.14)	0.37	.72
h (learning)	1.51 (0.25)	1.69 (0.33)	1.78	.08
k (strategy)	0.12 (0.21)	0.32 (0.41)	1.79	.08

selecting the wrong element from the memory set at retrieval. The general assumption is that the system selects the element with the highest activation at the moment of retrieval. The activation of the content elements comes from the context cues to which they are associated. A given context cue (e.g., a position in a list or a frame on the screen) will usually activate the target element most, but it will also spread activation to competing elements that are also associated to it (e.g., Burgess & Hitch, 1999). Crosstalk is one way to arrive at erroneous retrievals from long-term memory in ACT-R (Anderson & Lebiere, 1998). We incorporated the idea of crosstalk into our modelling framework by modifying the logistic performance function (equation 1) in such a way that it reflects the joint probability of an item i being activated above threshold *and* being activated higher than all other items in working memory. There is no limit to the activation resource, and no interference, so the effect of memory load is attributed entirely to increasing competition at retrieval.

The crosstalk model did not fit the data adequately. Overall G^2 was 3751.2 (range 45.2–231.8), a highly significant deviation from the data (*df* = 2975). The pattern of residuals suggests that the crosstalk model has similar problems as most of the resource models: It predicts a decelerated decline in performance for both asymptotic accuracy and speed, whereas the actual decline is accelerated for the asymptotes and approximately linear for the CPT's (ignoring the deviant point at memory demand 6).

DISCUSSION

We tested seven formal models of capacity limits in working memory with the same comprehensive data set. Only two models—one based on decay, one based on interference as the source of capacity limits—fit the data adequately. Several other models based on limited resources, a "magical number" limit, or crosstalk between context-content associations failed to reproduce the time–accuracy functions.

Implications for theories of capacity limits

The models we tested were designed to represent the most important hypotheses about the nature of capacity limits in the literature. We formalised these hypotheses within a common framework in order to make the models as comparable as possible. We also tried to keep the models simple (i.e., limiting the number of free parameters), while giving them the best chance possible to fit the data.

The failure of models tested here does not disprove conclusively the hypotheses on which they are based. It is possible that another model incorporating the idea of a limited resource pool, the assumption of a "magical number", or the crosstalk hypothesis will be able to reproduce the present data adequately. We suspect, however, that such a model will not be easily found. Where one of the models failed, we could identify the reason for its failure as one rooted in the underlying assumptions, not in some arbitrary feature of our formalisation.

As things stand, we regard the interference model as the best account of our data. The decay-based model also had an adequate fit, but it used two more free parameters, so that we prefer the interference model for reasons of simplicity.

Implications for Cognitive Ageing

Our data with the memory-updating task showed a pattern typical for the effect of ageing on working memory: Old adults performed worse on the task, in particular with higher memory load levels. Unfortunately, ordinal interactions like these are difficult to interpret, because a nonlinear monotonic scale transformation of the dependent variable (e.g., percentage correct) can make them disappear (Loftus, 1978; Kliegl et al., 1994). Formal models like those explored here can help to overcome this difficulty, because they make explicit assumptions about the transformations that translate a hypothetical variable (e.g., activation) into an observable outcome (e.g., percentage correct). For most of our models, we assume that a logistic function relates the activation value of an element into an observable performance score. Within a given model, we can therefore infer the hypothetical activation levels from the observable performance. To the degree that a model passes a rigorous test, we can be confident that the parameter estimates reflect theoretically meaningful constructs. A good model can then be used to measure hypothetical variables like activation, decay rate, or degree of interference. We can then ask, among other things, which of these variables is sensitive to an effect of ageing, and thereby attempt to pin down the source of ageing-related cognitive deficits.

The two models that accounted satisfactorily for the present data trace the source of the age difference to different parameters. In the decay model, it was mainly the Gaussian noise assumed for the activation levels of individual elements in working memory that distinguished the age groups. Although this model attributes the capacity limits of working memory to a speed factor (i.e., the speed of processing the computations and/or the speed of rehearsal, relative to the decay of information in memory), none of the two speed parameters reliably distinguished old and young adults. Thus, there is little evidence in our data for the speed theory of working memory decline in old age, as advanced by Salthouse

(1996). The results of the decay model are better compatible with the idea that ageing is associated with increased noise in the cognitive system (Allen, 1991; Allen, Kaufman, Smith, & Propper, 1998; Welford, 1958). Increased variability in the activation of working memory elements could also arise from non-optimal rehearsal strategies (e.g., rehearsing some items too often and others not often enough), which might point to a deficit in the control of attention as one aspect of executive functions (Engle, Kane, & Tuholski, 1999).

The results from the interference model suggest that old adults are more susceptible to interference than young adults. Consistent with this, Li (1999) reported that old adults suffer more from dual-task interference when an arithmetic task was combined with the memorisation of digits than when it was combined with memorisation of words. Presumably, the numbers involved in the arithmetic tasks have more feature overlap with the digit memory lists than with the words, resulting in a higher degree of interference which particularly impairs old adults.

The conclusion from the interference model seems to be at odds with results from a meta-analysis by Jenkins, Myerson, Hale, and Fry (1999). They compared simple memory spans with spans when a secondary task is added, and found that old and young adults did not differ in the amount of interference from the secondary task. Jenkins et al. (1999) noted, however, that the two age groups had different baselines (i.e., different mean simple spans). When subgroups of young and old adults with nearly equivalent simple spans were compared, the old subgroups showed larger interference effects than the young subgroups. A look at panel E of Figure 4 shows how the interference model proposed here can account for these data: Asymptotic accuracy declines over increasing complexity with positive acceleration. This implies that adding a constant amount of interfering material has a smaller absolute effect on performance when it is added at a lower complexity level than when it is added at a higher baseline of complexity. Thus, although old adults' performance drops steeper with increasing complexity, this is compensated by the fact that their baseline (i.e., simple spans) lies lower on the complexity scale. As a result, the drop in performance due to the same amount of additional interfering information is about equal for young and old adults.

One potential reason for the increased susceptibility to interference of old adults could be a reduced ability to inhibit irrelevant information (Hasher et al., 1999). Updating of working memory contents requires, among other things, to forget the old values when they are replaced. If old adults are less successful in getting rid of the old values, the remaining representations of old elements in working memory add to the total interference. In particular, each item suffers interference from $n-1$

present items plus n old elements, the latter weighted by the degree to which the old elements are still associated with the n frames.

Conclusions

A decline in working memory performance is a characteristic phenomenon of cognitive ageing. In this paper, we explored a number of potential factors that could be responsible for the limit of working memory capacity, and that could be affected by ageing. We think that our formalisation of a number of simple accounts of working memory capacity helps to chart the search space for an explanation of capacity limits in general, and of age-related declines in complex cognition in particular. Within this search space, we were able to identify two candidates that fit the time–accuracy data from one working-memory task particularly well, one based on decay and the other on interference. Decay and interference are the two main sources of forgetting in general theories of memory. It seems that we need no additional constructs, like limited resource pools or a "magical number" of free slots, to explain the limited capacity of working memory. Starting from the present results, we can now test specific predictions of the viable models in order to pin down more precisely the nature of one of the most important limiting factors in old adults' cognition.

Manuscript received September 2000

REFERENCES

Allen, P.A. (1991). On age differences in processing variability and scanning speed. *Journal of Gerontology: Psychological Sciences, 46*, 191–201.

Allen, P.A., Kaufman, M., Smith, A.F., & Propper, R.E. (1998). A molar entropy model of age differences in spatial memory. *Psychology and Aging, 13*, 501–518.

Anderson, J.R. (1983). *The architecture of cognition*. Cambridge, MA: Harvard University Press.

Anderson, J.R., & Lebiere, C. (1998). *The atomic components of thought*. Mahwah, NJ: Lawrence Erlbaum Associates Inc.

Anderson, J.R., & Matessa, M. (1997). A production system theory of serial memory. *Psychological Review, 104*, 728–748.

Anderson, J.R., Reder, L.M., & Lebiere, C. (1996). Working memory: Activation limits on retrieval. *Cognitive Psychology, 30*, 221–256.

Babcock, R. (1994). Analysis of adult age differences on the Raven's Advanced Progressive Matrices Test. *Psychology and Aging, 9*, 303–314.

Baddeley, A.D. (1986). *Working memory*. Oxford, UK: Clarendon Press.

Baddeley, A.D., Thomson, N., & Buchanan, M. (1975). Word length and the structure of short term memory. *Journal of Verbal Learning and Verbal Behavior, 14*, 575–589.

Brown, G.D.A., Preece, T., & Hulme, C. (2000). Oscillator-based memory for serial order. *Psychological Review*, *107*, 127–181.

Burgess, N., & Hitch, G.J. (1999). Memory for serial order: A network model of the phonological loop and its timing. *Psychological Review*, *106*, 551–581.

Byrne, M.D. (1998). Taking a computational approach to aging: The SPAN theory of working memory. *Psychology and Aging*, *13*, 309–322.

Cantor, J., & Engle, R.W. (1993). Working-memory capacity as long-term memory activation: An individual-differences approach. *Journal of Experimental Psychology: Learning, Memory, and Cognition*, *19*, 1101–1114.

Case, R. (1985). *Intellectual development: Birth to adulthood*. Orlando, FL: American Press.

Cerella, J. (1985). Information processing rates in the elderly. *Psychological Bulletin*, *107*, 260–273.

Conway, A.R.A., & Engle, R. (1996). Individual differences in working memory capacity: More evidence for a general capacity theory. *Memory*, *4*, 577–590.

Cowan, N. (in press). The magical number 4 in short-term memory: A reconsideration of mental storage capacity. *Behavioral and Brain Sciences*.

Engle, R.W., Kane, M.J., & Tuholski, S.W. (1999). Individual differences in working memory capacity and what they tell us about controlled attention, general fluid intelligence, and functions of the prefrontal cortex. In A. Miyake & P. Shah (Eds.), *Models of working memory* (pp. 102–134). Cambridge, UK: Cambridge University Press.

Halford, G., Wilson, W.H., & Phillips, S. (1998). Processing capacity defined by relational complexity: Implications for comparative, developmental, and cognitive psychology. *Behavioral and Brain Sciences*, *21*, 803–864.

Hasher, L., & Zacks, R.T. (1988). Working memory, comprehension, and aging: A review and a new view. In G.H. Bower (Ed.), *The psychology of learning and motivation* (Vol. 22, pp. 193–225). New York: Academic Press.

Hasher, L., Zacks, R.T., & May, C.P. (1999). Inhibitory control, circadian arousal, and age. In D. Gopher & A. Koriat (Eds.), *Attention and performance XVII* (pp. 653–675). Cambridge, MA: MIT Press.

Henson, R.N.A. (1998). Short-term memory for serial order: The start–end model. *Cognitive Psychology*, *36*, 73–137.

Henson, R.N.A., Norris, D.G., Page, M.P.A., & Baddeley, A.D. (1996). Unchained memory: Error patterns rule out chaining models of immediate serial recall. *Quarterly Journal of Experimental Psychology*, *49A*, 80–115.

Jenkins, L., Myerson, J., Hale, S., & Fry, A. (1999). Individual and developmental differences in working memory across the life span. *Psychonomic Bulletin and Review*, *6*, 28–40.

Just, M.A., & Carpenter, P.A. (1992). A capacity theory of comprehension: Individual differences in working memory. *Psychological Review*, *99*, 122–149.

Kaernbach, C. (1991). Simple adaptive testing with the weighted up–down method. *Perception and Psychophysics*, *49*, 227–229.

Kliegl, R., Mayr, U., & Krampe, R.T. (1994). Time–accuracy functions for determining process and person differences: An application to cognitive aging. *Cognitive Psychology*, *26*, 134–164.

Kyllonen, P.C., & Christal, R.E. (1990). Reasoning ability is (little more than) working-memory capacity?! *Intelligence*, *14*, 389–433.

Li, K.Z.H. (1999). Selection from working memory: On the relationship between processing and storage components. *Aging, Neuropsychology, and Cognition*, *6*, 99–116.

Loftus, G.R. (1978). On interpretation of interactions. *Memory and Cognition*, *6*, 312–319.

Mayr, U., & Kliegl, R. (1993). Sequential and coordinative complexity: Age-based processing limitations in figural transformations. *Journal of Experimental Psychology: Learning, Memory and Cognition*, *19*, 1297–1320.

Mayr, U., Kliegl, R., & Krampe, R.T. (1996). Sequential and coordinative processing dynamics in figural transformation across the life span. *Cognition, 59*, 61–90.

McCelland, J.L. (1979). On the relations of mental processes: An examination of systems of process in cascade. *Psychological Review, 86*, 287–330.

Meyer, D.E., & Kieras, D.E. (1997). A computational theory of executive cognitive processes and multiple-task performance: Part 2. Accounts of psychological refractory-period phenomena. *Psychological Review, 104*, 749–791.

Miller, G.A. (1956). The magical number seven, plus or minus two: Some limits on our capacity for processing information. *Psychological Review, 63*, 81–97.

Nairne, J.S. (1990). A feature model of immediate memory. *Memory and Cognition, 18*, 251–269.

Navon, D. (1984). Resources—a theoretical soupstone? *Psychological Review, 91*, 216–234.

Oberauer, K., Süß, H.-M., Schulze, R., Wilhelm, O., & Wittmann, W.M. (2000). Working memory capacity—facets of a cognitive ability construct. *Personality and Individual Differences, 29*, 1017–1045.

Salthouse, T.A. (1991). Mediation of adult age differences in cognition by reductions in working memory and speed of processing. *Psychological Science, 2*, 179–183.

Salthouse, T.A. (1992). Why do adult age differences increase with task complexity? *Developmental Psychology, 28*, 905–918.

Salthouse, T.A. (1994). The aging of working memory. *Neuropsychology, 8*, 535–543.

Salthouse, T.A. (1996). The processing speed theory of adult age differences in cognition. *Psychological Review, 103*, 403–428.

Salthouse, T.A., Babcock, R.L., & Shaw, R.J. (1991). Effects of adult age on structural and operational capacities in working memory. *Psychology and Aging, 6*, 118–127.

Schweickert, R., & Boruff, B. (1986). Short-term memory capacity: Magic number or magic spell? *Journal of Experimental Psychology: Learning, Memory, and Cognition, 12*, 419–425.

Süß, H.-M., Oberauer, K., Wittmann, W.W., Wilhelm, O., & Schulze, R. (2000). Working memory and intelligence. *Manuscript submitted for publication.*

Tehan, G., & Humphreys, M.S. (1998). Creating proactive interference in immediate recall: Building a DOG from a DART, a MOP, and FIG. *Memory and Cognition, 26*, 477–489.

Verhaeghen, P., Kliegl, R., & Mayr, U. (1997). Sequential and coordinative complexity in time-accuracy functions for mental arithmatic. *Psychology & Aging, 12*, 555–564.

Welford, A.T. (1958). *Aging and human skill*. London: Oxford University Press.

EUROPEAN JOURNAL OF COGNITIVE PSYCHOLOGY, 2001, *13* (1/2), 217–234

Modelling age-related changes in information processing

Daniel H. Spieler

Stanford University, CA, USA

Researchers in cognitive ageing seldom take advantage of explicit quantitative models of information processing to account for age differences in cognition. Where quantitative models have been used, these models typically remain silent about the details of information processing. The lack of explicit cognitive models has consequences for the interpretation of a number of empirical results. Using a specific class of models called random walk models, I review evidence showing that the empirical relations taken as support for global age-related changes are consistent with a number of possible age effects on information processing. In addition, I demonstrate that these models can be used to account for age differences within the context of individual experiments and such modelling has important implications for the interpretation of age differences in performance.

The central point that I argue for in this paper is not novel (Fisher & Glaser, 1996; Newell, 1973; Ratcliff, Spieler, & McKoon, 2000) but it is one that bears some reiteration, especially within the field of cognitive ageing. The point is that valid conclusions about the nature of age differences in cognition require the use of explicit information processing models that make quantitative rather than simply qualitative predictions. Quantitative modelling is particularly critical to research progress in cognitive ageing because of the unique inferential problems associated with using cognitive psychological paradigms in the context of between-group comparisons.

Requests for reprints should be addressed to D.H. Spieler, Department of Psychology, Stanford University, Stanford CA 94305-2130, USA. Email: spieler@psych.stanford.edu

This research was supported by NIA Grant RO1-AG16779. Thanks to Zenzi Griffin, Sabina Hak, Ulrich Mayr, and Justin Storbeck for helpful comments on an earlier version of this manuscript.

http://www.tandf.co.uk/journals/pp/09541446.html   DOI:10.1080/09541440042000287

In arguing for the importance of quantitative modelling in cognitive ageing, I will explore two specific instances where the lack of explicit information processing models led to a misunderstanding of what specific empirical results imply about age differences in cognition. First, I turn to the question of whether age differences in cognition are best characterised as general and global in nature or as a set of process-specific age effects. Second, I examine the role of modelling in the interpretation of the results of individual experiments. I turn first to the issue of general versus process-specific ageing.

EMPIRICAL EVIDENCE FOR GENERAL AGE EFFECTS

Older adults are slower than younger adults. While this statement is simple, the implications are not. Suppose (e.g., Faust, Balota, Spieler, & Ferraro, 1999) that for any task there is some amount of information that needs to be processed. Further assume that experimental manipulations influence the amount of information to be processed. Now assume that individuals (and groups) differ in the rate at which that information is processed. The changes in response time (RT) in response to experimental manipulations will be greater for the slow compared to the fast information-processing group (Cerella, 1985; Myerson, Hale, Wagstaff, Poon, & Smith, 1990; Salthouse & Somberg, 1982).

Creating a scatter plot (Brinley plot; Brinley, 1965) of young and old mean RTs for a set of conditions and tasks demonstrates this nicely. When the data is plotted in this manner, a striking regularity emerges. As shown in Figure 1, the mean RTs for younger and older adults are generally linearly related, and the function relating the two generally has a slope around 1.5 and a negative intercept (e.g., Brinley, 1965; Cerella, 1985; Salthouse & Somberg, 1982). Note also that the variance accounted for by this linear relationship is typically in excess of 90% (frequently over 95%).

This empirical relationship has been demonstrated across a wide range of tasks, conditions, and participant samples, suggesting that given the mean RT results from a group of younger adults, it may be possible to predict the speeded performance for a group of older adults. Because these data points are drawn from a range of tasks and conditions that tap a range of cognitive processes, age differences can be predicted with little regard for the specific processes and knowledge structures used in any individual task.

Following Cerella (1985) and Ratcliff, Spieler, and McKoon (2000), we can make this more explicit by developing a linear model of age-related slowing. If RT is a function of difficulty x with a minimum RT b even

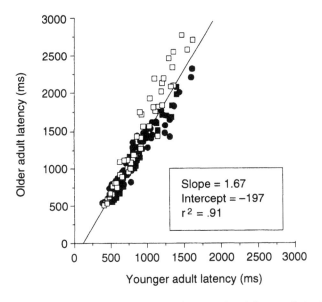

Figure 1. Brinley plot demonstrating the common result of linear relationship between young and older adult mean RTs. The different symbols represent different sets of tasks.

when processing is extremely easy, then:

$$RT = ax + b$$

Suppose that x remains constant with age but what changes is a and b. Thus

$$RT_{young} = a_{young} x + b_{young}$$

and

$$RT_{old} = a_{old} x + b_{old}$$

and using algebra to eliminate x we get:

$$RT_o = \frac{a_o}{a_y} RT_y + b_o - \frac{b_y a_o}{a_y}$$

Note that this function has a form exactly like the one observed in most Brinley plots, with a slope of a_o/a_y and an intercept of $b_o - b_y a_o/a_y$. This very simple derivation suggests that we should obtain slopes greater than one when $a_o > a_y$.

This linear model suggests that we might account for a wide range of empirical results in a very simple and elegant way. However, this formulation provides little information about what is actually influenced by the ageing process. It says only that older adults show a greater change in RT compared to younger adults in response to changes in difficulty.

INFORMATION-LOSS MODEL

Providing a more specific framework accounting for the general slowing results, Myerson et al. (1990) formulated a model intended to provide a quantitative account for the empirical Brinley plots and provide a mechanism for the influence of ageing on information processing. Within the model, the total time between the onset of a stimulus and an individual's response is the RT. This RT is the sum of a number of individual processing stages or steps.

$$RT = \sum T_k$$

The time for each individual processing stage, T_k is a function of the amount of information available at that stage, k.

$$T_k = \frac{D}{I_k}$$

where $I_k = I(1 - p)^k$ with D as a constant. The I_k defines the amount of information available at stage k, and p represents the loss of information at each processing stage. Thus, if there is less information available, then the amount of time required to complete that stage increases. Finally, the assumption is that a certain amount of information is lost at each processing stage. For example, as tasks become more complex, they require more processing stages, and with more processing stages, the amount of information lost increases. This loss of information parameter, p, is the parameter assumed to change with age. The model gives rise to a Brinley plot that is actually a positively accelerated power curve although within the range of RTs typically examined, the approximation to a linear function is quite high.

In both the linear model and the information-loss model, the primary goal has been to account for age differences in general, and empirical Brinley plots specifically. To varying degrees, these two models remain silent about any aspects of underlying processing not required by the between group comparisons.

In the linear model and the information-loss model, ageing influences a single parameter which in turn influences the type of Brinley function. The function that relates the young and older adults' performance provides the estimate of the model parameter (e.g., information loss or "difficulty"). If all points fall along a single function, then only a single parameter value is required, and if data points are better fit by two functions, then two parameter values are needed. Framing the research question in this way places considerable weight on the Brinley plot as a method for elucidating the nature of age differences in performance. The assumption is that the Brinley plot provides a way to determine how many parameters or parameter values are needed to adequately account for age effects. A single Brinley function suggests a single parameter or parameter value, and this in turn suggests a unitary influence of ageing on cognition.

To justify the central role for the Brinley plot method, it is not sufficient to show that a model can be formulated that is consistent with this interpretation of the Brinley plot. One should also show that Brinley plots constrain the interpretation of age effects in alternative but plausible models of information processing. Ideally these would be models that do not make a priori assumptions about the nature of age effects. In other words, the case for generalised slowing accounts would be greatly strengthened by showing not only that empirical Brinley plot results are consistent with general slowing models, but that the empirical Brinley pattern is inconsistent with a range of alternative models. If this empirical result is compatible with a number of plausible models, then no individual model gains much support by fitting these empirical results. To explore the constraint imposed by results of empirical Brinley plots, I turn to a traditional class of models commonly used in cognitive psychology and that are applicable to many of the tasks in which age effects have been examined.

RANDOM WALK MODELS OF INFORMATION PROCESSING

Random walk models, like other sequential sampling models (see Luce, 1986, for a review), make general assumptions about how information accumulates for a response. Assume a simple case where the task is a simple binary decision between two different responses based on the identity of a stimulus. This task could be a recognition memory judgement, a perceptual discrimination task, or any other choice task. Two basic parameters define the speed and accuracy of a decision. First, there is an amount of information that is necessary to make a decision, in other words, the response criterion. Second, there is the rate at which information accumulates toward a response. Following others (Luce,

1986; Ratcliff, 1978, 1988), I will refer to this as drift rate. In a binary decision, information is consistent with one of the response alternatives, moving the decision process toward the corresponding response boundary and away from the alternative, resulting in a relative decision criterion. At stimulus onset, the process starts equidistant from each response boundary, reflecting no bias for one response or another. (Response biases can easily be modelled but generally experiments are designed to discourage such biases).

Drift rate represents the quality or strength of information entering into the decision process. High drift rates result in the decision process moving quickly to one of the response boundaries while a low drift rate results in a slow rate of approach to the response criterion. The name "drift rate" gives the impression that this represents a speed parameter, but it is more accurately represented in terms of signal detection (for extensive discussion, see Luce, 1986; Ratcliff, 1978). If we assume that at each point in time, the information entering the decision process is either drawn from a signal or noise distribution and the decision process is an ideal observer attempting to minimise both misses and false alarms, then drift rate is directly analogous to the separation between the signal and noise distributions, d'. When the signal and noise distributions overlap considerably, the resultant drift rate will be relatively low and when the signal and noise distributions are far apart, the drift rate will be high.

On the assumption that the random walk is a model of the decision process and the response time includes time for other processes, there is a third parameter representing the residual time (Tr) and acts as an additive constant.

There is reason to believe that the parameters of the model tap real processes because it is possible to identify experimental manipulations that have selective influences on these parameters. For example, there are a range of manipulations that would seem to influence the quality of information entering the decision process and, as expected, these manipulations are modelled as changes in drift rate. Examples of these manipulations include perceptual noise (Ratcliff & Rouder, 1998) and ambiguity in categorisation (Ratcliff, Van Zandt, & McKoon, 1999). Moreover, instructions to individuals to emphasise either speed or accuracy or that bias individuals towards one of the response alternatives influence response criteria. Finally, this class of models has found support from recordings of neural activity in monkeys (Hanes & Schall, 1996).

RANDOM WALK MODELS AND BRINLEY PLOTS

Given the importance of Brinley functions, an obvious starting point is to demonstrate that this class of models can at least generate linear Brinley

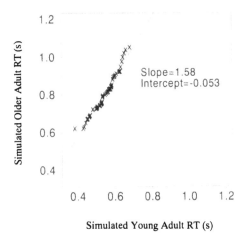

Figure 2. Brinley plot of mean RTs for simulated young and older adults using the diffusion model (adapted from Ratcliff, Spieler, & McKoon, 2000).

functions that are commonly found. As shown in Figure 2, this class of models is able to do so (Ratcliff, Spieler, & McKoon, 2000).

Brinley plots suggest that differences in overall response time have implications for the expected effect size for an experimental manipulation. Thus we might expect a slower group to show larger effect sizes. Exactly this scaling property is built into the general slowing models discussed earlier. The drift rate parameter in random walk models also exhibits such a relationship between speed and effect sizes. This is best demonstrated in signal detection terms. If the signal and noise distributions are already far apart, then increasing the separation further is likely to have only a small effect. However, if the two distributions overlap substantially, then even a small increase in separation will have large effects on performance. Similarly, if drift rate is already high, a further increase in drift rate because of some experimental manipulation will decrease RT only slightly, but at lower drift rates, a small increase in drift rate will result in a large decrease in RT. This is shown in Figure 3, where the faster group has a higher drift rate and the slower group has a lower drift rate and some experimental manipulation is assumed to result in an equal change in drift rate in the two groups. Ratcliff, Spieler, and McKoon (2000) showed that if young and old differ in drift rate overall, and experimental manipulations have identical effects on drift rate for both young and old, the diffusion model will produce a linear Brinley plot with a slope greater than unity and a negative intercept. Importantly, depending on the size of the experimental manipulations, changes only in

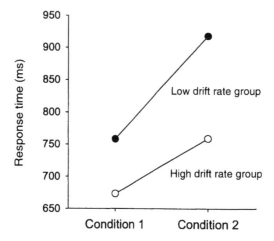

Figure 3. Example of overadditive interaction in slower group if both condition differences and group differences occur in drift rate.

drift rate can generate a range of Brinley slopes and intercepts. The actual slopes and intercepts depend on the size of the overall age difference in drift rate and the size of the differences in drift rate across conditions.

While the Brinley functions are influenced by age differences in drift rate, it is not possible to work backwards from the Brinley function to random walk parameters. The Brinley function does not sufficiently constrain the model parameters. For example, response criteria also influence RTs generated by random walk models. We (Ratcliff, Spieler, & McKoon, 2000) have shown that age differences solely in response criterion can also generate linear Brinley plots with a range of possible slopes and intercepts. There is an important distinction between drift rate and response criterion. While the effect of changes in drift rate on RT depends on the overall value of drift rate, the effect of changes in response criterion on RT is the same throughout the range of the parameter (e.g., Figure 4). Equal changes in response criterion for simulated young and old result in equal changes in RT for simulated young and old. One might think of this in terms of moving the finish line in a race (assuming constant speed of the runners).

These results lead to two insights. First, interpretations of age differences in the effect of some experimental manipulation depend on what parameter is influenced by the experimental manipulation and by the nature of the overall age difference in processing. If an experimental

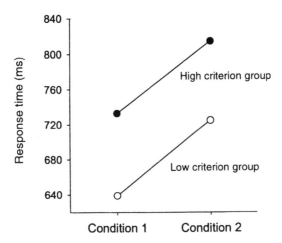

Figure 4. Example of additive effects if difference between conditions are in response criterion.

manipulation has a primary influence on an individual's criterion, then age differences in effect size may map closely onto age differences in underlying processing. Alternatively, if an experimental manipulation influences drift rate, then the interpretation of age differences in the effect of some experimental manipulation depends critically on how the overall age difference is modelled. Second, if a given linear Brinley plot can be generated by assuming age differences solely in drift rate or solely in response criterion, then a single linear Brinley function drawn from a range of tasks and conditions may reflect a heterogeneous mixture of age differences in drift rate and age differences in response criterion. Thus, while models attempting to account for age differences in cognition should be consistent with the empirical Brinley plots, these results alone are inadequate in determining the number or type of influences that ageing exerts on information processing.

CONSTRAINTS ON MODELLING OF AGE EFFECTS

If the random walk models can generate linear Brinley plots with changes either in response criterion or drift rate, then this suggests that the Brinley plots place insufficient constraint on these models and it suggests that additional empirical results are needed to adequately constrain these models. These constraints come from two sources.

Changes in model parameters have implications for the shapes of response time distributions and how those distributions differ across conditions. To characterise empirical RT distributions, it is common to use a mathematical function that, if successfully fit to the data, provides a description of the RT distribution via the parameters of the function. Ratcliff (1979) and many others (Heathcote, Popiel, & Mewhort, 1991; Hockley, 1984; Hohle, 1965; Luce, 1986) have shown that a convolution of a Gaussian and an exponential distribution, the ex-Gaussian, is generally successful in fitting empirical response time distributions from a range of experimental paradigms. Fitting the ex-Gaussian distribution yields three parameters that define the shape of the distribution. The parameters μ and σ are from the Gaussian distribution and reflect the leading edge and symmetric variability of the distribution, whereas the exponential parameter τ reflects the slow tail of the distribution (this is more of a heuristic rather than a definition because τ is influenced by RTs at other points in the RT distribution as well).

Figure 5 demonstrates how changes in the parameters of the random walk influence the shapes of the RT distribution as captured by the ex-Gaussian parameters. As the drift rate decreases, mean RT increases and this increase is particularly apparent in the slow tail of the RT distribution as reflected by the τ parameter. Figure 6 shows changes to the RT distribution as a result of changes in response criterion. Note that in this case, the change in mean RT is reflected as changes primarily in the μ

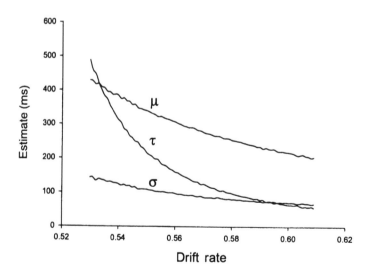

Figure 5.   Relation between ex-Gaussian parameters and drift rate.

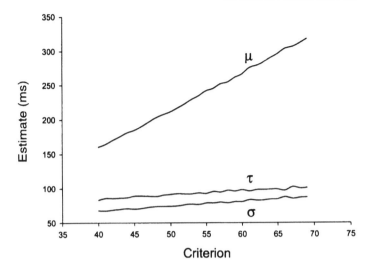

Figure 6. Relation between ex-Gaussian parameters and response criterion.

parameter. Thus, while drift rate influences the skew and variability of the RT distribution, response criterion tends to shift the RT distribution. As a result of these different influences of drift rate and response criterion, knowledge of how response time distributions differ across groups or across conditions provides an important constraint on the model. Of course, this also means that these models may not only account for effects on the mean of the RT distribution, but also for effects on the shape of the distribution.

A second source of constraint is error rates. If a decrease in drift rate is analogous to an increase in the overlap between the signal and noise distributions, a decrease in drift rate will result in slower RTs and an increase in the error rate. Increasing RTs may also result from increases in response criterion but the result will be a decrease in the error rate. For practical purposes, error rates under 5% across all conditions provide less constraint because a proportion of errors might arise from inappropriate response mapping or lapses in attention that are not directly related to the decision process modelled by the random walk. In practice, error rates will tend to be most informative when above the 10% range. This need not be a serious liability because this means that the random walk models are likely to be most informative in the range of error rates that can be particularly problematic for other information-processing models. Indeed, these models turn the liability of differential error rates and the possibility of speed–accuracy trade-offs into an asset because error rates help distinguish between changes in performance due to drift rate versus response criterion.

There are three possible outcomes from the application of these information-processing models. First, we may find that age differences are localised to one parameter. For example, across a wide range of circumstances, age differences may consistently be solely and uniformly in drift rate. This outcome is unlikely because of the relationship between model parameters such as response criterion and drift rate and error rates. Age differences solely in one of these parameters would enforce considerably more uniformity of age differences in RT and error rates than seems present in the literature. Lower drift rates in older adults with equal response criteria in young and old will generally result in larger error rates for older adults than for younger adults. However, we know that in some domains, age differences are present primarily in RT (e.g., many attentional paradigms), whereas in other domains, age differences are present to varying degrees in both RT and error rates. Moreover, in most studies, participants are instructed to minimise error rates. This will generally induce a negative correlation between drift rate and response criterion as individuals with low drift rates adopt more stringent response criteria. Thus it seems unlikely that age differences will be captured by a single parameter.

Second, the models may show that there is a single general transformation of the model parameters for younger adults that are able to fit older adults across a range of tasks and conditions. However, there is at least one instance in which young and old exhibit equal drift rates while old adopt more stringent response criteria (Ratcliff, Thapur, & McKoon, in press) and one case in which young and old show equal response criteria but different drift rates (Spieler & Balota, 2000). Nonetheless, it may be premature to rule out this second possibility, as it remains to be seen whether these results are exceptions to, rather than examplars of, the actual rule.

Third, we may find that what appeared to be a general relationship between young and old performance evaporates into a variety of age effects that are highly dependent upon the task and the sample of subjects used. It may be the case that in processing domains such as memory, age differences are modelled solely in drift rate; in some domains, age differences are perhaps solely in response criterion; in others, age differences are some various mixture of drift rate and response criteria. There is some preliminary evidence that appears to make this a likely outcome (e.g., Ratcliff, Thapur, & McKoon, in press; Spieler & Balota, 2000).

LOCAL ACCOUNTS IN COGNITIVE AGEING

In most experimental studies that include comparisons between younger and older adults, age differences are not observed in the context of a wide range of tasks with large samples of subjects. Rather, as is the case for most studies in cognitive psychology, a limited series of experiments is conducted with relatively small sample sizes. These experiments generally focus on one domain or one experimental paradigm. This approach makes it particularly difficult to test the traditional general slowing argument that relies on empirical relations from a range of tasks and conditions. In contrast, explicit information processing models allow us to capture age differences in conjunction with traditional task analyses, and allow for the interpretation of age differences in performance within the context of individual experiments. To demonstrate this, I turn to recent modelling efforts in which we examine the issue of age differences in Stroop performance (Spieler & Balota, 2000).

AGE DIFFERENCES IN INHIBITION

One of the landmark papers in cognitive ageing was a paper published by Hasher and Zacks (1988) that drew on a range of empirical results to suggest that older adults suffer from a decreased ability to suppress competing information. The inhibitory deficit framework was immediately applicable to a large range of tasks. Many of the tasks that appear to implicate inhibitory processing involve presenting individuals with distracting or competing information. In studies where RT is the primary dependent measure, the prediction is generally that older adults will show larger interference effects than do younger adults. Qualitatively, this is the identical prediction of generalised slowing. Indeed, across many experimental paradigms, evidence for an inhibitory deficit is also qualitatively consistent with generalised slowing (e.g., Connelly, Hasher, & Zacks, 1991; Gerard, Zacks, Hasher, & Radvansky, 1991; Spieler, Balota, & Faust, 1996).

As a specific example of this, take the Stroop task (Stroop, 1935). In this task, participants are required to name the colour in which a word is printed. In the conflict condition, the word names a nonmatching colour (e.g., BLUE printed in green), and the conflict between the colour and the word results in a slowing of colour naming compared to a neutral condition in which the word is colour unrelated (e.g., DOG printed in green). Efficient performance in this task requires suppressing the processing of the word information in order to name the colour. A deficit in the efficiency of inhibition should result in an increase in the processing of the word information and an increase in the size of the interference effect. Consistent with the inhibitory deficit account, older adults evidence larger Stroop interference effects than do younger adults (Comalli, Wapner, & Werner, 1962; Panek, Rush, & Slade, 1984; Spieler et al., 1996). Because this is also consistent with generalised slowing, it is common to try to show that the interference effects are larger or slower than some construal of generalised slowing. Unfortunately, this strategy is rarely successful because most general slowing models are not predictive but rather attempt to account for data after the fact. This gives the model a high amount of flexibility making it difficult to obtain empirical results that clearly refute general slowing (Perfect, 1994).

It is possible to translate a claim about inhibitory processing deficits into predictions about how random walk model parameters may differ across groups. The reasoning is as follows. Any Stroop trial can be seen as a selection between a word and colour response. The two boundaries in the random walk corresponds to the colour and word in the display. Sampling information from the word dimension moves one closer to the word boundary and sampling information from the colour dimension moves one closer to the colour boundary. Because the neutral condition contains word information not directly related to an appropriate response, there is less sampling of word information in the neutral condition and more in the incongruent condition. Thus, interference in the Stroop task is modelled as a reduction in drift rate in the incongruent relative to the neutral condition.

An application of a random walk model to Stroop performance in younger adults showed that the random walk model was able to account for these results (Spieler, Balota, & Faust, 2000). Recently we (Spieler & Balota, 2000) revisited the results of an experiment looking at Stroop performance in young and older adults (Spieler et al., 1996). In the original study, Spieler et al. (1996) also examined RT distributions from younger and older adults. The basic pattern is shown in Table 1. The older adults showed a much larger interference effect than did the younger adults. The increase in the interference for the older adults relative to the younger adults was evidenced as a large increase in interference in the τ parameter of the ex-Gaussian. It is this data that we sought to fit using the random walk model. There are three things to note about these data that suggest some general differences in random walk parameters for the two groups. First, there is a large difference between young and old in the leading edge of the distribution. Second, older adults show more variability and greater skew in the distributions than younger adults. Third, error rates (not shown) were nearly asymptotic ($\sim 3\%$). The greater variability and skew suggest that older adults have a lower overall drift rate than do the younger adults. However, the age difference in the leading edge of the distribution is greater than is obtained solely by drift rate differences suggesting that there are age differences in both drift rate and *Tr*. Assuming equal response criteria, the random walk fits to the young and old data are shown in Table 1.

TABLE 1
Ex-Gaussian parameter estimates reported in Spieler et al. (1996)
and corresponding random walk fits

	Neutral	*Incongruent*	*Effect*
Young adult data			
μ	608	659	51
σ	64	87	23
τ	64	100	36
Young adult model fit			
μ	609	658	49
σ	68	81	13
τ	64	101	37
Old adult data			
μ	811	878	67
σ	93	97	4
τ	98	195	97
Old adult model			
μ	810	875	65
σ	81	102	21
τ	100	196	96

Young parameters: Tr (400, 50); drift rate = .103–.078, response criterion = 57; old parameters: Tr (630, 50); drift rate = .079–.054, response criterion = 57.

For these results, the older adults had lower drift rates but surprisingly the best fit resulted by assuming that both groups were equally influenced by interference, with a change in drift rate of 0.025. This modelling result is inconsistent with our original account that argued support for an age deficit in inhibitory control. Indeed, these results argue against age differences in the processes that underlie Stroop performance.

One interpretation of these results is that age differences in the Stroop task are simply a result of overall differences between young and old and have nothing to do with the specific processes tapped by this task. In other words, our interpretation sounds quite similar to a general slowing account. Here it might be necessary to distinguish between general slowing *models* and general slowing *perspectives*. General slowing models are concerned with empirical relations between young and old adult performance (in practice this typically just means RT) across a range of tasks and conditions. I and others (e.g., Fisher & Glaser, 1996; Ratcliff, Spieler, & McKoon, 2000) have shown that such empirical relations underdetermine the nature of age differences. However, these models will be nearly impossible to disprove or even address in the context of a single experiment. In this case, these specific results have little to say about the status of general slowing models.

General slowing perspectives are more difficult to define. One perspective emphasises that age differences across a range of processing domains will be accounted for by a small number of explanatory constructs. The results of any individual study are unlikely to dissuade anyone committed to such a perspective although there are preliminary data suggesting age differences in drift rate (Spieler & Balota, 2000) but not response criterion, and age differences in response criterion (Ratcliff, Thapur, & McKoon, in press) but not drift rate. An alternative point of emphasis from a general slowing perspective is that the influence of experimental manipulations in different groups is related to group differences in overall RT. The present results may be quite consistent with this perspective although it is not clear that such a scaling of response times is a general phenomenon.

Rather than attempt to argue whether these results, or any other results, violate a general slowing perspective, it may be more useful to focus on what the present modelling perspective offers, particularly for researchers interested in cognitive theories of ageing. These models are not theories but are implementations of theoretical accounts of how processing is performed within a task. As such, the emphasis in this form of modelling remains on traditional task analyses. The models provide a way of translating our interpretation of how processing is performed in a task into an account of performance. In this case, performance includes a range of dependent measures including mean RT, RT distributions, error rates, and error RTs.

The class of models discussed here, specifically sequential sampling models, are unlikely to cover the entire range of tasks that have been identified as tapping executive control processes. In particular, tasks that involve complex problem solving and reasoning are likely to require alternative models such as that discussed by Meyer, Glass, Mueller, Seymour, and Kieras (this issue). Regardless of the particular model used however, the goal remains the same. Through the application of these models where appropriate, and in the development and use of alternative models where necessary, the goal is a formal and quantitative statement about how processing takes place and how this processing is influenced by ageing. The result is a theoretical account of some aspect of cognition and of how cognition is influenced by the ageing process.

Manuscript received September 2000

REFERENCES

Brinley, J.F. (1965). Cognitive sets, speed and accuracy of performance in the elderly. In A.T. Welford & J.E. Birren (Eds.), *Behavior, aging and the nervous system* (pp. 114–149). Springfield, IL: Thomas.

Cerella, J. (1985). Information processing rates in the elderly. *Psychological Bulletin, 98*, 67–83.

Comalli, P.E., Wapner, S., & Werner, H. (1962). Interference effects of Stroop color–word test in childhood, adulthood, and aging. *Journal of Genetic Psychology, 100*, 47–53.

Connelly, S.L., Hasher, L., Zacks, R.T. (1991). Age and reading: The impact of distraction. *Psychology and Aging, 6*, 533–541.

Faust, M.E., Balota, D.A., Spieler, D.H., & Ferraro, F.R. (1999). Individual differences in information processing rate and amount: Implications for group differences in response latency. *Psychological Bulletin, 125*, 777–799.

Fisher, D.L., & Glaser, R.A. (1996). Molar and latent models of cognitive slowing: Implications for aging, dementia, depression, development and intelligence. *Psychonomic Bulletin and Review, 3*, 458–480.

Gerard, L., Zacks, R.T., Hasher, L., & Radvansky, G.A. (1991). Age deficits in retrieval: The fan effect. *Journal of Gerontology, 46*, P131–136.

Hanes, D.P., & Schall, J.D. (1996). Neural control of voluntary movement initiation. *Science, 274*, 427–430.

Hasher, L., & Zacks, R.T. (1988). Working memory, comprehension, and aging: A review and a new view. In G.H. Bower (Ed.), *The psychology of learning and motivation* (Vol. 22, pp. 193–225). New York: Academic Press.

Heathcote, A., Popiel, S.J., & Mewhort, D.J.K. (1991). Analysis of response time distributions: An example using the Stroop task. *Psychological Bulletin, 109*, 340–347.

Hockley, W.E. (1984). Analysis of response time distribution in the study of cognitive processes. *Journal of Experimental Psychology: Learning, Memory, and Cognition, 4*, 598–615.

Hohle, R.H. (1965). Inferred components of reaction times as functions of foreperiod durations. *Journal of Experimental Psychology, 69*, 382–386.

Luce, R.D. (1986). *Response times: Their role in inferring elementary mental organization.* New York: Oxford University Press.

Myerson, H., Hale, S., Wagstaff, D., Poon, L.W., & Smith, G.A. (1990). The information-loss model: A mathematical theory of age-related cognitive slowing. *Psychological Review, 97*, 475–487.

Newell, A. (1973). You can't play 20 questions with nature and win: Projective comments on the papers of this symposium. In W. Chase (Ed.), *Visual information processing.* New York: Academic Press.

Panek, P.E., Rush, M.C., & Slade, L.A. (1984). Locus of the age–Stroop interference relationship. *Journal of Genetic Psychology, 145*, 209–216.

Perfect, T.J. (1994). What can Brinley plots tell us about cognitive aging? *Journal of Gerontology: Psychological Science, 49*, 60–64.

Ratcliff, R. (1978). A theory of memory retrieval. *Psychological Review, 85*, 59–109.

Ratcliff, R. (1979). Group reaction time distributions and an analysis of distribution statistics. *Psychological Bulletin, 86*, 446–461.

Ratcliff, R. (1988). Continuous versus discrete information processing: Modeling accumulation of partial information. *Psychological Bulletin, 95*, 238–255.

Ratcliff, R., & Rouder, J.N. (1998). Modeling response times for two choice decisions. *Psychological Science, 9*, 347–356.

Ratcliff, R., Spieler, D.H., & McKoon, G. (2000). Evaluating the effects of aging in response time with an explicit model of information processing. *Psychonomic Bulletin and Review*, 7, 1–25.

Ratcliff, R., Thapur, A., & McKoon, G. (in press). Effects of aging on reaction time in a signal detection task. *Psychology and Aging*.

Ratcliff, R., Van Zandt, T., & McKoon, G. (1999). Connectionist and diffusion models of response time. *Psychological Review, 106*, 261–300.

Salthouse, T.A., & Somberg, B.L. (1982). Isolating the age deficit in speeded performance. *Journal of Gerontology, 37*, 59–63.

Spieler, D.H., & Balota, D.A. (2000). Modeling age differences in Stroop performance. *Manuscript in preparation*.

Spieler, D.H., Balota, D.A., & Faust, M.E. (1996). Stroop performance in healthy younger and older adults and in individuals with dementia of the Alzheimer's type. *Journal of Experimental Psychology: Human Perception and Performance, 22*, 461–479.

Spieler, D.H., Balota, D.A., & Faust, M.E. (2000). Levels of selective attention revealed through analyses of response time distributions. *Journal of Experimental Psychology: Human Perception and Performance, 26*, 506–526.

Stroop, J.R. (1935). Studies of interference in serial verbal reactions. *Journal of Experimental Psychology, 18*, 643–661.

EUROPEAN JOURNAL OF COGNITIVE PSYCHOLOGY, 2001, *13* (1/2), 235–256

Age-related changes in brain–behaviour relationships: Evidence from event-related functional MRI studies

Bart Rypma and Mark D'Esposito

University of California, Berkeley, USA

A fundamental aim of studies in neurocognitive ageing is to understand age-related changes in brain–behaviour relationships. Neuroimaging techniques such as positron emission tomography (PET) and functional magnetic resonance imaging (fMRI) can be used for observation of these age-related changes only if the assumption of age-equivalent relations between neural activity and haemodynamic activity is valid. In one study, we characterised age-related differences in the coupling of the haemodynamic response to neural activity and found greater voxel-wise noise in older than in younger adults, but age-equivalent signal magnitude. These results suggested that alternative techniques may be necessary for analysing age-related differences in neuroimaging data. In a second study, we utilised one alternative method for comparing fMRI activation between younger and older adults performing a working memory (WM) task. Across three experiments, the results suggested that age-related functional changes in fMRI activation can be isolated to dorsolateral prefrontal cortex (PFC) during memory retrieval. These results suggest a plausible model for WM decline with normal ageing. In a third study we propose and test a model of age-related PFC dysfunction that may account for these and other age-related differences in cognitive performance.

A fundamental aim of studies in neurocognitive ageing is to understand how the ageing brain mediates age-related changes in the performance of cognitive tasks. The advent of neuroimaging techniques such as PET and fMRI permits more direct observation of these age-associated changes in the brain than has been possible in the past. Thus, hypotheses developed through behavioural comparisons of younger and older adults, and older

Requests for reprints should be addressed to B. Rypma, Department of Psychology, University of California, 3210 Tolman Hall, Berkeley, CA 94720-1650, USA.
Email: rypma@socrates.berkley.edu
Supported by the American Federation for Aging Research and NIH grants NS01762, AG13483 and AG15793.

http://www.tandf.co.uk/journals/pp/09541446.html   DOI:10.1080/09541440042000296

normal adults with older neurological patients (such as those with Alzheimer's or Parkinson's disease and focal brain injury; e.g., Gabrieli, 1991, 1996), may now be further tested and extended (Gabrieli & Rypma, 1997; Prull, Bunge, & Gabrieli, 2000; Raz, 2000; Rypma & Gabrieli, in press). The proposal that insights regarding age-related changes in cognitive performance may be gained from data acquired through functional neuroimaging techniques implies that the relationship between changes in *neural activity* with advancing age and changes in *performance* with advancing age must be examined directly.

Most neurocognitive ageing studies have tended to focus on age-group differences in mean or median neural activity and performance (a relatively *distal* level of analysis). Less emphasis has been placed on individual-subject variability in these measures or the relationships between them (a relatively *proximal* level of analysis; cf. Salthouse, 1991). Thus, age-related differences in activation have not been consistently linked to increases or decreases in cognitive performance. Regions of increased activity in older adults, relative to younger adults, have been observed in a number of studies using PET and fMRI (e.g., Cabeza et al., 1997; Grady et al., 1995; Reuter-Lorenz et al., 2000; Rypma, Prabhakaran, Desmond, & Gabrieli, 2000). Reuter-Lorenz, Marshuetz, Jonides, Smith, Hartley, and Koeppe (this issue) review studies that show age-related increases in activity that have been accompanied by age-equivalent performance in some cases (Cabeza et al., 1997), and age-differential performance in others (Reuter-Lorenz et al., 2000, this issue). Reuter-Lorenz and her colleagues (Jonides et al., 2000, and Reuter-Lorenz et al., this issue) have observed a third relationship between performance and neural activity, age-related reductions in PET activation associated with reduced cognitive performance in elderly relative to young. Such divergent patterns of results suggest that the relationship between neural activity and performance is quite complex. We propose that such complex relationships may be better understood by examining the relationship between neural activity and performance at the level of individual subjects; understanding the neural factors that underlie age-related changes in performance may best be approached by the study of individual differences in brain–behaviour relationships. There are at least two methodological requirements of this relatively proximal analysis level.

One requirement is that fMRI analytic methods must afford valid comparisons of neural activity between younger and older adults. Although it may seem trivially obvious, this requirement has proven extremely difficult to satisfy. For instance, many current methods of analysis assume that physiological consistencies exist between the individuals or groups under analysis. There are reasons to doubt the viability of this assumption however. The ageing brain undergoes dramatic changes involving global volume, synaptic density, oxygen uptake, and microvascular organisation. These assumptions are critical for valid observation of age-related changes in neural activity because many extant analysis methods use a common estimate (e.g., a gamma function or a Poisson function) of the haemodynamic response to model neural activity in both groups. In this paper, we will review evidence from our own laboratory, and from the laboratories of others, that suggests that the assumption of common haemodynamic response properties may be untenable. In the context of our own studies of age-related differences in neural activity, we will illustrate one method we have used (Rypma & D'Esposito, 2000) that permits circumvention of the assumption of common haemodynamic response properties.

The second methodological requirement of this proximal analysis level is the use of fMRI data collection methods that permit isolation of neural activity to particular task components (and thus, cognitive processes). Cognitive tasks used in neuroimaging experiments generally require a number of component cognitive processes. For instance, delayed-response tasks are comprised of at least three cognitive operations: encoding, maintenance, and retrieval of to-be-remembered information. There is behavioural evidence to suggest the importance of analysing neural activity in each of these task components. Burke and Light (1981), for instance, reviewed a broad literature on age differences in each of these component memory processes. Their analyses implicated retrieval deficits as a principal source of the age-related performance differences observed in memory tasks. Indeed, data from our laboratory suggests that some brain regions appear exquisitely sensitive to changes in performance specifically during memory retrieval and not other task components (Rypma & D'Esposito, 1999, 2000).

In this paper, we will first review data that address the assumption, implicit in many studies of age differences in cortical activity, that relationships between neural activity and haemodynamic activity are age-equivalent. These data have suggested to us one alternative analytic method that increases our confidence in the validity of our comparisons between younger and older adults. Second, we will review studies from our laboratory in which we have applied these alternative analytic methods in conjunction with event-related fMRI to more precisely interpret age-related differences in our fMRI data. From these data we have proposed a model of age-related changes in brain–behaviour relationships that we will test further using parallel distributed processing (PDP) modelling techniques.

TESTING HAEMODYNAMIC EQUIVALENCE
ASSUMPTIONS IN YOUNGER AND OLDER ADULTS

Observation of neural activity during cognitive performance using fMRI and some forms of PET depend critically on the reliability of haemo-dynamic responsiveness to neural activity. The haemodynamic response is the basis for blood-oxygen level dependent (BOLD) contrast fMRI. It is the change in fMRI signal that results from a brief (i.e., <1s) period of neural activity (e.g., Aguirre, Zarahn, & D'Esposito, 1998). Accordingly, the haemodynamic response has been carefully studied and characterised as a function that is delayed in onset and evolves over a 10–12s period following neural activity (e.g., Aguirre et al., 1998; Blamire et al., 1992). Studies of age-related differences in the neural substrates of cognitive processes (those studies that quantitatively compare changes in fMRI signal intensity across age groups), in turn, rely upon the assumption of age-equivalent coupling of neural activity to fMRI signal in time and space. As was stated previously, there are reasons to question this general assumption. First, histological studies of cerebral microvasculature have demonstrated considerable age-related variability in the organisation of intercerebral arterioles, capillaries, and venules. Fang (1976), for instance, observed age-related increases in the winding, coiling, and number of "blind-ends" in the cerebral vascular microlattice, most notably in the arteriole-venous-capillary bed. Because the BOLD fMRI signal has been shown to have a significant contribution from the capillary bed (Menon et al., 1995), these age-related differences in vasculature could conceivably produce age-related differences in BOLD fMRI signal responsiveness. Differences in experimentally induced fMRI signal change between younger and older subjects are indicative in general of differences in neural activity only if the coupling between neural activity and fMRI signal does not change with age.

In one study, we tested this assumption by measuring the temporal and spatial characteristics of the fMRI haemodynamic response in younger and older subjects to equivalent neural input (D'Esposito, Zarahn, Aguirre, & Rypma, 1999). Differences in the haemodynamic response between age groups in either time or space would indicate a failure of the assumption that the coupling of neural activity and haemodynamic activity are age-equivalent. In this study, random samples drawn from a young population (ages 18–32) and an older population (ages 65–82) were subjected to identical behavioural paradigms while being scanned with BOLD fMRI. The behavioural paradigm was a simple reaction time task that involved a visually cued, bilateral button press every 16s. Therefore, the spatial characteristics (i.e., where the stimulus was to appear and what kind of movement would be required) and the temporal characteristics (i,e., when the visual cues for movement appeared) were predictable. These task characteristics make tenable the assumption that neural activity was not different between younger and older subjects. We believe that this is a reasonable assumption for two reasons. First, movement-related electrical potentials in younger and older adults, recorded at a central scalp electrode, appear to be similar under conditions such as those present in our paradigm (Cunnington, Iansek, Bradshaw, & Phillips, 1995). Second, there is neuropathological evidence that primary motor cortex does not exhibit significant neuronal loss in normal ageing (Haug, 1997).

Analyses of the behavioural data from this experiment indicated that accuracy rates for younger (100%) and older subjects (98.9%) were similar. Older subjects' mean reaction time (414.8 ms), however, was significantly slower than that of younger subjects (368.1 ms). Three observations were made from the neuroimaging data. First, 32/32 (100%) of the young subjects exhibited suprathreshold activity in an anatomically defined region of interest (ROI) comprising primary sensorimotor cortex (along the central sulcus), whereas only 15/20 (75%) of the older subjects exhibited suprathreshold activation in the analogous region. Moreover, there was a significantly greater number of suprathreshold voxels in the central sulcus ROI of the younger compared to that of the older subjects (median of the young = 30.5 voxels; median of the older = 6.0 voxels; U = 60.5; $p < .0001$). This difference in spatial extent of activation could not be explained by age-related differences in the search-region volume. These search regions were slightly larger in the older (M = 385 voxels) group than in the younger group (M = 364 voxels).

For each subject, estimates of noise variance (i.e., the denominator of the F statistic), signal variance (i.e., the numerator minus the denominator of the F-statistic), and their ratio (i.e., signal : noise) were made from the time series of suprathreshold voxels. From this analysis, the second major observation was that the voxel-averaged noise magnitude was significantly greater in the older subjects than in the young (U = 125; $p = .009$), but signal magnitude was not (u = 194; $p = .29$). As expected from these results, the signal : noise ratio was significantly greater in the young than in the older group (median of the young = 7.6; median of the older = 5.9; U = 107; $p = .002$; Figure 1). Examination of the averaged power spectra from the suprathreshold voxels showed that the increased noise in the older over the younger subjects was greater in the lower than higher frequencies (Figure 1).

The third major observation was that of apparent age-related differences in the shape of the haemodynamic response function. Specifically, we tested the trial-averaged time series (from single, randomly chosen voxels) for age differences in shape and magnitude. This test was imple-

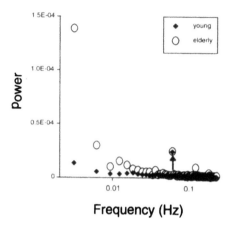

Figure 1. The average power spectra for the younger ($N = 32$) and older ($N = 20$) subject groups. For each group, frequency in Hertz is plotted on the x-axis and power (squared fMRI signal amplitude) is plotted on the y-axis. For both groups the spectrum is an average across subjects of the within-subject average spectra (across all suprathreshold voxels). It can be seen that the power at the fundamental frequency of the behavioural task (marked by the arrow) is nearly identical in the two groups. The greatest disparity between noise in the younger and the older groups is at the lowest frequencies, although the noise tends to be greater in the older group throughout the spectrum.

mented using a multivariate analysis of variance, which, for a basis-set of Fourier coefficients, compared the variability within each age group to the variability between age groups (with variability pooled across Fourier coefficients). A comparison of the within-group variability in the haemo-dynamic responses between the younger and older groups revealed no significant difference, $F(84, 186) = 1.18$, $p = .17$. The between-groups test yielded a trend towards a difference between young and older groups in the shape and scaling of the haemodynamic response, $F(6, 270) = 2.06$, $p = .06$. The individual and across-subject average haemodynamic responses (with each subject contributing the time series of one randomly selected voxel) for the older and the younger groups are presented in Plate 1. (The colour plate section is situated between pages 240 and 241. Online readers click here.)

One way to interpret the results of this study is to assume that the spatio-temporal pattern and intensity of neural activity in the vicinity of the central sulcus is the same between the populations from which the young and older groups were sampled (Cunnington et al., 1995; Haug, 1997). Given this assumption, any difference between groups in the

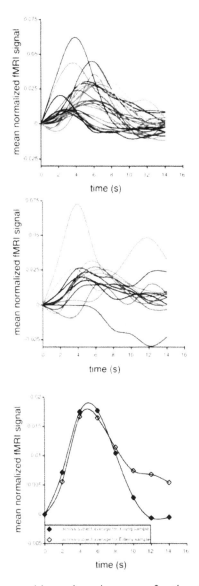

Plate 1. The trial-averaged haemodynamic response functions (HRF) from the younger (a) and older (b) samples. These haemodynamic responses are from single voxels that were randomly selected from among the suprathreshold voxels found in the central sulcus region of interest in each subject (one HRF per subject is shown). The HRFs are expressed as a fraction of the mean signal from within the selected voxel. The value at time = 0 peristimulus was subtracted from the time-series for display. The values of the HRFs at 2-s sampling intervals (starting at time 0) are actual data, whereas the intermediate values were obtained from these data by sinc interpolation. The across-subject averages for the younger and older subject groups are shown in (c).

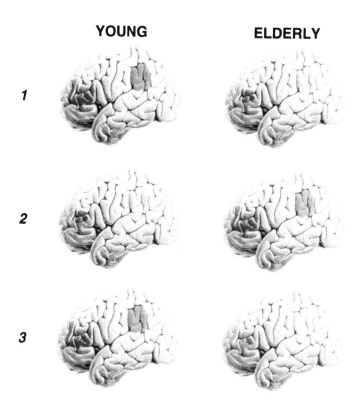

YOUNG   **ELDERLY**

1

2

3

Plate 2. Possible difference in patterns of brain activation between young and older individuals during the performance of a cognitive task. (Scenario 1) A similar pattern of activation between groups but greater activation in younger individuals in some of the brain regions. (Scenario 2) A similar pattern of activation between groups but greater activation in older individuals in some of the brain regions. (Scenario 3) A different pattern of activation between groups of individuals where new brain regions are activated in older individuals that are not active in young individuals.

spatial and temporal fMRI results would be attributable to differences in haemodynamic coupling between neural activity and BOLD fMRI signal change and/or other factors that can affect the BOLD fMRI signal (such as motion). There are a few possible explanations for changes in coupling between neural activity and BOLD signal in normal ageing. One hypothesis would be that age differences in the spatial properties of the vascular bed (Fang, 1976) cause changes in the spatial properties of this coupling. Another hypothesis would link vascular pathology (known to increase with normal ageing; Bohl & Hori, 1997) with spatial extent of this coupling.

The reduced spatial extent of fMRI activation we observed in the older subjects suggests that age-related comparisons of task-related fMRI activation using traditional statistical parametric mapping (SPM; Friston, 1994/1995) methods cannot be expected to yield age-equivalent fMRI activation in the presence of age-related neural activity. This is because, following the application of a Gaussian smoothing kernel, the intensity value of a given voxel will be a function of the intensity value of adjacent voxels, in addition to the intensity value of the given voxel. Thus, differences in the spatial extent of activation translate into differences in intensity after spatial smoothing of the imaging data. To illustrate this point, we performed a group analysis on our data and observed greater "activation" in primary sensorimotor cortex in the younger subjects as compared to the older subjects (Figure 2). If the results of Cunnington et al. (1995) are reliable, and evoked potentials are a reliable measure of spatially averaged neural activity, then this is an example of a positive fMRI result in the presence of a null neural result.

In addition to the differences in spatial extent between groups (in those subjects who had a detectable fMRI response), the observation that there was a substantial proportion of subjects in the older group who did not evince detectable responses bolsters the conclusion of the previous paragraph. That is, it is not likely that these subjects had no neural activity near the central sulcus associated with the button presses. Rather (based on Cunnington et al.'s 1995 results), it seems more likely that there was a greatly weakened, or perhaps non-existent, coupling between neural activity and fMRI signal in these subjects.

The implication of our finding that greater levels of noise per voxel may be observed in older compared to younger adults is that inferences based on statistical maps that rely on scaling of signal components by noise will yield potentially erroneous results in quantitative comparisons of younger and older adults. Several scenarios are possible (see Plate 2— colour plate section situated between pages 240 and 241; online readers click here). For instance, one is in an inferentially ambiguous situation if comparison of brain activity in younger and older adults yielded less

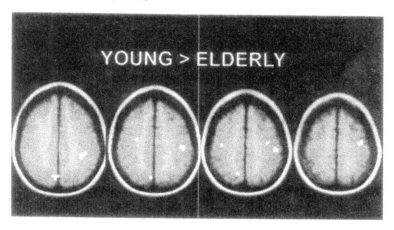

Figure 2. Random effects SPM{t} of younger vs. older motor response. The data from 11 older and 11 younger subjects were analysed using a modified GLM (Worsley & Friston, 1995). The covariate of interest was constructed with the first eigenvector obtained from a principal components analysis of haemodynamic responses from a separate group of subjects (Aguirre et al., 1998). Additional nuisance covariates were generated using the second and third eigenvectors. An SPM{t}, evaluating the covariate of interest, was generated for each subject. These maps were then normalised to standard Talairach space, smoothed with a three-dimensional Gaussian kernel (FWHM = 7.0 mm), and used to generate a new SPM{t}, which assessed the difference in task effects between younger and older subject groups. This map, which treated the task effect in each subject as a random effect, was thresholded at t = 4.2, corresponding to a = 0.05 (20 df, two-tailed, corrected for multiple comparisons, Worsley, 1994).

activation in the older, compared to the younger subjects across the entire statistical map, but no greater activation in the older compared to the younger (see Plate 2, scenario 1). In this scenario, it is possible that the observed age-related differences are not due to differences in signal intensity *per se*, but rather to other non-neuronal contributions, i.e., age-related differences in haemodynamic coupling. One may be on more solid inferential ground under circumstances where greater activation is observed in the older compared to the younger group (see, e.g., Grady, 1996; Rypma et al., 2000), at least in some regions (see Plate 2, scenario 2). In this scenario, it is unlikely that regional variation in haemodynamic coupling would account for such age-related differences in activation patterns. In a third possible scenario (see Plate 2, scenario 3), a different pattern of activation between groups (that is, new brain regions are activated in older individuals that are not active in younger individuals during performance of the same cognitive task) can be seen. This pattern could indicate some fundamental change in functional organisation with advanced age. It may also indicate compensatory mechanisms if it is accompanied by an improvement in performance over conditions where the activation is not present. Of course, any combination of these scenarios is also possible.

Our study of the haemodynamic response in normal ageing indicated that the magnitude of voxel-wise task-related signal *per se* was not detectably different between the age groups, nor was the shape of the average haemodynamic response. The implication of this finding is that more accurate inferences about age differences in cortical activity may come from analyses of the signal component of fMRI data, separate from the noise component.

STUDIES OF AGE-RELATED DIFFERENCES IN NEURAL ACTIVITY WITHOUT THE ASSUMPTION OF AGE-EQUIVALENT HAEMODYNAMICS

In a series of studies, we have implemented analyses that examined age-related differences in cortical activity that accompany age-related differences in cognitive performance. In one study, we (Rypma & D'Esposito, 2000) used an event-related fMRI design to explore the relative roles of dorsal and ventral PFC regions during specific components (Encoding, Delay, Response) of a WM task under different memory-load conditions. Our interest was in testing the hypothesis that age-related changes in the PFC may be the source of WM decline in normal ageing.

Evidence from behavioural and neuroimaging studies together suggests that the neural basis of age-related WM performance decline may be related specifically to age-related changes in one region of PFC, the dorsolateral region, whereas ventrolateral PFC regions may remain relatively unaffected by ageing. In behavioural research it has been observed that minimal age differences nearly always occur in memory-span tasks that do not involve delay components (e.g., Botwinick & Storandt, 1974; Bromley, 1958; Craik, 1968; Friedman, 1974; Gilbert & Levee, 1971; Taub, 1973). When memory demand is increased by (1) the imposition of delays between information encoding and retrieval, or (2) increases in the amount of information that must be maintained over a delay period, however, age-related declines in performance are often observed (Anders, Fozard, & Lillyquist, 1972; Craik, 1977; Marsh, 1975; Nielsen-Bohlman & Knight, 1995; Poon & Fozard, 1980; Smith, 1975). In neuroimaging research it has been observed that patterns of activity in PFC change with (1) increasing delay intervals (e.g. Awh et al., 1996) and (2) increases in the amount of information that must be maintained over a delay interval (Rypma & D'Esposito, 1999, 2000; Rypma & Gabrieli, in press; Rypma, Prabhakaran, Desmond, Glover, & Gabrieli, 1999). Specifically, low memory-demand conditions (e.g., maintenance of two or three letters) involved mainly ventrolateral PFC, whereas high memory-demand conditions involved dorsolateral PFC, in addition to ventrolateral PFC.

Behavioural studies demonstrating age differences in WM maintenance when memory loads exceed capacity, and neuroimaging studies demonstrating functional subdivisions of PFC in conditions under which age-related behavioural differences are observed, led us to hypothesise that the neural basis of age-related WM performance declines may be related specifically to age-related changes in dorsolateral, but not ventrolateral, PFC. Results from three experiments, described next, provided evidence to support this hypothesis.

In the first study, six younger subjects (mean age = 25.0) and six older community-dwelling subjects (mean age = 68.8) underwent fMRI while performing a delayed response WM maintenance task (see Figure 3) in which, on each trial, they first encoded either two or six letters, presented for 4 s; second, retained them across an unfilled 12-s interval; and, third, determined, within 2 s, whether or not that letter was part of the memory set. A 16-s intertrial interval that allowed fMRI signal to return to baseline followed each trial. We used an event-related fMRI design that allowed us to examine separately age-related differences in neural activity associated with stimulus encoding, memory maintenance, and memory retrieval during the WM task.

In our event-related design, least-squares parameter estimates were

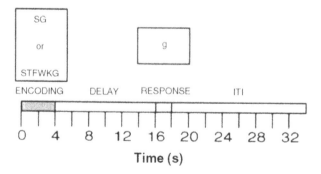

Figure 3. The trial sequence of the behavioural task. On each trial, subjects first encoded either two or six letters (in principal experiments and replication experiment 1), presented for 4 s. Second, they retained the letters across an unfilled 12-s interval. Third, a single letter appeared on the screen and subjects determined, within 2 s, whether or not that letter was part of the memory set. A 16-s intertrial interval followed each trial.

derived (for each subject) by modelling the hypothesised change in neural activity at each period of the task (Encoding, Delay, Response). Hypothesised neural activity in each task period was modelled with covariates comprised of blood-oxygen-level dependent (BOLD) haemodynamic response functions shifted in time to model activity at each task period. Details of this method can be found in, e.g., Zarahn, Aguirre, and D'Esposito (1997; see also Postle, Zarahn, & D'Esposito, 2000). The haemodynamic response function (HRF) used to construct the covariate was derived empirically for each subject from the (neuroanatomically defined) sensory-motor cortex (Aguirre et al., 1998). We assessed our hypotheses of age-related differences in PFC neural activity with random-effects tests of age-differences in the mean parameter estimates (i.e., the beta values derived from the least-squares solution of a linear model of the dependent data) that characterised fMRI signal during each task component. These parameter estimates were *not* scaled by the model error term (which would typically be used to obtain *t*-statistics for each voxel). This method avoided use of the noise component of fMRI signal since, in the study presented earlier, we observed reliable age-related differences in the noise component which could lead to the spurious inference of age-related differences in intensity of neural activity.

In the principal experiment, performance data indicated that subjects performed with high accuracy that did not differ between the two memory load conditions. Reaction times (RT) were faster in the two-letter than in the six-letter condition. Performance accuracy was not significantly different between younger and older subjects but younger subjects were faster than older subjects. Analyses of imaging data revealed no significant age-related differences in ventrolateral PFC regions, collapsed across hemispheres, in either of the memory load conditions during any of the task periods (i.e., stimulus encoding, retention interval, and response). In dorsolateral PFC, there were no significant age-related differences in regional activation during the encoding period and the retention period. Younger subjects, however, showed significantly greater activation than older subjects in the six-letter condition, during the response period (Mann-Whitney U, $p = .01$; Figure 4). No other effects reached significance (all $ps > .10$).

Similar to findings from our earlier study (Rypma & D'Esposito, 1999) with young adults, we observed considerable intersubject variability in fMRI signal in PFC in older adults. We therefore sought to further explore our findings of age group differences in dorsolateral PFC activity in terms of individual differences between subjects in the younger and older groups. To formally test relationships between cortical activity and performance, we performed regression analyses of subjects' RT and PFC activity (indexed by mean parameter estimates in dorsolateral and

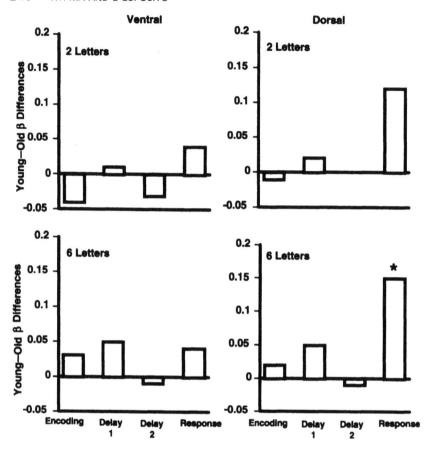

Figure 4. Age-group differences in activation by PFC region, memory-based condition, and task period. Age-group differences in regional mean parameter estimates (β) for dorsal and ventral PFC ROIs at each task period (encoding, delay, and retrieval) in the two- and six-letter memory load conditions. Activation differences above 0 indicate a difference favouring younger subjects. Asterisk denotes statistically significant age-group difference.

ventrolateral PFC in each task period). Tests of the regression coefficients that characterise the relationship between mean RT and ventrolateral PFC activity were nonsignificant. In dorsolateral PFC in younger subjects, *response* period regression coefficients showed a significant *positive* correlation (slope = .85, $p < .03$) between mean RT and cortical activity that accounted for 71% of the variance. In contrast, in dorsolateral PFC in older subjects, *response* period regression coefficients showed a significant *negative* correlation (slope = −.85, $p < .03$) between mean

RT and cortical activity that accounted for 72% of the variance. These relationships are presented in Figure 5a.

It is important to note that our finding of significant age-related differences in fMRI signal in dorsolateral PFC cannot be attributed to differences in HRF coupling for at least two reasons. The first and most obvious is that our measurement of neural activity was based on parameter estimates (which index age-invariant fMRI signal components independent of age-variable noise components) derived from our regression analyses. This method permitted us to circumvent those aspects of fMRI signal that appear to vary with age. Second, the hypothesis that this result could be attributed to age differences in HRF coupling would seem to require that it was observed in all task periods, not just during the retrieval period (that is, haemodynamic coupling would not be expected to vary as a function of cognitive factors).

These results are intriguing because they suggest that the pervasive age-related slowing observed across many different kinds of widely divergent behavioural tasks may result from a fundamental change in brain-behaviour relationships with age. Our proposal is that changes in the relationship between neural activity and performance that we observed in these data reflect an age-related decrease in neural efficiency. This age-differential neural efficiency provides a plausible neural mechanism for age-related changes that are observed in performance. It may be that age-

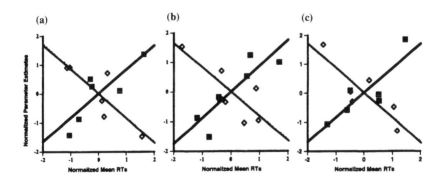

Figure 5. Scatter plots of the normalised regional mean parameter estimates during the response period in dorsolateral PFC plotted against normalised RTs in younger subjects (squares, principal exp. (a): slope = .84, r^2 = .71, p < .03; replication. exp. 1 (b): slope = .87, r^2 = .76, p < .01; replication exp. 2 (c) = .88, r^2 = .78, p < .05) and older subjects (diamonds, principal exp. (a): slope = –0.85, r^2 = .72, p < .03; replication exp. 1 (b): slope = –.82, r^2 = .68, p < .04; replication exp. 2 (c) slope = –.87, r^2 = .76, p < .03).

related changes in a *specific* region of the brain, dorsolateral PFC, may lead to a *generalised* age-related slowing of behaviour.

For such an argument to be plausible *prima facie* would seem to require that two minimal conditions be met. The first requirement is that this result would *replicate* with a different group of subjects performing a similar task. The second requirement is that this result would *generalise* to a different group of subjects performing a different kind of cognitive task. We therefore sought evidence for these two conditions in two subsequent experiments.

To test the *replicability* of our findings, we performed these analyses in a second experiment with a different group of six younger and six older subjects performing the same working memory task as was described previously. Analyses of the data from replication experiment 1 indicated that response period regression coefficients in dorsolateral PFC showed a significant positive correlation (slope = .87, $p < .01$, $r^2 = .76$) between mean RT and cortical activity in younger subjects but a significant negative correlation (slope = $-.82$, $p < .04$, $r^2 = .68$) between mean RT and cortical activity in older subjects (Figure 5b). No such correlations were observed in ventrolateral PFC.

To assess the *generalisability* of these findings, similar analyses were performed on data from a third group of younger and older subjects performing a different WM task (replication experiment 2). In this task, subjects initially viewed a series of three objects that sequentially appeared in three distinct locations in a 3 × 3 grid followed by an 8-s retention interval. Memory load was varied by requiring subjects to encode and maintain either two features (i.e., an object in a location) or only one feature (i.e., an object or a location). A test probe then appeared for 2 s, followed by a 12-s intertrial interval. On object trials, the test probe was a black and white object in the centre of a grid; subjects responded "yes" if the probe corresponded to a studied item on that trial and "no" if it did not. On location trials, the test probe was a black dot in one of the grid cells (other than the centre) and participants responded "yes" if it appeared in a location that an object had occupied on that trial and "no" if it appeared elsewhere. On combination trials, a black and white object appeared in one of the periphery cells and participants responded "yes" if the test probe corresponded exactly to a studied object/location pairing and "no" if it did not. Distractor items in this condition were always re-pairings of objects and locations from the current trial. The results indicated a replication of our main finding. Specifically, we observed (1) greater cortical activity in younger than in older in dorso- ($U = 3.0$, $p = .05$) but not ventrolateral PFC, and (2) significant patterns of RT–fMRI signal correlations that were positive for the younger age group (slope = .88, $r^2 = .78$, $p < .05$) but negative for the older age group (slope $= -.87$, $r^2 = .76$, $p < .02$; Figure 5c).

These results suggest that decreased speed of information retrieval at response (possibly reflecting less efficient memory-scanning processes, Sternberg, 1969) is related to increases in dorsolateral PFC activation for younger subjects, but to decreases in dorsolateral PFC activation for older subjects. Much converging evidence now exists to suggest that reductions in processing speed are related to age-related decreases in the overall efficiency of cognitive processing (e.g., Myerson, Hale, Wagstaff, Poon, & Smith, 1990; Salthouse, 1996). The current results suggest that there may be age-related differences in the neural correlates of processing efficiency.

Reductions in neural efficiency may lead to slowing of cognitive processes, specifically, the speed with which information can be activated in WM. Slower activation at memory retrieval may lead to degradation in the quality of information available for later response-stage processing. One correlate of low quality information available at the response stage could be reductions in the neural activation levels that permit discrimination between potential responses.

Some models of response processes suggest that the sigmoid relationship between a neuron's input activation and its firing probability may have consequences at the behavioural level (Kimberg, D'Esposito, & Farah, 1997; Servan-Schreiber, Printz, & Cohen, 1990). Response selection may be characterised as a signal detection mechanism in which the probability of a given response is determined by the relative strength of signal associated with each possible response. Thus, the sigmoid activation function relates neural activation levels to differences in signal strength between potential responses. Middle ranges of neural activation result in large differences in signal and easy discrimination between potential responses. As neural activation levels move above or below this range, potential responses become progressively less discriminable (Figure 6).

The age-related differences we observed in the relationship between neural activation and performance suggest that ageing may result in an overall reduction in neural activity in dorsolateral PFC. One consequence of this reduced neural activity may be that higher neural activation levels would be required to achieve optimal response discriminability. That is to say, for older adults, the sigmoid activation function may be shifted to the right (Figure 6). In this model, low levels of activation lead to optimum response discriminability for younger adults but to suboptimum response discriminability for older adults. As neural activation levels increase and move to the right of the sigmoid functions, response discriminability moves into the optimum range of older adults

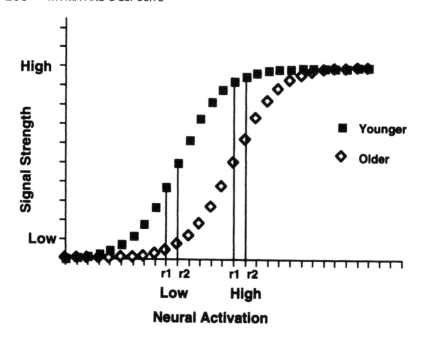

Figure 6. A sigmoid activation model of age-related differences in brain–behaviour relationships. The age-related differences we observed in the relationship between neural activity
and performance suggest that a sigmoid function may characterise the relationship between
neural activation levels and WM performance. In this model, potential responses (r1 and r2)
are selected on the basis of signal strength. The sigmoid activation function is shifted to the
right for older adults, suggesting that there may be age-related increases in the input activation required for cells to fire. This age-related change amounts to a bias-shift in the sigmoid
equation. At the behavioural level, the implication is that low levels of activation lead to
optimum response-discriminability for younger adults but to suboptimum response discriminability for older adults. As neural activation levels increase and shift to the right of the
sigmoid functions, response discriminability moves into an optimal range for older adults but
into a supraoptimal range for younger adults.

but into a supraoptimal range for younger adults. Such a model is
speculative at this stage but one implication is that increases in neural
activation will lead to improvements in performance for older adults but
to decrements in performance for younger adults. Just such relationships
between neural activation and performance were observed in the current
data.

SIMULATING AGE DIFFERENCES IN
BRAIN–BEHAVIOUR RELATIONSHIPS

The model we have proposed suggests that reductions in a single parameter, the overall neural activity level, lead to the neural inefficiency that underlies the inefficiency associated with age-related performance reductions. Can this fairly complex mechanism result from the adjustment of a single parameter? We and our colleagues have attempted to answer this question (Bretschneider, Viviani, Rypma, & D'Esposito, 2000; Viviani & Rypma, 1999) using PDP modelling techniques. The model we tested was based on the equation that renders a sigmoid function:

$$f_G(x) = \frac{1}{1 + e^{-(Gx + B)}} \qquad (1)$$

In equation 1, G refers to the level of gain in the function. Changes in the gain parameter alter the slope of the sigmoid function. B in the equation models the bias in the function. Changes in the bias parameter alter the X-offset, or left–right position, of the resulting function.

The prediction of the current model is that changes in the bias parameter, but not the gain parameter, result in the age differential patterns of brain–behaviour relationships that we have observed. Thus, age-related differences are modelled as different biases in the output. A positive bias is exactly equivalent to an activation function shifted to the left. A negative bias is exactly equivalent to an activation function shifted to the right. Thus, to test the model we gave older subjects lower biases in the output layer relative to younger subjects.

The input was set according to three parameters. The first is the input norm, i.e., the average total activation present in the input in each iteration. This parameter varied according to the differences in activation seen in the fMRI study presented earlier. The second is the average contrast between the highest and the lowest activation in the input. This parameter modelled the memory load in the two trial series. The third parameter regulated the variance of a noise term with a Gaussian distribution. The noise in the input translates into occasional incorrect responses, which are related to the accuracy level measured in the experiment.

To calculate the activation in the output, the sum of the input received from all connections was passed to the logistic function (equation 1). As is clear from equation 1, and as stated earlier, the output is regulated by two parameters. The first is the gain G (which regulates the slope of the logistic function). In the simulations, G was kept constant at a value of 2.5. The second is the bias B which regulates the shift of the logistic function in the x-axis direction of the output nodes. As dictated by our hypothesis, we modelled the older condition with a lower bias (−1.8) than the younger (−1.0). These parameters yielded age-differential sigmoid functions similar to those in Figure 6.

The raw data of the simulation are presented in Table 1. In the left column the input parameters are listed. The right column lists the measurements averaged over 5000 trials of the gradient (inversely related to reaction times), the activation levels, and the accuracy. The activation level in the output has no correspondence in the experimental data, but is useful to assess in what region of the logistic function are situated the input data. An activation level of 0.50 means that the input values are optimal.

The data on the input activation norm and the gradient are plotted in Figure 7. As the figure shows, the reaction times are a linear transformation of the inverse of the activation gradients. Hence, the relationship between neural activity recovered from the simulation closely resembles those we observed in the studies presented previously. These results are consistent with the idea of a single mechanism of age-related changes in which WM performance declines are mediated by overall reductions in neural activity in dorsolateral PFC.

TABLE 1
Results of simulation

Input			Output	
Younger adults, normal activation				
Norm	1.0	Gradient	0.073 (0.068)	
Contrast	0.145	Activation	0.50	
Noise	0.1	Accuracy	0.85	
Younger adults, higher activation				
Norm	1.8	Gradient	0.031 (0.030)	
Contrast	0.145	Activation	0.88	
Noise	0.1	Accuracy	0.84	
Older adults, normal activation				
Norm	1.0	Gradient	0.031 (0.030)	
Contrast	0.145	Activation	0.12	
Noise	0.1	Accuracy	0.84	
Older adults, higher activation				
Norm	1.8	Gradient	0.072 (0.069)	
Contrast	0.145	Activation	0.49	
Noise	0.1	Accuracy	0.85	

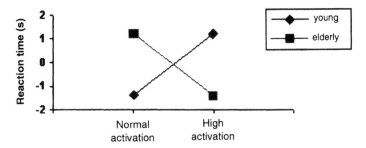

Figure 7. Reaction times as a function of activation levels. The data on the input activation norm and the gradient are plotted. The reaction times are a linear transformation of the inverse of the activation gradients.

CONCLUSION

These studies represent our initial efforts to understand the relationship between age-related changes in neural activity and performance. Our ability to make accurate observations rests not only on advanced technology but also on careful consideration of the potential pitfalls in this technology. The studies that we and others have conducted to understand the age-related differences in characteristics of fMRI signal have shown physiological changes in neural activity and fMRI signal with normal ageing and they have allowed us to develop techniques that take account of these differing signal characteristics. As a result, we have measurably greater confidence in our results than we might otherwise have.

The correlational methods we have employed to characterise brain–behaviour relationships allow us to tightly couple individual differences in performance to individual differences in neural activity. Thus, an understanding of age-related changes in the haemodynamic response to neural activity, the superior spatial resolution of fMRI, and the improved temporal resolution afforded by event-related fMRI methodology have permitted us to focus our analyses at a proximal analytic level. With these methodological improvements, we are able to advance more precise speculation about the nature of age differences in neural activity between younger and older adults.

The results of our studies suggest several empirically tractable hypotheses about the brain basis of age differences in performance that are consistent with emerging evidence that distinct neural systems in dorso-lateral and ventrolateral PFC selectively mediate different WM operations. First, they suggest that age-related decline in WM performance may be tied more to age-related physiological changes in dorsolateral than ventrolateral PFC. Second, they suggest that age-related differences in dorsolateral PFC function may exert their effects mainly during the retrieval of temporarily stored information and not necessarily during the encoding and maintenance of such information. Finally, they suggest that age-related WM performance declines may be mediated by overall reductions in retrieval-related neural activity in dorsolateral PFC.

Manuscript received September 2000

REFERENCES

Aguirre, G.K., Zarahn, E., & D'Esposito, M. (1998). The variability of the human BOLD hemodynamic responses. *NeuroImage, 8*, 360–369.

Anders, T.R., Fozard, J.L., & Lillyquist, T.D. (1972). Effects of age upon retrieval from short-term memory. *Developmental Psychology, 6*, 214–217.

Awh, E., Jonides, J., Smith, E., Schumacher, E., Koeppe, R., & Katz, S. (1996). Dissociation of storage and rehearsal in verbal working memory: Evidence from PET. *Psychological Science, 7*, 25–31.

Blamire, A.M., Ogawa, S., Ugurbil, K., Rothman, D., McCarthy, G., Ellermann, J.M., Hyder, F., Rattner, Z., & Shulman, R.G. (1992). Dynamic mapping of the human visual cortex by high-speed magnetic resonance imaging. *Proceedings of the National Academy of Sciences of the United States of America, 89*, 11069–11073.

Bohl, J.R.E., & Hori, A. (1997). Vascular changes. In S.U. Dani, A. Hori, & G.F. Walter (Eds.), *Principles of neural aging*. Amsterdam: Elsevier.

Botwinick, J., & Storandt, M. (1974). *Memory, related functions, and age*. Springfield, IL: Charles C. Thomas.

Bretschneider, V., Viviani, R., Rypma, B., & D'Esposito, M. (2000). A model of prefrontal cortical activation and performance in working memory tasks in younger and older subjects. *Abstracts of the Cognitive Neuroscience Society Meeting, 2000*, 141.

Bromley, J. (1958). Some effects of age on short-term learning and memory. *Journal of Gerontology, 13*, 12–21.

Burke, D.M., & Light, L.L. (1981). Memory and aging: The role of retrieval processes. *Psychological Bulletin, 3*, 513–546.

Cabeza, R., Grady, C.L., Nyberg, L., McIntosh, A.R., Tulving, E., Kapur, S., Jennings, J.M., & Craik, F.I.M. (1997). Age-related differences in neural activity during memory encoding and retrieval: A positron emission tomography study. *Journal of Neuroscience, 17*, 391–400.

Craik, F.I.M. (1977). Age differences in human memory. In J.E. Birren & K.W. Schaie (Eds.), *Handbook of the psychology of aging* (pp. 384–420). New York: Van Nostrand Reinhold.

Craik, F.I.M. (1968). Short-term memory and the aging process. In G.A. Talland (Ed.), *Human aging and behavior* (pp. 131–168). New York: Academic Press.

Cunnington, R., Iansek, R., Bradshaw, J.L., Phillips, J.G. (1995). Movement-related potentials in Parkinson's disease: Presence and predictability of temporal and spatial cues. *Brain, 118*, 935–950.

D'Esposito, M., Zarahn, E., Aguirre, G.K., & Rypma, B. (1999). The effect of normal aging on the coupling of neural activity to the BOLD hemodynamic response. *NeuroImage, 10,* 6–14.

Fang, H.C.H. (1976). Observations on aging characteristics of cerebral blood vessels, macroscopic and microscopic features. In S. Gershon & R.D. Terry (Eds.), *Neurobiology of aging.* New York: Raven.

Friedman, H. (1974). Interrelation of two types of immediate memory in the aged. *Journal of Psychology, 87,* 177–181.

Friston, K.J. (1994/1995). Statistical parametric maps in functional imaging: A general linear approach. *Human Brain Mapping, 2,* 189–210.

Gabrieli, J.D.E. (1991). Brain basis of changes in memory performance in aging and in Alzheimer's disease. *Experimental Aging Research, 17,* 96–97.

Gabrieli, J.D.E. (1996). Memory systems analyses of mnemonic disorders in aging and age-related disease. *Proceedings of the National Academy of Sciences of the United States of America, 93,* 13534–13540.

Gabrieli, J.D.E., & Rypma, B. (1997). Cognitive neuroscience and human aging. *The Cutting Edge: APA Division 20's Newsletter.*

Gilbert, J.G., & Levee, R.F. (1971). Patterns of declining memory. *Journal of Gerontology, 26,* 70–75.

Grady, C.L. (1996). Age-related changes in cortical blood flow activation during perception and memory. *Annals of the New York Academy of Sciences, 777,* 14–21.

Grady, C.L., McIntosh, A.R., Horwitz, B., Maisog, J.M., Ungerleider, L.G., Mentis, M.J., Pietrini, P., Schapiro, M.B., & Haxby, J.V. (1995). Age-related reductions in human recognition memory due to impaired encoding. *Science, 269,* 218–221.

Haug, H. (1997). The aging human cerebral cortex: Morphometry of areal differences and their functional meaning. In S.U. Dani, A. Hori, & G.F. Walter (Eds.), *Principles of neural aging.* Amsterdam: Elsevier.

Jonides, J., Marshuetz, C., Smith, E.E., Reuter-Lorenz, P.A., Koeppe, R.A., & Hartley, A. (2000). Brain activation reveals changes with age in resolving interference in verbal working memory. *Journal of Cognitive Neuroscience, 12,* 188–196.

Kimberg, D.Y., D'Esposito, M., & Farah, M.T. (1997). Effects of bromocriptine on human subjects depend on working memory capacity. *Neuroreport, 8,* 3581–3585.

Madden, D.J., Turkington, T.G., Provenzale, J.M., Denny, L.L., Hawk, T.C., Gottlob, L.R., & Coleman, R.E. (1999). Adult age differences in functional neuroanatomy of verbal recognition memory. *Human Brain Mapping, 7,* 115–135.

Marsh, G.R. (1975). Age differences in evoked potential correlates of a memory scanning process. *Experimental Aging Research, 1,* 3–16.

Menon, R.S., Ogawa, S., Hu, X., Strupp, J.P., Anderson, P., & Ugurbil, K. (1995). BOLD based functional MRI at 4 Telsa includes a capillary bed contribution: Echo-planar imaging correlates with previous optical imaging using intrinsic signals. *Magnetic Resonance in Medicine, 33,* 453–459.

Myerson, J., Hale, S., Wagstaff, D., Poon, L.W., & Smith, G.A. (1990). The information-loss model: A mathematical theory of age-related cognitive slowing. *Psychological Review, 97,* 475–487.

Nielsen-Bohlman, L., & Knight, R.T. (1995). Prefrontal alterations during memory processing in aging. *Cerebral Cortex, 5,* 541–549.

Poon, L.W., & Fozard, J.L. (1980). Age and word frequency effects in continuous recognition memory. *Journal of Gerontology, 35,* 77–86.

Postle, B.R., Zarahn, E., & D'Esposito, M. (2000). Using event-related fMRI to assess delay-period activity during performance of spatial and nonspatial working memory tasks. *Brain Research Protocols, 5,* 57–66.

Prull, M., Bunge, S., & Gabrieli, J.D.E. (2000). In F.I.M. Craik & T.A. Salthouse (Eds.), *Handbook of aging and cognition.* Mahwah, NJ: Lawrence Erlbaum Associates Inc.

Raz, N. (2000). Aging of the brain and its impact on cognitive performance: Integration of structural and functional findings. In F.I.M. Craik & T.A. Salthouse (Eds.), *Handbook of aging and cognition* (pp. 1–90). Mahwah, NJ: Lawrence Erlbaum Associates Inc.

Reuter-Lorenz, P.A., Jonides, J., Smith, E.E., Hartley, A., Miller, A., Marshuetz, C., & Koeppe, R.A. (2000). Age differences in the frontal lateralization of verbal and spatial working memory revealed by PET. *Journal of Cognitive Neuroscience, 12,* 174–187.

Rypma, B., & D'Esposito, M. (1999). The roles of prefrontal brain regions in components of working memory: Effects of memory load and individual differences. *Proceedings of the National Academy of Sciences, 96,* 6558–6563.

Rypma, B., & D'Esposito, M. (2000). Isolating the neural mechanisms of age-related changes in human working memory. *Nature-Neuroscience, 3,* 509–515.

Rypma, B., & Gabrieli, J.D.E. (in press). Functional neuroimaging of short-term memory: The neural mechanisms of mental storage. *Behavioral and Brain Sciences.*

Rypma, B., Prabhakaran, V., Desmond, J.E., & Gabrieli, J.D.E. (2000). Age differences in prefrontal cortical activity in working memory. *Manuscript submitted.*

Rypma, B., Prabhakaran, V., Desmond, J.E., Glover, G.H., & Gabrieli, J.D.E. (1999). Load-dependent roles of prefrontal cortical regions in the maintenance of working memory. *NeuroImage, 9,* 216–226.

Salthouse, T.A. (1991). *Theoretical perspectives on cognitive aging.* Hillsdale, NJ: Lawrence Erlbaum Associates Inc.

Salthouse, T.A. (1996). The processing speed theory of adult age differences in cognition. *Psychological Review, 97,* 475–487.

Servan-Schreiber, D., Printz, H., & Cohen, J.D. (1990). A network model of catecholamine effects: Gain, signal to noise ratio, and behavior. *Science, 249,* 892–895.

Smith, A.D. (1975). Aging and interference with memory. *Journal of Gerontology, 30,* 319–325.

Taub, H.A. (1973). Memory span, practice and aging. *Journal of Gerontology, 28,* 335–338.

Viviani, R., & Rypma, B. (1999). *A model of prefrontal cortical activation and performance in working memory tasks* (Technical Rep. No. 3). Ulm, Germany: University of Ulm, Dept. of Psychiatry.

Worsley, K.J. (1994). Local maxima and the expected euler characteristics of excursions sets of chi-squared, f and t fields. *Advanced Application Problems, 26,* 13–42.

Worsley, K.J., & Friston, K.J. (1995). Analysis of fMRI time-series revisited—again. *Neuro-Image, 2,* 173–182.

Zarahn, E., Aguirre, G.K., & D'Esposito, M. (1997). Empirical analyses of BOLD fMRI statistics: I. Spatially unsmoothed data collected under null-hypothesis conditions. *Neuro-Image, 5,* 179–195.

EUROPEAN JOURNAL OF COGNITIVE PSYCHOLOGY, 2001, *13* (1/2), 257–278

Neurocognitive ageing of storage and executive processes

Patricia A. Reuter-Lorenz, Christy Marshuetz, John Jonides and Edward E. Smith

Department of Psychology, University of Michigan, Ann Arbor, USA

Alan Hartley

Department of Psychology, Scripps College, Claremont, USA

Robert Koeppe

Division of Nuclear Medicine, University of Michigan, Ann Arbor, USA

Converging behavioural and neuropsychological evidence indicates that age-related changes in working memory contribute substantially to cognitive decline in older adults. Important questions remain about the relationship between working memory storage and executive components and how they are affected by the normal ageing process. In several studies using positron emission tomography (PET), we find age differences in the patterns of frontal activation during working memory tasks. We find that separable age differences can be linked to different cognitive operations underlying short-term information storage, and interference resolution. Some operations are associated with age-related increases in activation, with older adults displaying bilateral activations and recruiting prefrontal areas more than younger adults. Other operations are associated with age-related decreases in activation. We consider the implications of these results for understanding the working memory system and potential compensatory processes in the ageing brain.

Requests for reprints should be addressed to P.A. Reuter-Lorenz, Department of Psychology, University of Michigan, Ann Arbor, 48109-1109, USA. Email: parl@umich.edu

This research was supported by grants from the National Institute on Ageing (NIA AG8808, AG13027), all to the University of Michigan. The research assistance of Anna Cianciolo, Elisa Rosier, Michael Kia, Edward Awh, Leon Gmeindl, Andrea Miller, Anat Geva, and David Badre is gratefully acknowledged. C. Marshuetz is now at the Department of Psychology, Yale University, New Haven, CT.

http://www.tandf.co.uk/journals/pp/09541446.html   DOI:10.1080/09541440042000304

Baddeley's model of working memory postulates separable storage and executive components (Baddeley, 1986, 1992). The storage buffers are generally viewed as relatively passive, "slave" systems operating in the service of the executive processing components that mediate coding, manipulation, and selection of stored contents. A major focus of neuro-cognitive research on working memory is to define the neural and cogni-tive operations that underlie storage and executive processes and to specify the functional relationship between these components of the working memory system. This agenda has important implications for advances in cognitive ageing research because alterations in working memory play a central role in age-related cognitive decline (Engle, Kane, & Tuholski, 1999; Park et al., 1996; Salthouse, 1992; Salthouse & Babcock, 1991; Zacks, Hasher, & Li, 2000). There is broad agreement in the cognitive ageing literature that basic measures of short-term storage ability, as indexed by digit span and item recognition tasks, are less affected by ageing than working memory tasks that draw heavily on executive processing components, such as the reading span and operation span tasks (Babcock & Salthouse, 1990; Craik & Jennings, 1992; Dobbs & Rule, 1989; Salthouse, 2000; Salthouse & Babcock, 1991). Thus, on the face of it, ageing appears to honour the distinction between storage and processing components of the working memory system by affecting the latter disproportionately.

This apparent behavioural dissociation could result from any of several different neurobiological substrates. Most obviously, it could be that ageing selectively affects the neural operations associated with executive processing while sparing storage operations. If so, ageing would provide evidence for the structural and functional independence of these compo-nents of the working memory system. Furthermore, evidence that ageing affects only the processing components of the working memory system would challenge the idea that cognitive ageing effects stem from a unitary, globally acting mechanism (e.g., Salthouse, 1992).

An alternative account for the disproportional effects of age on tasks requiring executive processing turns on the notion of selective compensa-tion (cf. Cabeza et al., 1997; Grady et al., 1992). It may be that both storage and executive processes decline with age. However, during simple retention tasks executive operations can be recruited to compensate for storage decline, thereby ameliorating storage deficiencies.[1] Once enlisted

---

[1]According to some models, storage capabilities are inherent to the executive processes that are mediated by dorsolateral prefrontal cortex (DLPFC) (e.g., Cohen, Botvinick, & Carter, 2000; Goldman-Rakic, 1987). For example, Cohen and his colleagues propose that executive control entails the modulation of attentional and response processes by stored information about task demands (Cohen et al., 2000).

in the service of storage, however, executive operations are less available for other more demanding cognitive operations thereby accentuating impairments on executive processing tasks. According to this hypothesis, ageing affects multiple components of the working memory system at the level of neural substrate, but at the level of behaviour the effects appear selective. Note that these two hypotheses need not be mutually exclusive. Ageing could indeed have a disproportional effect on executive processes but to the extent that such operations remain functional they may be recruited to compensate for declining storage operations.

Evaluating these hypotheses will require defining the cognitive operations that mediate storage and executive processing demands, identifying the neural mechanisms and loci that implement these operations, and determining the structural and functional integrity of these mechanisms in the ageing brain. Towards these goals we have conducted a series of experiments on working memory in older adults (Jonides et al., 2000; Reuter-Lorenz et al., 2000). One of the key results to emerge from this work is that older and younger adults differ markedly in their patterns of frontal activation, while displaying similar patterns of activation in posterior cortical areas. We find that separable age differences can be linked to different cognitive operations underlying short-term information storage, and interference resolution. Some operations are associated with age-related increases in activation, with older adults displaying bilateral activations and recruiting prefrontal areas more than younger adults. Other operations are associated with age-related decreases in activation. Here we consider the implications of these results for understanding the working memory system and potential compensatory processes in the ageing brain. Before describing our work in detail, we highlight some of the evidence from primates and human patients with prefrontal lesions. These lines of work provide additional constraints on the localization and functional organisation of the working memory system that can inform our interpretation of the age-related changes we have observed.

FRONTAL CONTRIBUTIONS TO DELAYED RESPONSE PERFORMANCE: LESION EVIDENCE

Impaired delayed response performance has been traditionally associated with prefrontal damage. Variants of this task have become part of the canon of working memory research. It appears however that prefrontal lesions have different effects on delayed response performances in monkeys and in humans. Here we briefly review these differences and suggest several ways they may be instructive about the mechanisms of working memory.

Jacobsen's classic experiments (1931) on the delayed-response performance in monkeys were among the first to reveal the importance of prefrontal cortex to mnemonic processes. Basically, the delayed response task requires the monkey to view one of two identical stimuli (e.g., food wells) being baited with a reward, to retain this information while the stimuli are briefly hidden from view, and then to retrieve the reward. Thus, as in the item recognition task to be discussed later, a limited amount of information must be retained over a delay of only several seconds. The spatial delayed response task and certain of its variants are exquisitely and selectively sensitive to damage to the lateral regions of prefrontal cortex in monkeys, namely the caudal territory of the principal sulcus which corresponds to Brodmann's area (BA) 46/9 in humans (Goldman-Rakic, 1987; Petrides, 1994). This task would therefore seem to hold great promise in revealing the secrets of frontal lobe functions. Yet, despite its simplicity, the precise role of dorsolateral prefrontal cortex in the delayed response task in monkeys is still debated (see, e.g., Goldman-Rakic, 1998; Petrides, 1998).

In the human lesion literature, the link between prefrontal cortex and delayed response performance is less remarkable. In a recent review D'Esposito and Postle (1999) found significant delayed response deficits from prefrontal lesions in only three out of eight conditions[2] (across six different studies). Prefrontal deficits were more robust when the delay period was filled with distraction, in which case five out of seven conditions across five different studies yielded reliable differences between frontal patients and intact controls. As D'Esposito and Postle point out, the discrepancies among the human studies could be due to differences in task parameters, such as memory set size, delay period, material type, and response demands. In addition, the extent, loci, and aetiology of frontal lesions differ greatly among the patients in these samples, and thus lack the precision and uniformity of the primate studies.

But the species difference in delayed response deficits may stem from other factors as well. One important possibility is the laterality of prefrontal damage. The experimentally produced prefrontal cortex (PFC) lesions in monkeys typically are bilateral whereas the human lesion patients usually have damage confined to one hemisphere or the other. To the extent that both hemispheres can mediate working memory processes, human patients with unilateral prefrontal damage could

---

[2]A condition here refers to whether the delayed response test used spatial or non-spatial materials. D'Esposito and Postle (1999) categorise their meta-analytic observations with respect to test type and lesion subgroup (e.g., invading or sparing 46/9).

perform the tasks using the intact hemisphere. Two additional pieces of information are consistent with this suggestion. First, a comparison of patients with unilateral and bilateral frontal lobe excisions revealed more pronounced deficits in the two bilateral patients (Owen, Sahakian, Semple, Polkey, & Robbins, 1995). In the face of excellent simultaneous matching performance, the bilateral patients showed dramatic deficits when matching consecutively presented visual-spatial displays at a delay of 0 ms (Owen et al., 1995). The unilateral groups showed delayed matching deficits but only at delays of 4 s or more. Lesion size could have contributed to this difference assuming that the bilateral lesions were larger than the unilateral lesions. Nevertheless, the effects are consistent with the possibility that the differences between monkey and human studies may stem from compensation by the intact hemisphere in human patients.

The second relevant fact is that three of the four studies (Chao & Knight, 1998; Ptito, Crane, Leonard, Amsel, & Caramanos, 1995; Verin et al., 1993) for which D'Esposito and Postle find significant delay response deficits report that lesion side has no impact on the magnitude of the deficit. This is also true of lateralised groups studied by Owen et al. (1995). This lack of asymmetry suggests functional overlap of the left and right prefrontal regions, and potential compensation by the intact hemisphere in cases with unilateral damage. Here again is a caveat to bear in mind. These tasks may have made minimal demands on putative "material-specific" processors. For example, the spatial delayed response tasks used by Verin et al. and by Ptito et al. were modelled closely on those used with monkeys and required the retention of a single location. Likewise, Chao and Knight used a single sound, and Owen used a single pattern. Had the memory load (or other task demands) been greater, lesion side may have played a greater role thereby reflecting the limits of compensation from intact brain regions (for a review see Jonides et al., 1996).

Human lesion studies, particularly the older ones, do not provide precise information about the contributions of different frontal subregions in the delayed response task. One notable exception is the report by Ptito et al. (1995), in which patients were subgrouped according to whether or not their excision included Brodmann's area 46. Indeed, only those patients with involvement of 46 showed deficits relative to normal controls in the unfilled delay condition. Although this result is consistent with the monkey work, the excisions involving area 46 appear to be larger than those that do not (see Ptito et al., 1995, Figure 1). The possibility remains, then, that involvement of some other PFC subregions underlie impaired performance in this group. Fortunately, the roles of frontal subregions in the human brain can be addressed by functional neuroimaging studies of delayed-response type tasks using PET and fMRI. We turn now to consider this body of work.

FRONTAL CONTRIBUTIONS TO WORKING MEMORY

Neuroimaging evidence

Neuroimaging studies have left no doubt that prefrontal regions are engaged when humans perform delayed-response type tasks. Several recent reviews, based largely on positron emission tomography (PET) studies of healthy young adults, reach the same conclusion: tasks that require the simple retention of up to four items, and test memory with a yes/no recognition test, activate one or more sites within Brodmann's area 6 as well as ventral prefrontal areas including Brodmann's 44, 45, and/or 47 (for reviews see Cabeza & Nyberg, 2000; D'Esposito et al., 1998; Smith & Jonides, 1999). The pattern of laterality is orderly, with a predominance of left-sided activation in these areas, particularly areas 6 and 44 (Broca's area), for verbal tasks, and right-sided activation, particularly areas 6 and 47 for spatial location memory. Several groups have proposed that these regions mediate the maintenance or storage components of working memory in conjunction with parietal sites in Brodmann's areas 40 and 7 (e.g., D'Esposito, Postle, Ballard, & Lease, 1999; Owen et al., 1999; Smith & Jonides, 1997).

Of interest is the fact that significant activation of dorsolateral prefrontal sites, 46 and 9, is relatively rare in studies requiring simple retention. It is now widely believed, however, that when executive demands are increased, by requiring that the stored items be manipulated in some way, by recoding them or monitoring and tracking contextual codes, then dorsolateral prefrontal (DLPFC) sites are engaged (e.g., Cabeza & Nyberg, 2000; Owen et al., 1999; D'Esposito, Postle, Ballard, & Lease, 1999; Petrides, 1998; Smith & Jonides, 1999; see also D'Esposito et al., 1995). There are also indications that DLPFC involvement is increased by lengthening the retention interval (Barch et al., 1997) or by increasing the memory load to supraspan levels (i.e., greater than five for verbal items; Rypma & D'Esposito, 1999; Rypma, Prabhakaran, Desmond, Glover, & Gabrieli, 1999). There is some contention however about the laterality of DLPFC activation in relation to the type of material being employed in the working memory task. Studies that have directly compared well-matched verbal and spatial analogues of the same working memory task have found the expected left–right differences, although activations tend to be more broadly bilateral (e.g., Smith, Jonides, & Koeppe, 1996). This asymmetry is not always found however (e.g., D'Esposito et al., 1998), making the functional lateralisation of DLPFC operations a topic of ongoing investigation, and one that may be particularly relevant to ageing, as we shall see.

A summary

To summarise, the precise role of prefrontal cortex in delayed response and item recognition tasks is a matter of some debate. Bilateral damage to DLPFC in primates leads to frank and robust disruption, whether or not the retention interval is filled. Unilateral prefrontal lesions in humans (which may or may not include DLPFC) have more detrimental effects when interference occurs during the retention intervals. Some functional overlap between left and right prefrontal subregions is suggested by the inconsistent effects of unilateral damage, and by the absence of a clear laterality effect when deficits do emerge. For basic storage tasks, neuro-imaging studies reveal fairly reliable patterns of hemispheric dominance for verbal and nonverbal materials in ventrolateral prefrontal and premotor areas. There is little evidence for DLPFC activation for loads less than five, with several indications that this area is recruited for higher loads and/or longer delays. The evidence for DLPFC activation is highly consistent for tasks that include additional processing and manipulation of stored items (i.e., executive demands), with a tendency toward bilateral activations under these conditions. Thus, the picture in young adults is that DLPFC does not have an obligatory role in short-term retention as measured by delayed response and item recognition tasks. With these considerations in mind, we turn to our own neuroimaging evidence addressing the neural substrate of working memory in the ageing brain.

AGEING AND THE NEURAL SUBSTRATE OF WORKING MEMORY

In one of the first neuroimaging studies to examine the effects of age on verbal working memory, we found striking differences between older and younger adults. The participants were 16 older adults between the ages of 65–75, and 8 younger adults aged 21–30. All were females. After a session of practice, PET images were obtained for each subject in a memory task in which subjects viewed four uppercase letters, retained them for 3 s, and then responded manually to indicate whether a lower-case probe letter matched or did not match one held in memory (Stern-berg, 1966). Subjects were also scanned while performing a minimal memory control task that was matched for perceptual and response requirements (see Figure 1; see Reuter-Lorenz et al., 2000 for a detailed

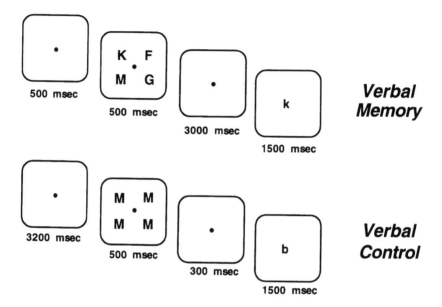

Figure 1. Cognitive tasks. Sequence of events and timing parameters for the verbal memory task and the minimal memory control. See Reuter-Lorenz et al. (2000) for more details.

description of methods). As expected, older adults had longer response latencies than younger adults on both tasks. For both groups control accuracy was at ceiling. The older adults were, however, less accurate than the younger adults on the memory task (92% vs 97%; $p < .02$).

Several different analyses were performed on the imaging data. First, we used a region of interest analysis to determine that the memory-related activations in the younger group were characteristic of previous results from our lab obtained with a similar task in young adults. Indeed, the regions of significant activation in our earlier study (see Smith et al., 1996), left 44 (Broca's area), left 6 (supplementary motor area), and left parietal sites in Brodmann's areas 7 and 40, were again active in our new sample of young adults. Moreover, the older adults showed reliable activation in each of these regions as well. Thus, there was an excellent correspondence between the left hemisphere areas activated in a verbal short-term retention task in younger and older adults.

However, visual inspection of the PET activation images and several additional analyses revealed a pronounced age difference (see Reuter-Lorenz, 2000, Figure 6.3): Older adults showed greater activity in the right hemisphere than the younger group, particularly in frontal regions. Even the most conservative analysis[3] revealed right 46/9 as one of the most active sites in older adults (see Reuter-Lorenz, et al., 2000, Table 2). We also devised additional analyses specifically to examine age differences in laterality of activations using documented evidence of the working memory circuitry. We compiled a corpus of active sites from published reports of verbal working memory tasks. Spherical volumes 1.5 cm in diameter were created around each reported peak pixel, and then a sister volume was created with the homologous coordinates in the opposite hemisphere. This allowed us to identify activation asymmetry (or its absence) throughout the working memory circuitry in both hemispheres for each age group.[4]

This circuitry analysis revealed significant activation in posterior regions including parietal areas 40 and 7 that was highly left lateralised in both younger and older adults. However, the differences in anterior asymmetry were striking. Overall, the older group activated the left and right anterior components of the working memory circuitry whereas younger adults showed only left hemisphere activation. A regional analysis indicated that the two RH areas that were uniquely activated in the older group were 44 (p = .02) and 46/9 (p < .0004; see Reuter-Lorenz et al., 2000, Table 3). These data were the first to indicate age differences in the lateral organisation of the verbal working memory circuitry.

We have since had the opportunity to replicate these results with a new group of older adults and here we report the results from this replication. Once again we used a four-item letter recognition task. One aim of this experiment, which we discuss later, was to examine age differences in resolving interference from prepotent responses (Jonides et al., 2000).

---

[3]Z-tests were performed on each pixel of the difference image resulting from the subtraction of the control image from the memory image. This analysis is conservative because it is entirely post hoc and requires corrections for numerous multiple comparisons.

[4]A set of 85 regions of interest (ROIs) was derived from published reports of peak pixels active during PET studies of verbal working memory tasks, including our own (see Reuter-Lorenz et al., 2000, Figure 2). The majority of these regions were in the left hemisphere and include frontal sites in Brodmann's 45, 46, 10 and 9, 44 (Broca's area), 6 (premotor and supplementary motor sites), parietal sites in areas 40 and 7, and temporal sites in 42 and 22. Spherical volumes were constructed around reported peak pixels, replicated in the symmetrical location in the opposite hemisphere, and then applied to each subject's memory-minus-control subtraction images, thereby permitting a comparison of the average activation changes across homologous regions. To assess differences in asymmetry in the front and back of the cortex, an anterior subset (n = 34) was defined in Talairach space as those ROIs with a y > 0 and a posterior subset (n = 33) with y < −10 and z > −10. The same approach was used to define spatial ROIs (see later) using a set of 98 regions from the published literature (see Reuter-Lorenz et al., 2000, Figure 2).

This required that in some conditions the probe item was familiar and thus highly associated with a "yes" response, while requiring a "no" response on that trial. Except for this manipulation and the fact that the memory set appeared on the screen for 750 rather than 500 ms, the task was the same as that used in the original ageing study reported by Reuter-Lorenz et al. (2000). There were 12 male participants in each age group (younger 19–30 years; older 61–72 years). Again, the older adults were significantly slower (e.g., 815 ms versus 683 ms for "yes" responses, $p < .001$) and slightly less accurate than the younger group (95% and 99% respectively, $p < .03$).[5] Our original ageing study armed us with a set of predicted sites of activation (ROIs) that could now be tested in a new sample of older adults, and we could test for age differences by applying them to the new group of young adults as well. Both age groups showed significant activation in the left hemisphere sites typically associated with verbal storage including supplementary motor area and parietal areas 40/7. However, only the older group showed activation in right 46/9 ($p < .008$). The younger group did not have reliable activation at this site.

The circuitry analysis based on working memory ROIs from the published literature again confirmed that younger adults activated prefrontal sites only in the left hemisphere, whereas older adults showed significant activation in prefrontal sites bilaterally. In this data set, the older group actually activated left 44 less than the younger group, while showing greater activation of right 44 (see Figure 2). The younger adults did not activate DLPFC in either hemisphere, whereas the older group showed marked right-sided activation in this site (see Figure 3). Unique to this replication experiment is the finding that older adults tended to activate left and right parietal sites in 40 and 7, whereas for younger adults activation in these regions was highly left lateralised.[6]

This pair of experiments demonstrates that in addition to activating the

---

[5]See Jonides et al., 2000 for detailed performance analyses. As we discuss subsequently, older adults performed more poorly than young adults in the high interference condition. However, only young adults showed a significant difference in activation between the high and low interference conditions which was exclusive to Brodmann's area 45 in the left hemisphere (Jonides, Smith, Marshuetz, Koeppe, & Reuter-Lorenz, 1998; Jonides et al., 2000). Therefore, the activation analyses we present here are from the average of the high and low interference conditions. For all of the analyses we report, the same patterns are also evident in each interference condition (versus the minimal memory control condition) alone.

[6]The subset of published ROIs that fell within Brodmann's areas 40 and 7 (see Reuter-Lorenz et al., 2000) was associated with 1.5% activation change in the left hemisphere ($p < .02$) and 0.3% change in the right hemisphere for younger adults. This left/right difference was significant ($p < .03$). For older adults there was 0.9% change in the left hemisphere and 0.8% in the right, both of which differed from zero ($p < .025$) and did not differ from each other.

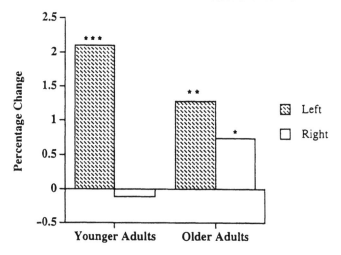

Figure 2. Working memory induced activation changes in Brodmann's area 44. Graph depicts percentage change in activation for the memory minus control subtractions in regions of interest falling within Brodmann's area 44. Asterisks denote significance levels when comparing activation changes to zero using one-tailed tests: * = $p < .06$; ** = $p < .001$; *** = $p < .0001$. The graph illustrates lateralised activation in 44 for younger adults but bilateral activation for older adults—left vs. right t-tests for younger and older respectively: $t(11) = 5.46$, $p = .0002$; $t(11) = 0.85$, $p > .20$. Younger adults activated left 44 more so than the older group, $t(22) = 1.63$, $p = .05$, whereas the opposite was true for right 44, $t(22) = 1.69$, $p = .05$.

canonical LH areas involved in short-term verbal storage, older adults activate several RH regions as well. One of these areas, DLPFC, is largely associated in young adults with working memory tasks that explicitly require executive processing operations in addition to storage. As noted earlier, two other manipulations have been shown to influence the magnitude of DLPFC activation in young adults in the context of working memory tasks. First, Barch et al. (1997) reported that lengthening the delay interval increased the magnitude of DLPFC activation, whereas visually degrading the memory items increased task difficulty but did not affect DLPFC. Second, Rypma and D'Esposito (1999) report an increase in the magnitude of right DLPFC activation as memory load increased from two to six items. Using an event-related fMRI design, they were able to isolate this load-dependent effect to the encoding phase of the trial. Thus, DLPFC involvement in younger adults appears to be modulated by load and storage duration manipulations. By specifically increasing the working memory demands, these manipulations could conceivably recruit executive operations such as attentional selection, contextual coding, or both.

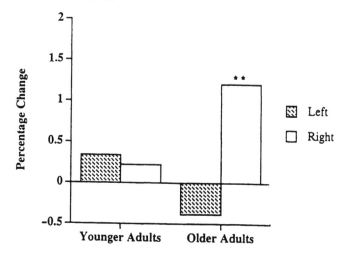

Figure 3. Working memory induced activation changes in dorsolateral prefrontal region. Graph depicts percentage change in activation for the memory minus control subtractions in regions of interest falling within Brodmann's areas 46/9. Asterisks denote significance levels when comparing activation changes to zero using one-tailed tests: ** = $p < .007$. Older adults show highly lateralised right-sided activity, whereas younger adults do not reliably activate this area in either hemisphere. The difference in the magnitude of right dorsolateral prefrontal cortex activation for older versus younger adults is reliable, $t(22) = 1.94, p = .03$.

These possibilities are important for our interpretation of right DLPFC activation in older adults. Their slower response times and reduced accuracies imply that older adults find these tasks more demanding than do younger adults. This difference in effective task difficulty could be driving the recruitment of DLPFC in older adults. In other words, in the ageing brain a memory load of four items retained for 3 s may be functionally equivalent to the same load at a longer delay or a greater load (six or more) at the same delay in the younger brain. Normally, DLPFC is recruited to meet these greater demands, and that is what we observe in older adults.

Our hypothesis, then, is that older adults recruit executive processes at lower levels of task demand than do young adults. By this account the additional sites of activation that we observe in older adults constitute a compensatory response to the age-related increase in task difficulty. Consistent with this proposal is the fact that combining the samples of older adults from both studies we find a significant inverse correlation between the magnitude of right DLPFC activation and response time ($r^2 = 0.143$; $p = .05$; see Figure 4). There was a non-significant trend toward a positive correlation between right DLPFC and right 44 activation (p = .08), although only the former was statistically related to performance.[7]

Several age-related changes could effectively increase task demands for older adults, such as decreased efficiency of rehearsal processes and increased vulnerability to interference. Indeed we have reason to think that both factors could be at work when older adults are performing

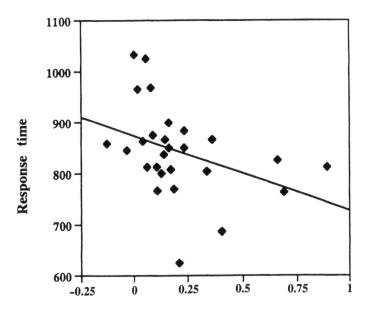

Percentage activation change

Figure 4. Scatter plot with regression line relating response times to the percentage activation change (verbal working memory vs minimal memory control) in right dorsolateral prefrontal cortex in older adults. The data include the set reported by Reuter-Lorenz et al. (2000) and those reported in the present paper.

---

[7]Using fMRI, Rypma and D'Esposito (2000, this issue) have found less DLPFC activity in older than younger adults at high memory loads (six items). This difference may stem from age differences in hemodynamic coupling (D'Esposito, Zarahn, Aguirre, & Rypma, 1999), although Rypma and D'Esposito (this issue) have developed new analysis methods to reduce this possibility. Nevertheless, Rypma and D'Esposito find that higher DLPFC activation in older adults is associated with better performance, a result that converges nicely with the pattern reported here.

these working memory tasks. Activation of right 44 could result if this right hemisphere homologue of Broca's area is recruited in the service of rehearsal in the older brain. This suggestion is motivated by several observations. Evidence indicates that left 44 contributes to overt and covert articulatory processes (e.g., rehearsal; Awh et al., 1996). There are also numerous indications that RH regions are capable of assuming some language functions of their LH counterparts (e.g., Baynes, Wessinger, Fendrich, & Gazzaniga, 1995; Kinsbourne, 1971). This compensatory potential is evident after early brain damage (e.g., Muller et al., 1999), and after LH injury occurring later in life (e.g., Buckner, Corbetta, Schatz, Raichle, & Petersen, 1996). Likewise, ageing may reveal the latent potential for RH compensation of certain language functions. Moreover, animal models of plasticity and recovery of function indicate that homologous regions in the opposite hemisphere provide a crucial substrate for functional compensation (see Nudo, 1999).[8]

On the other hand, DLPFC may be critical for modulating at least some forms of interference. Recall from our earlier review of the lesion literature that prefrontal damage including DLPFC is particularly detrimental when interference is high. Conceivably then, the DLPFC activation that we see in older adults may represent increased attention to rehearsal processes or contextual coding operations that can mitigate adverse effects of interference to which older adults are more prone (e.g., May, Hasher, & Kane, 1999). Although these suggestions are speculative they are clearly amenable to experimental analysis and our future studies will aim to test these hypotheses.

AGEING AND RESPONSE INTERFERENCE IN VERBAL WORKING MEMORY

Interference can arise from such varied sources as environmental input, irrelevant or no-longer relevant memory traces, or competing response

---

[8]In both of these observations plasticity and compensation are associated with the frankly compromised functioning of specialised regions. Our original study (Reuter-Lorenz et al., 2000) showed equivalent activation of Broca's area in younger and older adults. However, in the follow-up study reported here weaker left 44 activation was coupled with stronger right 44 activation in older compared to younger adults. It is conceivable that the global physiological, metabolic, and structural alterations that are part of the normal ageing process (e.g., Haug, 1997; Woodruff-Pak, 1997) compromise the efficiency of rehearsal mechanisms to an extent that can promote the recruitment of additional neural units in right 44. Accordingly, other lines of work have documented age-related reductions in left hemisphere dominance (i.e., greater bilaterality) for language with behavioural and electrical measures (see Bellis, Nicol, & Kraus, 2000).

tendencies. Prefrontal subregions may contribute differentially to resolving interference from these various sources. We have recently linked one particular site in ventrolateral prefrontal cortex (left 45) to the resolution of interference from prepotent responses (Jonides et al., 1998). Moreover, we have found that older adults are especially vulnerable to this form of interference and they are deficient in their activation of left 45 (Jonides et al., 2000).

This experiment used the basic letter recognition task with an important variation. Negative trials, requiring a "no" response, could be of two types. For "recent-negative" trials, the probe was a member of the memory set on the previous trial. Therefore it was highly familiar and had recently been associated with a "yes" response. As an example, the memory set on trial $n-1$ could consist of M, R, K, D and the set on trial n would consist of F, B, S, C. As a recent-negative probe for trial n, "k" would be familiar because of its membership in set $n-1$, but requires a "no" response. Recent-negatives were the predominant negative trial type in the high-recency condition (high interference). "Non-recent-negative" probes, on the other hand, had not been members of a memory set for at least the two prior trials. This type of negative trial defined the low-recency condition (low interference). Both younger and older adults required more time to reject recent-negative probes than non-recent negatives, but for older adults the difference between these conditions was disproportionately greater suggesting that it posed a particular challenge to them.

To identify the neural substrate associated with the processing of nonrecent compared to recent negative probes, blocks of trials with a preponderance of one trial type or the other were compared using PET. This analysis revealed a single site of activation in area 45 in prefrontal cortex that was present in younger adults but absent in their older counterparts (Jonides et al., 1998, 2000). We have proposed that this site is involved in processes that reduce response-related interference in younger adults, and that the inability to recruit this region by older adults contributes to their poorer performance.

The precise contribution of left 45 and its role in interference resolution is not yet known. However, event-related fMRI results from this task in younger adults (D'Esposito, Postle, Jonides, & Smith, 1999) indicate that area 45 activation emerges in the retrieval epoch of the task associated with the presentation of the probe. This temporal localisation implicates left 45 in mediating competing response tendencies and suggests that older adults have difficulty with this form of interference resolution. A related possibility is that area 45 is involved in resolving conflict between a familiarity code and a temporal code that, in the case of recent-negative probes, would lead to opposite responses.

It is interesting to note that, under the conditions where we observe an age-related absence of activation in area 45, we find that older adults are activating right DLPFC and right 44 to a greater extent than the younger group. This was established by our earlier comparisons of the high and low recency conditions to the minimal memory control condition (see earlier). The activations associated with these two levels of interference did not differ from each other in older adults, and, as described in the previous section, both were associated with significant activation of the right hemisphere homologues of the verbal working memory circuitry. These results suggest that rather than mediating verbal response inhibition *per se*, these right hemisphere regions may be contributing to contextual coding, attentional selection, or other processes that may be associated with working memory storage.

AGEING AND THE LATERAL ORGANISATION OF WORKING MEMORY

Our results indicate that ageing is accompanied by an alteration in the left lateralisation of neural activity associated with verbal working memory. As we noted previously, activation tends to be more bilateral in younger adults for high levels of working memory demand. The increased right anterior activation in our older group could reflect the same type of recruitment seen in the younger brain but at lower levels of task demand. Alternatively, the age differences in laterality could reflect adverse or compensatory changes that are unique to the ageing process. Whatever their functional significance, reports of age-related changes in the pattern of lateralised activity are becoming increasingly common.

For example, with a location recognition task (a variant of the spatial-delayed response task) we have shown an age difference in laterality that parallels that found in our work on verbal memory (Reuter-Lorenz et al., 2000). Designed as the spatial analogue of the verbal memory tasks, each trial consisted of a display of three dots at semi-random locations around a fixation cross. Subjects held these locations in mind for 3 s and, when the probe circle appeared, subjects indicated whether or not the probe encircled one of the remembered target locations. Region-of-interest analyses established that, as in previous work from our laboratory (Smith et al., 1996), the younger group showed a predominance of activation in parietal areas 7 and 40, and in right supplementary motor area (Brodmann's area 6) and ventral PFC (Brodmann's area 47). The older group also displayed significant activation in these areas; however as in the verbal study, their activation was more bilateral. Specifically, older adults significantly activated left supplementary motor area, and left

DLPFC (see footnote 4). It is noteworthy that the left DLPFC activation is nearly homologous to the right hemisphere activation in the verbal task. We cannot yet explain this paradoxical pattern of DLPFC asymmetry in the older group. The net result, however, is that tasks that produce asymmetrical activation in younger adults activate a bilateral network of prefrontal areas in older adults.

Other laboratories have also reported age differences in patterns of lateralised activity. Grady and her colleagues have found greater left DLPFC activation in older than younger adults in a short-term retention task using faces as the to-be-remembered items (Grady et al., 1998). This left-sided activation was coupled with less right ventrolateral prefrontal activity in the older than the younger group. In a series of studies on episodic memory, Cabeza and his colleagues (Cabeza, Anderson, Mangels, Nyberg, & Houle, 2000; Cabeza et al., 1997) found greater frontal bilaterality in older adults than younger adults have during the retrieval phase. Madden et al. (1999) have found a similar pattern in a semantic memory task. Outside the domain of memory, greater bilaterality in older adults has been found in a go/no-go task (Nielson, Garavan, Langenecker, Stein, & Rao, 2000) using fMRI, and in a phoneme processing task using ERPs (Bellis et al., 2000).

Do these age-related alterations in laterality have a common basis despite their emergence in seemingly diverse tasks? Do they stem from compensatory recruitment of additional brain regions or from a breakdown in inhibitory interactions between the two hemispheres? Definitive answers to these questions await future research. There are several reasons, however, to interpret these changes as compensatory. First, in our verbal working memory studies we find that activation of right DLPFC is positively correlated with performance speed among older adults. Similarly, in the spatial working memory task, the older adults were selected so that their level of accuracy was at least as good as the young adults in our sample. None the less, the older adults showed more bilateral anterior activation than the younger group. Second, the review of the human lesion literature presented in the introduction to this paper suggests functional overlap in the contribution of left and right prefrontal cortex to working memory, which could provide a substrate for compensation.

Another indication that bilateral activation is beneficial to older adults comes from our investigation of age-differences in a visual-matching task (Reuter-Lorenz, Stanczak, & Miller, 1999). This task was first developed by Banich and her colleagues (Banich, 1998; Belger & Banich, 1992) to examine the cognitive functions of interhemispheric interactions and the corpus callosum. Banich has shown that for easy matching tasks (e.g., smaller set size, physical identity match), young adults perform better when the matching letters are presented to the same visual field (i.e., hemisphere) than when they are presented to different hemispheres. However, as the match gets more complex (by including more letters or making the match more abstract) performance is better when the letters are presented to different hemispheres. We reasoned that if older adults benefit from engaging both hemispheres at lower levels of difficulty than do young adults, the bilateral presentation condition should be more advantageous for them. Indeed, this is what we have found. Older adults showed a performance advantage in the bihemispheric condition relative to the unilateral condition at lower levels of task difficulty than did the younger adults (Reuter-Lorenz et al., 1999; Reuter-Lorenz & Stanczak, 2000). The integrity of interhemispheric interactions in these matching tasks argues against the idea that changes in laterality result from a general decline in callosal function or impaired inhibition between the hemispheres with age (see Reuter-Lorenz & Stanczak, 2000). Instead, the ageing brain seems to benefit from engaging bilateral circuitry, as does the younger brain for higher levels of task demand.

CONCLUDING REMARKS

Our neuroimaging evidence suggests that for both verbal and spatial tasks that require simple storage, older adults recruit different brain areas with a greater bilateral distribution than do their younger counterparts. These differences occur even in the face of comparable accuracy levels suggesting that older adults achieve optimal performance by way of an altered neurocognitive route. We have proposed that older adults recruit executive processing operations controlled in part by DLPFC to mediate attentional or contextual coding operations, thereby bolstering their ability to meet the storage demands of the task. Yet, there are good reasons to believe that these executive operations are themselves vulnerable to ageing and will therefore be limited in the compensation they can offer. First, DLPFC is particularly vulnerable to age-related atrophy (Raz, 2000). Moreover, the greatest age-differences have been documented on tasks that draw heavily on executive operations (Fabiani & Wee, in press; Moscovitch & Winocur, 1995). It follows from our hypothesis that the disproportional decline in working memory tasks with explicit executive processing demands has at least two sources. Structural decline of DLPFC coupled with a compensatory role in storage tasks could severely limit the capacity of DLPFC to meet such demands. The compensatory application of executive mechanisms may exact a price on other tasks.

In conclusion, we have offered several hypotheses about the relationship between executive processing and storage components of the working memory system and the effects of ageing on this system. Although admittedly speculative, these hypotheses are testable. Clearly, the next decade of cognitive neuroscience promises to yield valuable new insights into the mechanisms of normal ageing. Likewise, studies of ageing should continue to raise important questions about the structure of the cognitive system and the life-long potential for plasticity, compensation, and neurocognitive reorganisation.

Manuscript received September 2000

REFERENCES

Awh, E., Jonides, J., Smith, E.E., Schumacher, E.H., Koeppe, R.A., & Katz, S. (1996). Dissociation of storage and rehearsal in verbal working memory: Evidence from positron emission tomography. *Psychological Science, 7*, 25–31.

Babcock, R.L., & Salthouse, T.A. (1990). Effects of increased processing demands on age differences in working memory. *Psychology and Aging, 5*, 421–428.

Baddeley, A.D. (1986). *Working memory.* Oxford, UK: Oxford University Press.

Baddeley, A.D. (1992). Working memory. *Science, 255*, 556–559.

Banich, M.T. (1998). The missing link: The role of interhemispheric interaction in attentional processing. *Brain and Cognition, 36*, 128–157.

Barch, D.M., Braver, T.S., Nystrom, L.E., Forman, S.D., Noll, D.C., & Cohen, J.D. (1997). Dissociating working memory from task difficulty in human prefrontal cortex. *Neuropsychologia, 35*, 1373–1380.

Baynes, K., Wessinger, C.M., Fendrich, R., & Gazzaniga, M.S. (1995). The emergence of the capacity to name left visual field stimuli in a callosotomy patient: Implications for functional plasticity. *Neuropsychologia, 30*, 187–200.

Belger, A., & Banich, M.T. (1992). Interhemispheric interaction affected by computational complexity. *Neuropsychologia, 30*, 923–929.

Bellis, T.J., Nicol,. T., & Kraus, N. (2000). Aging affects hemispheric asymmetry in the neural representation of speech sounds. *Journal of Neuroscience, 20*, 791–797.

Buckner, R.L., Corbetta, M., Schatz, J., Raichle, M.E., & Petersen, S.E. (1996). Preserved speech abilities and compensation following prefrontal damage. *Proceedings of the National Academy of Science, 93*, 1249–1253.

Cabeza, R., Anderson, N.D., Mangels, J.A., Nyberg, L., & Houle, S. (2000). Age-related differences in neural activity during item and temporal-order memory retrieval: A positron emission tomography study. *Journal of Cognitive Neuroscience, 12*, 197–206.

Cabeza, R., Grady, C.L., Nyberg, L., McIntosh, A.R., Tulving, E., Kapur, S., Jennings, J.M., Houle, S., & Craik, F.I.M. (1997). Age-related differences in neural activity during memory encoding and retrieval: A positron emission tomography study. *Journal of Neuroscience, 17*(1), 391–400.

Cabeza, R., & Nyberg, L. (2000). Imaging cognition II: An empirical review of 275 PET and fMRI studies. *Journal of Cognitive Neuroscience, 12*, 1–47.

Chao, L.L., & Knight, R.T. (1998). Contribution of human prefrontal cortex to delay performance. *Journal of Cognitive Neuroscience, 10*, 167–177.

Cohen, J.D., Botvinick, M., & Carter, C.S. (2000). Anterior cingulate and prefrontal cortex: Who's in control? *Nature Neuroscience, 3*(5), 421–423.

Craik, F.I.M., & Jennings, J.M. (1992). Human memory. In F.I.M. Craik & T.A. Salthouse

(Eds.), *Handbook of aging and cognition* (pp. 51–109). Hillsdale, NJ: Lawrence Erlbaum Associates Inc.

D'Esposito, M., Aguirre, G.K., Zarahn, E., Ballard, D., Shin, R.K., & Lease, J. (1998). Functional MRI studies of spatial and nonspatial working memory. *Cognitive Brain Research, 7*, 1–13.

D'Esposito, M., Detre, J.A., Alsop, D.C., Shin, R.K., Atlas, S., & Grossman, M. (1995). The neural basis of the central executive system of working memory. *Nature, 378*, 279–281.

D'Esposito, M., & Postle, B.R. (1999). The dependence of span and delayed response performance on prefrontal cortex. *Neuropsychologia, 37*, 1303–1315.

D'Esposito, M., Postle, B., Jonides, J., & Smith, E. (1999). The neural substrate and temporal dynamics of interference effects in working memory as revealed by event-related functional MRI. *Proceedings of the National Academy of Science, 96*, 7514–7519.

D'Esposito, M., Postle, B.R., Ballard, D., & Lease, J. (1999). Maintenance versus manipulation of information held in working memory: An event-related fMRI study. *Brain and Cognition, 41*, 66–86.

D'Esposito, M., Zarahn, E., Aguirre, G.K., & Rypma, B. (1999). The effect of normal aging on coupling of neural activity to the hemodynamic responses. *NeuroImage, 10*, 6–14.

Dobbs, A.R., & Rule, B.G. (1989). Adult age differences in working memory. *Psychology and Aging, 4*, 500–503.

Engle, R.W., Kane, M.J., & Tuholski, S.W. (1999). Individual differences in working memory capacity and what they tell us about controlled attention, general fluid intelligence, and functions of the prefrontal cortex. In A. Miyake & P. Shah (Eds.), *Models of working memory: Mechanisms of active maintenance and executive control* (pp. 102–134). New York: Cambridge University Press.

Fabiani, M., & Wee, E. (in press). Age-related changes in working memory and frontal lobe function: A review. In C. Nelson & M. Luciana (Eds.), *Handbook of developmental cognitive neuroscience*. Cambridge, MA: MIT Press.

Goldman-Rakic, P.S. (1987). Circuitry of the primate prefrontal cortex and the regulation of behavior by representational memory. In F. Plum (Ed.), *Handbook of physiology, the nervous systems, higher functions of the brain* (Section I, Vol. V, pp. 373–417). Bethesda, MD: American Physiological Society.

Goldman-Rakic, P.S. (1998). The prefrontal landscape: Implications for understanding human mentation and the central executive. In A.C. Roberts, T.W. Robbins, & L. Weiskrantz (Eds.), *The prefrontal cortex: Executive and cognitive functions* (pp. 87–102). New York: Oxford University Press.

Grady, C.L., Haxby, J.V., Horwitz, B., Schapiro, M.B., Rapoport, S.I., Ungerleider, L.G., Mishkin, M., Carson, R.E., & Herscovitch, P. (1992). Dissociation of object and spatial vision in human extrastriate cortex: Age-related changes in activation of regional cerebral blood flow measured with [^{15}O] water and positron emission tomography. *Journal of Cognitive Neuroscience, 4*, 23–34.

Grady, C.L., McIntosh, A.R., Bookstein, F., Horwitz, B., Rapoport, S.I., & Haxby, J.V. (1998). Age-related changes in regional cerebral flow during working memory for faces. *NeuroImage, 8*, 409–425.

Haug, H. (1997). The ageing human cerebral cortex: Morphometry of areal differences and their functional meaning. In S.U. Dani, A. Hori, & G.F. Walter (Eds.), *Principles of neural aging*. Amsterdam: Elsevier.

Jacobsen, C.F. (1931). The functions of frontal association areas in monkeys. *Comparative Psychology Monographs, 13*, 1–60.

Jonides, J., Marshuetz, C., Smith, E.E., Reuter-Lorenz, P.A., Koeppe, R., & Hartley, A. (2000). Changes in inhibitory processing with age revealed by brain activation. *Journal of Cognitive Neuroscience, 12*, 188–196.

Jonides, J., Reuter-Lorenz, P.A., Smith, E.E., Awh, E., Barnes, L.L., Drain, H.M., Glass, J., Lauber, E., & Schumacher, E. (1996). Verbal and spatial working memory. In D. Medin (Ed.), *Psychology of learning and motivation* (Vol. 34, pp. 43–88). San Diego, CA: Academic Press

Jonides, J., Smith, E., Marshuetz, C., Koeppe, R., & Reuter-Lorenz, P.A. (1998). The neural correlates of inhibitory processes in working memory as revealed by PET. *Proceedings of the National Academy of Science, 95*(14), 8410–8413.

Kinsbourne, M. (1971). The minor cerebral hemisphere as a source of aphasic speech. *Archives of Neurology, 25*, 302–306.

Madden, D.J., Turkington, T.G., Provenzale, J.M., Denny, L.L., Hawk, T.C., Gottlob, L.R., & Coleman, R.E. (1999). Adult age differences in functional neuroanatomy of verbal recognition memory. *Human Brain Mapping, 7*, 115–135.

May, C.P., Hasher, L., & Kane, M.J. (1999). The role of interference in memory span. *Memory and Cognition, 27*, 759–767.

Moscovitch, M., & Winocur, G. (1995). Frontal lobes, memory and aging: Structure and functions of the frontal lobes. *Annals of the New York Academy of Sciences, 769*, 115–150.

Muller, R.A., Rothermel, R.D., Behen, M.E., Muzik, O., Chakraborty, P.K., & Chugani, H.T. (1999). Language organization in patients with early and late left-hemisphere lesion: A PET study. *Neuropsychologia, 37*, 545–557.

Nielson, K.A., Garavan, H., Langenecker, S.A., Stein, E.A., & Rao, S.M. (2000). *Event-related fMRI of inhibitory control reveal lateralized prefrontal activation differences between healthy young and older adults*. Paper presented at the Frontal Lobes 2000 conference, Toronto, Ontario, Canada.

Nudo, R.J. (1999). Recovery after damage to motor cortical areas. *Current Opinion in Neurobiology, 9*, 740–747.

Owen, A.M., Herrod, N.J., Menon, D.K., Clark, J.C., Downey, S., Carpenter, T.A., et al. (1999). Redefining the functional organization of working memory processes within human lateral prefrontal cortex. *European Journal of Neuroscience, 11*, 567–574.

Owen, A.M., Sahakian, B.J., Semple, J., Polkey, C.E., & Robbins, T.W. (1995). Visuospatial short-term recognition memory and learning after temporal lobe excisions, frontal lobe excisions and amygdalo-hippocampectomy in man. *Neuropsychologia, 33*, 1–24.

Park, D.C., Smith, A., Lautenschlager, G., Earles, J.L., Frieske, D., Zwahr, M. & Gaines, C.L. (1996). Mediators of long-term memory performance across the life span. *Psychology and Aging, 11*, 621–637.

Petrides, M. (1994). Frontal lobes and working memory: Evidence from investigations of the effects of cortical excisions in nonhuman primates. In F. Boller & J. Grafman (Eds.), *Handbook of neuropsychology* (Vol. 9, pp. 59–82). Amsterdam: Elsevier.

Petrides, M. (1998). Specialized systems for processing mnemonic information within the primate frontal cortex. In A.C. Roberts, T.W. Robbins, & L. Weiskrantz (Eds.), *The prefrontal cortex: Executive and cognitive functions* (pp. 103–116). New York: Oxford University Press.

Ptito, A., Crane, J., Leonard, G., Amsel, R., & Caramanos, Z. (1995). Visual-spatial localization by patients with frontal-lobe lesions invading or sparing area 46. *Neuroreport, 6*, 1781–1784.

Raz, N. (2000). Aging of the brain and its impact on cognitive performance: Integration of structural and functional findings. In F.I.M. Craik & T.A. Salthouse (Eds.), *Handbook of aging and cognition, Vol. II*. Mahwah, NJ: Lawrence Erlbaum Associates Inc.

Reuter-Lorenz, P.A. (2000). The cognitive neuropsychology of aging. In D. Park & N. Schwarz (Eds.), *Ageing and cognition: A student primer*. Hove, UK: Psychology Press.

Reuter-Lorenz, P.A., Jonides, J., Smith, E., Miller, A., Marshuetz, C., Hartley, A., &

Koeppe, R. (2000). Age differences in frontal lateralization of working memory. *Journal of Cognitive Neuroscience, 12,* 174–187.

Reuter-Lorenz, P.A., & Stanczak, L. (2000). Aging and the corpus callosum. *Developmental Neuropsychology, 18,* 113–137.

Reuter-Lorenz, P.A., Stanczak, L., & Miller, A. (1999). Neural recruitment and cognitive aging: Two hemispheres are better than one especially as you age. *Psychological Science, 10,* 494–500.

Rypma, B., & D'Esposito, M. (1999). The roles of prefrontal brain regions in components of working memory: Effects of memory load and individual differences. *Proceedings of the National Academy of Sciences, 96,* 6558–6563.

Rypma, B., & D'Esposito, M. (2000). Isolating the neural mechanisms of age-related changes in human working memory. *Nature Neuroscience, 3,* 509–515.

Rypma, B., Prabhakaran, V., Desmond, J.E., Glover, G.H., & Gabrieli, J.D.E. (1999). Load-dependent roles of frontal brain regions in the maintenance of working memory. *NeuroImage, 9,* 221–226.

Salthouse, T.A. (1992). *Mechanisms of age-cognition relations in adulthood.* Hillsdale, NJ: Lawrence Erlbaum Associates Inc.

Salthouse, T.A. (2000). Steps toward the explanation of adult age differences in cognition. In T. Perfect & E. Maylor (Eds.), *Theoretical debate in cognitive aging.* London: Oxford University Press.

Salthouse, T.A., & Babcock, R.L. (1991). Decomposing adult age differences in working memory. *Developmental Psychology, 27,* 763–776.

Smith, E.E., & Jonides, J. (1997). Working memory: A view from neuroimaging. *Cognitive Psychology, 33,* 5–42.

Smith, E.E., & Jonides, J. (1999). Storage and executive processes in the frontal lobes. *Science, 283,* 1657–1661.

Smith, E.E., Jonides, J., & Koeppe, R.A. (1996). Dissociating verbal and spatial working memory. *Cerebral Cortex, 6,* 11–20.

Sternberg, S. (1966). High-speed scanning in human memory. *Science, 153,* 652–654.

Verin, M., Partiot, A., Pillon, C., Malapani, C., Agid, Y., & Dubois, B. (1993). Delayed response tasks and prefrontal lesions in man—evidence for self-generated patterns of behavior with poor environmental modulation. *Neuropsychologia, 31,* 1379–1396.

Woodruff-Park, D.S. (1997). *The neuropsychology of aging.* Malden, MA: Blackwell.

Zacks, R.T., Hasher, L., & Li, K.H. (2000). Human memory. In F.I.M. Craik & T.A. Salthouse (Eds.), *The handbook of aging & cognition* (2nd ed., pp. 293–358). Mahwah, NJ: Lawrence Erlbaum Associates Inc.

EUROPEAN JOURNAL OF COGNITIVE PSYCHOLOGY, 2001, *13* (1/2), 279–300

The impact of aerobic activity on cognitive function in older adults: A new synthesis based on the concept of executive control

Courtney D. Hall

University of Texas at Austin, USA

Alan L. Smith

Purdue University, West Lafayette, IN, USA

Steven W. Keele

University of Oregon, Eugene, USA

Numerous reaction time studies have suggested that age-related declines in cognitive function might be ameliorated by lifestyles involving aerobic activity or by interventionist programmes of aerobic exercise. These studies are far from conclusive, however, reflecting a failure to factor out cognitive from sensory and motor processes. Following a critical review of the literature, we report on recent developments that differentiate cognitive processes involving executive vs non-executive control, the former being associated with frontal lobe function. Three key studies suggest that aerobic exercise primarily improves executive control.

Research conducted over the last few decades has suggested that aerobic activity benefits physical health, reducing the incidence of age-related disease states including coronary artery disease, diabetes, hypertension, certain types of cancer and osteoporosis (Bouchard & Despres, 1995; Lee,

Requests for reprints should be addressed to S.W. Keele, Department of Psychology, University of Oregon, Eugene, Oregon, 97405, USA. Email: skeele@oregon,uoregon.edu

The authors gratefully acknowledge financial support for this project provided by an A.D. Hutchison Fellowship awarded by the University of Texas at Austin to Courtney Hall and a National Institutes of Health Grant NS-17778 awarded to Steve Keele, Robert Rafal, and Richard Ivry.

http://www.tandf.co.uk/journals/pp/09541446.html   DOI:10.1080/09541440042000313

1995; Vuori, 1995; see also US Department of Health and Human Services, 1996). Moreover, the claim has been made that such aerobic activity benefits cognitive health as measured by the efficiency of decision making, memory, and problem solving (see Dustman, Emmerson, & Shearer, 1994; Etnier et al., 1997 for reviews). The general argument, though not fully tested, has been that exercise programmes result in improved cardiovascular fitness, which in turn improves blood flow in the brain, thereby improving cognition.

The review we present here questions the validity of much of the research that has claimed cognitive improvement in the elderly resulting from exercise. We primarily restrict our detailed attention to studies that have employed reaction time methodologies, especially studies involving the retrieval of specific responses to specific stimuli. We argue that most of these studies failed to properly distinguish and isolate cognitive from non-cognitive components of rapid decision making. When we apply such a distinction, these studies almost uniformly fail to support the hypothesis that exercise ameliorates age-related declines in cognition. Indeed, some failed even to show an age-related decline in cognition. A cursory analysis of studies employing neither reaction time nor stimulus-dictated retrieval reveals similar methodological problems in failing to isolate cognitive from non-cognitive task components.

However, when we turn to studies that have, sometimes unknowingly, examined executive control, we find support for the link between aerobic activity and cognition. Later we will describe more fully what we mean by executive control, but in brief it refers to cognitive regulation of the relevant features of the environment and responding to them based on moment-to-moment changes in goals. Evidence suggests that ageing has a dramatically greater effect on executive than non-executive function. Executive function is highly dependent upon frontal lobes of the brain, and neuroimaging evidence suggests that such regions are particularly vulnerable to declines in blood flow with advanced age. We hypothesise that the vehicle whereby exercise improves frontally based cognition is improved blood flow to frontal brain regions. Finally, we review three studies that provide evidence that aerobic exercise preferentially benefits executive function. Together, these hypotheses provide a framework for more definitive analysis of the ameliorative effects of exercise on cognitive ageing.

ISOLATING COGNITIVE FUNCTIONS

Ever since the end of the 19th century (cf. Donders, 1969) it has been realised that reaction time—the time from stimulus onset to response onset—includes the time of non-cognitive sensory and motor processes as well as cognitive processes that link stimulus to response. The influence of any variable, such as age or exercise, on reaction time cannot be properly attributed to cognitive processes without some procedure for eliminating non-cognitive factors. The solution introduced by Donders was to employ two tasks differing from one another in a single critical way, such as complexity of decision. An estimate of the effect of decision complexity can be obtained by *subtracting* reaction time in the less complex condition from the more complex one. At least in the best of circumstances, sensory and motor components would be shared by the two conditions, so that a subtraction of their reaction times would isolate the influence of the variable of interest to decision complexity. Or, in related fashion, a function can be fit to a set of conditions varying in complexity with the slope of the function estimating the decision factor (cf. Posner, 1978; Sternberg, 1969). In yet other cases, a detailed model of processes can be fit to a set of data generated in response to manipulation of more than one variable, different variables being analytic to different processes (e.g., Meyer, Glass, Mueller, Seymour, & Kieras, this issue). The critical notion for attributing an effect such as improved reaction time to cognition, is to show a modulation of the effect of a *variable* rather than an effect on reaction time to individual conditions.

A favoured procedure in the analysis of ageing and exercise has been to examine both simple and choice reaction times. In the simple case, the particular stimulus that will occur is known in advance to the participant, as is the appropriate response. In the more complex case, the stimulus could be one of several possible stimuli, different stimuli requiring different responses. In order to implicate cognition, it is necessary to show that ageing slows choice reaction time *more* than simple reaction time and that exercise improves choice reaction time *more* than simple reaction time. This is not to say that simple reaction time does not include cognitive processes related to decision complexity. Rather, the argument simply is that choice reaction time is more complex, and an analysis of the effect of age or exercise on the choice process can be based only on the *differences* in two or more conditions varying in complexity. There is ample evidence that age-related reaction time deficits increase with choice difficulty (see Salthouse, 1985). However, the subtractive method, or its variants, long employed within cognitive psychology, typically has been ignored when examining ameliorative effects of exercise, thereby making it difficult to attribute any effects to cognitive rather than non-cognitive factors.

THE EFFECTS OF AGEING AND EXERCISE ON SIMPLE
AND CHOICE REACTION TIME

Cross-sectional studies

In her seminal study, Spirduso (1975) compared reaction times of younger and older men who were currently active in racquet sports or handball with subjects who were inactive. The active older subjects had played such sports for 30 or more years. Simple reaction time was measured from onset of a pre-specified light to movement initiation toward a key target. Three-choice reaction time was measured from stimulus to initiation of movement toward a key corresponding to one of three lights.

As seen in Table 1, reaction time slowed significantly with both age and reduced activity level. The advantage of high activity level was especially marked for older people, but only reliably so for simple reaction time. What is critical for attributing these effects to cognition, however, is to show that increasing cognitive complexity results in greater sensitivity to age and activity. In fact, the results are contrary to expectation. Both ageing and activity have greater effects on simple than choice reaction time.

Spirduso also measured movement time, the time following the release of a home key until a target key was touched. Less active participants moved more slowly than more active participants, especially for the older participants where movement time averaged 261 ms in the less active group and 161 ms in the more active one. Electromyographic recordings indicate that muscle activity may begin on the order of 65–75 ms prior to actual movement onset, the length of time of pre-movement muscle activity increasing with age (Weiss, 1965). Given Weiss' findings and the

TABLE 1
Simple and choice reaction time (ms) as a function of age and activity level
(Spirduso, 1975)

	Simple RT	Choice RT	Difference
Young active	243	287	44
Young inactive	264	303	39
Difference	21	16	
Old active	263	317	54
Old inactive	327	355	28
Difference	64	38	

significantly slower movement times of the older inactive participants in Spirduso's study, a portion of the observed age deficit in reaction time likely is attributable to non-cognitive, motor processes. The combination of slowed motor processes in addition to the lack of increased choice reaction time makes it difficult to attribute the fitness effects on reaction time to cognition.

Other explorations (Baylor & Spirduso, 1988; Emery, Huppert, & Schein, 1995; Rikli & Busch, 1986) of the relationship between amounts of habitual exercise and simple and choice reaction time are largely consistent with the initial study by Spirduso. Increasing age is correlated with slowed reaction time but is countered by an active lifestyle. In none of these studies, however, is there an indication that exercise in the old reduced choice reaction time more than in the simpler tasks. Two studies that employed an even more difficult choice reaction time task, in which digits are substituted for symbols, also failed to find the critical age by activity-level interaction (Lupinacci, Rikli, Jones, & Ross, 1993; Shay & Roth, 1992).

Only one cross-sectional study (Clarkson-Smith & Hartley, 1989) reports reaction time effects in accordance with expectations. More and less active subjects 55–88 years of age pressed a key to either a single digit (simple reaction time), to one of two digits (two-choice reaction time) or to one of four digits. Activity level was validated by the finding that more active subjects had lower resting heart rates and higher vital capacities. The more active group exhibited faster reaction time overall than the less active group, but more importantly showed a smaller slope of reaction time as a function of amount of choice (expressed in information theory terms). This slope effect is exactly what would be expected were high activity correlated with enhanced cognition. This study can be faulted in one manner, however. Because there was no control group of younger subjects, it is unclear whether physical activity retards age-related declines or is independent of ageing.

Clarkson-Smith and Hartley (1989) also found superior performance by the more active older subjects on other cognitive tasks. Of particular interest are their tests of memory, and we will return to that in the final discussion, offering an interpretation in line with our hypothesis regarding executive function. Overall, the evidence for activity-based improvements in cognition as assessed by amount of choice is quite weak, with six of seven studies (eight of nine including digit-symbol studies) failing to find the predicted effect. Cross-sectional investigations are further limited in that they fail to separate whether aerobic activity improves cognitive function or whether individuals with higher cognitive functioning are more active. A stronger test of the linkage between aerobic activity and cognitive function requires demonstration of improved cognitive function subsequent to exercise intervention.

Intervention studies

An intervention study by Rikli and Edwards (1991) is noteworthy in two regards, the length of the exercise intervention, which covered 3 years, and because the results are in partial agreement with the expectation that exercise improves choice reaction time more than simple reaction time. Their 3-year intervention with women averaging 70 years of age met American College of Sports Medicine guidelines (1986), including 20–25 minutes of aerobics and 20–25 minutes of calisthenics three times a week. They examined simple reaction time to depress a key in response to onset of a specific light and choice time to depress a key corresponding to one of two lights. A control group was tested initially and again after 3 years.

Pre- to post-test improvements were found for both simple reaction time and choice reaction time in the exercise group and less so for the control group. The interaction between group and test period was reliable, suggesting that the exercise regimen improved reaction time. Unfortunately, the authors did not report statistical analysis of the more critical interaction—amount of choice by group—that would implicate exercise in improving cognition. However, numerically the results are in accord with expectations: A 65 ms difference between choice and simple conditions prior to exercise interventions was reduced to 44 ms after 3 years of intervention. Little change was observed for the control group with the RT difference score being 95 ms in the pretest and 101 ms in the post-test. It is somewhat worrisome that the initial effect of choice for the control group (95 ms) was substantially larger than for the experimental group (65 ms), raising some issue regarding the adequacy of the control and casting doubt on whether the critical interaction would have been reliable. This concern is exacerbated by the fact that control and treatment were not random assignments and instead reflected voluntary choices in signing up for either an exercise class or non-exercise hobby classes. Such lack of random assignment engenders some of the same problems as cross-sectional studies.

Despite lack of a critical statistical test, lack of random assignment, and concerns about baseline pretest scores, the study of Rikli and Edwards (1991) is the only "interventionist" study with pre- and post-test scores we have found with numerical results in the predicted direction. Four other studies failed to find the predicted effect (Dustman et al., 1984; Madden, Blumenthal, Allen, & Emery, 1989; Panton, Graves, Pollock, Hagberg, & Chen, 1990; Whitehurst, 1991). Each of these examined older subjects who had participated in aerobic exercise programmes ranging from 2 to 8 months. Most used a control group that participated in non-aerobic activity over a comparable period. In each case the aerobic exercise groups showed cardiovascular fitness improvements relative to control groups. Three of these studies found no significant improvements at all in reaction time. Only the Dustman et al. (1984) study found aerobic activity to improve reaction time, but the effect was reliable only for simple reaction time, a result inconsistent with the hypothesis of improved cognition.

Discussion of studies of simple and choice reaction time

Overall, the intervention studies provide little evidence that exercise improves cognition. Four studies were negative in outcome and the only positive study, that of Rikli and Edwards (1991), failed to statistically evaluate the critical results. Perhaps the positive results of Rikli and Edwards can be attributed to the extremely long intervention period of 3 years. In addition, the study suffers from lack of random assignment to groups, giving it some of the character of a cross-sectional study. Cross-sectional studies reported in the prior section, which compare groups with long-standing activity level differences, with one exception, failed to support the hypothesis that exercise benefits cognition. Moreover, within the intervention paradigm the four negative studies themselves involved rather extensive exercise programmes of up to 8 months' duration. These studies report improvements in cardiovascular fitness without finding a concomitant improvement in cognition. Thus, it appears unlikely that duration of intervention was a critical factor.

Another possibility is that the subtraction of simple from choice reaction time does not appropriately assess choice difficulty. Subjects are able to anticipate precisely the next event and response in the simple case, and it is possible that such a factor is confounded with and perhaps even counter to choice differences. The point remains, however, that the great majority of reaction time studies have failed to demonstrate any cognitive effect and even those supporting such an effect are flawed.

Possibly alterations in choice difficulty via stimulus–response compatibility might be more susceptible to exercise influence than alterations in number of choices. Typically, responses that are not naturally related to the stimulus receive slower reaction times (cf. Keele, 1973, 1985). Dustman et al. (1984) did find exercise intervention to improve reaction time on an incompatible task of digit-to-symbol translation, but they failed to use a compatible control task that would allow isolation of a cognitive effect. Moreover, they did not include a control group of younger adults, so could not show the exercise effect to be larger for older than for younger subjects. Finally cross-sectional studies failed to find digit–symbol performance to be correlated with activity level (Lupinacci et al., 1993; Shay & Roth, 1992).

Some studies have used a variety of other cognitive measures, many of which are speeded and many of which form standard neuropsychological tests. These include such tests as WMS Visual Reproduction, WAIS Vocabulary, Verbal Fluency, Trail-making, Rey-Osterrieth Complex Figure Reproduction, and Culture Fair IQ tests. In general, these have failed to find physical activity, either of a lifestyle or interventionist type, to improve cognition (e.g., Blumenthal et al., 1991; Dustman et al., 1984; Kerr, Scott, & Vitiello, 1993), even when exercise resulted in clear aerobic fitness improvements. Shay and Roth (1992) likewise fail to find predicted effects for several of these tests, but do claim to find that elderly subjects with high activity levels show better performance on some visual tasks involving visual memory or visual assembly. Our primary complaint against this form of analysis is that while some complex, cognitive tasks may show an improvement associated with aerobic exercise, appropriate controls are lacking in order to pinpoint whether cognitive processes are involved and if so the nature of the processes. One cross-sectional study (Clarkson-Smith & Hartley, 1989) that also finds higher cognitive performance in more active elderly subjects will be discussed near the end of the next section. To this point, however, the overall evidence that exercise improves cognition is decidedly weak, most studies finding no effect or being contrary to predictions. We turn now to examination of "executive control" as a cognitive function that has been found to improve following exercise-based intervention in older adults.

EXECUTIVE FUNCTION AS A CLARIFYING CONCEPT

Recently psychologists have begun to investigate a high-level cognitive function called executive control (see Meyer & Keiras, 1997 and Monsell & Driver, 2000, for current analyses). Although different investigators use this concept in various ways, the core aspect that we emphasise here derives from a seminal paper by Norman and Shallice (1986). They described the situation where more than one concurrent stimulus allows multiple and conflicting actions. In such situations, goals or instructions provide additional constraint, a constraint called executive control. The necessity for accessory specification can also occur with a single stimulus for which the nature of response may vary depending on the current goal. Executive control is especially tapped when the instruction or goal that specifies the relevant stimulus component *varies* on different trials (e.g., Allport, Styles, & Hsieh, 1994; Rogers & Monsell, 1995; Spector & Biederman, 1976). In addition, executive control is tapped when more than one component of a stimulus requires response but in a particular order rather than independently (e.g., Meyer & Kieras, 1997; Umiltà,

Nicoletti, Simion, Tagliabue, & Bagnara, 1992). In this latter case, as in the former, additional instruction specifies when a *change* must be made in what or how to respond to a given event.

Simple and choice reaction time tasks, while differing in choice, do not clearly differ in the role of executive process. In both cases, trials typically occur in blocks, all trials within a block involving the same stimulus and response assignments. Because of the consistency of stimulus to response mapping, whatever stimulus occurs conveys sufficient response information without a need for additional constraint.

Ageing and executive control

Considerable evidence dating back at least to Birren (1965) has suggested that the speed of cognitive function declines as a function of age (see Meyerson, Hale, Wagstaff, Poon, & Smith, 1990 and Salthouse, 1985 for reviews). Lindenberger, Mayr, and Kliegl (1993) have argued that a large variety of age-related intellectual declines (e.g., in reasoning, memory, knowledge, and fluency) are associated with the decreases in processing speed that occur with ageing.

When Cerella (1985) plotted processing time of older adults for each of several tasks against the processing times of younger adults, a linear relationship emerged with slope of approximately 1.5. In other words, regardless of task, the older adults were 1.5 times slower than were the younger adults. Mayr and Kliegl (1993) re-examined this relationship for two situations, one involving executive control and the other not. In both situations, each object had three features: colour, relative size, and shading. In the non-executive condition, subjects matched each object against the object in the corresponding position in the second display until they found a pair that differed. They then indicated the dimension of difference. Having eight objects in each display required, on average, more comparisons than with only four. However, there is little or no need for an executive control becaues all the information required to make a decision is directly contained within the stimulus.

In the executive case there were always four objects in each display. The objects in one display were rotated 90 degrees clockwise or counter-clockwise with respect to the second display. Because of this rotation, each object differed from the object in the corresponding position of the second display. In order to match objects, the subjects first had to mentally rotate the objects in one display before comparisons of the other display could be made to determine the dimension of difference. One process, matching, is contingent on another prior process, rotation. Because rotational direction varies randomly from trial to trial, it involves a constraint that requires executive control. That is, how to compare the stimuli depends on another "instruction".

For both executive and non-executive situations, Mayr and Kliegl manipulated two levels of difficulty and three levels of required accuracy for a total of six processing time measurements upon which to compare old and young subjects. When the times for each condition for the older adults are plotted against the times for the young, two separate linear functions were obtained. The slope in the non-executive case was 1.95, roughly equal to that reported by Cerella (1985), indicating that older subjects were slower at all levels of difficulty and accuracy by a factor of about two. The slope for the executive case was 3.91, indicating that for all levels of difficulty, the older subjects took about four times as long. Thus, ageing appears more detrimental to tasks involving executive than non-executive processes, a result extended by Kray and Lindenberger (2000) and Mayr, Kliegl, and Krampe (1996) using other tasks analytic to the executive/non-executive distinction.

Executive control is primarily dependent on frontal lobes

Several studies suggest that executive function is heavily dependent on frontal cortical regions of the brain, more specifically the left, prefrontal cortex. We detail two such studies.

Stablum, Leonardi, Mazzoldi, Umiltà, and Morra (1994) compared control subjects to closed-head injury subjects with diffuse frontal lobe damage. Two letters, vertically arrayed, appeared either to the left or the right of a fixation point. For the single-decision task, subjects responded with a key press to the left–right position of the letters, the same task being constant over many trials. A dual-decision task likewise involved first response to the position of the letters and then a verbal report whether the letters were the same or not. Although the position judgement of the second task was identical to the first task, reaction to position was considerably longer in the dual-decision situation, even though it was the first response, presumably reflecting an executive process for controlling response order (Meyer & Kieras, 1997; Umiltà et al., 1992).

The increased time required for executive control is reflected in the *difference* in reaction times between the single- and dual-decision conditions. For the control subjects, adding the executive component increased decision time by 80 ms. For the head injury subjects, decision time increased significantly more by 197 ms, suggesting that frontal lobe impairment is especially problematic for tasks requiring executive control. Stablum, Mogentale, and Umiltà (1996) reported similar results.

Keele and Rafal (2000) compared performance of individuals with left frontal lobe injury (as a result of stroke or tumour) with control subjects. A non-executive task required the subject to respond to *unidimensional* colours or shapes by pressing a corresponding key. The stimulus—whether colour alone or shape alone—specified the correct response regardless of whether the subjects knew in advance what the dimension would be. On this task, frontal lobe subjects did not differ reliably from control subjects. Moreover, the groups were not differentially affected by number of choices, two or four.

In the executive case, however, a very different result occurred. In this instance the stimuli were *bidimensional*, with the shape surrounding the colour patch. An executive process was needed to implement an instruction, colour or shape, which indicated the relevant dimension on each trial. The reaction times for the control subject were 683 ms following a change in instructions. On the following trial, in which set remained the same, reaction time declined to 485 ms, a value little different from two-choice reaction time with unidimensional stimuli. Following a set switch, therefore, control subjects are able to effectively reconfigure for a change in relevant dimension. For the frontal patients, reaction time following an instruction switch was 1058 ms, a value much larger than for control subjects. Even subsequent to a switch, reaction time remained very high, averaging 987 ms, a value significantly greater than the two-choice times of the unidimensional case.

Thus, the patients with left frontal brain lesions have unusual difficulty when executive control is required to regulate relevance. Additional neuroimaging and patient data using somewhat similar paradigms (e.g., Frith, 2000; Konishi et al., 1998; McDowell, Whyte, & D'Esposito, 1998; Meyer et al., 1998; Rogers et al., 1998) have yielded similar conclusions.

Blood flow analysis

The cause of a differential decline in executive as opposed to non-executive functions in older adults may be related to a decline in the blood supply to the ageing frontal lobe. Such decline may result in chronic, low-level hypoxia of the frontal lobes leading to the observed cognitive changes. Shaw et al. (1984) demonstrated, in a sample of over 650 healthy participants, diminished resting cerebral blood flow in older adults, particularly in the prefrontal regions of frontal lobe and parietal lobe. These findings were consistent in both cross-sectional and longitudinal (up to 5 years) examinations of subjects. Such results have been corroborated in other studies of healthy, older participants (Gur, Gur, Obrist, Skolnick, & Reivich, 1987; Warren, Butler, Katholi, & Halsey, 1985). Both studies showed reduced resting blood flow in older adults compared to younger adults in frontal cortical regions. With mental activity, blood flow was increased by a similar degree in both younger and older adults, but older adults did not reach the same absolute levels. Thus, the evidence points to a differential reduction in blood flow to anterior brain regions with ageing, which could account for larger age-related declines in executive than non-executive function. West (1996) has reviewed other physiological evidence that supports these findings of differential effects of ageing on prefrontal cortex versus other cortical regions.

The effect of exercise on cerebral blood flow

Based on findings of reduced cerebral blood flow with age, particularly in frontal cortical regions, we hypothesise that aerobic exercise results in improved cardiovascular function and from that improved cerebral blood flow. Indeed, one cross-sectional study we reviewed found that more active elderly subjects exhibited superior cardio-pulmonary performance (Clarkson-Smith & Hartley, 1989). Several studies of aerobic exercise intervention of 2–8 months' duration likewise showed improved cardio-vascular function (Dustman et al., 1984; Kerr et al., 1993; Madden et al., 1989; Panton et al., 1990; Whitehurst, 1991). We know of no studies, however, that have demonstrated an important causative link in our argument whereby improved cardiovascular function results in improved cerebral blood flow, especially for frontal lobes. Such study would be an important line of investigation.

THE EFFECT OF EXERCISE ON EXECUTIVE AND NON-EXECUTIVE FUNCTION IN THE OLDER ADULTS

The preceding sections provide a foundation for suggesting that executive function is a likely candidate for exercise-based improvements in cogni-tion in the elderly. We detail three reaction time studies in support of this supposition and then extend the analysis to one study of memory. The first two reaction time studies were conducted without reference to execu-tive function, but analysis of their conditions suggests appropriateness of the concept. The third, by Kramer et al. (1999; see also Kramer et al., in press) was conducted with specific reference to executive function.

Abourezk and Toole (1995) employed two reaction time tasks. The first, not involving executive control, was a simple reaction time task. Subjects lifted a finger that corresponded to the position of a numeral (1, 2, or 3), the identity and position of a forthcoming signal being known in advance. In a second condition, any one of the three numerals could occur, the identity of the numeral also being correlated with the position of its occurrence (i.e., the digit 1 occurred in the left-most position, digit 2 in the middle position, and digit 3 in the right-most position). Prior to each numeral, the word "left" or "right" was presented. The word "left" required the subjects to lift the finger two positions to the left of the position of the given numeral; the word "right" required lifting the finger two positions to the right. A wraparound definition of left and right was employed. Thus, if the word "right" appeared, followed by digit 1, key 3, which was two positions to the right should be released. If digit 2 appeared, however, the appropriate key to release would be key 1. Because mapping of signal to key is dependent upon the immediately prior instruction, an instruction that can change on each trial, this condition requires executive control.

Two groups of women in their late 60s were compared in this cross-sectional study. One group participated in regular aerobic exercise, such as fast walking, aerobics, or dance. The other group did not participate in aerobic exercise, though they regularly engaged in stretching or flexibility activities. The groups did not differ reliably on simple reaction time, being on average 346 ms for the more active group and 374 ms for the less active group. In contrast, there was a massive group difference for the task requiring executive control. The more active group averaged 1101 ms; the less active group averaged 1819 ms. Of critical concern, the task by group interaction was highly significant, supporting the contention that exercise effects were localised to processes of executive control. Indeed, it is important, given the vastly differing difficulties of the two tasks, that the relative difference in reaction time for the two groups was 8% (non-significant) on the simple task but a remarkable 65% on the executive control task.

Two criticisms may be leveled against Abourezk and Toole's (1995) study. Their simple reaction time task is an inadequate control condition. The more difficult task involves not only executive process but also more choice (three-choice) than simple reaction time. This confound is cause for caution. Also, the cross-sectional nature of the study does not clarify causative links between exercise and cognition. These criticisms are at least partly countered in an intervention study by Hawkins, Kramer, and Capaldi (1992).

The non-executive task examined by Hawkins et al. (1992) involved responding with one of two key presses to one of two visual signals, or on a separate block of trials responding to auditory signals with key presses. Because the stimulus sufficiently specifies the appropriate response, no intervention of executive control is needed. In the executive case, the two signals, auditory and visual, occurred simultaneously. Subjects were asked to respond to the auditory signal first, followed by a response to the visual signal. Because the stimulus itself contains no information about response order, order must be imposed by executive processes—i.e., the stimulus component to respond to *changes* from one moment to the next in response to instruction (cf. Meyer & Kieras, 1997; Umiltà et al., 1992).

Consistent with the analyses of Mayr and Kliegl (1993) and Mayr et al. (1996) described earlier, the proportional age deficit in the Hawkins et al. (1992) study was larger on the task requiring executive control (50%) than on the tasks not requiring executive control (34%). Following a 10-week aquatic fitness programme, older participants showed significantly greater improvements on the executive control task, compared to the non-executive task. Averaging visual and auditory reaction times, dual-task performance improved by 154 ms whereas performance on the simpler tasks improved only 18 ms. This differential improvement, which is critical in implicating executive processing, was significantly larger than improvements due to practice alone. Age-matched controls who were not assigned the aquatic experience, improved 91 ms pre- to post-test for the executive case and 32 ms for the non-executive case.

Two major points stand out regarding the Hawkins et al. (1992) study. First, consistent with our prior review, this study provides no evidence for a beneficial effect of exercise intervention on the visual and auditory choice reaction time tasks when executive function is not required. The subjects receiving exercise improved 18 ms between pre- and post-tests, but the control subjects improved 32 ms. These improvements are likely due to practice provided by the two tests themselves. Second, exercise intervention improved reaction times on the task involving executive control (154 ms) more than for the control group (92 ms).

The Abourezk and Toole (1995) and Hawkins et al. (1992) studies, although fitting well to a theoretical framework of executive control, are interpreted on a post hoc basis. A recent study by Kramer et al. (1999; reported more fully in Kramer et al., in press) was couched in terms both of executive control and of frontal lobe function. They compared two groups of older adult subjects ranging in age from 60 to 75 years. One group participated in a 6-month aerobic walking programme and the other in a 6-month non-aerobic programme of stretching and toning. Tests of pulmonary performance showed the intervention to improve oxygen consumption only for the former group. We would, therefore, expect improvement in executive function only in that group. Three cases were examined, each case having an executive and a non-executive condition.

One case compared reaction time when switching between responding to digit and letter in compound stimuli. The cue regarding which stimulus aspect to attend to was provided by stimulus position within a matrix. Executive control would be especially involved when a switch in relevant stimulus was required. As predicted, only the aerobic group showed a pre-exercise to post-exercise improvement on the *difference* in reaction times between the switch and non-switch tasks. The groups did not differ on the non-switch condition.

Similar results appeared for two other cases. In the first, a compound stimulus occurred, and subjects were required to respond to the central stimulus, the flanking components being in conflict or not. When not in conflict, responses were completely congruent so that position of the stimulus was not critical. But when in conflict, response had to be specifically regulated not only by the identity of the central stimulus but also by the position. Although absolute reaction times improved pre- to post-test for both groups, only for the aerobic group did the *difference* in reaction time between conflict and no-conflict conditions diminish from pre- to post-test.

In the last case examined by Kramer et al. (1999), on some trials a second stimulus countermanded the first, requiring that action be stopped. Such countermanding requires executive control, because another signal modifies the meaning of the prior signal. In accord with predictions, only the aerobic group showed a pre- to post-test improvement in time to countermand. The control task where countermanding did not occur was not affected.

Thus, over a set of three different kinds of executive control—task switching, regulation by positional context, and countermanding—Kramer et al. (1999, in press) found an intensive programme of exercise to improve cognitive function. No such improvement was exhibited on control tasks not involving executive function. Together with the studies of Abourezk and Toole (1995) and Hawkins et al. (1992), the Kramer et al. study makes a strong case that exercise in older adults promotes cognitive well-being of executive control, a function dependent on frontal lobes of the brain.

An extension to "working memory"

Our argument that age-related declines in cognition and their remediation by exercise are most prominent for executive function has been based on reaction time analysis, but only for cases in which appropriate response to ambiguous stimuli must be regulated by specific instructional cue, with instruction changing frequently. Although it is not our purpose to review here other conceptions of executive function with respect to ageing and physical activity, it is useful to illustrate how the general approach can be extended to memory tasks in which success is measured by accuracy of recall rather than by reaction time.

Petrides (2000; see also West, 1996) argues for a differentiation of memory processes between those dependent and those not dependent on executive control. He suggests that paired associate recall, recall of themes from a story, or simple ordered recall from working memory are relatively "automatic" in that one association primes the next. These kinds of memory, he argues, depend primarily on posterior cortical brain regions. In contrast, other kinds of recall are more heavily influenced by constantly changing context, a notion very similar to what we have emphasised in our own definition of executive function. For example, in one task the same stimuli are randomly rearranged on each trial. The task is to pick an item from a set that was *not* selected on a previous trial. Thus, items in working memory that had been recalled on previous trials must be marked and eliminated from further recall. Petrides claims that subjects with lesions to dorsolateral prefrontal cortex show unusual difficulty with this kind of task, but not with tasks like digit recall that rely primarily on serial association with each other. In addition to these dissociations of memory type as a function of brain lesion location, Petrides cites neuroimaging analyses that point to prefrontal involvement in memory dependent on executive function.

Based on the analyses of Petrides (2000) and West (1996), we would predict that ageing effects would be more noted for memory tasks heavily dependent on executive processes and that performance on such tasks would be more susceptible to remediation by exercise. As we have argued repeatedly, however, appropriate control tasks are required to contrast with those involving executive function before any conclusions about the nature of cognitive effects can be made. An earlier study, though not couched in executive function terms, comes close to satisfying this requirement.

Clarkson-Smith and Hartley (1989) compared low and high activity groups of elderly subjects on three forms of "working memory". Activity level was validated by fitness testing. Two of the three forms of working memory we judge to heavily involve executive process and the third, while probably involving executive processes, may involve them to lesser extent. Thus, we would expect activity level to correlate more with performance of the first two tasks than with the third task.

In one task, subjects observed consecutive lists of letters and indicated which letter appeared in the second of each pair of lists but not the first. List lengths were varied in order to define a memory span. Such memory requires not mere recall from a buffer but context marking of items to specify lists and then explicit comparison of the two lists to decide which letter to recall. The second task, reading span, required subjects to listen to short sentences, and then recall the last word of each sentence. This task requires regulation of recall not only by the words in working memory, but also by word position within a sentence. Span again was determined based on numbers of sentences that could be dealt with. The third working memory task, backward digit span, was comparably difficult, being an assessment of maximum span, but did not clearly require executive process to as extensive a degree as the former two tasks (whether it does or not depends on specific theory). This task may be heavily loaded by serial readout (in backward order) from a buffer, a process that is impaired because ordered rehearsal cannot begin until the last item in the list. Indeed, Gregoire and Van der Linden (1997; cf. Meyer et al., this issue) report that though backward recall is worse than forward, decline of memory span with advanced age does not differ in the two cases as might be expected were backward span more laden with executive control. As we would predict, the high and low activity groups differed in memory span size on the letter and reading tasks, the high activity group being superior. But, they did not differ at all on backward digit span, this latter result being replicated by Blumenthal et al. (1991).

Of course, our analysis of the Clarkson-Smith and Hartley memory conditions is post hoc, and it suffers problems from the present view. Were the study done with the "subtractive" logic in mind, it would be important that the tasks differing in presence or absence of executive function be more similar than was actually the case. This is especially needed given controversy whether backward span does or does not employ executive processes more than forward span or other span tasks (e.g., Owen, 2000). Even if it were accepted that backward digit span did not involve executive processes as much as the other two tasks employed by Clarkson-Smith and Hartley, it would be important to demonstrate a reliable interaction between task and activity level, an interaction not examined by the authors. Such interaction would conform to the "subtractive" logic and also avoid the statistical pitfall of a null result. None the less, their results appear consistent with the view of ageing and exercise extracted from studies of reaction time and illustrate an appropriate course of action regarding memory.

Kramer et al. (in press) examined memory recall from an explicit executive-processes framework, employing the same subjects as previously described for reaction time assessment of executive control. Recall that one group of subjects engaged in aerobic walking activity over a 6-month period, while the control group engaged in stretching and toning exercises. In one test Kramer et al. compared recall of a list of words when it was the only one presented, with recall of the same list following a second list. In the latter condition, much as in the first of the Clarkson-Smith and Hartley tasks (1989), list context must be added to regulate recall, presumably making greater demands on executive control. Kramer et al. found exercise intervention to improve memory performance only in this second case. In another test, subjects indicated whether an item in either a spatial pattern or in a list of letters was in the same position as on the previous trial (one-back) or as two trials previously (two-back). Although the exercise group showed greater pre- to post-test improvements on the two-back conditions than the control group and little difference on the one-back conditions, these predicted results were not reliable. However, some of the subjects in the control group also showed pre- to post-test improvements in cardiovascular function, an outcome expected only for the exercise group. When the data were analysed not by group but by amount of improvement in cardiovascular function from pre- to post-test, improved memory scores on the two-back test (but not one-back) were reliably associated with improved cardiovascular function. Contrary to the results of Blumenthal et al. (1992) and Clarkson-Smith and Hartley (1989), backward serial recall (but not forward) also showed exercise-based improvement.

The contradictory effects on backward memory scan call for general caution regarding the conclusion that the ameliorative effects of exercise on memory in the older adult is primarily restricted to executive components. The problem is that memory tasks typically are much more complicated than those paradigms we have emphasised that are based on reaction time. It is not always clear on the surface that one memory task variation, though more difficult than another, actually differs in executive demands. For example, in the one-back and two-back memory tasks studied by Kramer et al., is it the case that one involves more in the way of executive process, or is it simply that memory demands are based on more degraded traces in the two-back case? A similar question can be asked about comparison of list recall immediately after list presentation versus recall after an intervening and different list. Are the differing results in these conditions due to differing reliance on context and executive control or are they due to differences in strength of memory trace? For such reason, we believe that memory tasks are in need of further analysis, both from a theoretical viewpoint regarding executive processes, but also from clear comparison of tasks that are very similar except for executive load. Meyer et al. (this issue) provide a step in this direction.

CONCLUSION

There would appear not to be many remedies for the decline of cognitive function with advanced age. According to the current analysis, however, vigorous exercise programmes over a lifetime provide one option, at least for executive functions based on frontal lobes of the brain. Moreover, exercise intervention of as little as a few months appears useful in recovering some lost function. Such analysis, if confirmed by further investigation, would support a national health policy that emphasises the importance of aerobic activity. Certain deficiencies in much of the past research need to be addressed in future investigation. Paramount among these is the employment of appropriate control conditions that, in accord with Donder's classic subtractive dictum, allow any effects of exercise in the older adult to be attributed to the cognitive process in question. We have emphasised a narrow aspect of executive process in this review. Future work needs to distinguish different aspects of executive control that are embodied in distinct frontal cortical regions. Petrides (2000) presented such a distinction regarding working memory functions. It is possible that not all forms of executive control respond in the same way to exercise. In addition to improvements in methodology and theoretical distinctions, additional studies need to clarify the causal links between exercise, improved cardiovascular function, and improved cognition. Particularly lacking at present is evidence that exercise intervention differentially improves blood flow to cortical regions subserving executive function compared to other cortical regions.

REFERENCES

Abourezk, T., & Toole, T. (1995). Effect of task complexity on the relationship between physical fitness and reaction time in older women. *Journal of Aging and Physical Activity*, *3*, 251–260.

Allport, D.A., Styles, E.A., & Hsieh, S. (1994). Shifting intentional set: Exploring the dynamic control of tasks. In C. Umiltà & M. Moscovitch (Eds.), *Attention and performance XV: Conscious and unconscious processing* (pp. 421–452). Cambridge, MA: MIT Press.

American College of Sports Medicine (1986). *Guidelines for graded exercise prescription* (3rd ed.). Philadelphia: Lea & Febinger.

Baylor, A.M., & Spirduso, W.W. (1988). Systematic aerobic exercise and components of reaction time in older women. *Journal of Gerontology: Psychological Sciences*, *43*, P121–P126.

Birren, J.E. (1965). Age changes in speed of behavior: Its central nature and physiological correlation. In A.T. Welford & J.E. Birren (Eds.), *Behavior, aging, and the nervous system* (pp. 191–216). Springfield, IL: Charles C. Thomas.

Blumenthal, J.A., Emery, C.F., Madden, D.J., Schniebolk, S., Walsh-Riddle, M., George, L.K., McKee, D.C., Higginbotham, M.B., Cobb, R.R., & Coleman, R.E. (1991). Long-term effects of exercise on physiological functioning in older men and women. *Journal of Gerontology: Psychological Sciences*, *46*, 352–361.

Bouchard, C., & Despres, J. (1995). Physical activity and health: Atherosclerotic, metabolic, and hypertensive diseases. *Research Quarterly for Exercise and Sport*, *66*, 268–275.

Cerella, J. (1985). Information processing rates in the elderly. *Psychological Bulletin*, *98*, 67–83.

Clarkson-Smith, L., & Hartley, A.A. (1989). Relationships between physical exercise and cognitive abilities in older adults. *Psychology and Ageing*, *4*, 183–189.

Donders, F.C. (1969). On the speed of mental processes. *Acta Psychologica*, *30*, 412–431.

Dustman, R.E., Emmerson, R., & Shearer, D. (1994). Physical activity, age and cognitive-neuropsychological function. *Journal of Aging and Physical Activity*, 2, 143–181.

Dustman, R.E., Ruhling, R.O., Russell, E.M., Shearer, D.E., Bonekat, H.W., Shigeoka, J.W., Wood, J.S., & Bradford, D.C. (1984). Aerobic exercise training and improved neuropsychological function of older individuals. *Neurobiology of Aging*, 5, 35–42.

Emery, C.F., Huppert, F.A., & Schein, R.L. (1995). Relationships among age, exercise, health, and cognitive function in a British sample. *The Gerontologist*, 35, 378–385.

Etnier, H.L., Salazar, W., Landers, D.M., Petruzzello, S.J., Han, M., & Nowell, P. (1997). The influence of physical fitness and exercise upon cognitive functioning: A meta-analysis. *Journal of Sport and Exercise Psychology*, 19, 249–277.

Frith, C. (2000). The role of dorsolateral prefrontal cortex in the selection of action. In S. Monsell & J. Driver (Eds.), *Attention and performance XVIII: Control of cognitive processes*. Cambridge, MA: MIT Press.

Gregoire, J., & Van der Linden, M. (1997). Effects of age on forward and backward digit spans. *Aging, Neuropsychology, and Cognition*, 4, 140–149.

Gur, R.C., Gur, R.E., Obrist, W.D., Skolnick, B.E., & Reivich, M. (1987). Age and regional cerebral blood flow at rest and during cognitive activity. *Archives of General Psychiatry*, 44, 617–621.

Hawkins, H.L., Kramer, A.F., & Capaldi, D. (1992). Aging, exercise, and attention. *Psychology and Aging*, 7, 643–653.

Keele, S.W. (1973). *Attention and human performance*. Pacific Palisades, CA: Goodyear.

Keele, S.W. (1985). Motor control. In L. Kaufman, J. Thomas, & K. Boff (Eds.), *Handbook of perception and performance*. New York: Wiley.

Keele, S.W., & Rafal, R. (2000). Deficits of task set in patients with left prefrontal cortex lesions. In S. Monsell & J. Driver (Eds.), *Attention and performance XVIII: Control of cognitive processes*. Cambridge, MA: MIT Press.

Kerr, B., Scott, M., & Vitiello, M.V. (1993). *Can aerobic exercise influence cognitive and motor functioning for older individuals?* Paper presented at the annual meeting of the Psychonomics Society, Washington, DC.

Konishi, S., Nakajima, K., Uchida, I., Kameyam, M., Nakahara, K., Sekihara, K., & Miyashita, Y. (1998). Transient activation of inferior prefontal cortex during cognitive set shifting. *Nature Neuroscience*, 1, 80–84.

Kramer, A.E., Hahn, S., Cohen, N.J., Banich, M.T., McAuley, E., Harrison, C.R., Chason, J., Vakil, E., Bardell, L., Boileau, R.A., & Colcombe, A. (1999). Aging, fitness and neurocognitive function. *Nature*, 400, 418–419.

Kramer, A.E., Hahn, S., McAuley, E., Cohen, N.J., Banich, M.T., Harrison, C.R., Chason, J., Vakil, E., Bardell, L., Boileau, R.A., & Colcombe, A. (in press). Exercise, aging and cognition: Healthy body, healthy mind? In A.D. Fisk and W. Rogers (Eds.), *Human factors interventions for the health care of older adults*. Hillsdale, NJ: Lawrence Erlbaum Associates Inc.

Kray, J., & Lindenberger, U. (2000). Adult age differences in task switching. *Psychology and Aging*, 15, 126–147.

Lee, I. (1995). Exercise and physical health: Cancer and immune function. *Research Quarterly for Exercise and Sport*, 66, 286–291.

Lindenberger, U., Mayr, U., & Kliegl, R. (1993). Speed and intelligence in old age. *Psychology and Aging*, 8, 207–220.

Lupinacci, N.S., Rikli, R.E., Jones, J., & Ross, D. (1993). Age and physical activity effects on reaction time and digit symbol substitution performance in cognitively active adults. *Research Quarterly for Exercise and Sport*, 64, 144–150.

Madden, D.J., Blumenthal, J.A., Allen, P.A., & Emery, C.F. (1989). Improving aerobic capacity in healthy older adults does not necessarily lead to improved cognitive performance. *Psychology and Aging*, 4, 307–320.

Mayr, U., & Kliegl, R. (1993). Sequential and coordinative complexity: Age-based processing limitations in figural transformations. *Journal of Experimental Psychology: Learning, Memory, and Cognition, 19*, 1297–1320.

Mayr, U., Kliegl, R., & Krampe, R.T. (1996). Sequential and coordinative processing dynamics in figural transformations across the life-span. *Cognition, 5*, 61–90.

McDowell, S., Whyte, J., & D'Esposito, M. (1998). Differential effect of a dopaminergic agonist on prefrontal function in traumatic brain injury patients. *Brain, 121*, 1155–1164.

Meyer, D.E., Evans, J.E., Lauber, E.J., Rubinstein, J., Gmeindl, L., Junck, L., & Koeppe, R.A. (1998). *The role of dorsolateral prefrontal cortex for executive cognitive processes in task switching*. Poster presented at the Cognitive Neuroscience Society, San Francisco, CA.

Meyer, D.E., & Kieras, D.E. (1997). A computational theory of executive processes and multiple task performance: Part I. Basic mechanisms. *Psychological Reviews, 104*, 3–65.

Meyerson, J., Hale, S., Wagstaff, D., Poon, L.W., & Smith, G.A. (1990). The information loss model: A mathematical model of age-related cognitive slowing. *Psychological Review, 97*, 475–487.

Monsell, S., & Driver, J. (Eds.). (2000). *Attention and performance XVIII: Control of cognitive processes*. Cambridge, MA: MIT Press.

Norman, D.A., & Shallice, T. (1986). Attention to action: Willed and automatic control of behavior. In R.J. Davidson, G.E. Schwartz, & D. Shapiro (Eds.), *Consciousness and self-regulation* (pp. 1–18). New York: Plenum.

Owen, A.M. (2000). The role of the lateral frontal cortex in mnemonic processing: The contribution of functional neuroimaging. *Experimental Brain Research, 133*, 33–43.

Panton, L.B., Graves, J.E., Pollock, M.L., Hagberg, J.M., & Chen, W. (1990). Effect of aerobic and resistance training on fractionated reaction time and speed of movement. *Journal of Gerontology, 41*, 645–649.

Petrides, M. (2000). Mid-dorsolateral and mid-ventrolateral prefrontal cortex: Two levels of executive control for the processing of mnemonic information. In S. Monsell & J. Driver (Eds.), *Attention and performance XVIII: Control of cognitive processes*. Cambridge, MA: MIT Press.

Posner, M.I. (1978). *Chronometric explorations of mind*. Hillsdale, NJ: Lawrence Erlbaum Associates Inc.

Rikli, R., & Busch, S. (1986). Motor performance of women as a function of age and physical activity level. *Journal of Gerontology, 41*, 645–649.

Rikli, R.E., & Edwards, D.J. (1991). Effects of a three-year exercise program on motor function and cognitive processing speed in older women. *Research Quarterly for Exercise and Sport, 62*, 61–67.

Rogers, R.D., & Monsell, S. (1995). The cost of a predictable switch between simple cognitive tasks. *Journal of Experimental Psychology: General, 124*, 207–231.

Rogers, R.D., Sahakian, B.J., Hodges, J.R., Polkey, C.E., Kennard, C., & Robbins, T.W. (1998). Dissociating executive mechanisms of task control following frontal lobe damage and Parkinson's disease. *Brain, 121*, 815–842.

Salthouse, T. (1985). The speed factor in cognitive aging. In *A theory of cognitive aging* (pp. 249–294). Amsterdam: North-Holland.

Shaw, T.G., Mortel, K.F., Meyer, J.S., Rogers, R.L., Hardenberg, J., & Cutaia, M.M. (1984). Cerebral blood flow changes in benign aging and cerebrovascular disease. *Neurology, 34*, 855–862.

Shay, K.A., & Roth, D.L. (1992). Association between aerobic fitness and visuospatial performance in healthy older adults. *Psychology and Aging, 7*, 15–24.

Spector, A., & Biederman, I. (1976). Mental set and mental shift revisited. *American Journal of Psychology, 89*, 669–679.

Spirduso, W.W. (1975). Reaction and movement time as a function of age and physical activity level. *Journal of Gerontology, 30,* 435–440.

Stablum, F., Leonardi, G., Mazzoldi, M., Umiltà, C., & Morra, S. (1994). Attention and control deficits following closed head injury. *Cortex, 30,* 603–618.

Stablum, F., Mogentale, C., & Umiltà, C. (1996). Executive functioning following mild closed head injury. *Cortex, 32,* 261–278.

Sternberg, S. (1969). Memory-scanning: Mental processes revealed by reaction-time experiments. *American Scientist, 57,* 521–457.

Umiltà, C., Nicoletti, R., Simion, F., Tagliabue, M.E., & Bagnara, S. (1992). The cost of a strategy. *European Journal of Cognitive Psychology, 4,* 21–40.

US Department of Health and Human Services. (1996). *Physical activity and health: A report of the Surgeon General.* Atlanta, GA: US Department of Health and Human Services, Centers for Disease Control and Prevention, National Center for Chronic Disease Prevention and Health Promotion.

Vuori, I. (1995). Exercise and physical health: Musculoskeletal health and functional capabilities. *Research Quarterly for Exercise and Sport, 66,* 276–285.

Warren, L.R., Butler, R.W., Katholi, C.R., & Halsey, J.H. Jr. (1985). Age differences in cerebral blood flow during rest and during mental activation measurements with and without monetary incentive. *Journal of Gerontology, 40,* 53–59.

Weiss, A.D. (1965). The locus of reaction time change with set, motivation, and age. *Journal of Gerontology, 20,* 60–64.

West, R.L. (1996). An application of prefrontal cortex function theory to cognitive aging. *Psychological Bulletin, 120,* 272–290.

Whitehurst, M. (1991). Reaction time unchanged in older women following aerobic training. *Perceptual and Motor Skills, 72,* 251–256.

Subject index

Action slips, 92
Additional-process hypothesis, 79–80, 83
Age × Task interaction, 8
Alternation cost, 166–168
Attention
  executive control fluctuations, 91–92, 96
  inhibitory control, 108, 117
  optimal times, 114–117
  selective, 184
  visual, 71–78
Attention-switching task, 15–16

Behavioural evidence, 2, 22, 235–256, 258
Between-set selection, 48, 57, 64
Brain changes, 21–24
Brain-behaviour relationships, 235–256
Brain-imaging studies, 2–3, 24, 235–278
Brinley ratios, 9–10, 49, 150–152, 218–225
Brodmann's area, 261–262, 264

CANTAB, 10, 15
Category cue memory test, 18–20
Catell Culture Fair test, 13–15, 17, 19, 21
Central nervous system, 14, 21–23
Circadian influences, 114–117
Cognitive ageing models, 5, 123, 165, 187, 217
Cognitive control, task switching, 165–186
Cognitive estimates, 16, 18–20
Cognitive processing
  aerobic exercise, 279–300
  brain-behaviour relationships, 235, 237, 249

unified computational theory, 149, 156
Cohort selection, 21–24
Construct
  evaluation, 33–34, 43–45
  group-related differences, 30–34, 36–41, 44–45
  specification, 31–32, 34, 44
  validity, 12–16, 32–33, 40–45
Context memory, 15–16

Distraction effects, 113–118
DMST, 15–16

EPIC (executive-process interactive control) model, 123–164
Episodic memory, 50–51, 53, 65–66
Event-related brain potentials (ERPs), 98–101
Executive control
  aerobic exercise effect, 279–300
  cognitive ageing models, 5–28
  efficiency fluctuations, 91–108
  formal models, 123, 165, 187, 217
  goal activation/maintenance, 71–89
  group differences research, 29–46
  inhibitory control, 107–122
  mental sets selection, 47–69
  modulatory role, 2
  processes, 35
  selective compensation, 258–259
  unified computational theory, 123–164
Executive-process interactive control (EPIC) model, 123–164
Exercise, aerobic, 279–300
Eye movements, 71–78

Fade-out paradigm, 47, 59–66

Failure-to-engage hypothesis, 79–80, 82–83, 85
fMRI (functional magnetic resonance imaging) study, 235–256
Frontal lobe
  aerobic exercise study, 280, 288–290
  age effects, 2, 5–7, 71–72, 165
  set-selection processes, 48
  task familiarity, 10–11
  task validity, 11–21
  working memory, 257, 259–263
Functional construct validity, 12–16
Functional magnetic resonance imaging (fMRI) study, 235–256

General-parameter accounts, 2, 29–46
gf scores, 5, 12, 14, 15, 17–18, 21
Goal activation and maintenance, 71–89, 99, 107
Goal neglect, 155
Group differences, research strategy, 29–46

Haemodynamic response, 235, 237–243, 245–247

Individual differences, 14–15, 31
Information-processing, 124–125, 148, 190, 217–234
Inhibition
  control processes, 96, 100, 107–122, 154
  frontal and executive tests, 6–9, 12–14, 18
  inhibitory-deficit hypothesis, 190–191, 229
Intelligence, 13–15, 17, 21
Intention, lapses, 92–94, 99–100
Interference
  cognitive ageing models, 7–8, 10, 12–13
  executive control fluctuations, 96, 100
  inhibitory control, 111–113
  mediation, 43–44
  working memory, 257, 270–272
Intrusion errors, 98–99, 101–102

ISPOCD, 10

Linear scaling effect, 8–9

Matching task, 15–16, 273–274
Memory
  see also Working memory
  inhibitory control, 108–113, 117
  retrieval, 54–55, 109, 117, 295–296
  short-term, 257–258
  span, 139–149, 153, 212, 294–295
Mental sets selection, 47–69

Name recognition, 18–20
NART test, 16–18
Negative priming, 7, 12, 15–16
Neuro-imaging studies see Brain-imaging
Neuropsychological tests, 10, 12, 15–21, 35–36, 286
Non-verbal recognition, 18–20
Numerical tests, 12–13, 16, 34, 39, 52, 195

Paired association task, 15–16
Parallel distributed processing (PDP) models, 237, 251–253
Perceptual-motor mechanisms, 148–149, 154
PET (positron emission tomography) study, 257–278
Physical fitness, 3, 279
Position recognition, 15–16
Positron emission tomography (PET) study, 257–278
Prefrontal cortex
  executive control processes, 91–92, 100–102
  fMRI studies, 235, 243–250, 253–254
  PET studies, 257, 259–263, 266, 271
Pro/anti cue paradigm, 73–77
Psychometric testing, 11, 56

Random generation task, 15–16, 34
Random walk models, 217, 221–225, 230
Reaction time

aerobic exercise effect, 280–286, 290–293
EPIC theory, 130–139, 149–154
executive control processes, 91
information processing, 218–232
mental set selection, 47–67
task switching, 80–81, 173–183
testing methods, 8–11, 13
Reading, inhibitory control, 110–111, 114
Research strategy, group differences, 29–46
Response selection, 165, 171–174, 180–184

Saccadic reactions, 72–78
Sentence completion test, 18–20
Set-selection processes, 47–69
Shape recognition, 15–16
Shor test, 14
Spatial span, 15–16, 272–274
Stroop test
cognitive ageing models, 7–10, 12–14, 16, 229–232
executive control fluctuations, 93–96, 99–102
research strategies, 34–35, 39, 41

Task familiarity, 10–11
Task performance
alternative strategies, 124, 134–139, 156
complexity, 8, 150–152, 187
dual, 123, 125, 131–139, 149, 155–156
skill acquisition, 124, 130–131, 148, 155–156
Task switching
cognitive control, 165–186
fade out paradigm, 59–66
goal activation/maintenance, 71, 78–86
research strategy, 36, 39, 41, 43–44
set-selection processes, 47, 53–56, 59, 66–67
Task validity, 11–21
Testing methods

cohort selection, 21–24
group differences research, 29–46
measurement problems, 8–9
task familiarity, 10–11
task validity, 11–21
Time-sharing ability, 123, 132–139, 155–156
Trails task
cognitive ageing models, 9–10, 13, 16
research strategies, 34–37, 40

Verbal fluency
executive processes testing, 16, 18–20, 34
set-selection, 54
working memory, 263–270
Verbal working memory, 139–148
Visual attention, 71–78
Visual search task, 15–16, 53

Wisconsin Card Sorting Test, 7, 16, 34
Within-set selection, 48, 56–57, 64–65
Word-recognition tasks, EPIC model, 130, 139–148
Working memory
complexity effects, 187–215
crosstalk model, 187, 190, 209–210
decay-based model, 187, 189, 206–207, 211–213
EPIC theory, 123–164
fMRI studies, 235, 243–250, 252–254
goal selection and maintenance, 71–72
inhibition-deficit hypothesis, 190–191
inhibitory control, 107–113, 118
interference effects, 187, 190, 207–209, 211–213, 270–272
lateral organisation, 272–274
limited resources model, 187–188, 200–205, 210–211
magical number model, 187, 189, 205–206, 211
physical exercise effect, 293–296
set selection, 51–53, 56
span, 15–16, 110–113
storage and executive processes, 257–278